# Śambūka and the *Rāmāyaṇa* Tradition

# Śambūka and the *Rāmāyaṇa* Tradition

## A History of Motifs and Motives in South Asia

Aaron Sherraden

ANTHEM PRESS

Anthem Press
An imprint of Wimbledon Publishing Company
*www.anthempress.com*

This edition first published in UK and USA 2025
by ANTHEM PRESS
75–76 Blackfriars Road, London SE1 8HA, UK
or PO Box 9779, London SW19 7ZG, UK
and
244 Madison Ave #116, New York, NY 10016, USA

First published in the UK and USA by Anthem Press in 2023



*British Library Cataloguing-in-Publication Data*
A catalogue record for this book is available from the British Library.

*Library of Congress Control Number: 2024951316*
A catalog record for this book has been requested.

ISBN-13: 978-1-83999-494-4 (Pbk)
ISBN-10: 1-83999-494-0 (Pbk)

Cover Credit: *Śambūkamokṣam* painting by the artist Murali T.

This title is also available as an e-book.

In memory of my father (1946–2023)

# CONTENTS


*List of figures* xi

*Acknowledgments* xiii

*Foreword: Śambūka's Story across Time and India's Regions* xvii

*A Note on Transliteration* xxi

*Abbreviations* xxiii

1. **Introduction: Śambūka's Death Toll** 1
   The Traditions of the *Rāmāyaṇa* and Śambūka 6
   The Plan for This Book 15

2. **Śambūka's Earliest Death** 21
   Understanding the *Uttarakāṇḍa* 23
   The Development of *Varṇadharma* in Texts Composed between the Empires 28
      *Varṇadharma, tapas,* and Śūdra exclusion 28
      The *Mānava Dharmaśāstra* 34
      The *Arthaśāstra* 36
      Śambūka in the *Vālmīki Rāmāyaṇa* 38
   Why Is the Śambūka Story in the *Rāmāyaṇa* Narrative? 43
   How to Read Vālmīki's Śambūka 53

3. **First Responders** 57
   Kālidāsa's Śambūka Attains the Course of Virtuous Men 58
   Setting the Record Straight in the *Paümacariya* 66
   Forming the Foundations of Śambūka's Future 72

4. **The *Uttararāmacarita* and Śambūka's Purpose in Death** 75
   Connections and Divergences between Kālidāsa and Bhavabhūti 76
   Pity in Bhavabhūti's *Uttararāmacarita* 79
   The Hand that Swings the Sword 81
   Śambūka Speaks … in Sanskrit 83

Śambūka's Death, It's All a Part of the Plan 87
Śambūka's New Importance 90

5. **The Accident or the Execution** 93
Placing *Bhakti* 94
The Vernacular *Rāmāyaṇas* of Kampaṉ and Tulsīdās 98
Bringing Vālmīki into a New Era 101
Śivasahāya's commentary on the *Vālmīki Rāmāyaṇa* 101
The *Padma Purāṇa* 103
The *Kaṇṇaśśa Rāmāyaṇa* 107
Kṣemendra's *Rāmāyaṇamañjarī* 109
The Salvation of Śambūka 110
Kṣemendra's *Daśāvatāracarita* 110
The *Adhyātma Rāmāyaṇa* 112
E̲lutacchan's Malayalam *Adhyātma Rāmāyaṇam* 113
The *Rāmcaritmānas'* Afterword 115
It Was an Accident! 117
Nāgacandra's *Pampa Rāmāyaṇa* 118
The *Raṅganātha Rāmāyaṇa* 120
Eknāth's *Bhāvārtha Rāmāyaṇa* 121
Kerala shadow puppetry: *tolpāvakūttu* 122
Raviṣeṇa's *Padma Purāṇa* 124
Svayambhūdeva's *Paümacariu* 126
Hemacandra's *Triṣaṣṭiśalākāpuruṣacarita* 126
Who is narrating Śambūka's accidental death? 127
The Curious Case of the *Ānanda Rāmāyaṇa* 128
Borrowing Śambūka's Death: Narrative Exchange between Jains and Hindus 132

6. **Śambūka Lives on Ramtek Hill** 137
Ramtek and the Vākāṭakas 138
Ramtek and the Yādavas 143
Ramtek and the Marāṭhās 149
Ramtek Today 158
Śambūka's Layered History on Ramtek Hill 165

7. **The Anti-Caste Revolutionary** 167
The Politics of Caste 168
Tripuraneni Ramaswami Chaudari's *Śambuka Vadha* 173
Comparing Śambūka's Crimes: Swami Achhutanand's *Rām-Rājya-Nyāy* and Santram B.A.'s *Niraparādh kī Hatyā* 177

Dr. B.R. Ambedkar on Śambūka 187
Two Periyars Censure the *Rāmāyaṇa* 190
A Battle over the Details: Śambūka in the Twentieth Century 198

8. **Śambūka in the Twenty-First Century** 201
The Aadi Dharm Samaaj and The Martyrdom Day of the Great Sage Śambūka 204
Śambūka in *The Last Letter* 211
Śambūka, Rohith Vemula, and the Lynching of African Americans in the United States 215
Controlling the Narrative: Śambūka's Slaughter 218

9. **Conclusion: Śambūka and the *Rāmāyaṇa* Tradition** 221

*Bibliography* 227

*Index* 239

# LIST OF FIGURES


| | | |
|---|---|---|
| 6.1 | The Dhūmreśvara temple viewed from the East | 137 |
| 6.2 | Ramtek Hill viewed from the South | 138 |
| 6.3 | The Dhūmreśvara *liṅga* | 138 |
| 6.4 | Hanumān *mūrti* wielding a bow at Rām Talāī | 163 |

# ACKNOWLEDGMENTS

I would like at the outset to recognize the generous financial support I have received at various stages of this project's life from the Department of Asian Studies at the University of Texas at Austin, the South Asia Institute at the University of Texas, the American Institute of Indian Studies, and the Dolores Zohrab Liebmann Fund. Without the assistance I received from all these sources, this book or any of the work that led to its creation would have not been possible.

My efforts to put this study together would have been doomed at the outset without the guidance of many teachers over the course of several years. The first iterations of this project—which would ultimately become my dissertation—came from a series of term papers I wrote for a few of my Sanskrit classes taught by Joel Brereton at the University of Texas. His insights in the early phases of my journey with Śambūka gave me the momentum I needed to get this study off the ground. Special thanks must be reserved for my advisor, Donald Davis, who patiently guided me through my graduate (and undergraduate) education and, in the process, unfailingly encouraged my efforts on this and other projects for many years. It is hard to articulate how influential he has been on my work, but I can certainly say that his mentorship and support have been constant and have come in many forms. Also instrumental in helping me shape this project and the skills needed to take it on are Martha Selby, Cynthia Talbot, Darsana Manayathu Sasi, Oliver Freiberger, Dalpat Rajpurohit, Rupert Snell, Patrick Olivelle, Kashika Singh, Brajesh Samarth, Mithilesh Mishra, Lalita du Perron, Jishnu Shankar, Ratheesh R. Nair, Bindu Rajasenan Nair and everyone at AIIS Thiruvananthapuram, Achyuta Nand Singh and everyone at AIIS Jaipur, the late M. R. Unnithan, Sumit Guha, Shenghai Li, and Edeltraud Harzer. I thank them all for their patience, support, and generosity. I extend my thanks also to Mary Rader, who, in addition to several generally helpful gestures, has been instrumental in tracking down obscure materials in the cavernous library system. I wish to acknowledge Paula Richman for patiently offering her comments on this book throughout many phases of its creation. We discussed the larger scope and finer details of it over several conversations. Her work has long been an inspiration for how I understand the *Rāmāyaṇa* and its impact. To have her be involved in this project is a great honor for me. Many people—several named here and others who have remained anonymous—have offered their comments on various drafts of this book, which has greatly improved the final product. I thank them all for sharing their knowledge and time to help me deliver a better product. Whatever imperfections remain are of my own doing.

I am greatly indebted to many people in India who have provided me with incredible new insights and materials on the subject of Śambūka, among many others. I was warmly welcomed by numerous people into the vast network of publishing houses in Uttar Pradesh and New Delhi. I thank especially A. R. Akela at Anand Sahitya Sadan (Aligarh), Avanish Kumar at Bahujan Kalyan Prakashan (Lucknow), and Shanti Swaroop Bauddh at Samyak Prakashan (New Delhi). J. N. Aditya at the Periyar Lalai Singh Charitable Trust (Kanpur) also showed immense generosity to me over the course of several days. I spent an enlightening period with *tolpāvakūttu* artist K. K. Ramachandra Pulavar at his home and studio in Koonathara, Kerala. Among many other acts of kindness, he arranged for a private performance of the Śambūkumāran episode of *tolpāvakūttu*'s *Rāmāyaṇa* narrative. Also in Kerala, I extend my thanks to Chandramohan S, with whom I had many great conversations about poetry and activism as we roamed about Thiruvananthapuram, stopping in various libraries, bookstores, and coffee shops. The incredible artist, Murali T, whose work graces the cover of this book, welcomed me into his home in Kannur for hours of great conversation, food, and fun. I thank him and his family for many great memories. Thanks to Hemanth N. S. and his family for frequently opening their home to me during my various visits to Kerala. My deepest thanks to Darshan "Ratna" Raavan, Surekha Sujata, and the entire AADHAS family for welcoming me to many of their events during 2016–2017. Their willingness to share their ideas and experiences has greatly enriched my understanding of the hard work being done to address social injustice in India. I will forever be grateful to Sudhanva Deshpande, Brijesh Sharma, Moloyashree Hashmi, and everyone with Jana Natya Manch for their extremely welcoming nature and willingness to give me a peak behind the curtain of how they produce their work and present it to their audiences. My time in Ramtek was made exponentially more enjoyable and productive thanks to the help and kindness of Ishwar Akat, Dilip R. Patil, and Sunil C. Jain. They showed me around Ramtek, provided me with several helpful resources, and spoke with me at length about the history of their town.

I have a long list of friends to acknowledge. They served not only as sounding boards for my ideas but also pillars of support and necessary distraction.

My greatest appreciation and admiration goes—in no particular order—to Andrea Gutierrez, Hillary Langberg, Charlotte Giles, Justin Ben-Hain, Michael Mitmoen, Matthew Guckenberg, Shirin Afsous, Kathleen Longwaters, Daniel Dillon, Matthew Milligan, Rupali Warke, Parvathy Prem, Aniruddhan Vasudevan, Gwen Kirk, Soham Pain, Sucheta Arora, Shivee Gupta, Zeyn Kermani, Megha and Ankur Sheel, Dhruv Nagar, Christopher Fleming, Akhilesh Jain, Gunja Pandav, Subhamoy Das, Riddhi Dattani, Garima and Siddharth Jain, Ani Dasgupta, Pallavi Abiktar, Esha Kothari, Suyog Jain, Avni Jain, Michael Fiden, Katie Lazarowicz, Emily Beissner, Jeff Wilson, Imran Khan, Akshay Singh, Keely Sutton, Abhishek Baradia, Kelly Hanner, and the entire Sharma family—Suresh, Rani, Lokpriya, and Devyani. A special thanks goes to Ashay Rane for not only being an excellent friend but also patiently sitting with me to help me understand a trove of Marathi materials.

Any accomplishment of mine, big or small, has my family's imprint on it; this book is no different. I thank my grandmother Edith O'Toole, my brother Collin and sister-in-law Alexandra, my brother Brian and his immensely talented child Angel, and my brother-in-law Raghav. You all inspire me and keep my life vibrant. My heartfelt gratitude goes to my cousins Shubhra Gupta and Anuj Sharma for many insightful conversations and adventures out in New Delhi. To my mom and dad: thank you for all your support and love, even when my path through life has been hard to keep track of. Tragically, my father will not see this book come to fruition, but his impact is on every page. My wonderful mother- and father-in-law, Dipali Sanghi and Inder Bhullar, have been more influential than they likely realize. Their genuine curiosity about the latest twists and turns in my work has been a true blessing that kept me pushing to complete the next step. Dinesh Chandra and Chanchal Sanghi (Papu-Naani) opened their home and hearts to me for many months while I completed my fieldwork in India and helped me in too many ways to count while I was there. Vasant Kunj has now truly become my home, and I am extremely grateful for that. Without their love, openness, motivating spirits, and generosity, none of this work would have come to fruition. Our little dog, Bucky, provided me with much-needed solace in times of stress. Our walks forced me out of the house to clear my head, gather my thoughts, and find new avenues for communicating my ideas. Finally, and most importantly, my greatest appreciation goes to my incredible partner in life, Neha, who has been a truly unshakable force of love and support even in the toughest, most stressful times. I would have given up on this project long ago if it weren't for her enduring compassion and unending patience.

Aaron Sherraden
Columbus, OH

# FOREWORD: ŚAMBŪKA'S STORY ACROSS TIME AND INDIA'S REGIONS

I commend Aaron Sherraden's *Śambūka and the Rāmāyaṇa Tradition* to you. This monograph takes as its starting point a terse account of Śambūka's decapitation, found in the earliest, extant, full literary telling of the life and deeds of Rāma in the ancient Sanskrit *Rāmāyaṇa* attributed to Sage Vālmīki. One of Hinduism's two preeminent ancient epic narratives, Vālmīki's *Rāmāyaṇa* and its subsequent retellings have played key roles in later devotional practices to Viṣṇu and his *avatāras*. Textual historians generally date the text (which first circulated orally in several recensions) as taking its fixed form starting approximately the mid-sixth century BCE and ending no later than the second or third century CE.[1] Śambūka's story appears in the final of the seven books of the *Rāmāyaṇa* attributed to Vālmīki, which many philologists consider a later interpolation.

Over time, however, Śambūka's story has grown into a narrative tradition of its own. During the last two thousand years, its events have appeared in multiple literary retellings characterized by literary strategies such as elaboration, concision, major reinterpretation, and alternate endings. These retellings depict Śambūka variously as a miscreant and enemy of the social and moral orders, a victim of upper-caste prejudice and violence, a pioneer who engaged in ascetic practices previously monopolized by upper castes, a recipient of Rāma's divine grace, one who has achieved release from the cycle of death and rebirth, a social and political revolutionary, a wise teacher and moral exemplar, and a venerated martyr in the cause of Dalit liberation. Accounts of Śambūka's rigorous asceticism have appeared in both cosmopolitan languages (e.g., Sanskrit and Prakrit) and regional literary ones (e.g., Tamil,

---

1 For detailed discussion of debates about the text's dating, see vol. 1, pp. 22–23 (1984) and vol. 7, p. 69 (2017) of the authoritative translation and annotations of the critical edition of *The Rāmāyaṇa of Vālmīki: An Epic of Ancient India*, edited by Robert P. Goldman and various translators (Princeton, NJ: Princeton University Press, 1984–2017).

Awadhi, Malayalam) across India from ancient times to the present. Moreover, in addition to Hindu texts, his story also appears in a lineage of texts composed by Jain authors in which Rāma does not kill Śambūka. Sherraden reveals how Śambūka's story continues to perform its cultural work in the twenty-first century, serving as the basis for ritual devotion, modern poetry, and even cover art for publications envisioned through a range of religious and social lenses.

Yet the story of Śambūka's motivations and actions has been repeatedly reframed as Indian social norms have changed over time. On the one hand, by practicing the asceticism limited exclusively to upper castes, Śambūka's behavior is perceived by some critics as so destabilizing to the social order that the king must execute the criminal immediately. On the other hand, since the practice of asceticism is believed to result in a higher level of religious knowledge, Śambūka's supporters viewed him as a spiritually motivated advocate of "equal opportunity" asceticism that should be open to all, rather than just a small upper caste elite.

This monograph could be said to have "backed into" the tail end of the oldest extant *Rāmāyaṇa* and then moved from this earliest iteration to a far-reaching examination of Śambūka's story in ancient, medieval, early modern, and contemporary tellings, extending all the way to the present day. Sherraden's analysis of carefully selected texts and religious practices serves as an unsurpassed magnifying glass that focuses on a story that has received only rare attention in the past from scholars who have hitherto mainly limited themselves to its Sanskrit retellings. Further, Sherraden reveals how frequently Dalit texts and street theater have revivified the story in their struggle to advance social justice.

Sherraden has skillfully and engagingly contextualized each iteration of Śambūka's story in its historical, religious, political, and social circumstances of patronage, philosophical and religious discourse, devotional sentiments, and anti-caste advocacy. His careful detective work and insightful analysis make visible the many reinterpretations of the story within regional literary traditions and ritual practices, ranging from Marathi and Telugu to Gujarati and Hindi languages. The sole pilgrimage site featuring worship of Śambūka is Ramtek in Maharashtra, where devotees of Rāma and Sītā have been promised that they will gain the fruits of their worship if they venerate Śambūka first. An organization that promotes the dignity of Dalit culture and the education of Dalit children, especially females, has created an annual set of calendrical and memorial days: on the Sunday closest to the widespread Hindu festival of Diwali, they remember Śambūka's martyrdom, when he sacrificed his head to protest that asceticism should be available to all people.

Given these achievements, I invite readers to enter Sherraden's fascinating and superbly documented book. Readers who are already steeped in the *Rāmāyaṇa* tradition and those coming to it afresh will understand and appreciate the *Rāmāyaṇa* tradition from a perspective informed by the long—and continually changing—tellings of Śambūka's story.

Paula Richman
William Danforth Professor of South Asian Religions, Emerita
Oberlin College

# A NOTE ON TRANSLITERATION

This study makes use of several languages that are expressed in a variety of scripts. For ease of comparison between these languages, I have chosen to represent all the source languages cited in this study using Roman transliteration. However, because this project deals simultaneously with multiple languages that have unique systems of transliteration, I have chosen to combine them all in a single system throughout the text, adopting conventions of both and making some alterations of my own. This is especially relevant when combining Malayalam with Indo-European languages. All languages follow their standard mode of transliteration with the following exceptions:

- Hindi and Sanskrit do not have short vowels for *e* or *o* while Malayalam does. Normally, Malayalam would show the short vowels as *e* and *o* and the long as *ē* and *ō*. So as not to create confusion between representations of these languages, *e* and *o* (e.g., *tolpāvakūttu* in place of *tōlpāvakūttu*) will consistently represent their respective long vowels in all languages while *ĕ* and *ŏ* (e.g., *Eklavyan̲t̲ĕ* in place of *Ēklavyan̲t̲e*) will represent their shortened counterparts as found in Malayalam.
- Malayalam transliteration often retains *r̲* when in a cluster with other consonants. However, to better reflect pronunciation, I will change *r̲* to *t̲* when in a consonant cluster (e.g., *Eklavyan̲t̲ĕ* in place of *Eklavyan̲r̲ĕ*).
- When it appears at the end of certain words, the Malayalam *virāma* (schwa vowel) is represented using the character *ŭ* (e.g., *kiḷippāṭṭŭ*).
- The typical final *anusvāra* (*ṃ*) in Malayalam is represented simply as *m*.
- The vocalic "*r*" sound in Sanskrit and Hindi is represented with the character *r̥*. This is to distinguish it from the retroflex "*r*" sound of Hindi, which is represented by *ṛ*.

There are occasions where Hindi and Sanskrit, though represented by the same characters in Devanagari script, are transliterated slightly different due to the languages' respective conventions in pronunciation and transliteration. In particular, Hindi will often drop the *a* vowel when in final or, in some cases, medial position. For example, *vadha* in Sanskrit becomes *vadh* in Hindi. I will maintain the appropriate conventions for Sanskrit and Hindi throughout this study. This means that names like Śambūka and Rāma, when coming from Hindi sources, will be reproduced in Roman transliteration as Śambūk and Rām.

# ABBREVIATIONS

| | |
|---|---|
| AADHAS | Aadi Dharm Samaaj |
| *AdhR* | *Adhyātma Rāmāyaṇa* |
| *ĀR* | *Ānanda Rāmāyaṇa* |
| *AŚ* | *Arthaśāstra* |
| *DAC* | *Daśāvatāracarita* |
| JPTM | Jat-Pat Todak Mandal |
| *KR* | *Kaṇṇaśśa Rāmāyaṇa* |
| *MBh* | *Mahābhārata* |
| *MD* | *Meghadūta* |
| *MDh* | *Mānava Dharmaśāstra* |
| *PadP* | *Padma Purāṇa* of Raviṣeṇa |
| *PC* | *Paümacariya* |
| *PP* | *Padma Purāṇa* |
| *RaV* | *Raghuvaṃśa* |
| *Rām-Rājya-Nyāy* | *Rām-Rājya-Nyāy (Nāṭak): Śambūk-Muni-Balidān* |
| *RCM* | *Rāmcaritmānas* |
| *RM* | *Rāmāyaṇamañjarī* |
| *Sammān* | *Sammān ke liye Dharm Parivartan Karem* |
| *ŚĀŚ* | *Śūdrācāraśiromaṇi* |
| *SGM* | *Sindūrāgirimāhātmya* |
| *True Reading* | *The Ramayana (A True Reading)* |
| *TŚPC* | *Triṣaṣṭiṣalākāpuruṣacarita* |
| *URC* | *Uttararāmacarita* |
| *VR* | *Vālmīki Rāmāyaṇa* |

# Chapter 1

# INTRODUCTION: ŚAMBŪKA'S DEATH TOLL

A ravenous jackal emerges from his den at the edge of a cremation ground and observes a vulture speaking to a grieving family as they prepare to leave the corpse of a young boy to be cremated. As the sun sets, the vulture rushes the family along lest he be forced to resign the boy's body to the nocturnal creatures of the cremation ground, including the jackals. Reminding the family of the inevitability of death, the vulture tells them, "You've stayed long enough in this dreadful cremation ground, teeming with vultures and jackals and filled with skeletons—a terror for all beings. Nobody who has been subjected to the rule of Death has come back to life, be they friend or foe. This is the way of all beings" (*MBh* 12.149.8–9). With their hopes dashed, the family leaves the boy's body to the delight of the famished vulture.

The jackal, hoping to stall the family until darkness falls over the cremation ground so that he can claim his next meal, challenges the family's affection for the boy, and questions how they could give up hope so quickly. The vulture and the jackal go back and forth, commanding and manipulating the emotions of the lamenting family as they each seek to dine on the boy's flesh. The jackal urges them to wait a bit longer—anything can happen. Perhaps the boy is alive, or perhaps he could even be revived. In an attempt to instill hope in the family, the jackal tells them that he knows of a time when a deceased boy did, in fact, come back to life.

"There is nothing to stop you in your affection or your weeping lament," the jackal explains, "but you will constantly ache from abandoning this dead boy. It has been heard that the child of a Brahmin was revived because Rāma, courageous and true, upheld righteousness and killed the Śūdra Śambūka" (*MBh* 12.149.61–62). The jackal and the vulture debate at length about the fate of the boy as the family wavers between surrendering their child to the cremation grounds and turning back to wait for any sign of life. As the arguments rage on, Śaṅkara, the god Śiva, appears before them all, prepared to grant everyone present a boon. For the grieving family, he restores the boy back to life, and he eliminates the hunger afflicting the two flesh-eating scavengers.[1]

This story occurs in the *Mahābhārata* (*MBh*), one of two major Sanskrit epics in India, the other being the *Rāmāyaṇa*. The *MBh*, a massive composition of some 100,000 verses attributed to the legendary sage Vyāsa, details the circumstances surrounding a massive war fought between warring cousins stemming from a dispute over the rightful claim to the throne of the Bhārata kingdom. The *Rāmāyaṇa*, a shorter but still extensive work of about 20,000 verses and attributed to yet another legendary sage, Vālmīki, chronicles the exile of its hero, Rāma, to the forest just prior to his coronation as king of Ayodhyā. While in the forest, his wife, Sītā, is kidnapped and much of the story follows his attempts to locate her and recover her from the demon king, Rāvaṇa. The epic sees Rāma reclaim the throne of Ayodhyā and ends with an account of his rule—perfect at times, fraught with hardship at others. Though there are naturally numerous differences between the epics and their development,[2] both were initially bardic compositions that gradually accumulated numerous didactic and religious accretions during their respective developmental histories, which overlapped considerably during the last few centuries BCE and the first few centuries CE. The *Rāmāyaṇa*, though, appears to have reached its completed form before the *MBh*.[3]

Aside from a common developmental trajectory, there are also many thematic similarities between the two epics. For example, both include a devastating sentence of exile to the forest and a climactic battle between the stories' opposing forces. The connections between the two epics go beyond vague thematics, however, and the plot material of the *Rāmāyaṇa* appears scattered throughout the *MBh* with noteworthy frequency.[4] The most obvious instance of that would be the fact that the *MBh* actually contains an entire account of

---

1 This is a summary of a story that occurs in *MBh* 12.149.1–117.

2 For a survey of such differences between the *MBh* and *Rāmāyaṇa* epics in terms of plot, thematics, structure, and compositional history, see Brockington (1998) and Goldman (1984, pp. 14ff.). Goldman and especially Brockington provide detailed explorations of how the two texts converge and diverge on these points.

3 The precise dating of either the *Rāmāyaṇa* of Vālmīki or the *MBh* has been the subject of considerable debate for decades. Among the most comprehensive accounts of the temporal interrelationship between the two epics and the scholarship that attempts to sort it out can be found in Brockington (1984, pp. 226–233 and 308–312), Brockington (1998, pp. 473–484), and Goldman (1984, pp. 14ff.).

4 The reverse is not true. Vālmīki's *Rāmāyaṇa* is largely silent on the events and central characters of the *MBh*. See Brockington (1998, p. 481).

Rāma's life within it called the *Rāmopākhyāna* (The Episode of Rāma).[5] Though abbreviated in comparison with Vālmīki's *Rāmāyaṇa*, the *Rāmopākhyāna*—at about seven hundred verses—is still a lengthy subsection of the *MBh* that follows a comparable narrative arc to Vālmīki's text. But beyond including this entire account of Rāma's life, the *MBh* calls on stories from the *Rāmāyaṇa* in subtler, more isolated ways. There are numerous passing references to Rāma's deeds scattered throughout the *MBh* epic and the jackal's brief mention of a deadly interaction between Rāma and Śambūka is one of them.[6]

Briefly, the story of how Rāma came to kill Śambūka is as follows: Śambūka was a Śūdra, the lowest of four classes (*varṇas*) within the stratified system of social segregation known as the *cāturvarṇya.*[7] He was performing rigorous austerities (*tapas*) with the intent of gaining access to heaven in his worldly body. As a Śūdra, Śambūka was forbidden to engage in *tapas* and his doing so was said to have disrupted the balance of righteousness (*dharma*) in Rāma's kingdom—so much so, in fact, that it resulted in the death of a young Brahmin, the highest of the four *varṇas*. As king, it would have been Rāma's responsibility to prevent these types of transgressions and remedy them should they occur. Under such obligations, he sets out to find Śambūka and kill him to prevent him from continuing his illegal *tapas*. Once Rāma finds Śambūka and extracts the necessary information to identify him as the offending Śūdra, Rāma decapitates him. In so doing, he instantly restores the balance of *dharma* in the kingdom, thus reviving the Brahmin boy.

---

5 The *Rāmopākhyāna* (3.258–275) occurs in the third book of the *MBh* called the *Vanaparvan*. There is a long history of argumentation as to which of these Rāma stories predates the other. For a survey of such scholarship, see Van Buitenen (1975, pp. 207–214). However, Goldman has presented a convincing refutation of the *Rāmopākhyāna* as being a source of the *Vālmīki Rāmāyaṇa*, arguing instead that the latter is clearly the earlier text (1984, pp. 33–39).

6 For more instances of references to the Rāma story in the *MBh*, see Brockington (1998, pp. 473–484).

7 The term *varṇa* (lit. color) is sometimes translated as "caste," but the parallel, while not altogether incorrect, is imprecise. A caste is a specific birth-based social group that is often endogamous and typically associated with a specific occupation. One's connection to that occupation—whether real or imagined—is intimately tied to one's social standing in society based on the desirability and relative purity or impurity associated with carrying out that occupation. In the Indian context, the term *jāti* (lit. birth) is a closer approximation to caste. *Varṇa* is also strictly birth-based, connected to occupation, and signifies stratification, but the term is much more general in its application and a single *varṇa* can and does include many distinct castes. When discussing *varṇa* in modern social contexts, it is still common and even useful to lean on the parallels between the concept of caste and *varṇa*, even if those parallels are not exact.

The origins of this story about the killing of Śambūka lie in the *Rāmāyaṇa* of Vālmīki, yet the jackal from the story at the opening of this chapter is to referring the story in the *MBh.* That such a thing might happen—a character in one epic calling on a story from the other—is testament to the fact that the impact of the story of Rāma's life extends far beyond the limits of a singular *Rāmāyaṇa* text. Just one small invocation of even the briefest moments from the Rāma story can instantly orient (or reorient) an audience based on their presumed familiarity with Rāma's actions. It then becomes possible to import the *Rāmāyaṇa*'s influence in the service of some particular goal. This type of intertextual borrowing is precisely what is happening in the cremation ground.

The story of the jackal occurs as a side story, supplemental to the primary plot of the *MBh.* In fact, much of the material in this enormous text is made up of these tangential side stories. At this point in the main narrative, we are near the end of the epic when the Great War between rival family members on the Kurukṣetra battlefield is over and Yudhiṣṭhira—whose side was narrowly victorious—laments the losses on both sides that accompanied the war. Faced with the horrible notion that he has only attained such a victory by striking down his own kin, he curses the warrior code of the Kṣatriyas (*kṣatradharma*) that has put him in such a position.[8] Now set to rule the Bhārata kingdom over which the Great War was fought, Yudhiṣṭhira remains conflicted about the nature of *dharma* and threatens to renounce the kingdom and worldly life altogether. Many attempt to persuade him not to abandon his duties and accept his position as ruler, but he continues to have doubts. Ultimately, Yudhiṣṭhira is told to go to see Bhīṣma, his cousin and a commander in the opposing Kaurava army, who lies mortally wounded on a bed of arrows in the very spot where he fell in battle some days earlier. There, Bhīṣma imparts to Yudhiṣṭhira an extraordinarily long lesson regarding the nature of what is right and wrong to quell Yudhiṣṭhira's concerns. As a part of this lesson, Bhīṣma narrates the story of the jackal and the vulture to demonstrate to Yudhiṣṭhira the virtue of optimism as he confronts his feelings of guilt and loss in the aftermath of the war.[9]

We have, then, a story (the *MBh*) in which one character (Bhīṣma) tells another character (Yudhiṣṭhira) a story (the cremation ground tale); in this story, one character (the jackal) tells another set of characters (the deceased boy's family) a story (the story of Śambūka)—it is a story within a story within a story.

---

8 Kṣatriyas form the ruling and warrior *varṇa*, subservient only to the Brahmins.

9 For an account of the structure of the *Śāntiparvan*, where this story about Bhīṣma and Yudhiṣṭhira occurs, and its place within the *MBh* epic generally, see Fitzgerald (2004, pp. 79–164).

Each of these stories has a purpose that connects it to the meta-story that contains it.[10] The jackal tells the Śambūka story as a part of his efforts to convince the boy's family not to abandon their son's body so quickly; Bhīṣma tells the story of the cremation ground to console Yudhiṣṭhira in his time of great distress and convince him that all hope is not lost; and the author(s) of the *MBh* told the story of Yudhiṣṭhira's plight in order to explore the complexities of *dharma* and communicate those complexities to the epic's audience through what amounts to "the longest deathbed sermon on record," courtesy of Bhīṣma. (Van Buitenen, 1973, p. xxiii).

I draw attention to the story of the jackal in the cremation ground because the jackal's use of the *Rāmāyaṇa* in this anecdote is an excellent illustration of how the *Rāmāyaṇa* is a pervasive, amorphous phenomenon that wields extraordinary narrative and cultural power. That power can be, and often is, directed toward some particular end, either encapsulated within a narrative, as is the case with the jackal in the *MBh*, or in real-world situations that profoundly affect people's lives, as we will see throughout this study. It will become clear as the chapters progress that the *Rāmāyaṇa* is not a rigid, monolithic entity. It is instead an entire tradition of near-infinite bounds that includes texts, poems, dramas, paintings, sculptures, films, novels, songs, posters, temples, phrases and idioms, speeches, dances—the list goes on. These expressions of the Rāma story need not be located within a "*Rāmāyaṇa*" at all. In fact, I very intentionally opened this book with an instance of the Śambūka story—a story native to the *Rāmāyaṇa*—that occurs outside of a *Rāmāyaṇa* text. I did this to demonstrate that this book is not an exploration of the Śambūka story within a text called the *Rāmāyaṇa*. It is not even a census of the Śambūka story's appearance across many texts. Rather, it is a study of connections and divergencies between innovations in literature, art, performance, politics, and religion as a single story—the story of Śambūka's death, and occasionally the story of his life—charts a network of pathways through Indian history, actively or passively utilizing the gravity of the *Rāmāyaṇa* tradition the entire time. Because the *Rāmāyaṇa*

10 The *Rāmopākhyāna*, too, is narrated for a very particular purpose. Yudhiṣṭhira has been exiled to the forest and his wife, Draupadī, whom he shares with the other Pāṇḍava brothers, has just been kidnapped. He asks the sage Mārkaṇḍeya if anyone has suffered as great a misfortune as him, whereupon the sage narrates the story of Rāma to pacify him because Rāma has experienced the exact same type of hardship. The *Rāmopākhyāna* ends with Rāma's coronation and thus does not account for Sītā's second exile, one of the most contentious moments in the *Uttarakāṇḍa*, the final book of the *Rāmāyaṇa*. This should come as no surprise, however, because narratively speaking, if Mārkaṇḍeya were to have told Yudhiṣṭhira of Sītā's exile in his time of grief, it would have done very little to console him. On this point, see Goldman and Sutherland Goldman (2017, pp. 70–72).

tradition is so profoundly important to an understanding of the development of the Śambūka story, it is necessary to spend some time getting familiar with the *Rāmāyaṇa* tradition and the Śambūka tradition that runs at times parallel to it and at times against it.

## The Traditions of the *Rāmāyaṇa* and Śambūka

Literature does not simply appear and it does not simply relate stories, nor do literary traditions simply pass stories along with blind devotion. Literature and the traditions rooted in that literature always have something to tell us about why these stories exist and the purpose behind their reappearance in new contexts. Consider the legends of the Trojan War, some of the most famously revisited stories that find new relevance century after century. The war was immortalized in Homer's Greek epics the *Iliad* and the *Odyssey* of the eighth century BCE. The historicity of the Trojan War is murky, but that is rather inconsequential to my purpose here. I am instead more concerned with what happened after Homer and, most importantly, after there existed a story about the Trojan War.[11]

Countless poets and authors have taken the account they received from Homer and others and reframed it to work for their own purposes. Perhaps the most consequential of reworking of the story of the Trojan War and especially its aftermath came in the first century BCE when Virgil wrote his Latin epic, the *Aeneid*. Through his work, argues Classicist W. F. Jackson Knight, Virgil attempts to show us "how it had happened that Rome grew to greatness after a process which began in weakness and despair" (1956, p. 14). These circumstances of weakness and despair are those of Aeneas and the few surviving Trojans who managed to escape after their city was sacked by the Greeks. Homer also tells us a tale of hardship in the wake of the Trojan War in his *Odyssey* by telling us about the Greek soldier Odysseus and the tribulations he endured as he made his way back home to Ithaca. Yet, despite the Greeks' victory in Troy, Homer's *Odyssey* nevertheless marks the end of the Greek Heroic Age and it lacks a strong orientation toward a prosperous future (Thompson, 2004, p. 114). Virgil, however, shows quite the opposite fate. He tells us about a different aftermath to the war at Troy—one that is decidedly more Roman in its leanings and more hopeful in its exposition. In her account of Trojan War stories throughout history, Diane Thompson suggests that, in receiving Homer's epic account of Troy,

---

11 For a concise overview of the problems of Troy's history, its relationship to the literature that depicts it, and some of the scholarship surrounding it, see Thompson (2004, pp. 13–24).

Virgil has "transformed Homer's individualistic, crafty Greek heroes into villains, and Homer's Trojan losers into the noble, pious, community-minded, heroically suffering, finally victorious ancestors of Rome" (ibid., pp. 113–114). He turned a story of crushing defeat into a story of unparalleled valor that begins the history of Rome. After Aeneas arrives in Italy and navigates a contentious relationship with the Latins, he eventually marries the daughter of the native king. Their descendants, we are to understand, are none other than the progenitors of Roman civilization itself.

Virgil used the fame of Trojan War stories, especially Homer's, and adjusted their thrust toward formulating a prideful history that turns the rubble of the ruined city of Troy into the foundations of the Roman Empire. Virgil proved so successful in his task that his *Aeneid* eventually "became widely accepted as the foundation story of Latin Catholic European civilization," as stories of Troy were retold in the Middle Ages (ibid., p. 112). And the story of Troy has found new life in literature continuing into the present day.[12]

In line with the true mark of a literary tradition, stories about the Trojan War are in no way confined to the page. The power of their characters, messages, and imagery have inspired artists and entrepreneurs of various media to create new ways of revisiting the story of Troy continuously since Homer composed his interpretation. Even today, references to the Trojan War are ubiquitous and show up in settings as far flung as film, sports, and reproductive health. Many Homeric themes and characters have even taken a firm hold on popular culture in recent years. Among many other examples one could cite, Odysseus covertly entered the twenty-first century through the Coen Brothers' film *O Brother, Where Art Thou?* (2000), which satirically and rather loosely follows Homer's *Odyssey* as if it were set in Mississippi during the Great Depression.

Countless stories have worked their way deep into the cultural fabric of communities all around the world and self-contained studies dedicated to their histories of reception appear to be very much in vogue.[13] One tradition that has dug itself especially deeply into the society that produced it is that of the *Rāmāyaṇa*. The *Rāmāyaṇa* tradition, though massive, can be remarkably subtle and flexible in its application. The many literary, cultural, religious, and artistic dimensions of the tradition's expression allow those tapping into its influence to shape what they want us to receive as consumers of the story.

12 The most concise survey of such appearances and reappearances of Troy legends can be found in Thompson (2004).

13 See, for example, Lieb et al. (2011), Gillingham (2018), Leonard (2013), Ivanova (2018), and Ziolkowski (2011). Though broader in scope than a single story, see also Hunt et al. (2017).

In the case of the jackal from the opening of this book, calling on the Śambūka story in the way that he does and in the context that he does ensures that we as an audience receive a very particular framing to the story. Our setting is a cremation ground where a family is grieving the loss of a son and a jackal is attempting to instill a sentiment of hope in them. When the jackal explains to the family that there was once a Brahmin boy who was revived when Rāma killed the Śūdra Śambūka, the setting helps us identify the boy's revival as one of the most salient aspects of the Śambūka story, at least in the mind of the jackal. After all, the jackal's entire purpose for mentioning the story at all is to convince the deceased boy's family that there is always a chance that he could suddenly be revived, thus stalling them until nightfall so he, in place of the vulture, can eat the boy's corpse. In this very specific situation, Śambūka's significance as an individual is dismissed in favor of the means he provides to something the jackal considers to be greater. Śambūka the person is expendable to the jackal. He wants the family to hear about the boy who miraculously came back to life. It is a story of *revival* that he's after, not a story of death, and he uses this story to trick the family into holding out hope for a little while longer. The basis of the jackal's trick lies in the fact that the grieving family would have been familiar with the tale of Rāma and invoking it was meant instill a sense of unassailable legitimacy to his argument. When the jackal mentions that Rāma was once himself responsible for the revival of a young boy, the family immediately falls for the jackal's ploy.

Telling the story of Rāma or any smaller aspect thereof is as widespread today as it was when the epic was first committed to writing. The story has worked its way into nearly every aspect of India's cultural heritage and it has been depicted in almost every expressive medium imaginable. With over two thousand years of continuous transmission in a land as socially and culturally diverse as India, the permutations in narrating the life of Rāma are endless. Describing the *Rāmāyaṇa* tradition's breadth most concisely, A. K. Ramanujan famously wrote in his 1991 essay, "Three Hundred *Rāmāyaṇa*: Five Examples and Three Thoughts on Translation," that

> [t]he number of *Rāmāyaṇas* and the range of their influence in South and Southeast Asia over the past twenty-five hundred years or more are astonishing. Just a list of languages in which the Rāma story is found makes one gasp: Assamese, Balinese, Bengali, Cambodian, Chinese, Gujarati, Javanese, Kannada, Kashmiri, Khotanese, Laotian, Malaysian, Marathi, Oriya, Prakrit, Sanskrit, Santali, Sinhalese, Tamil, Telugu, Thai, Tibetan—to say nothing of Western languages. Through the centuries, some of these languages have hosted more than one telling

> of the Rāma story. Sanskrit alone contains some twenty-five or more tellings belonging to various narrative genres (epics, *kāvyas* or ornate poetic compositions, *purāṇas* or old mythological stories, and so forth). If we add plays, dance-dramas, and other performances, in both classical and folk traditions, the number of *Rāmāyaṇas* grows even larger. To these must be added sculpture and bas-reliefs, mask plays, puppet plays and shadow plays, in all the many South and Southeast Asian cultures. (1991, p. 24)

The *Rāmāyaṇa* tradition is not only astonishingly broad, as Ramanujan points out, it is also remarkably self-aware. Ramanujan even opens "Three Hundred *Rāmāyaṇas*" with a folk tale that illustrates such awareness. The story describes the efforts of Hanumān, a faithful confidant of Rāma and general in the monkey army that helps find and recover Sītā, to find Rāma's ring that had fallen into a hole. When Hanumān goes to the netherworld to find it, he encounters the King of Spirits, who presents Hanumān with an entire platter of rings. Baffled about which ring to pick, the king explains that "[t]here have been as many Rāmas as there are rings on this platter. When you return to earth, you will not find Rāma. This incarnation of Rāma is over. Whenever an incarnation of Rāma is about to be over, his ring falls down. I collect them and keep them" (ibid., p. 24). Even Hanumān, a crucial actor from within the *Rāmāyaṇa* narrative itself, becomes aware that many *Rāmāyaṇas* have been told and many more will be told in the future as Rāma incarnates again and again.

Such self-awareness is by no means limited to folk renderings of the Rāma story. Consider this famous passage from the Sanskrit *Adhyātma Rāmāyaṇa* (*AdhR*), written in the fifteenth century, wherein Rāma's wife, Sītā, explains to Rāma that she will accompany him to the forest during his exile despite his concerns that she is not suited for the hardships such a life entails. She says to Rāma,

> I will tell you something else. And after you hear it, do take me to the forest. I have heard many *Rāmāyaṇas* from many Brahmins. Tell me, does Rāma go to the forest without Sītā in any of them? So, I will go with you as your companion in every respect. (*AdhR* 2.4.77–78)

In its pervasiveness and self-awareness of its own multiplicity, the *Rāmāyaṇa* tradition works its way into nearly every aspect of India's sociocultural heritage. To borrow from Ramanujan yet again, it is no exaggeration to say that "[i]n India and in Southeast Asia, no one ever reads the *Rāmāyaṇa* or the *Mahābhārata* for the first time. The stories are there, 'always already'" (1991, p. 46). No matter where you go in India, the *Rāmāyaṇa* has been there first and its breadth and pervasiveness are certainly not limited to encounters through reading. One cannot even set foot in India without *experiencing* the story. Aside from the literary and performative manifestations of the Rāma story, it easily finds its way into one's mundane daily routine and society's most consequential moments. Posters of Rāma and Sītā surrounded by their companions hang prominently in shops and rickshaws alike. Towering statues of Hanumān are peppered through many Indian cities while small ornaments of him carrying a mountain hang from many rearview mirrors (Lutgendorf, 1994). Turn on the TV and you're likely to see either a cartoon rendition of the story of Rāma or one of the multiple live-action serializations of the epic that have appeared over the last thirty-some years.[14] The *Rāmāyaṇa* is so ubiquitous that receiving it quickly becomes an unconscious habit.

Yet even as the *Rāmāyaṇa* expresses itself in nearly every cultural context to the point of mental and sensory overload, there are also those instances when the habitual reception of the *Rāmāyaṇa* is disturbed by an event so momentous that we are forcefully pushed into being fully aware of its effect on society. One of the more recent of such events is undoubtedly the Ayodhyā controversy. Contestations over the meaning and history of Ayodhyā have been raging for centuries and reached a tipping point in 1992 when Hindu extremists destroyed the Babri Masjid believing that it sat on the ruins of a temple marking the birthplace of Rāma. Some thirty years later, the Supreme Court of India has ruled that the land must be used for a Rāma temple, with a separate tract of land being allocated for a new mosque. The process of reaching this decision has been rife with communalism and strife with the *Rāmāyaṇa* sitting at the center of the conflict.

A tradition is defined, in part, by the connections that sustain it across time and space. In order to responsibly label the totality of the discrete expressions of the *Rāmāyaṇa* as a tradition, we have to understand how those expressions relate to one another. The problem, of course, is that taking on the *Rāmāyaṇa* tradition as a whole is a task too large for any one study or any one person. The web of connections that make up the entire *Rāmāyaṇa* tradition is overwhelming and seemingly infinite in scope. How, then, can we follow the history of this tradition without sacrificing the vastness of its reach? I believe I have found a viable and representative solution in the Śambūka episode.

This book argues that the Śambūka story boasts its own tradition—a much more manageable tradition that nevertheless permeates the farthest reaches of

---

14 For more on Ramanand Sagar's massively popular serialization of the *Rāmāyaṇa*, which ran from 1986 to 1987, see Thapar (1989). Other subsequent serializations appeared in 2008 and 2012.

the larger *Rāmāyaṇa* tradition. To chart a pathway through the Śambūka tradition is, in a sense, to simultaneously chart a pathway through the *Rāmāyaṇa* tradition; it is just more focused in breadth. Just like the development of the *Rāmāyaṇa* itself, the development of the Śambūka story is a series of connections and contestations over time and space that come together to form an entire tradition made up of a combination of different languages, communities, and expressive media from all over India and abroad over the course of the story's history.

When new historical and social contexts invite new expressions of the *Rāmāyaṇa*, the exposition of the Śambūka episode becomes a useful barometer for positioning a particular *Rāmāyaṇa* in a specific context or ideology. Its usefulness in this way comes from the fact that the circumstances of the Śambūka story present a controversial complexity to Rāma's character that is at odds with how audiences have been conditioned to know him throughout most of the *Rāmāyaṇa* tradition's existence. The various ways of negotiating or exploiting this controversy provide us with a captivating survey of the *Rāmāyaṇa*'s effect on so many aspects of Indian culture. We hear about Śambūka in epics, poetry, dramas and puppet plays, novels, pamphlets, speeches, and court rulings. We see him in paintings and on posters, on TV, and in films. We can visit him in a temple where he lives as a devotee of Rāma or commemorate him as a martyr for the downtrodden. This study follows the developments in telling the story of Śambūka, the sociohistorical circumstances that are behind those developments, and what it all means for the development of the *Rāmāyaṇa* tradition itself.

In addition, the Śambūka story is especially useful for my purposes because it affords me the opportunity to present facets of the *Rāmāyaṇa* tradition that openly challenge the prevailing social and moral assumptions present in mainstream *Rāmāyaṇa* narratives. By accounting for those challenges via this exploration of the Śambūka tradition, I can more clearly demonstrate that any *Rāmāyaṇa* story is part of the *Rāmāyaṇa* tradition, even those that challenge the tradition from within. It is not a prerequisite of any narrative rooted in the *Rāmāyaṇa* tradition to always accept the *Rāmāyaṇa* as a singular, unassailable account of truth. This fact is easily demonstrated by the existence of so many different narrations of the Śambūka story as his death toll rises with iteration upon iteration appearing century after century, some of which align very closely with the first mention in Vālmīki's *Rāmāyaṇa*, and some of which depart from it to an almost unrecognizable degree.

Throughout this book, I will be detailing three prominent ways of engaging with the Śambūka episode, four if we include the trend of ignoring it outright. The first is to frame the story in such a way that elevates Rāma by justifying his punitive action against Śambūka. Justification on this front typically manifests in two ways: a sociocultural justification and a religious justification.

The sociocultural justification takes shape by using the narrative to reinforce the *varṇa*-based social structures that place a high value on the life of the deceased Brahmin boy and a low value on the life of Śambūka, a Śūdra. This social stratification puts Rāma and Śambūka in their respective positions of wielder of state-sanctioned power on the one hand and recipient of systemic subjugation on the other. Religious justification of the Śambūka story is, in many cases, not altogether different from sociocultural justification. It is instead an elaboration on it. The same caste-based social systems often inform the narrative, but Rāma is now not merely a worldly authority, he is a divine one as well. Despite Śambūka's transgressions of the prevailing social order, Rāma in these versions of the tale does kill Śambūka, but in doing so grants him his heavenly ambitions. Śambūka's contact with the god-king Rāma, deadly though it may be, is an immediate pathway to liberation.

The second way of engaging with the Śambūka story involves absolving Rāma of any involvement in Śambūka's death. In stories that utilize this method of narration, Rāma's brother, Lakṣmaṇa, kills Śambūka. Moreover, Śambūka's death is accidental. This method of narrating the Śambūka story first appears in a Jain version of the *Rāmāyaṇa* and it is indeed especially prevalent in Jain tellings of the story. However, this version of events also appears in several Hindu texts. It suits the Jain tradition particularly well because Rāma, depicted in Jain *Rāmāyaṇas* as an ideal Jain himself, could never be involved in any situation of violence. Similarly, by making the death accidental, all criminal and caste-based social structures that are foreign to the Jain tradition are easily removed from the story, including any mention of a deceased Brahmin boy.

Śambūka narratives following the accidental death scenario and especially those that justify his death on sociocultural or religious grounds have been predominant for most of the Śambūka tradition's history. A third method of narrating the Śambūka story, though, has taken shape over the last 150–200 years. Several anti-caste activists rose to prominence starting around the turn of the twentieth century as India witnessed a massive shift in caste consciousness that fundamentally changed the way in which the so-called lower castes interacted with society around them. Numerous prominent anti-caste leaders of Dalit and other non-Brahmin communities starting in the late-nineteenth century and throughout the twentieth century explicitly called on the Śambūka story as a means of demonstrating that caste-based discrimination is deeply ingrained in Indian society. That the *Rāmāyaṇa*, a beloved story all over India, would so openly endorse the execution of a Śūdra, among the most socially vulnerable within India's citizenry, remains a point of anger even today. But instead of merely calling attention to the injustice of Śambūka's death, Dalit and non-Brahmin authors, poets, and playwrights—many of whom were or still are activists themselves—took control of the narrative and depicted Śambūka as a revolutionary leader, an enthusiastic educator, and a martyr for the anti-caste movement.

In these narrations, Śambūka mobilizes education as a means of creating an awareness among India's Dalits and non-Brahmins through education and providing a vocabulary to challenge their systemically oppressed position. It was this challenge to the prevailing social order that condemned Śambūka to death. This Śambūka embodied the various anti-caste movements' most pressing concerns and most effective strategies. For Dalit and non-Brahmin author-activists, he became one of the most useful tools for challenging the dominance of the upper castes and used the *Rāmāyaṇa*—an iconic and infallible text from within that social paradigm—to do it. This image of Śambūka as a revolutionary and martyr finds many expressions in the twenty-first century through depictions in dramas, films, poems, paintings, and more. His potential as a symbol of education, collective pride, and sacrifice ensures that this particular use of the Śambūka narrative remains consequential and vibrant in the current age, especially as India continues to grapple with caste inequities.

I will be referring to a great number of *Rāmāyaṇa* works in this study that, for the most part, fall within one of the three narrative structures just listed. I will, however, have occasion to mention a few outliers—*Rāmāyaṇa* creations that may not fit any of these categories; even some that fit more than one simultaneously. The aim in gathering iterations of the Śambūka story in all these compositions of various media will be to establish a developmental history of the Śambūka episode by following these various narrative tracks and, wherever possible, securing them in a particular moment of Indian history. This project of describing the development of the Śambūka story and positing some reasons for how that development came to be is useful for two reasons. First, the temporal, linguistic, geographic, and social landscapes that the Śambūka episode traverses throughout its history mirror those same landscapes as traveled by the *Rāmāyaṇa* itself. The purpose of this exercise of viewing the *Rāmāyaṇa* tradition through the lens of the Śambūka story is to get a real, palpable sense of the epic's persistent impact on Indian history and culture. And should the Śambūka narrative deviate from its mainstream exposition, we have the occasion to ask what is behind that deviation and what that means for our understanding of the *Rāmāyaṇa* tradition.

Second, the Śambūka story is of great social consequence in today's India and it has been for much of India's history, yet it is an episode in the *Rāmāyaṇa* tradition that is woefully understudied. The importance of the Śambūka episode stems from that fact that Rāma, one of Hinduism's most beloved figures, is at the center of Śambūka's death, as is the caste system. Rāma, a revered representative of the state, kills a Śūdra, someone of low social standing, for violating his station in life by practicing asceticism. That asceticism, we are to understand, creates enough upheaval within Ayodhyā's social norms that a young Brahmin dies as a result. Śambūka is thus sentenced to death. Yet Śambūka's execution is not an eye-for-an-eye punishment. His death results in the *revival* of the Brahmin boy. The value of lives is not equal in this story. Śambūka was not killed so that the same violence would be inflicted on him that he is alleged to have inflicted on the Brahmin boy through his asceticism. Instead, Śambūka's life is traded for the life of someone of higher social standing.

There are numerous potential sources of discomfort within these narrative circumstances. For ardent devotees of Rāma, his involvement in Śambūka's execution may be dissonant with their views of him as an ideal figure and a bestower of grace. For members of India's subjugated classes—those who can most easily identify with Śambūka's social rank—his death is an injustice and his life and death have both been misrepresented. Whatever the case may be, many throughout the history of the *Rāmāyaṇa* tradition believed that the Śambūka story had to be changed and it was changed by both Rāma's harshest critics and his fiercest defenders. Many have seen points of controversy within the story, but prevailing social trends at a particular point in history and the community or communities of which one is a part dictate what is controversial about it and what strategies are most appropriate for addressing the issues it presents. This book explores the different paths the Śambūka story has taken as the stakeholders in its exposition attempt to negotiate the flaws in its many narrations. There is undoubtedly more work to be done on the character of Śambūka, but what I am presenting here is an initial account of what about the Śambūka story needed to be changed, by whom, and why.

Before moving on to describe the layout of this book, it is important to address some basic assumptions I am making about the material I am presenting. First, I will often refer to the *Vālmīki Rāmāyaṇa* as a text written by Vālmīki. Even though the bulk of this text was likely written by a single person accepted popularly to be the legendary sage Vālmīki, it has gone through a centuries-long period of redaction with many contributors to the project. Nevertheless, any time I refer to the *Rāmāyaṇa* of Vālmīki, I am referring to it in its final, completed form even though a figure named Vālmīki may not have written the parts under investigation. This clarification is particularly relevant to this study because the Śambūka story appears for the first time in the *Vālmīki Rāmāyaṇa*'s *Uttarakāṇḍa*, the last of the epic's seven books and one that is most certainly a later accretion to Vālmīki's core text.

The second overarching assumption I will be making (and have already made) is that what I am calling the Śambūka tradition—the entirety of works dedicated to Śambūka and the communities that produce and receive those works—is a component of a larger *Rāmāyaṇa* tradition. To be sure, the Śambūka story is a part of the *Rāmāyaṇa*. However, some who develop certain works on Śambūka, especially those offering a rather stern indictment of Rāma's actions or the social structures on which the incident is based, may not consider themselves as part of any sort of tradition rooted in the *Rāmāyaṇa*. The disconnect, should there be any, will likely be explained by a dissonance between my perspectives and goals as a scholar and the perspectives and goals of a participant from within the tradition as either a content creator or audience member. For example, the act of creating a work wherein Śambūka operates as a central figure may be—and often is—a form of protest against the most prevalent currents of the *Rāmāyaṇa* tradition. While my academic categorization of the *Rāmāyaṇa* tradition includes those protests within the *Rāmāyaṇa* tradition itself, some emic participants in what I am calling the Śambūka tradition might resist such an inclusion. However, the enterprise at hand is meant to develop a comprehensive look at the various voices within this Śambūka tradition and to do so most effectively I will be discussing them within the same overarching framework. That framework is what I am referring to as the *Rāmāyaṇa* tradition.

That brings me to my third assumption, which is that the *Rāmāyaṇa* tradition as I am using it in this study encompasses anything that is either itself a *Rāmāyaṇa* work or anything that can be traced back to some iteration of the *Rāmāyaṇa* or its influence. The *Rāmāyaṇa* tradition as I am defining it also encompasses any person or group that creates a work related to the *Rāmāyaṇa*, receives the *Rāmāyaṇa* in any form, or is otherwise impacted by the story's existence. That definition of the *Rāmāyaṇa* tradition is admittedly and intentionally broad. It is, in fact, meant to account for the *Rāmāyaṇa*'s farthest reaches.

## The Plan for This Book

The narrative specificities for each iteration of the Śambūka episode are never an accident. The Śambūka story appears in the ways that it does for a reason, or perhaps multiple reasons. There are moments and connections throughout Indian history that can help us explain why a specific iteration of the Śambūka story appears when and in the way that it does. An exploration of those moments and connections, though focused on Śambūka, can also help understand a *Rāmāyaṇa* text within a particular context that imbues that text with meaning. Presenting the Śambūka episode in a particular way could simply be following some precedent or it could be a piece of a larger social revolution. The ensuing chapters follow a chronological path through the nearly two-thousand-year development of the Śambūka story, utilizing numerous expressions of and references to the episode to locate trends in narrating the Śambūka story and matching those trends to particular moments and, at times, prolonged movements in Indian history.

Chapters 2–4 are focused on specific texts that fit two basic criteria: first, they are especially consequential to the *Rāmāyaṇa* tradition overall; second, they introduce a significant innovation to how the Śambūka story can be narrated. To properly set a foundation for moving chronologically through histories of the Śambūka tradition and, by extension, the *Rāmāyaṇa* tradition over the course of the book, Chapter 2 explores the Śambūka episode's earliest appearance in the *Vālmīki Rāmāyaṇa*, the first *Rāmāyaṇa* text and a keystone for the *Rāmāyaṇa* tradition. The inclusion of the Śambūka episode in Vālmīki's *Rāmāyaṇa* as part of the *Uttarakāṇḍa*, the epic's final book, marked the *Rāmāyaṇa* contribution to a widespread consolidation of a Brahmin-centric social order happening in the first few centuries of the Common Era. Once the Śambūka story was part of the *Rāmāyaṇa*, it solicited reactions from numerous participants in what was to become an entire tradition of narrating the story of Rāma's life and exploits.

Chapter 3 details the Śambūka episode in two texts of the *Rāmāyaṇa* tradition that appeared in the middle of the first millennium CE, shortly after the final compilation of the *Vālmīki Rāmāyaṇa*: Kālidāsa's *Raghuvaṃśa* and Vimalasūri's *Paümacariya*. Informed by prevailing trends in their respective religious traditions, each frames Rāma's involvement in Śambūka's death in a way that sheds a favorable light on Rāma's conduct. Kālidāsa introduces a concern for Śambūka's afterlife by mentioning that Rāma, in killing Śambūka, sends him along the path of virtuous men (*satāṃ gatim*). In doing so, he makes Rāma a figure worthy of his subjects' admiration, even when he is tasked with enforcing Ayodhyā's social norms in a rather brutal way. Kālidāsa, as a court poet for the Gupta Empire, is doing a very specific kind of work in depicting the Śambūka episode in this way. The Guptas oversaw an elaborate imperialization of Vaiṣṇavism that increasingly viewed Rāma as a god-king whom the Guptas themselves could emulate. In modifying the circumstances of Śambūka's death, Kālidāsa made it easy for the Vaiṣṇava kings of the Gupta Empire to identify with a Rāma who was simultaneously capable of maintaining an authoritative hold on his subjects while bestowing some level of grace on them. Rāma, in Kālidāsa's telling, is just but fair and divine in his delivery of both punishment and salvation.

As a Jain, Vimalasūri was operating in an entirely different religious paradigm than Kālidāsa. In the first millennium CE, Jain teachers were forced to confront the rising popularity of Hindu Vaiṣṇava figures like Rāma and

Kṛṣṇa and many did so by incorporating them into the Jain tradition. Vimalasūri helped catalyze Rāma's incorporation into Jainism—a stringently nonviolent tradition—through his *Paümacariya*, which understood Rāma to be a Jain Śalākāpuruṣa (an illustrious figure). Successfully bringing Rāma in line with the characteristics of a Śalākāpuruṣa—an ideal Jain, to be sure, but ultimately not a divine incarnation—required Vimalasūri to drastically revise the content of Rāma's actions throughout the entire *Rāmāyaṇa* story, including the episode of Śambūka's death. Depicting Rāma as a Śalākāpuruṣa and distancing him from all acts of violence throughout the epic, including Śambūka's death, allowed Vimalasūri to develop a narrative that capitalized on Rāma's popularity without having him run contrary to Jain tenets.

Chapter 4 explores Bhavabhūti's monumental Sanskrit drama, the *Uttararāmacarita*. This play deals exclusively with the latter portion of Rāma's life based largely on Vālmīki's *Uttarakāṇḍa*. The *Uttararāmacarita* marks the first time that Śambūka is given a detailed developmental focus as an integral part of the plot of the work within which he appears. Bhavabhūti transforms Śambūka's death from a brief encounter into a sustained interaction between Rāma and Śambūka that extends *beyond* the execution. The circumstances around Śambūka's death even set off a series of events that lead to the eventual reunion of Rāma and Sītā, whom Rāma had controversially banished from Ayodhyā while she was pregnant with their twin boys. We also find a highly introspective Rāma hesitate in killing Śambūka, a small but radical detail in the moment of Śambūka's death.

With Chapter 5 we move away from very detailed explorations of single texts to more general observations that involve several texts following larger patterns set, in large part, by the texts covered in Chapters 2 and 3. The setting is a critical period in the development of the *Rāmāyaṇa* tradition around the turn of the second millennium CE. Thanks in large part to a massive increase in dedicated devotion to Rāma as a god in this period, both the *Rāmāyaṇa* tradition and the Śambūka tradition along with it grew exponentially. An additional reason for such exponential growth alongside this increasingly prevalent devotion to Rāma is the vernacularization of the *Rāmāyaṇa*, which came from myriad poets from all over India rendering the Rāma story into regional languages, often enhanced with local sentiments and regional streams of influence. Perhaps the most valuable artifact of this period in the Śambūka narrative's development comes with the realization that the precise type of narrative a poet employs does not always correlate to religious tradition. The boundaries between these traditions appear to have been quite fluid: many Hindu texts employ an accidental death motif that parallels the Śambūka episode of Vimalasūri's Jain *Paümacariya*. The reverse, however, is not true. Because of the unacceptability of violence in Jainism—especially on the part of revered figures—we find no execution motif (whether salvific as in Kālidāsa or damning as in Vālmīki) in any Jain *Rāmāyaṇa*, although there are Jain texts that remain silent on Śambūka.

One of the most extraordinary examples of Śambūka's adaptability over an extended period can be found at the center of a small Maharashtra town known today as Ramtek. A small temple sits about halfway up the hill at the center of the town. The temple houses a rather unassuming *śiva-liṅga* known today by the name of Dhūmreśvara, the Lord of Smoke. That *liṅga* is the divinized form of none other than Śambūka, who was made into this form by Rāma as part of a series of boons granted to Śambūka at the time of his death. The temple on this hill marks the site of the paradoxically deadly and immortalizing encounter between Rāma and Śambūka. The literary and epigraphic records associated with Ramtek reveal a gradual maturing of the Śambūka story over fifteen hundred years that combines the salvific execution motif with regional literary networks, localized material culture, and temple practices that continue to produce an entirely unique and living history of the Śambūka story into the present day. The process of maturation in the story's details is intimately tied to centuries of religious innovation, political turmoil, and refinements in literary craft. Chapter 6, which outlines this history of Śambūka and his home at Ramtek from the middle of the first millennium up till today, thus serves as something of an epilogue to the preceding chapters and a transition to the modern focus of the subsequent chapters. It is an account of how this story has become inseparable from the religious environment of a particular place and how people have used the story to demonstrate Rāma's continued grace and the benefits of devotion to him even in transgression.

The study up to this point will have covered a period of approximately fifteen hundred years of a very active *Rāmāyaṇa* tradition. The Śambūka narratives produced during this time remained largely supportive of Rāma. Any modifications made to the Śambūka story from one context to the next were made to align Rāma with the prevailing ideological sentiments of that specific context. In other words, the intent of these modifications was to match Rāma's interaction with Śambūka to the expectations of the audience for which the story was intended. Bending the Śambūka story to elevate Rāma's character may have been the most prominent trend in narrating the episode for much of its history, but that was rather quickly overtaken in the early twentieth century by a strong contingent of Dalit and non-Brahmin author-activists who, simultaneously feeding and following the momentum of increasingly widespread anti-caste movements, elaborated on the Śambūka story to place Śambūka in the position of honorable protagonist. We now find self-contained works that are focused on Śambūka's life, not Rāma's. In many of these tellings,

Śambūka is an educator intent on spreading awareness of a systematic and unjust oppression imposed on members of India's most subjugated peoples. He is, in this way, a revolutionary leader who provides his followers with the tools they need to push back against their oppressors. Śambūka's challenge to Ayodhyā's caste system and his boldness in educating the lower castes are what attracted the attention of the state and pushed Rāma to execute the rebel. Chapters 7 and 8 outline how this novel telling of the Śambūka story took hold, spread throughout the twentieth and into the twenty-first century, and inspired numerous new expressions of Śambūka as an embodiment of the tragedies of casteism, a figurehead around which an anti-caste resistance could be mobilized, and a challenge to the complacency of those who blindly accept the *Rāmāyaṇa* narratives that have been handed down for centuries.

While this version of Śambūka as a compelling symbol of resistance, leadership, and martyrdom has taken a strong hold in recent decades, it has not gone unchallenged. As Śambūka became a more versatile, unapologetic, and widely promoted figure in these circles, opposing voices would often denounce Dalit and other non-Brahmin expressions of the Śambūka story as egregious affronts to Hindu sentiments, even resulting in a few criminal cases, at least one of which reached the Supreme Court of India. The more contentious these battles over the Śambūka story became, the more engrained he became in the minds of anti-caste activists. Eventually, the image of Śambūka as a revolutionary and martyr for the causes of the oppressed that had been developing throughout the twentieth century began to transcend the limits of the literature that produced such an image. As caste tensions have increased steadily since the 1990s, Śambūka has frequently been invoked in speeches, poems, plays, paintings, and films. Those invocations serve to connect the caste violence of the Rāma-Śambūka interaction to current caste discrimination in India today. In fact, the circumstances of Śambūka's death are often recalled when attempting to express grief, outrage, and frustration for contemporary examples of caste discrimination and violence.

Śambūka has travelled far and wide during his two thousand or so years as a part of the South Asian literary universe. His story has forced hundreds, if not thousands, of participants both within and tangential to the continuously evolving *Rāmāyaṇa* tradition to carefully consider how to frame his death in the face of prevailing social or religious trends. There are many ways to mobilize Śambūka and as I piece together his tradition throughout the course of this study, I hope my readers will find that his story not only reflects the impact of major moments in India's history, but that he has also contributed volumes to that history. An understanding of the Śambūka tradition's contributions will most certainly help us read, experience, and view the *Rāmāyaṇa* tradition and its position in society from an entirely new perspective.

# Chapter 2

# ŚAMBŪKA'S EARLIEST DEATH

Near the end of the *Rāmāyaṇa*, Rāma returns to Ayodhyā to be installed as king after fourteen years of exile to the forest. His reign brings with it a long-awaited era of peace and prosperity. However, that peace is eventually disturbed when a Brahmin father brings the body of his dead son to the palace gates. The Brahmin questions how such a thing can happen, going so far as to accuse Rāma of failing to live up to his kingly responsibilities. Rāma becomes distressed and calls a meeting of his closest advisors. One among them, Nārada, explains to Rāma that when society loses sight of *dharma* as the ages progress, the birth-based system of societal segregation—the *cāturvarṇya* or system of four *varṇas*—begins to break down. By the time of the final age, known as the Kali Yuga, the lowest of these *varṇas*, the Śūdras, will begin to do the work of Brahmins, the highest of the *varṇas*. Nārada specifies that only in the Kali Yuga will a Śūdra be able to practice very intense austerities (*tapas*). Before that time, practicing of *tapas* is a crime for a Śūdra. Indeed, Nārada identifies the cause of the Brahmin boy's death as being a Śūdra engaged in *tapas* on the outskirts of Rāma's kingdom. He tells Rāma to survey his kingdom and rid it of all wrongdoing, including this errant Śūdra. Rāma obliges and, after traveling throughout his kingdom, finds an ascetic hanging upside down from a tree on a mountainside in the southern reaches of the Ayodhyā kingdom

> Then, going near to the man engaged in difficult *tapas*, Rāma said these words to him—"You are virtuous, O Great Ascetic.
> "Of which birth are you, O Resolute Ascetic? I am asking you out of curiosity. I am Rāma, the son of Daśaratha.
> "What objective do you desire from practicing such difficult *tapas*? I wish to hear, O Ascetic.
> "Are you a Brahmin? Prosperity be to you. Or are you an unconquerable Kṣatriya? Or are you a Vaiśya? Or if you are a Śūdra, tell me so truthfully." (*VR* 7.66.14–17)
> He heard the words of Rāma—resolute in his action—and, with his head still hanging down, he said this—

> "I was born of a Śūdra womb. I am engaged in formidable *tapas* because I wish to obtain renowned divinity with this body, O Rāma.
> "Out of a desire to obtain the world of the gods, I do not speak untruthfully, O King. Know me to be a Śūdra known by the name Śambūka, O descendant of Kakutstha." (*VR* 7.67.1–3)

Upon hearing this, Rāma unhesitatingly decapitates him without uttering a word. The gods praise Rāma for his swift action against Śambūka and rejoice in the fact that a Śūdra has been denied his socially untenable ambitions of divinity through these dubious means. Śambūka's beheading even brings with it a very specific reward: the revival of the deceased Brahmin boy. The gods inform Rāma that the boy has regained his life the moment that Śambūka was struck down.

This is the earliest version of the Śambūka story. We find it in the *Uttarakāṇḍa*, the seventh and final book of the *Vālmīki Rāmāyaṇa* (henceforth *VR*).[1] The episode's appearance in the *Uttarakāṇḍa* has specific consequences for how we should understand it both historically and narratively. In this chapter, I will detail how we can account for this first iteration of Śambūka's death by following these two pathways—the historical and the narrative. Each are critical to properly conceptualizing the episode and placing it in its proper context, but an informed reading of this episode requires a thorough understanding of both.

The historical setting for this chapter is the period between the fall of the Maurya Empire and the rise of the Gupta Empire, that is "between roughly the fourth century BCE and the fifth century CE, a period that saw unparalleled developments within the Indian subcontinent, developments that defined classical Indian culture and society" (Olivelle, 2006, p. v). These developments involved the "extensive use of writing and the flowering of literature and scholarship: grammar, philosophy, law, political science, epics, drama, poetics, art, architecture, and so on" (ibid., p. v).[2] Of greatest concern here, of course, are the epics, but it is important to contextualize the developments in India's epic literature within this period that witnessed extensive production in numerous areas of literary, ideological, and material output. To that end,

1 See 7.64.1–7.67.4 for the full episode; there is also material relevant to the Śambūka episode in Appendix I, no. 11 of the Baroda Critical Edition of the *VR*.

2 These quotes are taken from the volume *Between the Empires: Society in India 300 BCE to 400 CE* (Oxford University Press, 2006) edited by Patrick Olivelle. The book comprises essays delivered during a conference hosted at the University of Texas at Austin in 2003 covering the historical and social developments that occurred during the period between the Maurya and Gupta Empires.

I will situate the *VR* generally and the Śambūka episode specifically within the transformative currents of the period by discussing it alongside other texts that help define and amplify the developments of these several centuries.

Following this discussion, I will detail some of the narrative nuances of the Śambūka story that help elucidate some of the reasons why it does not fit so well in the overall epic and some reasons why it does. When we consider the fact that the *VR* in its final form was written over the course of centuries, contributions from a collective of poets from different eras and sociopolitical conventions are bound to introduce some heterogeneity in the narrative's flow. I nevertheless find it important to also take the Śambūka episode and its function within the epic seriously as a legitimate piece of the completed narrative. Uncomfortable to modern sentiments though it may be, there is a logic to the Śambūka story appearing where it does and unfolding as it does that tracks with the overall narrative and historical trajectory of the *VR*.

However, before proceeding with my goal of shedding light on the historical and narrative circumstances that imbue the Śambūka episode with much of its meaning, it is worthwhile spending some time with the *Uttarakāṇḍa*, wherein the episode occurs.

## Understanding the *Uttarakāṇḍa*

Most scholars now believe that the *VR* originally ended with Rāma's triumphant return to Ayodhyā after his defeat of Laṅkā's demon king, Rāvaṇa, and the rescue of Rāma's wife, Sītā.[3] In this ending, Rāma ascended the throne to the Ayodhyā kingdom, which was denied to him fourteen years prior. With his installation as king of Ayodhyā, it would appear that all of the epic's major conflicts are resolved. But this is no longer how Vālmīki's text ends. This ending excludes the *Uttarakāṇḍa*, which is now the last book of the epic. Following the meticulous work of J. L. Brockington (1984), the latest scholarship largely agrees that the first written expression of the *Rāmāyaṇa* epic consisted roughly of what is now books 2–6: the *Ayodhyākāṇḍa*, *Araṇyakāṇḍa*, *Kiṣkindhākāṇḍa*, *Sundarakāṇḍa*, and *Yuddhakāṇḍa*, respectively. The narrative highlights from these books include the denial of Rāma's coronation as king of Ayodhyā at the insistence of his stepmother, his fourteen-year exile to the forest

3 For an extensive overview of the compositional history of the *VR*, see Brockington (1984). For a more concise account of the epic's evolution, see the introduction to Goldman (1984, pp. 14–23). L. A. van Daalen has conducted a thorough look into the grammatical features of the *VR*'s Sanskrit language wherein he includes some observations on interpolated passages and other issues related to the epic's development; see Van Daalen (1980).

following that denial, Rāvaṇa's kidnapping of Rāma's wife, Sītā, the search for Sītā aided by the monkey army of Kiṣkindhā, Hanumān's reconnaissance mission to Laṅkā where he finds Sītā, the battle between Rāma's and Rāvaṇa's armies, the rescue of Sītā, and Rāma's return to Ayodhyā. In none of these books do we get any significant mention of Rāma's childhood or his rule over Ayodhyā once he becomes king after his exile. These parts of the story come with the *Bālakāṇḍa* and *Uttarakāṇḍa*—the epic's first and seventh books, respectively—which were added later. Many have attempted to date this late layer of the epic with varying results, as tends to be the case when dealing with anything produced in classical India. Nevertheless, scholarly consensus seems to have settled on the fact that the *Uttarakāṇḍa*, our focus here, most likely reached its completed form as part of the *VR* sometime in the first few centuries of the Common Era.[4]

The most basic narrative purpose of the *Uttarakāṇḍa* is to provide a glimpse of life in Ayodhyā with Rāma on the throne.[5] It is the final bookend to the epic, one that brings to rest the tension that came with denying Rāma his rightful place as king. In resolving this tension, it asserts that Rāma's rule brings about a revival of life as it was in the Kṛta Yuga, a time defined by moral perfection and freedom from hardship of any kind, including the loss of a son.[6] Though this account of Rāma's reign is the part of the book that is most contiguous to the epic's main narrative, the *Uttarakāṇḍa* surprisingly takes its time before Rāma makes an active appearance in his capacity as king. The book opens with a detailed history and genealogy of the demon Rākṣasas, including Rāvaṇa's exploits before the events of the *Rāmāyaṇa* (*sargas* 1–34). Hanumān's early life also features in *sargas* 35 and 36 of the book. We hear about material related to Rāma starting in *sarga* 37, over one-third of the way through the book, and it is not long before we encounter Rāma's famously controversial exile of Sītā based on rumors circulating in Ayodhyā of her infidelity while being held captive in Laṅkā (*sargas* 42–51).

An aura of anxiety undercuts a considerable portion of the content detailing Rāma's efforts in maintaining a reign of perfection throughout the *Uttarakāṇḍa*, particularly when it comes to ensuring the comfortable disposition of the Brahmins. That anxiety is captured well by the descriptions of previous kings'

---

4 For a sampling of such scholarship, see Goldman (1984, p. 15), Guruge (1991, p. 41), and Brockington (1984, pp. 53–59, 329).

5 For a complete synopsis of the plot of the *Uttarakaṇḍa*, see Goldman and Sutherland Goldman (2017, pp. 1–11).

6 The connection between Rāma's rule and the return to this perfected state of existence is explicitly stated in 1.1.71–76, among the final verses of the *Bālakāṇḍa*, and 6.116.82–90, the very end of the *Yuddhakāṇḍa*.

failures to uphold their obligations to Brahmins[7] and, later, Rāma sending his brother, Śatrughna, to protect sages in the forest and destroy the demon Lavaṇa who has been harassing them.[8] Nowhere else in the *Uttarakāṇḍa* is the anxiety over Brahmins' well-being more clearly expressed than in the episode of Śambūka's execution, which centers around placating the Brahmins' concerns about a transgressive Śūdra.

Many streams within the *Rāmāyaṇa* tradition, through their constant reimagining of the circumstances of Śambūka's death and the apologetics surrounding it, have deemed the episode one of the most controversial and incongruous moments in the epic. In the *Uttarakāṇḍa*, it is second in terms of infamy only to Rāma's abandonment of Sītā, perhaps the greatest blemish on Rāma's career. If these stories complicate the image of Rāma to such a great extent—especially when the *Yuddhakāṇḍa* ended with his perfectly conclusive and triumphant return to Ayodhyā—why include the *Uttarakāṇḍa* at all?

Numerous scholars have wrestled with the controversies of the *Uttarakāṇḍa* and the book's thematically imperfect fit within the epic's framework.[9] Brockington, for example, offers that the *Uttarakāṇḍa* "originated basically as a response to the natural curiosity felt by the audience to hear about the later events in Rāma's life," in particular those that follow his installation as King of Ayodhyā (1998, p. 393). Indeed, the entire epic depicts Rāma's eventual trajectory toward the throne of Ayodhyā, which is tragically denied to him near the outset of the story. The *Rāmāyaṇa* then details his trials and tribulations as he is exiled to the forest for fourteen years, during which time Sītā is kidnapped by Rāvaṇa. While the bulk of the *Rāmāyaṇa* deals with his effort to recover her from Rāvaṇa's clutches, that mission is ultimately subservient to installing Rāma in his position as king. The *Rāmāyaṇa* is not fully resolved until we see Rāma on the throne and the *Uttarakāṇḍa* provides us with the only glimpses into his reign.

---

7 Goldman and Sutherland Goldman note that these stories detailing the strenuous interactions between kings and Brahmins have been relegated to appendices in the Baroda Critical Edition of the *VR*. They have, for good reason, restored them to the main body of the text in their own translation (2017, pp. 7, n. 14 and 212–216).

8 The example of the conflict between Śatrughna and Lavaṇa is comparable to instances in the *Bālakāṇḍa* wherein Rāma and Lakṣmaṇa's had similar encounters with the demons Tāṭakā, Subāhu, and Marīca. These demons were disrupting the sacrifices of forest-dwelling Brahmins and Viśvāmitra called on Rāma and Lakṣmaṇa to eliminate them (see *VR* 1.23–29).

9 A useful outline of various positions on the *Uttarakāṇḍa* throughout *Rāmāyaṇa* scholarship appears in the introductory material to Goldman and Sutherland Goldman (2017).

Even in terms of poetics, argue Goldman and Sutherland Goldman, leaving the *Rāmāyaṇa* with a happy reunion of Rāma and Sītā and an uncontested ascension to the throne would detract from the underlying sentiment of the poem (2017, pp. 59–63; see also Gerow, 1984, p. 58). Vālmīki, so the legend goes, composed his poem in a metrical verse he called a *śloka* after seeing a hunter kill a male *krauñca* bird while mating with its lover. Witnessing such a terrible incident drove him to poetically invoke the feelings of the female *krauñca*'s grief (*śoka*) to depict the pain of separation experienced by Rāma and Sītā. With Rāma and Sītā happily united in the end, there is a poetic dissonance that would be untenable. The bereaved *krauñca* has no opportunity to reunite with its deceased mate; the Rāma story—modeled on the pain felt by this bird—should conclude with a similar result. The *Uttarakāṇḍa* delivers that result.

Aside from pure narrative curiosity and aesthetically sound poetics, there are functional concerns as well that would appear unresolved if the epic stopped with the *Yuddhakāṇḍa*. Drawing again on the work of Goldman and Sutherland Goldman, they observe that the epic "serve[s] as a guide to social and political behavior, as both a *dharmaśāstra* and an *arthaśāstra*" (2017, p. 57). Without the *Uttarakāṇḍa*, we would have only brief accounts of the duties of a king and certainly no examples with Rāma on the throne, thus losing out on some rather critical perspectives on the political happenings (*arthaśāstra*) of Ayodhyā. As a part of this loss, the issue of heirs—perhaps a monarchy's most urgent concern—would be completely lacking in the absence of the last book. It is, after all, only in the *Uttarakāṇḍa* that we find out that Rāma has fathered twins, Lava and Kuśa, to further his Ikṣvāku lineage (ibid., p. 58).

Goldman and Sutherland Goldman go far in demonstrating the logic behind the book and its relationship to the entire epic. In particular, the seemingly disconnected stories all tie together with an underlying theme of a constant risk of widespread dharmic imbalance whenever Rāma fails to live up to his own *dharma* as king.[10] Arshia Sattar has also engaged directly with the problem of the *Uttarakāṇḍa* and she also works to justify the book's existence rather than dismiss it wholesale as an interpolated work of little poetic or narrative merit. She notes that with the *Uttarakāṇḍa* dedicating considerable space to the genealogies of Rāvaṇa and Rāma, it functions more like a Purāṇa than an epic. As such, it provides the Rāma story with a "multi-generational, multi-yuga and essentially cyclical narrative" that "elevates the story of the Ramayana to the cosmic level, to the eternal

10 See Goldman and Sutherland Goldman (2017), esp. pp. 145–148.

struggle for power between the gods and their opponents. Rama, Vishnu's current avatara, is merely doing what Vishnu has always done" (Sattar, 2016, pp. 205–206). With the *Uttarakāṇḍa* (and the *Bālakāṇḍa*) fulfilling such a role, Sattar suggests that "we are able to understand why there is such a marked difference between [the *Uttarakāṇḍa* and *Bālakāṇḍa*] and the middle books of the Valmiki Ramayana, not just in style and language, but also in intent and purpose" (ibid., pp. 214–215). These additions to the core of the epic, in other words, round out the loose ends of the epic's mythological coherency.

In addition to these insights, Sattar also articulates a very elegant account of the *Uttarakāṇḍa* that tightens its evidently loose narrative continuity and provides the epic with a sense of closure.

> The word *uttara* had many meanings, among them, 'after', 'epilogue', 'ultimate' and 'answer'. This Uttara Kanda performs the functions of all those meanings: it comes after Rama's adventures as an exiled prince and then as a reinstated king are over; it acts as epilogue to the main story where loose ends are tied up and narrative closure is provided with Rama's ascent to heaven; it is the ultimate moment in his long tale and in his theology; and it provides a series of complex answers to questions that the previous story suggests. (Sattar, 2016, p. 7)

Whatever its imperfections or virtues, the *Uttarakāṇḍa* is now a part of the *VR* and it appeared in a certain time with certain purposes. What those purposes are or what message is being conveyed may differ from episode to episode. Thinking specifically of the Śambūka episode, one might say that it updated the type of "cultural work" the "storyworld" of the *Rāmāyaṇa* does to shape the audience's perceptions of an evolving social ideology in a new era of political turbulence and scholastic exuberance.[11] That social ideology is *varṇadharma* and that new era is the period between the Maurya and Gupta Empires.

11 The concept of the "work of culture" as a process whereby subconscious thoughts become public expressions in the form of myths, rituals, and so on comes from Gananath Obeyeskere (1990). The concept of "storyworlds," the visualized space we create in our minds and the interactions that take place in those spaces based on the narrative, comes from David Herman (2009). I borrow the synthesized use of these two ideas and their application to the Hindu mythological context from Adheesh Sathaye (2015, pp. 6–7, 244–249). Sathaye states concisely that "the cultural work of Hindu mythology is to bind storyworlds to the real world" (ibid., p. 244).

## The Development of *Varṇadharma* in Texts Composed between the Empires

In the section that follows, I explore the ideological expansion of Brahminism as reflected in two non-*Rāmāyaṇa* texts: the *Mānava Dharmaśāstra* and the *Arthaśāstra*. Following an examination of these texts and their role in participating in the project of expanding Brahminical influence, I will show how the Śambūka episode helps situate the expanded *VR* within that same project. Ultimately, the Brahminical institution with the clearest presence in the Śambūka narrative is *varṇadharma*, a theological construct that sought to solidify an idealized social stratification of Indian society and gained its clearest expression during Brahminism's major overhaul in the period between the decline and eventual fall of the Maurya Empire (ca. third–second century BCE) and the beginnings of the Gupta Empire (ca. fourth century CE).

Before proceeding into the material just mentioned, it would be prudent to start with a disclaimer. Texts from this period are notoriously difficult to date with exact precision. It may be possible to narrow down a century or range of centuries within which a text was composed, but that is usually as close as we can get, and even that can be a tenuous enterprise. In addition, we must be mindful of the conditions of the text's composition. It becomes necessary, for instance, to establish whether a text was ever revised or redacted—with developmental histories that extend over centuries in some cases—so as not to read anachronisms into certain layers of the text or the society the text is said to reflect. It is also important to consider how true the society portrayed in the text actually is. Does the text promulgate a realistic vision of society or an idealized one? In most cases, the latter is true and we must resist the temptation to take these texts as an account of the social and political realities of the time. This is not to say that we cannot learn about Indian society by examining these texts, but rather that we should focus what we are able to say. For example, we may not be able to say with confidence that Indian society strictly adhered to the prescriptions and proscriptions of social stratification (i.e., the *varṇa* system) as portrayed in Brahminical texts, but we can often infer that the texts' authors intended to put forth the impression that society did, in fact, toe that line because the authors—most often Brahmins—positioned themselves at the top of that social hierarchy and had a vested interest in promoting an ideology that would keep them there.

### Varṇadharma, tapas, *and Śūdra exclusion*

The first step in understanding the relationship between the Śambūka episode and the texts I intend to highlight here requires an understanding of *varṇadharma*, which operates as a central concept in much of Sanskrit literature.

Splitting this compound up, the term *varṇa* signifies a birth- and occupation-based social class that operates within a four-tiered stratification of society (*cāturvarṇya*). The term *dharma* in the compound then qualifies *varṇa* as the moral and legal code by which members of these *varṇas* are supposed to conduct themselves. Both component terms deserve a closer look.

The four *varṇas* are, in decreasing order of social status, the Brahmins (the priestly class and most socially dominant), Kṣatriyas (the class of kings, other political elite, and warriors), Vaiśyas (merchants and cultivators), and Śūdras (servants). The theology of *varṇa* and society's division into these four classes has its origins in the Puruṣasukta of the *Ṛg Veda* (10.90). Historically, however, the Puruṣasukta hymn was a late interpolation to the *Ṛg Veda*, perhaps added, in part, to "provide a Ṛgvedic charter for such a division of society" (Jamison & Brereton, 2014, p. 1538). In other words, the *varṇa* system matured outside the *Ṛg Veda* and 10.90 was added to the text to impart this hierarchical system with a sense of timeless Vedic authority. The central figure in the hymn is the cosmic man, the Puruṣa, who is sacrificed as a means of creation. The sacrifice yields, among other things, the four *varṇas*. From the Puruṣa's mouth comes the Brahmin, from the arms comes the Kṣatriya, from the thighs comes the Vaiśya, and from the feet comes the Śūdra (10.90.12). With the addition of the Puruṣasukta to the *Ṛg Veda* came a powerful Vedic precedent for the ritual supremacy of the Brahmins and ritual subjugation of the Śūdras. Later Vedic texts, operating within that precedent, then "formalized *varṇa* as a basic discourse of social power based on ritual status" (Sathaye, 2015, pp. 62–63) that helped the *varṇa* ideology spread alongside Vedic religion around the turn of the first millennium BCE.

However, with the rise of the Maurya Empire, particularly by the time of the emperor Aśoka in the middle of the third century BCE, came a decline in animal sacrifice, a cornerstone of the Brahmins' livelihood and a source of their religious and political dominance. Even with their ritual specialization stunted under the Mauryas, Brahmins did not necessarily vacate their relatively high social stature. On the contrary, Aśoka himself, in his famous rock edicts, appears to consider Brahmins to be a group of disciplined holy men who are to be honored and supported. Importantly, however, their ritual functionality and their position within the *varṇa* system are muted in the edicts (Lubin, 2013, pp. 33, 35ff.). Aśoka often mentions the Brahmins alongside another group of revered religious professionals: the ascetics (*śramaṇa*), that is, Buddhists, Jains, and others. Brahmins and ascetics were now counterparts of sorts in the Mauryan imperial worldview. This new relationship and the high degree of prestige asceticism attained under the Mauryas would have a lasting effect on the Brahmins' religious professionalism, even after the decline of the empire.

The power vacuum left by the fall of the Maurya Empire allowed for a kind of revived yet revised vision of *varṇa*. With the Buddhist political structures dissolved after the fall of the Mauryas, Brahmins could reestablish their intimate relationship with the ruling class, reinstate the importance of ritual sacrifice and their exclusive rights to its performance, and reexamine the theoretical foundations of *varṇa*. The return of Brahmins to a position of widely recognized political and social supremacy was, however, not a return to a conceptualization of Brahminism or *varṇa* of the pre-Mauryan era. The prestige of asceticism that found a foothold under the Mauryas left an irreversible mark on *varṇa* and the scope of what it meant to be a Brahmin in particular. To that end, Johannes Bronkhorst offers that "[t]he core ideology of Brahmanism is of a socio-political nature; it is a vision in which Brahmins are at the apex of society, and society as a whole is primarily classified into four caste-classes, *varṇas*" (2016, p. 24). A main tenet of Brahminism, then, is to keep Brahmins in a socially superior position. Doing so very often requires flexibility in expressing that superiority and adopting new means of maintaining it as sociopolitical circumstances warrant change. Within Brahminism, the maintenance of the *varṇa* system is paramount and that maintenance was carried out not through religious conversion or military conquest, but through the imposition of an ideology.[12] That ideology is most clearly expressed in scholastic treatises known as Śāstras, to which we will return shortly.

Moving on to the *dharma* component of *varṇadharma*, this concept eventually became central to Brahminical-Hindu theology signifying, among other things, a moral, ethical, or even legal code of conduct. However, it did not always occupy such a prominent position. The Brahminical appropriation of *dharma* in this sense appears instead to have come in the wake of the Maurya emperor Aśoka and his promotion of *dharma* in its Buddhist sense, making it "the cornerstone of his imperial ideology" in the third century BCE (Olivelle, 2017, p. 11). Once Aśoka utilized *dharma* as a framework for the conduct of his empire, it became central to the political ethos of classical India and the Brahminical segments of society could no longer relegate it to specialized contexts, as was the case throughout the early, middle, and late Vedic periods (ca. mid-second millennium BCE to ca. 500 BCE).[13] As *dharma* became

---

12 This spread of Brahminical ideals is part of the larger reinvigoration of Sanskrit in the early centuries of the Common Era whereby the language moved from the exclusively religious realm to the literary and political realms. The extent of the spread of these ideologies, carried by the prestige of Sanskrit, has been identified by Sheldon Pollock as the "Sanskrit Cosmopolis." See Pollock (2006).

13 For more on the history of *dharma*, see the introduction to Olivelle (2017), esp. pp. 8–13 and Hiltebeitel (2010).

a contested term in imperial and religious arenas, however, so too came the expert tradition of defining what *dharma* means in Brahminical settings. That expert tradition is known as Dharmaśāstra, which has produced an incredible array of treatises on *dharma* and its role in society. A primary focus of these texts is the importance and preservation of *varṇadharma*, especially as it relates to the dominant position of the Brahmins.

The social supremacy of Brahmins and the position of kings to sustain that supremacy underpins the functionality of *varṇadharma*. That supremacy has been called many things in scholarship including political Brahmanism (McClish, 2009), Brahmin power (Sathaye, 2015, pp. 62–64), and Brahmanical power (Bronkhorst, 2016, pp. 221–240). Olivelle offers that the *varṇa* system was "from the start an ideologically driven enterprise designed to place the Brahmin at the top of a pyramidal social hierarchy, supporting the claim to power of the Kṣatriya class, and in a special way reducing the Śūdras and other lower classes to a marginal and oppressed status" (2019, p. 121). It is important to clarify that the claim to power of the Kṣatriya class mentioned by Olivelle was largely limited to worldly affairs of government. They were still subjected to the higher moral order of *dharma*, a power schematic that was controlled by Brahmin jurists of the Dharmaśāstra tradition. Some of the most salient features of the Brahmins' superior position in Indian society includes their relative immunity to sovereignty of the king and their ability to place all other classes of society—including the king himself—in a subordinated position.

In conveying the prominent position of Brahmins, I generally prefer Mark McClish's "Brahmanical exceptionalism," which he has defined in different places as "the belief that Brahmins were deserving of special rights and privileges within the greater political order" (McClish, 2009, pp. 11–12) and "various immunities of the Brāhmaṇas as a class," that grant them "some degree of emancipation from the king's sovereign power" (McClish, 2019, p. 190). My preference for this term should not imply that I believe the term to be more accurate than the others; each is appropriate to various circumstances. I appreciate the term "Brahmanical exceptionalism" because it contrasts well with a concept that I would like to emphasize in the context of the Śambūka episode. That concept is Śūdra exclusion.

Our textual sources—written largely by Brahmins—portray the political and social landscape of classical India in an idealized way. That landscape was designed by Brahmin scholars to keep them in a socially dominant position, often out of reach of even the king's authority. The king's role in this social system was to enforce this design conceptualized by the Brahmins. In the end, what we get is a model of society that is engineered through the scholarship of Brahmins, enforced through the authority of the Kṣatriyas, and sustained by the enterprises of the Vaiśyas. The Śūdras, we are told, support the general functioning of this society through service to these other classes of people. That service, though, comes with systemic social, economic, legal, and ritual subjugation by means of a careful exclusion of the Śūdra *varṇa* from the leniencies and privileges enjoyed by the other three, particularly the Brahmins.[14]

Take, for example, this passage from the *Āpastamba Dharmasūtra* (12.27.17–20), which demonstrates Dharmaśāstra's tendency to err on the side of leniency when inflicting punishments on Brahmins for crimes they may commit.

> If a Brahmin is guilty of these crimes [of murder and theft], however, he should be blindfolded. Alternatively, those who transgress their specific duties should be kept in secret confinement until they relent. If they do not relent, they should be banished. A teacher, an officiating priest, a bath-graduate, and the king may save him from punishment, except in the case of a capital crime.[15]

Compare this to 12.27.14–16 of the same text, immediately preceding 12.27.17–20 just cited. Here we find a statement on appropriate punishments for a Śūdra for various illegal acts.

> If a Śūdra hurls abusive words at a virtuous Ārya, his tongue shall be cut out. If, while he is speaking, walking on the road, lying in bed, or occupying a seat, a Śūdra pretends to be equal to Āryas, he should be flogged. If a Śūdra kills a man, steals, or appropriates land, he should be executed and his property confiscated.[16]

---

14 Though speaking of the disparity between the Brahmins and the so-called Untouchables, Louis Dumont extrapolates similar thinking to the much larger idea of caste-based stratification generally. Based on the dichotomy of these two extremes and the web of relationships that governs the interactions of all societal participants within those extremes, he finds that "the actual society is a totality made up of two unequal but complementary parts." Those two parts are defined especially by their relationship to purity—how they interact with impurities of various kinds and how that plays out in the ritual universe dictated by Brahmins. The Brahmins thus use concerns of purity and impurity to justify the existence of the caste system and the stratification within it. However, while the "Untouchables" serve as the social opposite of the Brahmins in the observable world, they receive even less attention in the legal literature than the Śūdras, who are spotlighted in texts on *dharma* as counterparts to the Brahmins. See Dumont (1980, p. 55).

15 Olivelle's translation (1999, p. 71). A bath-graduate (Skt. *snātaka*) is one who has completed his Vedic education. This designation is only available to Brahmins, Kṣatriyas, and Vaiśyas. See Lubin (2018) for more on the *snātaka*.

16 Olivelle's translation (1999, p. 71).

This example of the contrasting circumstances between Brahmins and Śūdras is not unique. Numerous examples exist of a Śūdra's punishment being articulated in direct contrast to a Brahmin's for the same or similar transgressions.[17]

In addition to these examples of punishments, which ultimately fit under a kind of law enforcement, the *dharma* texts focus heavily on socioreligious purity and access to education and ritual. This is predicated primarily on the fact that the upper three *varṇas*—also referred to as twice-borns (*dvija*)—are eligible for Vedic education by way of the *upanayana* ceremony. This ceremony marks the "second birth" symbolized by the investiture of a sacred thread to wear as they commence this education. The Śūdras are specifically excluded from receiving this initiation or actively participating in the religious schematics available to the twice-born *varṇas* and overseen by the Brahmins. The most violent denial of a Śūdra's access to the knowledge and rituals described in the Vedas appears in the *Gautama Dharmasūtra*, which prescribes that if a Śūdra "listens in on a vedic recitation, his ears shall be filled with molten tin or lac; if he repeats it, his tongue shall be cut off; if he commits it to memory, his body shall be split asunder" (12.4–6).[18]

The discussion above reveals that one purpose for promoting *varṇadharma* was to restrict Śūdras' access to the privileges and benefits of the religious institutions of the higher *varṇas*. The demarcation between Śūdras and the other *varṇas* in this way could, according to our sources, be violently enforced. The terms of violation were defined by Brahmins and punishments carried out by kings. As we are about to see, this aspect of *varṇadharma* appears in several venues throughout Sanskrit literature. The concept appears explicitly and implicitly in the traditions of Dharmaśāstra and Arthaśāstra (statecraft) and figures into the epic narratives as well; and, importantly for my purposes, it is central to the Śambūka episode. In the intervening centuries between the Maurya and Gupta Empires, we see a deep preoccupation in Sanskrit texts with *varṇadharma* culminating in several theoretical and narrative explorations of the subject meant to bolster the hierarchization of society in unequivocal terms. Two of these texts—the *Mānava Dharmaśāstra* and Kauṭilya's *Arthaśāstra*—are worth exploring in some detail.

---

17 By way of example, see *Āpastamba Dharmasūtra* 2.27.8–10. Both earlier and later *Dharmaśāstra* texts have a generally unfavorable view of Śūdras. Olivelle has, however, identified examples of positive treatment. Pointing toward *Āpastamba Dharmasūtra* 2.28.11 and 15, he notes that "Āpastamba … even says that one may learn aspects of *dharma* from Śūdras" (2005, pp. 39–40).

18 Olivelle's translation (1999, p. 98).

### *The* Mānava Dharmaśāstra

The first text I will be looking at to help establish the larger historical and literary context for Śambūka's appearance in the *VR* is the *Mānava Dharmaśāstra* (*Manu's Treatise on Dharma*, henceforth *MDh*), a text attributed to the figure Manu, the son of the self-existent and imperishable creator. It was and continues to be an extremely consequential text in the field of Dharmaśāstra, a tradition that sought to codify and promote a Brahminical conceptualization of *dharma*. Before moving forward, however, it is necessary in a discussion of these scholastic texts on *dharma* to distinguish between how I will be representing the tradition within which these texts exist and the texts themselves. I use the unitalicized Dharmaśāstra to refer to the expert tradition of scholarship on *dharma* as it is codified, categorized, and systematized within a Brahminical Hindu worldview. I use the italicized *Dharmaśāstra* when referring to texts within that expert tradition written after and including the *MDh*. It is important to note, though, that prior to *Dharmaśāstra* texts came works referred to collectively as the *Dharmasūtras*, which are written in an aphoristic prose. These earlier *Dharmasūtra* texts are included in the broadly conceived Dharmaśāstra tradition, but they are distinct in style, content, and time period from the later, versified *Dharmaśāstra* texts.

The landmark *MDh* helps us delineate between the two categories of *Dharmasūtra* and *Dharmaśāstra* because it "occupies the middle position at the point of transition from the prose and scholastic *Dharmasūtras* to the metrical *Dharmaśāstras* ascribed to authoritative divine beings" (Olivelle, 2005, p. 20). Many of the key features that separate the *Dharmaśāstra*s from the *Dharmasūtra*s are innovations of Manu. By way of example, his text was the first *Dharmaśāstra* that was composed entirely in verse, which gave the text an aura of religious authority reflecting a trend in other areas of Sanskrit literature, including the epics (ibid., pp. 25–26). The *MDh* was also given a divine narrative frame by which the prescriptions and proscriptions on *dharma* were claimed to have come straight from the self-existent creator. The *MDh*, then, begins to drift away from a reliance on multiple sources of *dharmic* authority—namely the Vedas, the authority *par excellence*, as well as traditionally authoritative texts known as *smṛti*s and the conduct of virtuous people (*ācāra*)—that characterized the earlier *Dharmasūtra*s and instead moves toward promulgating *dharma* as coming from a single, divine source (ibid., pp. 26–28).

As for the date of the *MDh*, I rely on Patrick Olivelle's assessment that the text was composed by a single individual writing around the second or third century CE, a couple of centuries shy of the rise of the Gupta Empire

(2005, pp. 18–25).[19] The earliest *Dharmasūtras* were composed several centuries earlier in the wake of the Aśoka's politicization of *dharma* as discussed above. Therefore, the segment of Dharmaśāstra's development that encompasses the creation of the *Dharmasūtras* and the early *Dharmaśāstras* aligns with the period "between the empires" that I am exploring here and the reason for that alignment is no coincidence. Throughout this phase of maturation in Dharmaśāstra culminating in the composition of the *MDh*, thinkers within the tradition became increasingly concerned with *varṇadharma*, a concept narrativized in the Śambūka episode. I find ruminations on *varṇadharma* in the Dharmaśāstra tradition—the *MDh* in particular—and the addition of the Śambūka story to the *VR* to be part of the same sociopolitical project.

The *MDh* contains many expressions of Śūdra exclusion. Verses 2.36–37 describe the appropriate time for each of the *varṇas*' Vedic initiation (*upanayana*) but leave Śūdras out of the discussion. In 2.80, a verse describing the necessity of reciting the syllable *ōṃ* along with the Sāvitrī verse as well as the timely performance of one's rites, Manu mentions only Brahmins, Kṣatriyas, and Vaiśyas. Śūdras are also excluded from the ritual universe altogether through restrictive marriage proscriptions. In 3.14–15, Manu prohibits Brahmin and Kṣatriya men from taking Śūdra wives lest they violate the purity of their bloodline, though in 3.12–13 he does appear to follow the standard *anuloma* ("with-the grain") sexual relationship where a man of a higher *varṇa* may have intercourse with a woman of a lower *varṇa*. He specifies, however, that a man's first marriage should be to a woman of his own class. In 3.249, Śūdras are excluded from receiving leftover food from ancestral offerings. 4.80–81 prohibit Vedic graduates from engaging with Śūdras in various ways, including instructing them in the law or prescribing certain observances. Chapter 11 of Manu's text presents a few telling situations that reflect a deep-seated anxiety surrounding a Śūdra's access to ritual practices. In 11.13, for instance, Manu declares that someone who is looking to conduct a sacrifice but is unable to do so because he is missing some necessary implement can take those things from others. He is especially encouraged to take those things from a Śūdra because a Śūdra should have nothing to do with sacrifices. 11.24 prohibits begging a Śūdra for money to conduct a sacrifice. It might not be a stretch to say that this verse makes such a prohibition because of the legal gray area that brings a Śūdra too close to patronizing a sacrifice in the first place. 11.42 would seem to

19 Like many other texts produced in classical India, though, the *MDh* did go through phases of redaction after completion but the majority of the text seems to have been penned by this singular author. According to Olivelle, only about twelve percent of the text is interpolated material (2005, pp. 50–62).

confirm that point. Manu states: "Those who perform their daily fire sacrifice by obtaining money from a Śūdra are considered reprehensible among vedic savants, for they are the officiating priests of Śūdras."[20] The existence of such statements would seem to suggest that these types of behaviors were happening and, from the perspective of the upper eschelons of ancient Hindu religious society, needed to be legislated against.

The impact of the *MDh* was swift and wide-reaching. We have already seen that it inspired a new way of conceptualizing Dharmaśāstra as a tradition and *Dharmaśāstra* texts as compositions representing that tradition, but its influence extended rather far beyond its own field of expertise. Manu's vision of *dharma*—and *varṇadharma* within it being of particular concern here—became so pervasive that it led intellectuals in other areas to apply this new paradigm of *dharma* to their own endeavors. This periodically even meant revisiting extant works and bringing them in line with the worldview promoted by Manu. The epics were one such venue where redactors expanded existing material to include the social philosophy of Manu. Another such venue was statecraft and the implementation of political and judicial policy within Indian society. For example, one innovation of Manu in his treatise on *dharma* that went unstated above was his incorporation of "a long exposition on the king, state administration, and especially judicial procedure derived at least partly from Kauṭilya's *Treatise on Politics* [=*Arthaśāstra*]" (Olivelle, 2017, p. 73). The relationship between the *MDh* and the *Arthaśāstra* is bolstered, in part, by an always implicit and sometimes explicit concern for the preservation of *varṇadharma*. Olivelle's observation that Manu's unprecedented inclusion of matters of statecraft in the world of *dharma* needs a slight, but significant, qualification that bears heavily on my own concerns with Manu's influence on textual traditions outside of Dharmaśāstra. The compositional timelines of the *MDh* and the *Arthaśāstra* overlap. Portions of the *Arthaśāstra* as we know it today were composed before the *MDh* and some portions were composed after (and appear to be influenced by) the *MDh*. To help me illustrate why these developments are important in this discussion of the Śambūka episode, I will shift the discussion to the *Arthaśāstra*.

## *The* Arthaśāstra

In a recent study detailing the developmental history of the *Arthaśāstra* (*Treatise on Politics*, henceforth *AŚ*), Mark McClish has demonstrated that the history of the *AŚ* as we have it today consists broadly of two main compositional

20 Olivelle's translation (2005, p. 217).

landmarks: the original text, which McClish has called the "*Daṇḍanīti*" ("*The Policy of Governance*," literally "*The Policy of the Rod*") and the redaction of that base text done by someone by the name of Kauṭilya.[21] The former, which McClish places around the first century BCE, was a rather realist view of political strategy and technique that had little to say about a king's sovereign power or its limitations.[22] Kauṭilya's redaction from the third century CE, however, inserts a theological layer to the text that puts the king in a subordinate position to his *dharma*—*dharma*, in this case, being subdivided into *rājadharma* (the *dharma* of kings) and *kṣatradharma* (the *dharma* of Kṣatriyas, the *varṇa* within which kings are born).[23] What sets the king apart from the general population of Kṣatriyas is his specialized *rājadharma*.

The concept of a specialized *dharma* for kings is not a development native to the tradition of statecraft; it is instead an innovation of the Dharmaśāstra tradition. From the earliest stratum of Dharmaśāstra literature, represented by the *Āpastamba Dharmasūtra*, the king is not merely a member of the Kṣatriya *varṇa*. As king, he is charged through his *rājadharma* with enforcing and, in so doing, upholding *varṇadharma* itself (McClish, 2019, p. 262). There are many examples of such enforcement throughout the Dharmaśāstra tradition. *MDh* 8.410–420, for instance, gives numerous details about the expected conduct of each of the four *varṇa*s. I cite 8.418 here:

> The king should strenuously make Vaiśyas and Śūdras perform the activities specific to them; for when they deviate from their specific activities, they throw this world into confusion.[24]

In essence, through *rājadharma*, the king becomes subject to an idealized moral order that sets the expectation that he will preserve and protect *varṇadharma*. This expectation is solidified in the Dharmaśāstra tradition and becomes represented in the redacted *AŚ* when Kauṭilya introduced certain theological developments of Dharmaśāstra into this text on statecraft.

The timing of the two strata of the *AŚ* is telling. The *Daṇḍanīti* was composed several centuries prior to the *MDh*. The *MDh* itself represents the culmination of the philosophies of statecraft and *dharma*—once independently

---

21 This is not to say that there were no other contributors to the extant text at different moments. McClish notes several passages relating to the exceptional position of Brahmins, for example, that may have been added by other redactors or even potentially overzealous scribes adding notes in the margins of the text (2019, pp. 193–197).

22 On the dating of the *Daṇḍanīti*, see McClish (2019, pp. 151–152).

23 On the dating of Kauṭilya's redaction, see McClish (2019, pp. 144–150).

24 Olivelle's translation (2005, p. 189).

functioning intellectual endeavors—coming together, fortified by the enforcement of *varṇa*. The unification of these ideas, though, was not instantaneous. The Dharmaśāstra tradition appropriated the structures of statecraft between the third century BCE and the second century CE whereupon it matured with the composition of the *MDh*. After Manu, there occurs a sort of pendulum effect whereby the field of statecraft absorbs theological innovations within Dharmaśāstra (especially the *MDh*). That absorption then becomes manifest in the redaction of the *AŚ* by Kauṭilya. The driving force behind the appropriation of statecraft in the Dharmaśāstra tradition and the subsequent appropriation of *dharma* in the practice of statecraft was the increasing influence of Brahminical theology, which is represented especially by the adherence to and enforcement of *varṇadharma* in the theoretical and narrative literature leading up to the Gupta period (see McClish, 2019, pp. 217–219). This time frame—from the composition of the earliest Dharmaśāstra texts in the wake of the Maurya Empire, through the composition of the *MDh*, up to the redaction of the *AŚ* just before the Gupta Empire—corresponds to the same period "between the empires" that saw the addition of the Śambūka episode to the *VR*, which, as we shall now see, also reflects rising Brahminical influence in the form of *varṇadharma*.

## *Śambūka in the* Vālmīki Rāmāyaṇa

As we move away from theoretical treatises into the realm of narrative, I find Adheesh Sathaye's observations on the role of *varṇa* in the *Dharmaśāstras* versus the epics helpful. He points out that while the *Dharmaśāstras* "conceived of *varṇa* as a totalizing system of social order, the Sanskrit epics and purāṇas offered unusual cases that compelled the consumer to wrestle with the real-world applicability of such rules and regulations" (2015, p. 11). Unusual cases that could appear within the narrativized epic framework include "violations, counter examples, or failures of Hindu social norms, creating sites of slippage and rupture in the storyworld where one could find, at least in principle, cracks within the normative social doctrine" (ibid., p. 11). In other words, whereas theoretical treatises like the *Dharmaśāstras* present idealized perspectives of a prevailing social order, the epics venture into the weeds by problematizing those conventions. The "cracks within the normative social doctrine," however, are nearly always resealed—to continue using Sathaye's apt metaphor—with "scholastic caulk" in the form of cautious characterizations of unconventional behavior or clever narrative framing that explains the rationale behind some potentially controversial action (ibid., p. 11). We see this time and time again in the epics.

One of the clearest examples of the *VR* using narrative framing to navigate moral gray areas would be when the monkey king Vālin attempts to chastise

Rāma for shooting him from a concealed position while he was engaged in battle with his brother, Sugrīva (4.17). He argues that Rāma violated his Kṣatriya *dharma* and, in so doing, committed a sinful act. After hearing Vālin's rebuke, Rāma himself swiftly and firmly responds to the accusations. The crux of his argument comes in 4.18.15 where he says that *dharma* is subtle and hard to understand for even the most capable people. He then details the subtleties behind his specific actions against Vālin by telling him that his lust for his brother's wife is grounds for death. Rāma, as a representative of the Kingdom of Ayodhyā, is authorized to carry out the punishment and, in killing Vālin, he is upholding his ancestral *dharma*—a *dharma*, we are told, that is too complex for Vālin to fully comprehend (e.g., 4.18.39). Vālin is apologetic upon hearing Rāma's lesson in *dharma* and Rāma assures him that in receiving his due punishment, he is freed of his sins (4.18.55). Vālin then dies of his wounds. The epics and purāṇas are replete with examples of this kind of nuanced look at *dharma*, the most famous example—this time appearing in the *MBh*—being Kṛṣṇa's quelling of Arjuna's conflicted mind as he weighs the burden of battling his kin in the Great War on the Kurukṣetra battlefield. The resolution to this conflict comes in the form of Kṛṣṇa's long, *dharma*-heavy discourse in the form of the *Bhagavad-Gītā*.

In addition to building lectures on *dharma* into the narrative, poets of the epics also seem to have found unconventional characters useful in illustrating the complexities of *dharma* and closely related issues of *varṇa*. A prime example of such characters is Viśvāmitra, the subject of Sathaye's study quoted above and a figure famous for crossing the boundaries of *varṇa* by utilizing intense *tapas* to traverse the usually impossible gap between being a Kṣatriya and being a Brahmin. Śambūka is another unconventional character who violated the Brahminical social order and was made an example of by the poet(s) of the *Uttarakāṇḍa*. In this episode, even Rāma's action against Śambūka introduces another avenue of moral exploration. The audience may wonder why Śambūka had to die and the *Uttarakāṇḍa* applies the caulk to this crack preemptively by having Nārada explain why Śambūka (though not directly named by the sage) must die before the execution is even carried out. The caulking seems to have worn thin, however, as some streams of thought have deemed the basis for Śambūka's death and Rāma's involvement in it questionable. Charting the development of these critiques is, of course, the primary purpose of this book.

The very first iteration of the Śambūka story in any context appears in the last book of the *VR*, the *Uttarakāṇḍa*. As mentioned above, this final book is widely believed to be a late addition to the core of Vālmīki's text from around the second century CE. The expansion of the *VR*, then, occurred in the same historical context as the composition of the *MDh* and Kauṭilya's redaction of the *AŚ*. We might expect, then, that some of the same issues surrounding *varṇadharma* would be raised in these sources in a similar way as in the *VR* and that is precisely what we find.

Meditations on *varṇadharma* after the fall of the Maurya Empire often exhibited Brahmin exceptionalism and Śūdra exclusion simultaneously. They are, after all, two sides of the same coin. In the ideological world of Brahminism, Śūdras are exceptional, but in the exact opposite way as their Brahmin counterparts. Śūdras receive as much severity in the attention paid to them as Brahmins receive leniency. We have seen this exclusion put forward rather explicitly in the *MDh*, though other texts also put forth similar sentiments.

In balancing Brahmin supremacy with Śūdra subjugation and charging the Kṣatriyas—kings in particular—with upholding that balance, *varṇadharma* afforded Brahmins a paradigm by which they could control social interactions and maintain a position of dominance in society. That dominance even extended to Brahmins' relationship with the king. Both the *MDh* and the redacted *AŚ* took the latest theological ruminations on *varṇadharma* and applied it to the world of statecraft, previously an entirely worldly enterprise with little to say about the limits of a king's sovereignty. The king's enforcement of *varṇadharma* became a duty of the highest order—a *dharma* in its own right. In this new conceptualization of a king's sovereignty, a failure to uphold the limits of *varṇadharma* would not only be a lapse of governance, but it would also be a lapse of a king's divine duty. In this theological system of *varṇa* hierarchy, the king became subservient to both *dharma* and the dominance of Brahmins.

This Brahminical schematic of social organization with all its nuance is on full display in the Śambūka episode. The narrative captures the social dominance of Brahmins along two vectors: one where Brahmins are viewed relative to Śūdras and one where they are viewed relative to the king. The former is depicted through the panic over—and eventual rectification of—the young Brahmin's death. The Brahmins' supremacy vis-à-vis Śūdras is clear from the fact that the life of Śambūka, as a Śūdra, is expendable when the life of a Brahmin is at stake. As soon as Śambūka is killed, the Brahmin boy comes back to life and the gods rejoice in this fact. Even the superior position of Brahmins in relation to the king—Rāma himself—finds mention when the father of the deceased Brahmin boy approaches Rāma's court chastising his lax governance and blaming him for the death of his son.

In addition to depicting the social dominance of Brahmins, the Śambūka episode also makes the ritual exclusion of Śūdras a central point to the plot by describing his engaging in *tapas* as a criminal act punishable by death. Nārada explains to Rāma that by practicing *tapas*, Śambūka has transgressed the limits of his *varṇa* and he has done so to so severe a degree that he has caused the death of a Brahmin. In his new role as king, Rāma is now beholden to the obligations set forth by *rājadharma*, which stipulates that he must ensure that all his subjects adhere to their *varṇadharma*. In this situation, that means that Rāma must counter the consequences of Śambūka's crime—that is, the death of the Brahmin boy—by executing him.

In the Śambūka episode, then, we get all the major highlights of *varṇadharma* as it was conceptualized in the early centuries of the Common Era and described in texts like the *MDh* and the *AŚ*. I find this to be no coincidence. When the *Uttarakāṇḍa* was added to the *VR* at roughly the time of the *MDh*'s composition and the redaction of the *AŚ*, there was a prime opportunity to infuse the *VR* with similar ideological principles, particularly those related to *varṇadharma*. The result is the addition of the Śambūka episode, which falls in line with the ruminations on *varṇadharma* happening in these other areas of Sanskrit literature.

Though *varṇadharma* is a foundational concept in the Śambūka episode, it is articulated in the context of a Śūdra violating *varṇadharma* through the specific practice of *tapas*. In this case, Śambūka engages in *tapas* so that he may enter heaven with his body. It is worth briefly considering the idea of *tapas* as it relates to Śūdra exclusion. In the *VR*, Nārada charges Śambūka with the capital offense of practicing *tapas* outside the Kali Yuga, the only time, according to him, when a Śūdra would be able to practice such a thing. The *VR* may depict Nārada stating Śambūka's guilt plainly and encouraging Rāma to act swiftly thereon, but a survey of Brahminical literature reveals conflicting views on a Śūdra's ability to engage in *tapas* (Olivelle, 1993, pp. 193–194). Following Nārada's line of thinking, *Brahmāṇḍa Purāṇa* 1.31.60 explains that a Śūdra practicing *tapas* signifies the Kali Yuga. Overall, though, passages in Brahminical texts that explicitly deny a Śūdra the right to practice *tapas* are quite rare; and they are even rarer in texts of the Dharmaśāstra tradition specifically. Nevertheless, Olivelle draws our attention to the fact that some texts place *tapas* among a list of six practices that cause the downfall of Śūdras as well as women and he cites *Atri Smṛti* 136–137 in support of this (ibid., p. 194).[25] Looking elsewhere, Olivelle believes that we find "a more liberal attitude toward Śūdra asceticism" in the epics, especially if we consider the *MBh* (ibid., p. 194).

---

25 Though significantly later, similar statements can be found in the *Jātiviveka* as well as the *Nāradīya Purāṇa*. See Benke (2010), pp. 102 and 140 for citations of the *Nāradīya Purāṇa* and *Jātiviveka*, respectively, as found in the sixteenth-century text on *śūdradharma* entitled *Śūdrācāraśiromaṇi*.

The references that Olivelle cites all deal with a Śūdra participating in the various *āśramas* or "life-modes" one adopts after completing a Vedic education.[26] Since *tapas* and these life-modes (especially in the more conventionally ascetic modes of the forest hermit and the renouncer) are often closely connected, there is an implied exclusion of Śūdras from the practice owing to the fact that they have no access to the *āśrama* system because they have no rights to the ceremonial initiation (*upanayana*) into Vedic education that such access presupposes.[27] The apparent connection between the *āśrama*s and the specific practice of *tapas* leads Olivelle to consider examples of a Śūdra adopting an ascetic life-mode as representing this "liberal attitude" pertaining to a Śūdra's legal ability to practice *tapas*.

Although Olivelle's observations certainly identify a conflict in how Sanskrit literature envisions a Śūdra's engagement with the *āśrama*s and *tapas*, I find it necessary to note that there need not always be an inherent connection between *tapas* and an associated *āśrama*. I have argued elsewhere that the *VR*, for example, does not exhibit much concern with a codified system of *āśramas* (Sherraden, 2019), but we nevertheless find numerous examples of characters engaging in *tapas* outside the context of a committed ascetic *āśrama*. There are even examples of socially subordinated characters other than Śambūka living an ascetic life with no mention of their *āśrama*; yet, as part of their ascetic lifestyle, they nevertheless engage in *tapas*. Some prominent examples of such characters would be the tribal woman Śabarī and the young ascetic accidentally killed by Daśaratha. Both episodes are addressed more fully below when considering the overall place of the Śambūka episode in the wider *Rāmāyaṇa* narrative.[28]

Bringing the above discussion to a close, the story of Śambūka's death involves, in actuality, two deaths. The one we are most concerned with here, of course, comes with Śambūka's execution. The second death in the episode is the untimely death of the young Brahmin boy, which sparks the series

26 Indeed, a Śūdra's denial of *tapas* in the literature is rather implicit this way; a Śūdra is generally prohibited to access of more ascetic lifestyles that go along with being a *parivrājaka* or, even more so, a *vānaprastha*. I thank Patrick Olivelle for this observation.

27 For a useful account of *tapas* and its connection to the *āśrama*s in the context of "Brāhmaṇic asceticism," see Kaelber (1989, pp. 101–124).

28 It is telling to note, however, that these episodes appear in earlier strata of the *VR* and the characters are not subjected to the same severity of punishment that we see in the Śambūka story. It is only with the addition of the *Uttarakāṇḍa*, a work of literature contemporary to the *MDh* and the redacted *AŚ*, that we get this fully matured vision of politicized *varṇadharma* whereby Śambūka's execution for *varṇa*-based crimes is condoned in the Brahminical social schematic and carried out by the king.

of events culminating in Śambūka's execution. These two characters' relative social value, defined by *varṇadharma*, drives the narrative of the entire incident wherein the life of Śambūka is traded for the life of the Brahmin and the office of the king serves as the mechanism for ensuring that this trade takes place. When instructing Rāma on the cause of the boy's death and the means of rectifying it, Nārada, as the king's divine advisor, reminds Rāma of the Brahminical institutions the king is charged with protecting. Nārada makes it clear that Śambūka transgressed the limits of his social class (*varṇa*), which disrupted the balance of *dharma* in Ayodhyā and ultimately led to the death of the young Brahmin. Rāma, as a king beholden to *rājadharma*, is obligated to restore the proper functioning of *varṇadharma* within his jurisdiction. That restoration equates to Śambūka's death and puts Rāma in the position to mete it out.

Recalling the aspects of the *MDh* and the *AŚ* highlighted above, we have here in the Śambūka episode of the *VR* a clear expression of the primacy of *varṇadharma* in conceptualizing society, the Brahmins' superior position within the *varṇa* system, the Śūdras' inferior position within that system, and the king's role in upholding the demarcations between *varṇas*. The Śambūka narrative hits all the major features of the Brahminical project occurring in other areas of Sanskrit literature at the time providing us with a story that fits both ideologically and temporally within the developments in Brahminism that emerged "between the empires."

## Why Is the Śambūka Story in the *Rāmāyaṇa* Narrative?

The preceding remarks have related mostly to the historicity of the Śambūka episode and its place in the overall development of the *VR* into the form we know today. But how does the story fit thematically into the completed epic? The episode introduces considerable dissonance into the image of Rāma's character and is at odds with certain elements of earlier portions of the narrative, so it is worth spending some time discussing how we can read Śambūka's death in the context of the epic overall. Given the controversial subject matter of the Śambūka story and its appearance in an interpolated book of the epic, it is tempting to dismiss it outright as a later accretion that lends little narrative value to the epic. After all, the story's mere existence introduces a turbulence into the narrative that violently derails the positive perception of Rāma's perfect rule in Ayodhyā. Be that as it may, I want to look at the Śambūka episode as a legitimate piece of a complete *VR*, accounting for the ways in which it does and does not fit.

Simply put, the Śambūka story is not perfectly flush with the narrative of the *VR*. Some aspects of its narrative do not fall in line with the spirit and plot of the epic. For instance, as soon as Śambūka identifies himself as a Śūdra and reveals the intent behind his *tapas*, Rāma unhesitatingly executes him without another word. The rigidity and unforgiving nature with which Rāma kills Śambūka represents a drastically different demeanor than he displays during interactions with other characters of a similar social standing in other parts of the epic. His friendship with the tribal leader Guha comes to mind, as does his pleasant and amicable experience in the hermitage of the ascetic woman Śabarī.

At the outset of Rāma's exile, he is introduced to Guha, the king of the Niṣādas, a forest-dwelling tribe of hunters and fishermen, and the two exhibit great mutual respect.[29] Guha's status as a Niṣāda would normally preclude a close relationship with Rāma, a member of Ayodhyā's royalty. In fact, the quick and unlikely friendship between the two gave later commentators on the *VR* considerable pause.[30] The text itself seems aware of the unconventional nature of the friendship between Rāma and Guha and appears to shed some light on why the interaction played out the way it did. Guha, for example, offers Rāma his entire kingdom but Rāma declines, telling Guha that he is now an ascetic and has no use for such things. His focus now is on *dharma* and a life of asceticism (*VR* 2.44.14–22). The narrative makes clear that Guha attempted to act in the subordinate fashion that would normally be expected of him, but Rāma dismisses the offer due to his newly formed identity in exile. In fact, Rāma's identity at a given moment during exile is rather fluid. Whether Rāma chooses to be a disconnected ascetic or a duty-bound Kṣatriya changes according to the circumstances he finds himself in and the decisions he and those around him make.[31] Whatever the case may be, Guha shows Rāma, Lakṣmaṇa, and Sīta great hospitality and dispatches his kinsmen to guide them across the Ganges as they travel deeper into the forest. Rāma, in turn, demonstrates great appreciation for Guha and his assistance as they get further away from Ayodhyā in the early days of their exile.

The second example of Rāma forging a friendship with the epic's marginalized characters is Śabarī.[32] Śabarī is a member of the Śabara tribe,

29 The Guha episode occurs in *VR* 2.44.9–2.46.79.

30 For more on the commentarial reactions to the friendship between Rāma and Guha, see Pollock (1984a, p. 404).

31 An opposing example to Rāma's refusal of Guha's kingdom based on his newly acquired position as a forest-dwelling ascetic would be his clear expression of his Kṣatriya identity and status as a representative of Bharata's rule in Ayodhyā when he kills Vālin in the *Kiṣkindhākāṇḍa*.

32 The Śabarī episode occurs in *VR* 3.69.19–3.70.27.

a group indigenous to the Deccan region of India.[33] Perhaps unexpectedly given her non-Aryan tribal identity, she develops a close association with Vedic ritual and the observation of *dharma* by tending to the needs of the disciples of sage Mataṅga's hermitage on the shores of Lake Pampā. These disciples, just before ascending to heaven, prophesized to Śabarī that Rāma and Lakṣmaṇa would come to her hermitage and that she was to welcome them. Her reward for doing so would be her ascension into heaven. Upon meeting Śabarī, Rāma admires her asceticism and grants her leave to attain heaven as soon as she fulfilled her obligation to welcome him and Lakṣmaṇa to the hermitage on Lake Pampā. The rapport between Rāma and Śabarī is very amicable, quite distinct from the situation between Rāma and Śambūka despite the similarities in circumstance and power dynamics informing the two sets of interactions.

The difference in Rāma's demeanor between the episodes of Śambūka and Śabarī is easily explained by the context of his respective interactions with these characters. Śabarī was a pious servant to Brahmin sages and a gracious attendant to Rāma when he had just lost Sītā. Śambūka, on the other hand, was a transgressor and an enemy of the state who had caused the death of a young Brahmin through his *tapas*, thus contributing to the decline of *dharma* in Ayodhyā. He had to be dealt with as a criminal who violated his *varṇadharma*. And Rāma, now king of Ayodhyā, had to fulfill his own *rājadharma* by enforcing the boundaries of that *varṇadharma*. When Rāma entered in Śabarī's hermitage, he was under no obligation to follow the *dharma* of kings because, quite simply, he was not a king.

What is not so easily reconciled, however, is Rāma's ambivalence toward Śabarī's asceticism when compared to the severity of his treatment of Śambūka for his acts of asceticism. Śambūka's *tapas* disrupted the peace of Ayodhyā and brought about the death of a Brahmin and Nārada makes it clear that Rāma was in the appropriate position—and under the necessary obligation—to rebalance the scales of *dharma* and revive the Brahmin boy.

33 For more on this aspect of Śabarī's identity, see Pollock (1984b, pp. 354–355), Lutgendorf (2001, pp. 120–124), and Brockington (1984, pp. 121, 177 n. 22). The names of some tribal communities, including the Śabaras, became stereotyped to refer generically to "barbarous tribes" that fall outside the Brahminical Aryan fold (see Parasher, 1991, pp. 179ff.). The Śabaras also figure into the *MBh*. Brockington notes that the Śabaras—alongside other groups including the Niṣādas, Ambaṣṭhas, and Māhiṣakas, for example—were seen as "culturally and probably racially distinct" (Brockington, 1998, pp. 211–212) from the Aryans and were depicted at various points in the *MBh*'s development as "potential foes" (in the earlier portions of the epic) and culturally deviant, "relegating them to a low status" (ibid., p. 211).

The inconsistency that clouds this rationale, however, is the fact that Śūdras—and characters of a similar, non-twice-born station—from other parts of the epic do engage in *tapas* without causing the deaths of anyone else, let alone Brahmins in particular. Śabarī is herself an example of a socially subordinate character being an ascetic without disrupting the balance of *dharma* in greater Ayodhyā. She is referred to repeatedly as an ascetic woman either in the narrative frame or by Rāma himself. In *VR* 3.70.7, Rāma says to Śabarī, "I hope that any obstacles you have faced have been overcome and that the *tapas* you undertake is prosperous." Immediately after that, in 3.70.8, he proceeds to call her a great ascetic (*tapodhanā*). And in the following verse, the text refers to her simply as an ascetic woman (*tāpasī*). Rāma evidently had no issue with Śabarī's *tapas* despite her social standing and his position as a representative of Ayodhyā's ruling class.

Another example of the *VR*'s lenient attitude toward socially subordinate characters practicing *tapas* is the instance of the ascetic accidentally killed by Daśaratha.[34] After Rāma departs for the forest in exile, Daśaratha pines for his lost son and reflects on what has brought on this tragedy. He tells Kausalyā—Daśaratha's wife and Rāma's mother—about when he was a young, prideful prince and expert bowman known to be able to hit his target by sound alone. He recalls a time when he thought he had heard the sound of an elephant in the Sarayū River and released an arrow in its direction. The sound was actually an ascetic collecting water from the river. The arrow pierced the ascetic, mortally wounding him. As he lay dying, the ascetic told Daśaratha that he was collecting it for his blind, aged parents. The ascetic lamented that there is no reward for *tapas* or sacred learning and instructed Daśaratha to go to his father's hermitage and beg forgiveness. As he prepared to die, the ascetic assured Daśaratha that he is not a Brahmin, thus absolving him of the sin of Brahminicide; he is, in fact, the son of a Vaiśya father and a Śūdra mother.[35] Daśaratha obliged and went to confess to the ascetic's ailing parents, who requested to be brought to the body of their son. Daśaratha brought them to the corpse whereupon they lamented their loss. Their son's spirit appeared before them, assuring them that they, too, will

34 This episode occurs in *VR* 2.57.8–2.58.57.

35 The parentage of the ascetic is variable between recensions of the text. The Northern Recension even refers to the boy as the son of Brahmins, making his statement of reassurance to Daśaratha in *VR* 2.57.37 somewhat unusual. See 1416* in the Baroda Critical edition; see also Pollock (1984a, p. 435). A Brahmin identity for the ascetic would effectively negate my argument for the role this episode plays in demonstrating a contrasting treatment between Śambūka with other ascetic characters in the *VR*.

earn a place in heaven. After the ascetic's spirit departed for heaven, the father cursed Daśaratha to live out his last days lamenting over the loss of a son. After relating the story to Kausalyā, Daśaratha dies of grief from the loss of Rāma and guilt for bringing on the curse by which Rāma was doomed to be exiled.

The incident between Daśaratha and the ascetic has several plot points that warrant a comparison with the Śambūka episode. In particular, the contradictory positions each episode takes regarding who can practice *tapas* and how violations of *varṇa* boundaries are enforced deserve a close look. In the episode of Daśaratha's accidental killing of the young ascetic, that ascetic is active in both *tapas* and Vedic ritual—or, at the very least, he is in close contact with others who are.[36] Yet, his mixed parentage makes his close engagement with these Brahminical institutions unexpected. Despite this, the ascetic's freedom to practice *tapas* appears to be taken for granted in the narrative. At no point, even after the ascetic reveals himself to be born of a Vaiśya father and Śūdra mother, does Daśaratha exhibit any concern that this person may be in violation of *varṇadharma*. For instance, he has no issue describing the wounded forest-dweller as an ascetic using vocabulary derived from the word *tapas*. He refers to his victim as either *tapasvin* or *tāpasa* two times (*VR* 2.57.27, 2.58.14) during his recollection of the incident and twice in 2.57.18 and 2.58.7 as reported speech from the ascetic himself and his parents, respectively. Daśaratha likewise refers to the ascetic's father as *tāpasa* in 2.58.43. That same ambivalence applies to the ascetic's engagement with Vedic learning and ritual despite his occupying a gray area between twice-born and non-twice-born. Several medieval commentators on Vālmīki's text even felt compelled to clarify how it is possible that the son of a Vaiśya father and Śūdra mother could participate in Vedic rituals by citing passages from the *Dharmaśāstras* that specify revised worship practices suitable to a Śūdra's low, non-twice-born status.[37]

Neither Vedic education nor ritual factor heavily into the Śambūka episode, but *tapas* figures directly into his death. The role of *tapas* and its connection to the death of the ascetics in each of these episodes reveals an inconsistency in the level of leniency shown to them. Śambūka's *tapas* is framed as a crime. The *tapas* of the ascetic killed by Daśaratha, on the other hand, is framed as an

36 Pollock notes that in *VR* 2.57.32, when the ascetic laments that asceticism and sacred learning have brought no reward, he may be referring to his father's asceticism and learning (1984a, p. 434). Nevertheless, the ascetic is in close orbit to these twice-born institutions.

37 See Pollock's notes to *VR* 2.58.27–28 (1984a, pp. 436–437).

achievement of great power, as is clear from Daśaratha's panic at the thought of killing an ascetic, regardless of his birth status. And that panic proves justified because this disastrous misstep is the basis for a devastating curse that forces Daśaratha to endure the loss of a son and die broken-hearted with grief. Śambūka's death, though, is neither a misstep nor a cause for retribution against Rāma. Quite the contrary, the gods praise Rāma for obstructing Śambūka's passage to heaven. The basis for that praise is the fact that Rāma, as Ayodhyā's highest ruling authority, fulfilled his *rājadharma* by killing Śambūka and preserving the prescriptions and prohibitions of *varṇa*. The power dynamics between low-born ascetic and ruling elite are reversed in Daśaratha's situation. When Daśaratha killed the ascetic, *he* was the transgressor.

On these points alone, the two episodes stand in stark contradiction with one another. But there is more to consider. One major distinction between Rāma and Daśaratha at the time of their respective actions is that Rāma was king—and thus subject to *rājadharma*—while Daśaratha was merely a prince.[38] Another distinction between these two incidents is that Śambūka's death was an adjudicated capital punishment while the boy in Daśaratha's situation was killed accidentally. These differences help rectify some of the disparities in how these episodes unfold, but we are still left with an inconsistent philosophy on who has permission to perform *tapas* and what is an acceptable outcome for all those involved in the deaths of these ascetics from marginalized backgrounds. Daśaratha is doomed to die grieving for his son while the slain ascetic ascends to heaven. Rāma is praised by the gods while Śambūka fails in his attempts to gain entry to heaven. In Śambūka's case, Nārada's lament about the decline of *dharma* and the unauthorized *tapas* of Śūdras being a transgression is in full force; but that same social theory does not seem to be informing the narrative when Daśaratha kills the ascetic. There is nothing inherent in the narrative that helps settle that glaring inconsistency. Instead, we can only explain that disconnect by recalling that the *VR* was composed over a period of centuries and that the layer that contains Daśaratha's slaying of the ascetic reflects a different social worldview than the younger layer of the text that contains the Śambūka episode.

One more episode from the *VR*, the story of Triśaṅku, deserves our attention in this effort to determine Śambūka's fit in the overall narrative. The Triśaṅku episode represents one of the Śambūka episode's closest

38 It is worth noting that Rāma acts as a representative of the Kingdom of Ayodhyā on more than one occasion during his exile. Even though he professes himself to have fully adopted the life of an ascetic several times (e.g., *VR* 2.44.19–20), he reclaims his role as an enforcer Ayodhyā's laws when the situation warrants. A primary example of this comes during the death of Vālin (4.18, esp. vv. 9–11).

narrative parallels in the epic with each sharing a great deal of thematic material. It is worthwhile to consider them side by side. The story of Triśaṅku appears toward the beginning of the epic in the *Bālakāṇḍa*.[39] Its appearance in this book makes it a particularly useful comparison with the Śambūka story because the *Bālakāṇḍa* was added to the *VR* around the same time as the *Uttarakāṇḍa*, thus placing the theoretical social constructs portrayed in the episodes at a comparable point in history, unlike the other examples discussed above, which come from older layers of the epic. Aside from sharing a similar date, the Triśaṅku story also shares numerous prominent themes with the Śambūka episode. Whether explicitly or implicitly, both stories are centered around *varṇa*, transgression, and strained attempts to access heaven. Despite their shared subject matter, however, the two stories have very different outcomes. Triśaṅku does ultimately enter heaven—a heaven specifically created for him by a powerful advocate—while Śambūka's denial of heaven is final and deadly. A closer look at the story of Triśaṅku and a close comparison with the Śambūka story reveals how characters facing similar obstacles receive very different treatments based on their social class and the societal structures these stories intend to portray.

According to the *VR*, Triśaṅku was a king in the Ikṣvāku lineage, making him an ancestor to Rāma. He wanted to enter heaven with his body. As would be standard practice, he asks for help in conducting the necessary sacrifice from Ayodhyā's court seer, Vasiṣṭha. Vasiṣṭha refuses, saying only that it is not possible. Undeterred, Triśaṅku heads to the forests to ask Vasiṣṭha's ascetic sons to conduct the sacrifice. Sufficiently offended by Triśaṅku's disobeying of their father's order, they not only refuse to help him, they also curse him to take the form of a *caṇḍāla*, a class of social outcasts in the Brahminical worldview that are believed to be so impure that they fall outside the system of *varṇas* altogether. Still determined, the now outcasted Triśaṅku approaches Viśvāmitra—a figure with a history of conflict with Vasiṣṭha and subversion of the norms of *varṇa*—and asks *him* for help. Known to be somewhat of a renegade, Viśvāmitra agrees and begins soliciting various seers, disciples, and priests to assist in the impending sacrifice. Though reluctant, they agree to help due to their fear of Viśvāmitra's ascetic powers. As Triśaṅku makes his way toward heaven in his body (*saśarīra*)—now the body of a *caṇḍāla*—Indra intervenes and refuses to allow him to enter. Indra's reasoning is that he is afflicted by the curse. Indra sends Triśaṅku flying back to Earth. Viśvāmitra, though, invokes his ascetic powers to create an entirely new

39 The story is covered in *VR* 1.56.10–1.59.33. Śatānanda, Janaka's family priest, narrates the story to Rāma as a means of providing Rāma with some insight into Viśvāmitra's past deeds.

set of heavens and insists that Triśaṅku be allowed to dwell there. The gods oblige but demand he remain there upside down.

The most direct vector for comparison between the episodes of Triśaṅku and Śambūka is, without question, the fact that both characters attempt to enter heaven in their bodies (*saśarīra*). This theme of characters entering heaven in their bodies is rare in the *VR*, occurring only a few times throughout the course of the text. Most notably, both Lakṣmaṇa (in 7.96.17) and Rāma (in 7.100.10) enter heaven this way as Rāma's time as an *avatāra* of Viṣṇu comes to an end and the epic draws to a close.[40] Triśaṅku and Śambūka are the only characters that struggle with their bodily passage to heaven and, of those two, only Śambūka dies in pursuit of it. The disparity in the outcome of Triśaṅku's and Śambūka's attempts to get into heaven in this way is colored by the perception of their transgressions and the respective punishments in seeking out this heavenly aim; and underlying all these points is *varṇa*.

The theme of *varṇa*, critical to the Śambūka episode, appears more covertly in the Triśaṅku episode, but its role in the latter is nevertheless valuable to consider. *Varṇa* exists in the story of Triśaṅku in two ways. First, the sons of Vasiṣṭha curse Triśaṅku—a Kṣatriya by birth—to be a *caṇḍāla*, which ultimately means a total loss of *varṇa* identity given that the *caṇḍāla*s fall outside the *varṇa* system. Triśaṅku's new outcasted identity becomes the basis for Indra to deny him entrance into heaven. The societal structure within which Triśaṅku and Śambūka exist ensures that their low social standing proves detrimental to their heavenly goals, at least initially. The difference, however, is that Triśaṅku was cursed to a lower station while Śambūka was born into one. The distinction between Triśaṅku's temporary marginalization and Śambūka's permanent marginalization proves crucial to the respective outcomes of their shared aim of entering heaven with their bodies. In the end, Triśaṅku achieves his goal but Śambūka does not.

The second conduit for *varṇa* to enter the Triśaṅku story is more subtle and comes with the figure of Viśvāmitra. Viśvāmitra was a legendary king, a Kṣatriya, who managed to upwardly change his *varṇa*—normally an impossible task—and become Brahmin through incredible feats of asceticism. Viśvāmitra's movement from one *varṇa* to another and the incompatibility

40 There is only one other instance of a character entering heaven in their body outside the Triśaṅku and Śambūka episodes. *VR* 1.33.7–12 describes Viśvāmitra's sister, Satyavatī, who entered heaven this way and subsequently was transformed into a river. In 2.102.10, we also get an additional reference to Triśaṅku entering heaven when Vasiṣṭha is explaining the origins of the world to Rāma during his failed attempt to dissuade Rāma from embarking on his exile.

of that progression with the Brahminical worldview underscores how other characters interact with him. His abilities simultaneously inspire awe and fear as those around him attempt to seek his help and avoid the wrath of his notorious temper. In his study of Viśvāmitra, Adheesh Sathaye offers that "[a]bnormality and narrative conflict occur when these *varṇa*-mapped bodies cross boundaries and move out of place, whether by will or by coercion" (2015, p. 7). Though speaking about Viśvāmitra legends, Sathaye's observation works equally well in the case of Śambūka. The rarity of Śambūka's ambition in *tapas* is bolstered, in some sense, by the Hindu tradition's knowledge of Viśvāmitra, a figure who has come to represent the impossible transformation of caste—from Kṣatriya to Brahmin—by virtue of his *tapas*. Viśvāmitra's grasp of *tapas* and the power it provides makes him a figure at the edge of Brahminhood, but there is a deep anxiety about his ability to use *tapas* to achieve impossible aims that becomes apparent in those who interact with him. The transfer of that anxiety to a Śūdra hoping to achieve the impossible aim of attaining heaven with his body becomes untenable within the power structures of Brahminism, which is defined, in part, by the exclusion of Śūdras from the privileges of and access to religious and social power enjoyed by the twice-borns, Brahmins in particular.

Continuing with the similarities in these episodes, both involve a punishment for a failure to obey Brahminical conventions. Śambūka's violation of Brahminical norms is clear. As a Śūdra in the Tretā Yuga, he was not permitted to engage in *tapas*. He nevertheless did in hopes of achieving his aim of entering heaven with his body. The response from Rāma, a representative of Brahminical interests, was swift and unforgiving. Triśaṅku's crimes against the authoritative structures of Brahminism are slightly more complicated. He attempted to enter heaven in his body through sacrifice. Though Vasiṣṭha deems the final goal of Triśaṅku's proposed sacrifice untenable, patronizing a sacrifice in general is something that Triśaṅku, as a Kṣatriya, would have been allowed and, in fact, encouraged to do. In this situation, Triśaṅku is operating well within Brahminical conventions. He erred not in his attempt to conduct a sacrifice or even in his desire to enter heaven in his body. Instead, his transgression came when he disregarded his Brahmin advisor's determination that his goal was impossible and the sacrifice was not to be done. That transgression brought with it a revoking of his Kṣatriya status through the curse imparted on him by Vasiṣṭha's sons. The curse forces Triśaṅku to seek out a means to his goal elsewhere, made even more difficult given the fact that he is now a *caṇḍāla* and thus ineligible to perform any Brahminical sacrifices. He ultimately finds an advocate in Viśvāmitra, whose relationship to Brahminical structures and the boundaries of *varṇa* is famously tumultuous.

Viśvāmitra's advocacy for Triśaṅku is an interesting point of contrast with Śambūka's condition. It was only by virtue of Viśvāmitra's interference that Triśaṅku was able to circumvent Indra's denial of heavenly access. Viśvāmitra built an entire cosmos for Triśaṅku so that his goal of entering heaven in this body could be realized. It may not have been exactly what Triśaṅku was imagining at the outset, but, in the end, he achieved his goal—and in quite a miraculous fashion. Śambūka, a Śūdra lacking any advocate, suffers not only a denial of his goal, but the ultimately consequence of death. That fate appears to never have been a possibility for Triśaṅku, a Kṣatriya supported by the powerful and *varṇa*-defying Viśvāmitra.

Even with the differences in the treatment of Triśaṅku and Śambūka, there is not a contradiction in worldview. Triśaṅku began his embodied journey to he ven from a privileged position (that of a Kṣatriya) and through an acceptable means (sacrifice). The context of Śambūka's journey to heaven in his body, on the other hand, was flawed from the outset. He attempted to achieve his goals through *tapas*, which was inherently unacceptable given his position as a Śūdra. That common worldview explains how Triśaṅku and Śambūka ended up in very different places on their embodied journey to heaven and their respective destinations are punctuated by the difference in their *varṇa*.

As is clear from the examples cited above, there is a great deal of thematic material from the Śambūka story that is found in other parts of the epic, but how that material is presented from episode to episode can vary considerably. Some of the thematic inconsistencies between episodes can be explained away by accounting for the social standing of the characters involved as well as the context of their interactions, but there are also situations where comparable episodes present opposing worldviews without a justification built into the narrative. By way of example, we have seen that the degree of leniency toward who has access to *tapas* exhibits a fluidity from episode to episode. The ripples introduced by these inconsistences in prominent themes shared between the Śambūka episode and other episodes from across the *VR* can make it challenging to reconcile the Śambūka story's fit into the epic. It is easy and tempting to sink into the minutiae of sorting out why characters behave one way in one context and another way in a different context and, on that basis, find ground to dismiss this episode as an anomaly. In fact, calling on the historical development of the epic is sometimes the only way to navigate the inconsistencies. Unsurprisingly, characters appearing in older layers of the epic often behave in a similar way to each other, but a contrasting way to characters in other parts of the epic. This explains why the stories of Triśaṅku and Śambūka—both from a similarly late period in the *VR*'s development—share a compatible worldview, but Rāma's slaying of Śambūka and Daśaratha's slaying of the young ascetic—two episodes written centuries apart—are considerably more mismatched. That added historical perspective can be critical when attempting to justify the Śambūka episode's existence in the *VR*.

## How to Read Vālmīki's Śambūka

The Śambūka episode sits at a point of contact between the historical and the narrative development of the *VR*, and the convergence for these two developmental pathways is centered on *varṇadharma*. Historically, as we have seen, *varṇadharma* had grown into an integral concept within post-Mauryan Brahminism and the composition of the *Uttarakāṇḍa* occurred at the height of Brahminism's reformation of *varṇadharma*. What is left for my purposes here is to demonstrate how this concept guides the Śambūka episode into a harmonious position within the *VR*. I have already detailed how *varṇadharma* and its transgressions are central to both the Śambūka episode itself and its buildup, but placing this episode within the larger *Uttarakāṇḍa* and, with that, the *VR* as a whole requires us to go beyond using Śambūka alone as the litmus test for *varṇadharma* and look at Rāma. Paying close attention to his character development and his own successes and failures with respect to *varṇadharma* and the closely related concept of *rājadharma* can help us smooth out the rough edges of the Śambūka episode's seemingly imperfect fit within the epic. Since Rāma is the most consequential character in the epic, understanding his condition at the time of Śambūka's death is the last logical step to properly placing the Śambūka episode within the narrative of the *VR*.

With the *Uttarakāṇḍa*, the audience finally gets to see Rāma as king of Ayodhyā after a denial of his near ascension to the throne early in the epic made worse by a heartbreaking exile. This closure marks one of the most potent aspects of the *Uttarakāṇḍa*. With Rāma on the throne, we also get to see how Rāma becomes subject to *rājadharma*, a paradigm of duty that has never applied to Rāma directly. The *Uttarakāṇḍa*, then, gives us a whole new way of envisioning Rāma as a character. How Rāma engages with *rājadharma* informs how we are to read the Śambūka story: not as an immaterial episode with little connection to the epic, but instead as a consequential part of Rāma's career and a logical development within the text.

Goldman and Sutherland Goldman, in the introductory material to their translation of the *Uttarakāṇḍa*, clearly lay out several aspects of the *Uttarakāṇḍa* that instill in the book a sense of logic and cohesiveness. Most critical for my purposes here are their observations on Rāma's neglect of *rājadharma* (2017, pp. 145–148), which I have already alluded to several times above. After Rāma ordered Lakṣmaṇa to escort his pregnant wife to the forest for her exile, Rāma's grip on his kingly obligations slipped, something of which he himself was aware (ibid., p. 139). He found himself unable to execute his duties and his failures to adhere to *rājadharma* brought about two incidents symptomatic of a lapse in *dharma* and the detrimental effect this can have on his kingdom's well-being. Both incidents, it is worth noting, directly affect the well-being of Brahmins in particular. The first is the harassment of Brahmin sages by the demon, Lavaṇa. Rāma dispatches Śatrughna to remedy this situation. Immediately after this is addressed, however, we hear about the death of the Brahmin boy. To rectify this, realign with the principles of *rājadharma*, and restore the balance of *dharma* generally in Ayodhyā, Rāma kills Śambūka.

The Śambūka episode, then, serves as the linchpin for reestablishing the ideals of *varṇadharma* in Ayodhyā after Rāma's inability to live up to his own *dharma* as king. After a period of utopian conditions in Ayodhyā at the outset of his rule, Rāma briefly falters when faced with following his *rājadharma*. That lull had terrible consequences for life in Ayodhyā, depicted in the narrative as hardships suffered by the Brahmins. By killing Śambūka, Rāma stabilizes the Brahmin community and, by extension, the kingdom at large. Śambūka, in this sense, is far from being an inconsequential character. He is one reason for the disruption of peace in Ayodhyā, and in death, he is the catalyst for Rāma to reinstate the ideals of Brahminism in Ayodhyā.

Although *varṇadharma* shows up in many forms and contexts throughout the *VR*, the Śambūka episode represents the most clearly articulated and most up-to-date exposition on the duties and limitations of *varṇa* that the text has to offer, placing Śambūka's death squarely within the Brahminical renaissance coming out of the Mauryan era. Historically speaking, it is an extremely consequential moment in an extremely consequential text. Indeed, understanding the importance of *varṇadharma* and the ideological weight it carried within Brahminism during the historical moment that the *Uttarakāṇḍa* appeared as a part of the *VR* is critical to properly appreciating the Śambūka episode as a part of this text, not just as a standalone piece that incidentally appears within it.

When taken at face value, the problems of the Śambūka episode might lead one to disregard it as an unnecessary foray into controversial territory that does little more than damage Rāma's reputation on top of the damage already done through his exile of Sītā. The episode also introduces several inconsistencies into the narrative when it is placed side by side with other similar moments in the text. Be that as it may, the story is a part of the epic and it has logical reasons for being there. Historically, it injects into the epic a refined vision of *varṇadharma* that reflects the prevailing social ideologies within Brahminism. Narratively, the death of the Brahmin boy marks the consequence of Rāma's failure to live up to his *rājadharma* while distracted by the torment and guilt of exiling Sītā. The death of Śambūka is what rights that apparent wrong. However, even though one can argue for the Śambūka story's fit within the *VR* and within the historical moment of its composition, there was something—or perhaps many things—about the way Śambūka died in the *VR* that warranted further explanation and exploration. Many contributors to the *Rāmāyaṇa* tradition working after Vālmīki found reason to revisit this story; to revise it, retell it, reframe it, contradict it, or support it. This study provides evidence that the Śambūka narrative was, and continues to be, an extraordinarily influential moment in the *Rāmāyaṇa* tradition and subsequent chapters in this book explore some of the ways others have grappled with the problems and questions it posed.

# Chapter 3

# FIRST RESPONDERS

After Brahminism gained a strong footing in post-Mauryan South Asia—a footing typified by the codification of *varṇadharma*—the next great South Asian empire, the Guptas, crafted their own schematic for an imperial religion. With the Guptas came an imperially sponsored Vaiṣṇavism marked by a burgeoning temple culture that involved elaborate structures and public spaces that provided the public with a new kind of access to religion (Willis, 2009). The Guptas' presentation of Vaiṣṇavism opened Viṣṇu worship up to an unprecedented level of popularity, which extended to Viṣṇu's various incarnations (*avatāras*), including Rāma. Naturally, a text that frames Rāma as both divine figure and *avatāra* of Viṣṇu as well as a hero in his own right was bound to benefit from the momentum of the religious movement spearheaded by the Guptas. The story of the *Rāmāyaṇa*, then, saw a rejuvenated life in this new era of South Asian history.

The story of Rāma was, at this point, still largely defined by Vālmīki's *Rāmāyaṇa*. As interest in the story grew, critical perspectives on this quintessential Rāma text began to emerge. In the world of the *VR*, it is Rāma's responsibility as king to maintain the prevailing social order by which his kingdom is to be governed and mete out the necessary punishments when that order is violated. The text's Śambūka episode exemplifies both a violation by a member of Ayodhyā's society and the proper response to it, carried out by the king himself. Be that as it may, Rāma's unquestioningly swift action against Śambūka placed him in a role of enforcer that is at odds with the compassionate image of Rāma that pervades a great deal of the epic. The difficulty in reconciling these two seemingly conflicting images of Rāma created a troubling puzzle for later authors who lived in a world where Rama's divinity and the idealism it represented were becoming increasingly accepted. How could they reframe Rāma's involvement in Śambūka's death to better suit the changing expectations of their audience without abandoning the issue of Rāma upholding Ayodhyā's social structures? This was an important question for many early authors who included the subject matter of the *Uttarakāṇḍa* in their narrations of the Rāma story.

This chapter explores two of the first critical reactions to the Śambūka episode after its earliest appearance in Vālmīki's *Uttarakāṇḍa*. These responses set powerful precedents for reexamining the terms of Rāma's involvement in Śambūka's death in light of evolving religious sentiments. A significant shift came with exploring Śambūka's life *after* death. Where Vālmīki focused on Śambūka's death as final and retributive, some early poets after Vālmīki softened that stance by transforming Rāma's contact with Śambūka into a moment of deliverance. As an example of a text that utilizes such a motif, I will be discussing Śambūka's appearance in Kālidāsa's *Raghuvaṃśa*. Developments represented in his work became a precursor to the developments in the Śambūka story that would accompany the *Rāmāyaṇa*'s entrance into a period in Indian religious history when we find the clearest expressions of devotion (*bhakti*) toward Rāma. But to focus exclusively on these developments happening within an ultimately Brahminical paradigm would be to ignore another significant line of contributions to the Rāma tradition coming from the Jains. In the Jain context, the *Uttarakāṇḍa*—indeed, Vālmīkis *Rāmāyaṇa* as a whole—is seen as a gross misrepresentation of Rāma's life. In the earliest Jain telling of the *Rāmāyaṇa*, the *Paümacariya*, author Vimalasūri has no issue challenging Vālmīki's understanding of Rāma's exploits entirely, including the notion that Rāma is in any way involved in Śambūka's death.

The two Śambūka episodes explored in this chapter represent a range of motivating factors for taking a second look at the way the circumstances around Śambūka's death unfolded in the *VR*. Kālidāsa largely follows the general structure of Vālmīki's take on the story, but he does change key elements of the narrative that are at odds with his contemporary environment. The distinctiveness of Vimalasūri's Śambūka episode is markedly more extreme to the point of being nearly unrecognizable when placed side by side with that of his predecessor in Vālmīki. Whatever the final form the episode took, both Kālidāsa and Vimalasūri felt a need to address the issue of Śambūka, but it is important to keep in mind that they were not moved to do so as because they perceived Śambūka's death to be a tragedy. In general, their efforts should be understood as attempting to rescue Rāma's image from Vālmīki's rather cold portrayal of summary capital punishment.

## Kālidāsa's Śambūka Attains the Course of Virtuous Men

At most a few centuries after the *Uttarakāṇḍa* was appended to the *VR*, Kālidāsa wrote his *Raghuvaṃśa* (*The Lineage of Raghu*, henceforth *RaV*). He used the text to present a history of the Raghu dynasty, including a concise narration of the best known of Raghu's descendants: Rāma Rāghava, the hero of the *Rāmāyaṇa*. Despite the brevity of his account, Kālidāsa chose to include the story of Śambūka within this abridgment of Rāma's exploits, dedicating sixteen verses out of the Rāma story's 630-some verses spanning seven *sargas* (9–15). Kālidāsa's rendering of the Śambūka episode in his *RaV* occurs in vv. 42–57 of the fifteenth *sarga*.

Kālidāsa largely follows Vālmīki in telling the story: Śambūka is guilty in his transgression of *varṇa* boundaries; Rāma is approached by a grieving Brahmin father who blames Rāma's lapses in kingly responsibility for bringing about the death of his son; Rāma surveys his kingdom in search of wrongdoing; Rāma decapitates Śambūka after the latter identifies himself as a Śūdra practicing *tapas* with heavenly ambitions; and, after killing Śambūka, Rāma makes his way to Agastya's *āśrama*. But aside from the basic differences that stem from Kālidāsa simply presenting an abbreviated episode, there are several significant and, it would seem, deliberate departures from the *VR*.

First, Nārada's long reflection on the declining efficacy of *dharma* as the Yugas progress is removed in its entirety. Additionally, Nārada's entire counsel pointing Rāma toward a defiant Śūdra is replaced by the formless Sarasvatī explaining to Rāma that he is to put an end to any misconduct in his kingdom without specifically mentioning a Śūdra engaged in *tapas* (15.46–47). Once Rāma does locate Śambūka, Kālidāsa details the specifics of his *tapas* by describing him as hanging upside down from a tree branch inhaling smoke (15.49–50). This is more descriptive than Vālmīki, who simply has him hanging upside down. However, the most innovative changes Kālidāsa introduces to the Śambūka story work toward two goals: to highlight the virtues of contact with Rāma—even deadly contact—and the unfailing righteousness of Rāma's character. To the latter point, the Brahmin recants his earlier chastisement of Rāma and praises him for bringing his son back to life, reinforcing the impossibility of Rāma's susceptibility to error (15.57). To the former, Kālidāsa drastically changes the outcome of the Rāma–Śambūka interaction and sets a precedent for narrating the Śambūka episode that ripples through the *Rāmāyaṇa* tradition for centuries to come.

Vālmīki portrays a rather jubilant scene after Śambūka's death, with the gods heaping praises and showers of flowers onto Rāma for preventing the Śūdra's entrance into heaven. The episode closes off its loose ends with the revival of the Brahmin boy and the definitive death of Śambūka. Kālidāsa does not include this scene of the rejoicing gods and this deletion allows him to entirely redirect the focus of Śambūka's fate. In 15.53, Śambūka "attains the course of virtuous men" (*lebhe* [...] *satāṃ gatim*). In the same verse, Kālidāsa lets his readers know that this course is not attainable "through even the most difficult of austerities that go beyond one's own path" (*tapasā duścareṇāpi na svamārgavilaṅghinā*). In other words, Śambūka's position as a Śūdra negates the efficacy of his *tapas*. But, fortunately for

Śambūka, his crimes got Rāma's attention and brought the two in contact. Through this elaboration, Kālidāsa demonstrates that any sort of contact with Rāma is enough to transcend the limits of *varṇa* and bring about a desirable outcome. Most notably, Śambūka's attainment of the "course of virtuous men" exhibits a concern for what happens to Śambūka after his death that is absent from the *VR*.[1] This change is Kālidāsa's major innovation to the Śambūka story.

Robert Goldman makes the same observation about Kālidāsa's attention to Śambūka's afterlife (2019, pp. 97–98) and also calls attention to the fact that the fourteenth-century commentator, Māllinātha, when commenting on *RaV* 15.53, refers his readers to 8.318 in the *MDh*, which states, "When men who have committed sins are punished by kings, they go to heaven immaculate, like virtuous men who have done good deeds."[2] Kālidāsa himself does appear to employ the teachings of Manu's text elsewhere in his *RaV*, as is evident from 14.67, where Sītā tells Lakṣmaṇa to pass along a message to Rāma after her exile:

> Manu has established that it is the king's *dharma* to uphold the system of *varṇāśrama*. Therefore, even though you have cast me out like this, I shall observe the condition of an ascetic. (*RaV* 14.67)

Mallinātha's suggestion is thus a promising interpretation from within the tradition, that also seems to align with the idea in *RaV* 15.53 that receiving a punishment from the king carried with it a fast-track to expiation and "the path of virtuous men." This places Rāma somewhere at the intersection of a worldly king and a divine figure. It seems reasonable

---

1 The phrase *lebhe satāṃ gatim* occurs in more explicitly devotional texts including the *Bhāgavata Purāṇa* (10.81.40) and the *Śiva Purāṇa* (*Koṭirudrasaṃhitā* 16.8). In both cases, the usage suggests a passage to heaven. In other instances when *gati* is meant to indicate a divine or heavenly state, it is often modified with words like *paramā* (excellent) or *uttamā* (highest). Considering just the *VR*, see, for example, 2.58.35–38, 4.55.12, and 4.56.11. See also 7.97.3; here, the word *gati* appears without any modifying adjectives. Instead, Rāma describes how he will go along the course already taken by his brother, Lakṣmaṇa (i.e., the preordained course of Death, *pūrvanirmāṇabuddhā hi kālasya gatir īdṛśī VR* 7.96.2). The precise phrase *satāṃ gatim* does appear in 2.103.6, though it does not carry with it a sense of heaven. Here, Vasiṣṭha explains to Rāma—who has already departed Ayodhyā in exile—that "you would not stray from the course of virtuous men" (*nātivarteḥ satāṃ gatim*) if he were to do the bidding of his guru, follow *dharma* on behalf of his people, and listen to the pleas of his mother for him to come back. In this passage, then, the "course of virtuous men" is one defining Rāma's personal conduct.

2 Olivelle's translation (2005, p. 184).

that Kālidāsa would have elected to exalt Rāma as both a king *and* a god by granting Śambūka his aims of attaining heaven. After all, by the time Kālidāsa was writing, Rāma was a significant part of the increasingly pervasive Vaiṣṇavism of the Guptas, with whom Kālidāsa was associated.[3]

In his exposition of the episode, Kālidāsa is the first to direct some attention to Śambūka's redemption, and he places Rāma in the position of delivering it. But, as I have already cautioned, we should hesitate in painting Kālidāsa with too progressive a brush. Given that he maintains a Brahminical paradigm for criminalizing Śambūka, I would argue that Kālidāsa ruminates on Śambūka's fate in death not so much to demonstrate compassion for the Śūdra or a discomfort with his death *per se*, but instead to elevate Rāma and demonstrate the power of contact with him. Kālidāsa makes it clear that by practicing *tapas* as a Śūdra, Śambūka was chasing his divine ambitions in vain. His crimes, however, brought him into contact with Rāma and his purifying authority. Death at Rāma's hand absolved him of his transgressions and brought his objectives within reach.

What may have motivated Kālidāsa's new perspective on the Śambūka story? Goldman and Sutherland Goldman offer that "the summary execution of the *śūdra* ascetic Śambūka has proven to be a source of unease among some audiences of those versions of the *Rāmāyaṇa* that include some form of the *Uttarakāṇḍa*" (2017, p. 104). They appear to attribute this unease to not only the audiences but to the authors as well, saying that early poets, namely Kālidāsa and Bhavabhūti, "begin to express some concern at what happens to be at best an excessively harsh and violent action on Rāma's part" (ibid., pp. 106–107).[4] Both Kālidāsa and—as we will see in the next chapter—Bhavabhūti expressed this concern narratively via a trope that would become common in devotional literature that sees "the exaltation of even an evil and degraded being through death at the hands of a divinity" (ibid., 107). What led these poets to employ this trope, however, is challenging to pin down. In the case of Kālidāsa, the preoccupation with Śambūka's afterlife and exaltation of Rāma may not reflect a personal concern of the poet. Instead, I would like to offer that Kālidāsa's modifications to the Śambūka story and the sentiments they represent were the result of external motivations. Aside from simple discomfort with Vālmīki's rather cold exposition of the episode, I argue that Kālidāsa redirected the trajectory of the Śambūka episode in his *RaV* to suit the tastes of the expansive and culturally innovative Gupta Empire, during

3 For Kālidāsa's relationship to the Guptas, see Mirashi (1963, pp. xxiii ff.), Ingalls (1976, pp. 15–26), and Bakker (1986, p. 30).

4 For a more in-depth discussion of Bhavabhūti's role in the development of the Śambūka tradition, see Chapter 4 in this study.

which time the poet was a significant figure. In addition to being exceptional specimens of artistry in Sanskrit literature, many of Kālidāsa's works depict and promote Gupta religious and political ambitions.

The Guptas exerted their influence over large swaths of northern India and the epigraphic record from that period details several conquests that resulted in those expansive territories. There are numerous inscriptions referring to Gupta kings' conquests and victories in battle.[5] Likewise, the fourth *sarga* of Kālidāsa's *RaV* outlines Raghu's *digvijaya* (lit. victory in all directions), a circling of the subcontinent in an effort to gain territory and tribute, as might be expected from a *cakravartin* (emperor) (Ingalls, 1976, p. 16; Willis, 2009, p. 68). Paying particular attention to *RaV* 4.60–68, Kālidāsa narrates Raghu's encounters with the Pārasīkas (Persians), Yavanas (Greeks), and the Hūṇas (Huns). This likely corresponds to historical Gupta campaigns of expansion under Samudragupta and Candragupta II, who each added considerable territory to the Gupta Empire.[6]

There is another commonality between the Gupta inscriptional record and Kālidāsa's work. The following is an excerpt from the Bhitari stone pillar inscription[7]:

> The son of the *Mahārājādhirāja*, the glorious Samudragupta,—who was the exterminator of all kings; who had no antagonist (*of equal power*) in the world; whose fame was tasted by the waters of the four oceans; who was equal to (the gods) Dhanada [=Kubera] and Varuṇa and Indra and Antaka [=Yama]; who was the very axe of (the god) Kṛitānta; who was the giver of many millions of lawfully acquired cows and gold; who was the restorer of the *aśvamēdha*-sacrifice, that had been long in abeyance; who was the son of the son's son of the *Mahārāja*, the illustrious Gupta [...][8]

---

5 For example, the Udayagiri cave inscription of Candragupta II and the Allahabad stone pillar inscription referring to Samudragupta. Fleet (1960); see no. 6, pp. 34ff. and no. 1, pp. 1ff.

6 Ingalls (1976, pp. 16–17). The actions of Skandagupta, ruling in the mid-fifth century, may also be significant as he fended off the Hūṇas in the face of their increasing encroachment into Gupta territory (ibid., p. 18). Skandagupta was known to compare himself to Rāma, with Kālidāsa's *RaV* perhaps contributing to this image depending on when, precisely, we can place the text within the Gupta period (Bakker, 1986, p. 30).

7 The village of Bhitari is in Uttar Pradesh about 10 km to the northeast of the town of Saidpur, itself approximately 40 km to the northeast of Varanasi. The inscription is undated, though comes from the period of Skandagupta (mid-fifth century). See Fleet (1960, no. 13, pp. 52ff.).

8 Fleet (1960, no. 13, pp. 52ff.). Fleet's translation.

Similar comparisons between Samudragupta and either some or all the gods Kubera, Varuṇa, Indra, and Yama appear in several other Gupta-period inscriptions as well.[9] It perhaps comes as no surprise to find that Kālidāsa compares Daśaratha, one of his subjects in the *RaV*, to this same set of divine figures not once, but twice.[10]

> In his fairness and his pouring down showers of riches—and because of his subduing of evil people—the king equaled Yama and the Lord of the Puṇyajanas [=Kubera] along with Varuṇa; and he equaled the sun in his radiance. (*RaV* 9.6)

And

> Now the spring has returned to serve the king with new flowers as if he were the only one—distinguished in his valor and having a burden equal to that of Yama, Kubera, the Lord of Water [=Varuṇa], and the Thunderer [=Indra]. (*RaV* 9.24)

Similarly, Kālidāsa's *Meghadūta* (*The Cloud Messenger*, henceforth *MD*) seems to be participating in the same promotion of Gupta excellence. The narrator of the text is a Yakṣa, a semidivine being who has been banished to Rāmagiri, a place far to the south of his home in the Himalayas. At the onset of the monsoons, he enlists a cloud to deliver a message to his lover as the cloud is sure to be headed north as the monsoons sweep across India. The *MD* is a poetic description of the cloud's path that emphasizes numerous prominent Gupta sites that extend from its southern-most influence at Rāmagiri (the site of the Yakṣa's banishment), up into the empire's central territories, and cutting through the northern reaches of Gupta presence toward the Himalayas. A key example of the text's emphasis on Gupta preeminence comes with the Yakṣa's

---

9 Cf., Fleet (1960, no. 2, pp. 18ff.): the Eran stone inscription of Samudragupta wherein Samudragupta is compared to Dhanada (=Kubera) and Antaka (=Yama). Ibid. (no. 4, pp. 25ff.): Mathura stone inscription of Candragupta II wherein, among his other attributes, Samudragupta is compared to Dhanada (=Kubera), Varuṇa, Indra, and Antaka (=Yama) precisely as in the Bhitari inscription of Skandagupta. The same is true of the Bilsad stone pillar inscription of Kumaragupta (ibid., no. 10, pp. 42ff.) and the Mankuwar stone image inscription of Kumaragupta (ibid., no. 12, pp. 47ff.).

10 Michael Willis also notes how *RaV* 17.81 describes what qualities these four deities bestow on a king (not with specific reference to Daśaratha) and how this appears to resemble *MDh* 7.4–6, though with a shortened list of deities (2009, p. 59).

instruction the cloud to go out of his way to visit the Gupta capital of Ujjain, which does not even fall along the direct route to his beloved.

> Though out of your way as you head to the North, do not be averse to the welcome of the palace roofs in Ujjain. It would be a mystery if you did not find delight in the quivering eyes of the ladies there, trembling and shaking like flashes of lightning. (*MD*, *Pūrvamegha* 28)

The correlations between Kālidāsa's works and in the epigraphic record of the Guptas suggest that Kālidāsa was invested in promoting Gupta political dominance through his literature. There is also evidence to suggest that Kālidāsa's project of elevating the Gupta civilization extended into the realm of religion by contributing to the Gupta vision of Vaiṣṇavism.[11] Of course, one would expect to find significant Vaiṣṇava signifiers in narrating the Rāma story in the *RaV* and indeed, nearly all of *sarga* 10 in the text—which describes the gods approaching Viṣṇu to descend to earth to eliminate Rāvaṇa—details the greatness of Viṣṇu. Throughout the rest of the work, Kālidāsa periodically draws attention to Rāma's position and self-awareness as an *avatāra* of Viṣṇu, but, unlike Rāma stories of later centuries, the devotionalism in the *RaV* is more directed toward Viṣṇu himself.[12] However, this attention to Viṣṇu is somewhat generalized and not necessarily unique to the Guptas, nor does Kālidāsa envision Rāma to be especially more divinized than we find in the final form of the *VR* (i.e., with the addition of the *Bāla* and *Uttara kāṇḍas*, where the vast majority of Rāma's connections to Viṣṇu are highlighted). While the Vaiṣṇavism present in the *RaV* is thus rather inconclusive in its connection to the Guptas, Kālidāsa's contributions to the Guptas' promotion of Vaiṣṇavism is evident in another way.

Candragupta II was especially expressive of a Vaiṣṇava identity for the Guptas through his development at Udayagiri, a site which displays several religious innovations. Michael Willis' study on Udayagiri provides us with a picture of these energetic religious developments. He notes that "Udayagiri was reworked under Candragupta II … to articulate a revitalised form of early

---

11 Whereas Vaiṣṇavism was the preferred mode of religious expression among Gupta leadership, this was not to the exclusion or suppression of other religious practices present within their territories. As Gupta influence expanded under Candragupta II's reign, he appointed ministers to oversee new territorial additions and showed considerable religious tolerance in doing so. Aside from appointing Śaiva ministers, the religious worldview under Candragupta allowed for his officials to donate land and money to the Buddhists as well (Ingalls, 1976, p. 17). Cf. *Epigraphia Indica* (1909–1910, pp. 70 ff.) and Fleet (1960, no. 5, pp. 29ff. and no. 6, pp. 34ff.).

12 See, for example, *RaV* 11.85 and 13.1.

Hindu kingship in which the ruler was envisaged as a paramount sovereign (*cakravartin*) and supreme devotee of Viṣṇu (*paramabhāgavata*)" (2009, p. 3). The devotion to Viṣṇu is especially evident from his superimposition of Vaiṣṇava iconography onto Udayagiri's systems for keeping time and observing the skies. For instance, Candragupta appears to have placed a large relief of Viṣṇu Nārāyaṇa in such a way as to take advantage of the site's natural features to dramatize the *varṣāmāsavrata* festival in which Viṣṇu is put to sleep at the outset of the monsoons (during the month of Āṣāḍha) and subsequently awakened four months later (in the month of Kārttika). The relief, which depicts Viṣṇu laying on a serpent, is shaded by rock formations for most of the year, but is illuminated around the summer solstice (i.e., the beginning of Āṣāḍha) so as to predict and dramatize the onset of the festival (Willis, 2009, p. 30ff.).

As for Kālidāsa's contributions to this aspect of Gupta identity, his *MD* is framed entirely around the *varṣāmāsavrata* (Willis, 2009, p. 32). In only the second verse, we hear about how the banished Yakṣa is heartbroken from the curse of separation from his beloved. He sees a cloud forming at the mountaintop where he is staying in exile.

> Having spent several months on that mountain, the lover—who was separated from his beloved and whose golden armlets had fallen from his arms—saw a cloud clinging to the summit on the first day of Āṣāḍha, looking like an elephant bent over, nudging a little hill. (*MD*, *Pūrvamegha* 2)

After the Yakṣa is finished describing the path to be taken by the cloud, he explains when his curse will come to an end and he can finally be reunited with his lover.

> When Viṣṇu gets up from his serpent bed after sleeping these next four months, my curse will be over. Then we both will delight in our every desire—intensified by our separation—during the nights lit up by a full autumn moon. (*MD*, *Uttaramegha* 50)

This verse is only ten verses from the end of the poem, which is one hundred twenty-five verses in total. By ending his work this way and starting the poem in the month of Āṣāḍha, Kālidāsa has not only framed the *MD* according to the commencement and culmination of the *varṣāmāsavrata* festival—an important occasion for the Guptas—but he has also signaled the end of the Yakṣa's curse (and the end of the *MD*) in one of the most Vaiṣṇava ways possible: with Viṣṇu's awakening after a four-month slumber atop the serpent Śeṣa.

All of this suggests that Kālidāsa was heavily involved in promoting an idealized imperial image of the Gupta kings that is woven into the epic and religious lore of the times. I find this to be the true motivating factor for the poet to revisit Śambūka's death. The Vaiṣṇavism and conceptions of kingship developed under the Guptas was at odds with the image of Rāma as seen in Vālmīki's Śambūka episode—it had to be changed. Kālidāsa's reframing of the episode and focus on Śambūka's fate in death would have an enormous effect on later authors who engaged with the challenges of the *Uttarakāṇḍa*. But Kālidāsa's personal involvement in the evolution of the Śambūka story does not end here. I will have occasion to revisit his relationship to the Guptas and his compositional choices in the *MD*, which play an important role in Rāmagiri—modern Ramtek, Maharashtra—the site of the world's only temple to Śambūka, to be discussed in Chapter 6.

## Setting the Record Straight in the *Paümacariya*

Kālidāsa's new perspective on the Śambūka incident aligned with evolving Brahminical sentiments and political circumstances. Despite his changes, however, key features of the Śambūka narrative endured. Rāma's involvement in the violence of Śambūka's death still pervades the account as we find it in the *RaV*, as does the issue of *varṇa*. Yet not everyone engaging with the *Rāmāyaṇa* accepted even this much about the Śambūka story. I turn now to another early respondent to the Śambūka problem: Jain poet Vimalasūri. His issues with the epic extend far beyond the single issue of Rāma's unflinching killing of Śambūka. In fact, Vimalasūri takes issue with Vālmīki's entire rendering of Rāma's story, and he dedicates his *Paümacariya* (*The Deeds of Padma*, henceforth *PC*) to setting the record straight on Padma, his name for Rāma. His vision of the Rāma story has had a lasting effect on the *Rāmāyaṇa* tradition, both within and outside Jain contexts. In fact, his specific detailing of Śambūka's death is found with only minor changes in Rāma narratives originating from many different time periods, religious traditions, and regions, as will become clear in Chapter 5.

The addition of the *Bāla* and *Uttara kāṇḍas* to the core of Vālmīki's *Rāmāyaṇa* signals, among other things, a growing institutionalized affinity for Viṣṇu in his many manifestations and a means of expressing that affinity through the widely appealing genre of the epic. Being that the Jain community—and the Jain laity, in particular—was not isolated from the broad cultural trends of the world around them, the Jain teachers (*ācāryas*) had to contend with the rising popularity of the story of Rāma and the potential for members of their own religious tradition to accept, however passively, the Brahminical messages that came with it. There was a prominent concern on the part of the Jain teachers to acknowledge the impressionable lay community as a primary target for their teachings in order to secure a future for the religion. While discussing the sustained success of Jainism in comparison with the fading Buddhist presence in India, Jainism scholar Padmanabh Jaini notes that "for the Buddhists ... dealing with philosophical issues seems to have been the chief preoccupation of the learned ācāryas. Jaina teachers, while also deeply interested in such questions, nevertheless showed equal or perhaps even greater concern with the creation of works intended for the ordinary layperson" (1979, p. 285). This concern led to the creation of a body of extracanonical texts aimed at the Jain lay community.

One manifestation of these extracanonical texts came in the form of literature adopting the mythology of gods from traditions outside of Jainism and redesigning that literature to fit Jain ethical models.[13] One of the more prominent examples of this process are Jain treatments of the story of Rāma, who, by the time Vimalasūri was writing, had already been elevated to being an *avatāra* of Viṣṇu via the later accretions of the *Rāmāyaṇa* and the Purāṇas. This divine status characterized through accessible mediums of literature made Rāma and his story an influential presence in the South Asian landscape of the time. Considering this widespread popular accessibility and the concern with the lay community of Jainism, Jaini postulates that "had Jaina teachers ignored the tremendous fascination which these figures [i.e. Rāma, Kṛṣṇa, etc.] held for the average layperson, regardless of his religious affiliation, they would have done so at the peril of their own society's disintegration" (1979, p. 304). It would be no coincidence, then, that the nascent propagation of Rāma's divinity roughly corresponds to the first Jain accounts of his life. In the early centuries of the Common Era, we find the Jains undertaking a similar project with respect to the *Rāmāyaṇa* as the Brahminical Hindus of the same period. They began infusing the narrative with their respective traditions' religious ethics and tailoring the story to the audience they sought to attract (Cort, 1993, p. 190; Thapar, 2000, p. 14). It is also noteworthy that a sizable portion of the Jain community would likely have been converts from Brahminism.[14]

Of course, Jain *ācāryas* acknowledging Rāma's divine status as an incarnation of Viṣṇu was clearly out of the question for many reasons. Most obviously,

13 For an in-depth look at the relationship between Jain ethics and the *Rāmāyaṇa*, see Clines (2022).

14 Jha (1978, p. 15). Referring to Ācārya Jinasena's *Ādipurāṇa* (*Mahāpurāṇa*) 39.1–80, Jha further notes that the *dīkṣānvayakriyās* (initiation rites) enjoined to converts suggest a largely Brahminical audience as evidenced by the heavy use of terminology from the target audience's worldview. 39.19–24, for instance, depicts Bharata relaying the fallacies surrounding Brahmanical conceptions of sacred texts to convince a group of *dvijas* to undertake the Jain *dīkṣānvayakriyās*.

promoting a Brahminical deity in the literature, extracanonical though it may be, would have proven detrimental to the Jain cause. Also, attributing any sense of divinity to Rāma would be contrary to the Jain worldview. Instead, Vimalasūri describes the hero of his epic as one of the sixty-three Śalākāpuruṣas, great men who, though endowed with extraordinary abilities, are ultimately not divine figures (Kulkarni, 1990, p. 5). Specifically, Rāma is the eighth incarnation of Baladeva. Similarly, Lakṣmaṇa is identified as the eighth Vāsudeva and Rāvaṇa as the eighth Prativāsudeva to even out the trinity that recurs age after age in different incarnations with the same relationships maintained between the three. Baladeva and Vāsudeva are stepbrothers, Baladeva being more even-tempered and pious and Vāsudeva being more temperamental—characteristics that roughly fit the portrayal of Rāma and Lakṣmaṇa in the *VR*. Prativāsudeva is antagonistic to the other two. He is often portrayed as a noble, albeit periodically tyrannical, ruler. Vāsudeva kills Prativāsudeva and subsequently inherits his kingdom. Since he has engaged in violence by killing Prativāsudeva, he goes to hell after his death. Baladeva, finding no joy in worldly existence, renounces it and ultimately attains salvation (ibid., pp. 7–8). It is clear then, that with some specification and modification, the trinity of Baladeva-Vāsudeva-Prativāsudeva lends itself quite well to parallel characterizations of Rāma, Lakṣmaṇa, and Rāvaṇa.[15]

Integrating Rāma into this Jain conception of idealized beings necessitated several sweeping changes to Rāma's character and many actions attributed to him. Indeed, matching the *Rāmāyaṇa* generally to a Jain moral schematic required large-scale changes to the narration, including a wholesale jettisoning of Rāma's involvement in violence.[16] Vimalasūri proudly took it upon himself to mobilize his *PC* toward the task of correcting Vālmīki's account of Rāma's life. In the process of aligning the Rāma story with Jain ethics, Vimalasūri criticizes the Brahmin poets before him for misrepresenting how the events of Rāma's exile unfolded. It is quite apparent that Vimalasūri is challenging Vālmīki himself, though he never mentions him by name. Instead, he generalizes his criticisms to take aim at "the *Rāmāyaṇa* composed

15 As another example of integrating Brahminical deities into Jain mythology, Kṛṣṇa is considered the ninth incarnation of Vāsudeva. His more numerous exploits in violence and sex were harder to mitigate, thus disqualifying him from identification with Baladeva (Jaini, 1979, p. 305).

16 Other general features of the *VR* that had to be changed or abandoned to match the Rāma story to Jain sentiments include emptying the story of Brahminism and divinity and replacing them with Jain didactics and socioreligious structures and figures; providing ostensibly realistic interpretations of impossibilities or exaggerations found in the *VR*; and providing a less explicitly antagonistic relationship between Rāma, Rāvaṇa, and other characters (Kulkarni, 1959, pp. 199–204).

by the poets."[17] By the time Vimalasūri wrote his *PC* around the middle of the first millennium CE, the core of Vālmīki's *Rāmāyaṇa* had already been around for several centuries and had only recently been expanded upon with the additions of the *Bāla* and *Uttara kāṇḍas*. Vimalasūri knew Vālmīki's text in its final form since he was familiar with events from these two late *kāṇḍas*.[18] Vimalasūri had a long list of contentions with the Brahminical *Rāmāyaṇa*, which are dramatized in the *PC* through a line of questioning between King Śreṇika and the sage Gautama, a disciple of Mahāvīra. In the second chapter (*pavvan*), we learn that the king has been reflecting on worldly texts like the *Rāmāyaṇa* and finds that the stories told by its poets to be lies; they defy reason and belief.[19] King Śreṇika then appeals to Gautama to tell him the true account of the *Rāmāyaṇa*. He wonders, for instance, how Rāvaṇa was overpowered by monkeys, how those monkeys could have built a causeway over the ocean, how Rāma could have been involved in acts of violence like the killing of the golden deer and the slaying of Vālin, and how Kumbhakarṇa could sleep for six months straight.[20] Gautama responds:

> Then the best of *gaṇadharas* [Gautama] said, "Listen, O bull among men, give me your full attention. As was taught by the *kevalin*, so I also will tell you.[21]
> "Rāvaṇa is not known to be a demon, nor even did he eat meat. All this that those foolish pseudo-poets have said is false.
> "And things said without a sense of restriction do not give truthful meaning, O King; and moreover, these words are faulty as if cut from the root." (*PC* 3.14–16)

---

17 *kaīhi rāmāyaṇaṃ raïyaṃ*. *PC* 2.116. For more on the relationship between the works of Vimalasūri and Vālmīki, see Kulkarni (1959, pp. 199ff.).

18 For example, the marriage of Rāma and Sītā (*PC pavvan* 27, *VR* 1.72), Śatrughna's killing of Lavaṇa (*PC pavvan* 86, *VR* 7.60–62), and Rāma's exiling of Sītā's due to rumors of infidelity (*PC pavvans* 93–94, *VR* 7.42–47).

19 Cf. *PC* 2.104–117.

20 For this line of questioning, see *PC* 3.7–13.

21 The *gaṇadharas* are disciples—generally converted Brahmins—of the *tīrthaṅkaras* or "fordmakers" who teach truth and the path to salvation according to an imperishable tradition; Mahāvīra is the last of the *tīrthaṅkaras*. See Dundas (2002, p. 37) and Jaini (1979, pp. 2–3). Most prominent among *gaṇadharas* is Gautama, who often appears as "an interlocutor with Mahāvīra and occasionally as a converter of heretics" (Dundas, 2002, p. 37). A *kevalin* is anyone who has attained *kevalajñāna*, or infinite knowledge (Jaini, 1979, p. 2). In this passage, Gautama is referring to Mahāvīra, who attained *kevalajñāna* after his departure on the mendicant path, thus becoming the twenty-fourth and final *tīrthaṅkara* or *jina* of the present cycle (ibid., pp. 27–28).

King Śreṇika's questions and Gautama's response demonstrate that some of Vimalasūri's major problems with the Brahminical *Rāmāyaṇa* center around issues of improbable feats, slanderous misrepresentations of the Rākṣasas, and Rāma's involvement in violence. This last point is especially crucial for our purposes because it forced Vimalasūri to challenge Vālmīki's understanding of Śambūka's death.

The first thing to note about Vimalasūri's Śambūka episode is its placement in the narrative. Śambūka is somewhat obscured at the end of the *VR* during the resolution of the epic as a whole and, though important to demonstrating the condition of Rāma's rule in Ayodhyā, he is not entirely crucial to the body of the narrative. Vimalasūri's Śambūka, on the other hand, is more integrated into the main narrative and he appears in a very different portion of the epic. We hear about him in the forty-third *pavvan* of a total of one hundred eighteen, approximately halfway through the text and at one of the crucial dramatic turning points of the narrative: immediately preceding the abduction of Sītā.

In the *PC*, Śambūka is the very strong and capable son of Rāvaṇa's sister, Candraṇakhā and her husband, Kharadūṣaṇa.[22] Despite the warnings of his gurus, Śambūka enters the forest carrying the *sūryahāsa* sword with him. As he enters the forest, he is seen by Maraṇa (Death), who warns that whoever enters his line of sight while devoid of the proper mental and meditative qualities will be killed. Śambūka goes deep into a bamboo grove and begins to practice *tapas* near the sword to appease Maraṇa and he remains there for twelve years and four days. Three days before his *tapas* is to be completed, Lakṣmaṇa approaches and stumbles upon the sword. Fascinated, he picks it up and uses it to slash at a patch of bamboo.

> And just then, he saw there a fallen head, ornamented with earrings, and a body, wet with blood and mud as if the branch of a coral tree. (*PC* 43.27)

The head is Śambūka's. Lakṣmaṇa has accidentally decapitated him while engaged in *tapas*. He runs to confess to Rāma. Candraṇakhā comes to visit her son, sees his head separated from his body, and weeps. She sets out in pursuit of her son's killers, but when she encounters Rāma and Lakṣmaṇa, she becomes enchanted with their beauty.

---

22 In many *Rāmāyaṇa*s from the Hindu tradition, Khara and Dūṣaṇa are two separate figures, both brothers of the Rākṣasa king, Rāvaṇa.

At this point, the *PC* converges somewhat with the *VR* in that Candraṇakhā (Śūrpaṇakhā in Vālmīki's text) becomes the catalyst for Rāvaṇa's abduction of Sītā. As in the *VR*, Rāma and Lakṣmaṇa reject Candraṇakhā's advances in the *PC*. In Vimalasūri's text, however, Lakṣmaṇa does not mutilate her. Instead, having mutilated *herself*, Candraṇakhā goes to Kharadūṣaṇa and explains that their son was slain and she was molested and mutilated. Kharadūṣaṇa then asks Rāvaṇa for his help in avenging his son's death. During the search for Rāma and Lakṣmaṇa who are under attack by Kharadūṣaṇa and his troops, Rāvaṇa comes across Sītā, becomes infatuated with her, and abducts her.

In re-positioning the Śambūka story and narrating it as he does, Vimalasūri was able to eliminate several issues inconsistent with Jain doctrine. I have already discussed his tactic of removing Rāma—as Baladeva, an ideal Jain—from any acts of violence. Another example of purging the story of details would be the deemphasis of *varṇa*. When Rāma kills Śambūka at the end of the *VR*, he does so as a king upholding his *rājadharma* to protect society and ensure the proper maintenance of *varṇadharma*. Śambūka's transgression of *varṇa* provides the entire impetus behind his capital punishment. Making the death accidental in the *PC* avoids any *varṇa*-based motivations for Śambūka's death. Lakṣmaṇa did not know he was killing anyone until it was too late. By removing issues of *varṇa* from entering his narration of the Śambūka story, Vimalasūri is removing a key Brahminical social structure at odds with the Jain vision of society.[23] Furthermore, the issue of *rājadharma*—a central motivating feature for Rāma's execution of Śambūka in the *VR*—is eliminated by relocating the episode because Rāma is still in exile at the time of his death. Vimalasūri's restructuring of the Śambūka episode thus allows the narrative to circumvent some of the Brahminical ideology of the story as found in Vālmīki's text.

Vimalasūri's Śambūka is nearly unrecognizable when juxtaposed with the Śambūka of the *VR*. In fact, there is some room to question whether they are the same character at all. However, despite the narrative divergences, several parallels remain. Most generally, both tellings deal with the decapitation of a defenseless ascetic killed during his *tapas*, there is a lamenting parent in each case, and hero is transformed into villain while the villain is transformed into an

---

23 Vimalasūri was not entirely successful in cleansing the story of Brahminical imagery. For instance, there is reference on more than one occasion to the "code of honor" absolving mendicants, Brahmins, cows, women, children, and the elderly from guilt and they are not to be killed or injured even if they commit some sort of offense (Kulkarni, 1990, pp. 78, 80). Cf. *PC* 35.15 and 65.30.

object of sympathy.[24] These plot points are easily manipulated to suit the specifics of the authors' intents, creating a number of consistencies between these two episodes despite producing different results. Also, considering that Vimalasūri knew the *Uttarakāṇḍa* and does not include a Śambūka story in some analogous portion of his own *PC*, it seems entirely plausible to me that he was consciously excising the story from the end of the epic and relocating it to a more narratively prominent place. In fact, Śambūka's appearance at this point draws a considerable amount of attention to the episode and, accordingly, to its deviation from Vālmīki's version. Thus, I contend that not only is this the same Śambūka, but Vimalasūri uses his narration of the Śambūka episode to explicitly counter Vālmīki and further the aims of his *PC* as a whole. Each of the discrepancies between the episode as portrayed in the *PC* and the *VR* do the double work of discrediting Vālmīkis knowledge of the Rāma story while simultaneously elevating Rāma as a Jain Śalākāpuruṣa. Śambūka's accidental death thus participated in Vimalasūri's larger project of laying claim to the Rāma story on behalf of the Jain laity.

## Forming the Foundations of Śambūka's Future

Kālidāsa and Vimalasūri each left early and significant impressions on the tradition of narrating Rāma's life. They each sought to elevate Rāma, whose image had become complicated with the addition of the *Uttarakāṇḍa* to the *VR*—Śambūka's death being a major contributing factor in that complication. Kālidāsa strove to match Rāma's reputation to contemporary political and Brahminical expectations while keeping the story's essential elements intact. His major innovations lie in bolstering Rāma's divinity and demonstrating mercy toward Śambūka. This mercy is limited, however, being that it is only in the service of demonstrating Rāma's compassion and divine authority; it is not an acknowledgement that Śambūka was innocent.[25] Vimalasūri was more iconoclastic. While criticizing the Brahminical narration of the Rāma story as lies and exaggerations, he sought to definitively establish Rāma in the pantheon of Śalākāpuruṣas, thereby simultaneously draining

24 Stuart Blackburn makes these observations in his study on the Kerala shadow puppetry tradition *tolpāvakūttu* (1996, pp. 72–73). This tradition, based almost entirely on Kampaṉ's Tamil-language *Irāmāvatāram*, includes a scene that very closely resembles Vimalasūri's Śambūka story (for more, see Chapter 5 in this study).

25 I concede that Śambūka's crimes are deemphasized in Kālidāsa's work. For instance, he completely removes Nārada's lament on declining *dharma* and Śambūka's transgressive anticipation of *dharma* in the Kali Yuga, when Śambūka's *tapas* would have been acceptable.

Rāma of his divinity and giving the Jain laity access to this increasingly popular figure. His understanding of the Śambūka episode served as one aspect of a massive overhaul of the entire epic dedicated to correcting Vālmīki's misconstrued versions of events associated with Rāma's life.

In receiving the *VR* as at least one of their primary sources for the Śambūka story, both poets discussed in this chapter had to contend with the unwaveringly cold legality of the episode. For Kālidāsa, the Śambūka episode presented an opportunity to replace symbols of retribution with symbols of redemption. In the *RaV*, Rāma is transformed from an enforcer to a liberator. For Vimalasūri, neither system of symbols—the retributive depiction of Vālmīki or the redemptive depiction of Kālidāsa—would have been fitting for his Rāma. He needed to change the entire paradigm of Śambūka's death. Rāma could in no way be associated with that violence, nor could he or anyone else be endowed with the divine authority to single-handedly and instantly grant Śambūka liberation. In fact, one could easily argue that Lakṣmaṇa's interruption of Śambūka's austerities—a decidedly Jain means of attaining release—was detrimental to Śambūka's aims. Ultimately, Vimalasūri uses the Śambūka episode in the service of his de-Brahmanizing of the epic.

Whatever the ultimate result of including Śambūka in their works, both poets accepted him as a part of the story to be told. They embraced his story and allowed it to serve their ultimate aims: to exalt Rāma in a world where Vaiṣṇavism was permeating larger swaths of India in Kālidāsa's case or to demonstrate the fictiveness of a competing mythological tradition in Vimalasūri's. Their reflections of Śambūka's death set new foundations for the flurry of *Rāmāyaṇas* that would appear in subsequent centuries. Some of these new *Rāmāyaṇas* incorporate themes explored in this chapter while others revert to a telling of the story more in line with the *VR*. Some chose to excise any material of the *Uttarakāṇḍa*, including the Śambūka story while some kept the *Uttarakāṇḍa* but avoided the Śambūka story. The next two chapters deal with a large number of these texts. Chapter 4 is narrow in its scope, focusing on one of the most beautifully composed and innovative accounts of the Śambūka story—that of Bhavabhūti in his drama, the *Uttararāmacarita*. Chapter 5 broadens this focus and takes a bird's-eye view of the *Rāmāyaṇa* tradition as it flourished in medieval India, a period of intricate connections between many South Asian Religious traditions, linguistic communities, and regional populations as they contributed to an immense array of variation in narrating the story of Rāma's life and Śambūka's death.

# Chapter 4

# THE *UTTARARĀMACARITA* AND ŚAMBŪKA'S PURPOSE IN DEATH

This chapter analyzes Bhavabhūti's eighth-century *Uttararāmacarita* (*The Later Deeds of Rāma*, henceforth *URC*),[1] a text that dives deeper into Śambūka's death than any considered so far. Aside from it being a beautifully crafted piece of literature, I choose to focus on Bhavabhūti's play because it ties into developments related to Śambūka's depiction in Kālidāsa's *RaV*. In creating the *URC*, though, Bhavabhūti was not beholden to political oversight in the way Kālidāsa was, nor was he involved in a large-scale revisionist project like Vimalasūri. He did, however, have a framework within which to work as he redesigned not only how we are to understand Śambūka, but how we are to understand the entire *Uttarakāṇḍa*.

The *URC* is a Sanskrit drama, a genre with its own conventions. Characters, plot, and structure all follow elaborate formulae most clearly laid out in the *Nāṭyaśāstra*, a dramaturgical text compiled around the time of Kālidāsa (Gerow, 1984). The aesthetic effect of a Sanskrit drama relies on an intricate system of poetics centered around the theory of *rasa*, which Edwin Gerow summarizes in the dramatic context as being "a resolution of sentiments sufficiently general to abolish the mundane distinctions between audience, actor, and author" (ibid., p. 43). In blurring these boundaries between a work of art, the artist, and the audience, *rasa* is a poetic tool that underpins the enjoyment and appreciation of art.

Briefly, *rasas*—of which there are eight or nine, depending on the theoretician—are the various emotional catalysts in a work of art that exist as a product of the play's composition and the actors' portrayal as well as their ability to resonate with a person's inherent experiences and emotions. The universally acknowledged eight *rasas* are *śṛṅgara* (erotic), *hāsya* (comic), *karuṇa* (piteous), *raudra* (furious), *vīra* (heroic), *bhayānaka* (terrifying), *bībhatsā* (disgusting), and *adbhūta* (wondrous); the debated ninth *rasa* is *śānta* (peaceful).

---

1 For a discussion on the date of Bhavabhūti, see Mirashi (1974, pp. 1–11).

While a drama may utilize any number of these *rasas* as the context warrants, it will have a single dominant *rasa* that best relates to the overarching plot.[2]

Bhavabhūti exploits these structural and poetic conventions of Sanskrit dramaturgy to reexamine the sometimes controversial events of Rāma's later life as we know it from the *Uttarakāṇḍa*. With this chapter, I explore how he accomplishes this reexamination. Because of the resemblance between the Śambūkas of their respective texts, I begin by outlining the relationship between Kālidāsa and Bhavabhūti, which includes a note concerning legendary accounts about the personal connection between the two poets as well as a close look into some of the motifs present in the texts they produced. After that, I focus in on the *URC* itself and Śambūka's role in it. I show how Bhavabhūti employs the conventions of Sanskrit drama and the play's dominant *rasa* in service of elevating Śambūka's character and helping us understand Rāma's condition as he carries out the execution.

The tone and function of Śambūka's death and Rāma's involvement therein undergoes enormous modification in Bhavabhūti's work.[3] For the first time, we see Rāma hesitate in killing Śambūka during an instance of deep inner turmoil. Once Rāma does kill him, Śambūka takes a divine form and shares a touching moment with Rāma. No longer just a subordinated figure used to demonstrate the consequences of violating the limits of one's *varṇa* or an exemplary case of the power of contact with the divine, Bhavabhūti's Śambūka plays a significant connective role in the drama and serves as a critical source of momentum in the progression of its narrative, which centers around Rāma's exile of Sītā. In fact, Bhavabhūti's Śambūka sparks a series of events that lead to their eventual reunion, a far cry from the condemned criminal of Vālmīki's text and even the passive beneficiary of Rāma's redemptive powers as king as found in Kālidāsa. The play is an extraordinary and—at the time of its composition—unprecedentedly detailed and emotive contribution to the *Rāmāyaṇa* and Śambūka traditions alike.

## Connections and Divergences between Kālidāsa and Bhavabhūti

Even though Kālidāsa and Bhavabhūti are separated by some three centuries (ca. fifth century and eighth century, respectively), there are still clear markers

2 There is much more to the theory of *rasa* that falls outside the scope of this study. It is a topic that has been debated, revised, and transformed repeatedly for centuries. For an overview of Indian poetics, see Gerow (1971) and Vijayavardhana (1970).

3 For a concise contextualization on the innovative sentiments regarding Śambūka in the *URC*, see Goldman (2019, pp. 98–99).

for comparison. In his translation of Bhavabhūti's *URC*, Pollock notes that the work appears to be a "counterpart to, and competitor of, [Kālidāsa's] masterpiece" (2007, p. 34). The "masterpiece" Pollock is referring to is his drama *Śakuntalā*, based on the love story between Śakuntalā and King Duṣyanta found in the *MBh.* Aside from representing portions of each of India's two major epics, the two works share a great number of thematic and structural similarities, which have solicited a number of comparisons between the two plays and between the two poets in their roles as dramatists.[4] Such scholarly comparisons are in addition to a popular legend that the two were contemporaries.[5] However unlikely this may be, there is a particularly noteworthy legend pertaining to Kālidāsa's supposed contribution to the *URC.* According to this legend, Bhavabhūti approached Kālidāsa for his opinion on the play and Kālidāsa offered a single correction. In its original form, Verse 27 of Act I, when Rāma is recalling his time with Sītā on Mount Prasravaṇa in Janasthāna, is said to have been:

> *kim api kim api mandāṃ mandam āsattiyogād aviralitakapolaṃ jalpator akrameṇa* |
> *aśithilaparirambhavyāpṛtaikaikadoṣṇor aviditagatayāmā rātrir evaṃ vyaraṃsīt* ||

> Talking about anything aimlessly with cheeks joined together in close union, our arms one upon the other engaged in a tight embrace, the night thus ended with the late hours having passed by unnoticed.

Kālidāsa's one recommendation in the entire play was that Bhavabhūti remove the *anusvāra* (*ṃ*) at the end of the word *evaṃ* (thus) found in this verse. With this suggestion, the meaning of the verse becomes:

> Talking about anything aimlessly with cheeks joined together in close union, our arms one upon the other engaged in a tight embrace, only the night ended with the late hours having passed by unnoticed.

This new meaning suggests that *only* the night ended, signaling to us as readers that the love shared between Rāma and Sītā continued. Of course, there is no historical basis for such a legend given their incompatible dates. Nevertheless,

---

4 See Pollock (2007, pp. 33ff.), Kale (1934, pp. 21–23), Mirashi and Navlekar (1969, pp. 453–454), and Mirashi (1974, pp. 7–8). For a specific comparison of the Śambūka episode between the two poets, see Goldman and Sutherland Goldman (2017, pp. 107–109).

5 For legendary accounts of Kālidāsa and Bhavabhūti's interactions, see Mirashi (1974, pp. 68–70).

given elaborate legends like this and the resonances of Kālidāsa in Bhavabhūti's own work, the range of associations between the two dramatist-poets are powerful enough to create a haze of real stylistic and narrative borrowings between the two poets' works that are colored by their legendary interactions.

There are clues in the text of the *URC* to suggest that Bhavabhūti was continuing Kālidāsa's specific innovations relating to Śambūka as found in the *RaV*, a point to which I will return shortly. However, it is worth acknowledging that, as pieces of literature, Kālidāsa's *RaV* and Bhavabhūti's *URC* are doing two very different kinds of work. In the previous chapter, I identified some political and social motivations that underpin the *RaV*'s composition. The poem was created to elevate the Raghu lineage and sustain resonances of Gupta predominance at the same time, thus blurring together the worlds of political reality and mythological narrative. Also, Kālidāsa's *RaV* is an immense work. The Rāma story occupies only a fraction of the text, and the Śambūka story a fraction of that. The role of the Rāma story in general is subservient to the project at hand, leaving the smaller episodes of the text rather unconnected to the work as a whole. Neither of these situations is true in the case of Bhavabhūti's *URC*. Not only does he use the Rāma story to constitute the drama's subject matter, he also limits his narrative frame to the events portrayed in the *Uttarakāṇḍa*. This drastically restricts the temporal boundaries of the play's setting and allows Bhavabhūti to focus on narrative connections and dwell on issues routinely passed over in epic renditions of the Rāma story. Also key is the fact that, unlike Kālidāsa, Bhavabhūti's aim is not to *universalize* the story of Rāma and draw parallels to his sociopolitical reality. Instead, he appears to have sought to *personalize* the epic and enter Rāma's psyche to help his audience understand the difficult choices Rāma had to make during his reign over Ayodhyā.

While the *RaV* and *URC* diverge in their compositional framework, Bhavabhūti is clearly taking cues from his predecessor. You may recall that Kālidāsa removes Nārada's *varṇa*-based lament from the *RaV*'s Śambūka story altogether and has "Sarasvatī, whose form was hidden" (*gūḍharūpā sarasvatī*) convey to Rāma that the young Brahmin's death was due to some unspecified misconduct (*kaścid apacāraḥ*) in the kingdom. Bhavabhūti does something similar in the prelude to Act II. Here, he eliminates Nārada's speech and replaces it with a statement from a "disembodied voice" (*aśarīriṇī vāk*), though this voice does mention Śambūka by name and identifies him as a Śūdra.[6] Even more explicit, however, is Kālidāsa's description of Śambūka inhaling

6 Instead of "voice," the Sanskrit term *vāc* could just as easily be translated as speech, or even Speech personified. The goddess Sarasvatī is closely associated with speech, often identified as Speech itself (cf. *Taittiriya Saṃhitā* 3.4.3.4), making Bhavabhūti's *áśarīriṇī vāk* resonate that much more with Kālidāsa's *gūḍharūpā sarasvatī*.

smoke (*dhūmapaḥ*) as part of his *tapas*.[7] Bhavabhūti uses the exact same word to describe Śambūka in the *URC*.[8] Nowhere in the *VR* (or any other text prior to Kālidāsa that I am aware of) is Śambūka described as inhaling smoke. When Rāma finally finds Śambūka in Vālmīki's text, all he sees is an ascetic performing very difficult austerities while hanging upside down; smoke plays no part in his *tapas*. For another point of comparison, Śambūka's life in Kālidāsa did not end with his death. There was more for Śambūka along "the course of virtuous men." This rings true with Bhavabhūti, who follows his predecessor in demonstrating an interest in Śambūka's afterlife, but Bhavabhūti takes the story further than Kālidāsa and, in the *URC*, we get our first glimpses of what Śambūka experiences after his punishment is carried out.

As mentioned above, Kālidāsa looked to create a bridge between the epic and his political environment while Bhavabhūti built a bridge between the epic's characters and his audience based on a sympathetic emotional experience. That being the case, my focus here will be on how Bhavabhūti crafts the play's plot and emotional backdrop rather than the specific political and historical contexts within which the work was composed. A major part of Bhavabhūti's project involves revamping how we understand Śambūka's relationship with Rāma and to best understand how he integrates this novel perspective into his drama, we must first understand how he crafts its structural and emotional environment. To do so, it is imperative to acknowledge how Bhavabhūti utilizes *rasa* to overhaul the basis of the interaction between Rāma and Śambūka.

## Pity in Bhavabhūti's *Uttararāmacarita*

Śambūka's death is undoubtedly a troubling incident, but, taking the *Uttarakāṇḍa* as a whole, it is often overshadowed by Rāma's exile of a pregnant Sītā upon their return to Ayodhyā. Despite proving her innocence in a literal trial-by-fire, rumors abound in the kingdom that Sītā did not remain chaste while held captive in Rāvaṇa's house. As the king of Ayodhyā, Rāma finds himself duty-bound to quell the suspicions of his citizenry. With his *URC*, Bhavabhūti accepts the challenges of the *Uttarakāṇḍa* and explores the complex emotions Rāma feels as he is torn between his heart and his *dharma*. The play is framed by Sītā's exile and Bhavabhūti constantly illustrates the heart-wrenching guilt that Rāma lives with as a man tormented by memories of his beloved, whom he has cast out of the kingdom and home they share while she was pregnant.

---

7 Cf. *RaV* 15.50. See also *RaV* 15.49, where Śambūka is described as having eyes reddened with smoke (*dhūmābhitāmrākṣa*).

8 Cf. Vāsantī's line in the prelude to Act II just after v. 2.8.

These insights into a wounded Rāma were entirely unfamiliar to a tradition so used to knowing Rāma as composed and steadfast in all his obligations.

Bhavabhūti's work is poetic in the technical sense. He strives to produce for his audience an aesthetic experience through the creation of a sympathetic resonance of emotional states between characters and audience members. This resonance is accomplished by the manipulation of the various *rasas*. The different elements of the plot all contribute to bolstering the emotions Bhavabhūti hopes to elicit throughout the play and, in so doing, he deepens our understanding of Rāma's suffering. In particular, Bhavabhūti repeatedly calls on the piteous *rasa* (*karuṇa-rasa*) to frame Rāma's troubled state of mind, thus providing an intensification of *karuṇa-rasa* in the *Rāmāyaṇa* narrative.

Manipulating *rasa* as a means of reexamining or reframing existing narratives is a not unique enterprise in South Asian literature, even within the *Rāmāyaṇa* tradition alone. Gregory Clines has recently demonstrated how Jain poet Raviṣeṇa has rewritten the Jain Rāma story as a *kāvya* with special attention to *rasa* and manipulating his poetics to convey a very particular schematic of Jain ethics. However closely Raviṣeṇa adheres to Vimalasūri's narrative, Clines (2022) argues that his attuned application of *rasa* to convey Jain priorities of renunciation through *śānta rasa*—the peaceful *rasa* closely associated with the desire to renounce the world—is itself an innovation in the way the *Rāmāyaṇa* was told in Jain contexts.

In a wide-reaching survey of *rasa* in the *URC*, David Shulman points out that when reading Bhavabhūti's work, we should "think of a ripening faculty of empathy which is the necessary substratum for all other forms of emotional or aesthetic experience, and for understanding other people, including those closest and most loved" (2001, p. 74). Indeed, Bhavabhūti explicitly calls attention to the fact that *karuṇa-rasa* suits Rāma's dejected state in the *URC* and it is, in fact, the one true *rasa* from which all others derive.

> It is imperceivable due to his profoundness: a piercing pain hidden inside as if wrapped in clay and kiln-fired. The *rasa* of pity is Rāma's. (*URC* 3.1)
> There is only the *rasa* of pity. It is divided into separate parts because of myriad causes as it conforms to their differences just as water can change from whirlpool to wave to bubble; it is all just water. (*URC* 3.47)[9]

Pity is not the only *rasa* to appear, however. In fact, Bhavabhūti spends considerable time building his way up to *karuṇa-rasa* by developing feelings

9 *URC* 3.48 in some editions; all citations provided here will be according to Kale (1934).

in the realm of the erotic (*śṛṅgāra-rasa*), itself divisible into love in union (*sambhoga-śṛṅgāra-rasa*; e.g., *URC* 1.27 discussed above) and the more mournful love in separation (*vipralambha-śṛṅgāra-rasa*). Sentiments of love in separation happen at numerous occasions in the play, especially in two contexts: when Rāma is remembering his time spent in the forest away from Sītā and when he is plagued with guilt for having to exile Sītā.[10] Within many conceptions of *rasa*, the *vipralambha-śṛṅgāra* and *karuṇa rasas* are considered quite similar to each other, and likewise the technical poetic elements contributing to its portrayal.[11] In fact, some poeticians contend that the only difference between the two sentiments is that in *karuṇa-rasa*, the object of affection is deceased and there is no possibility for reunion; in *vipralambha-śṛṅgāra*, on the other hand, the object of affection (especially a lover) is still alive so the possibility of reunion remains.[12] The similarity between *rasas* gives Bhavabhūti the opportunity to play with the subtle difference between the two in the form of a one-sided reunion between Rāma and Sītā in Act III, for which Śambūka is at least indirectly responsible, as we will see below. The closeness in *rasa* also makes possible a smooth transition from *vipralambha-śṛṅgāra-rasa* to *karuṇa-rasa*, the overarching *rasa* that Bhavabhūti imagines for his play. This consistent and nuanced handling of *rasa* gives the audience a context designed by Bhavabhūti to understand Rāma's state as he encounters difficult situations beyond the obviously troubling banishment of Sītā—for example, the death of Śambūka.

## The Hand that Swings the Sword

In the *URC*, we first hear about Śambūka in the prelude to Act II during a conversation between Ātreyī, an ascetic woman, and Vāsantī, a forest deity and friend of Sītā. Ātreyī is in the forest after having unsuccessfully tried to

10 There are many examples of the former, especially throughout Act I. Cf. *URC* 1.31. For the latter, cf. *URC* 1.45 and 1.47.

11 These elements include *vibhāvas* (stimuli), *anubhāvas* (consequents), and *vyabhicārins* (transitory states). The stimuli provide the context in which a *rasa* can be realized, the consequents are its perceivable effects, and transitory states are fleeting emotions that intensify the overarching *rasa*. The proper manipulation of all these elements gives rise to *rasa*.

12 See Vijayavardhana (1970, p. 100) and Pollock (2007, p. 57 n. 13). The distinction is blurry in the case of the *URC* because Sītā has gone into the ground, back to the Gaṅgā, effectively symbolizing her death—subsequently making the dominant *rasa* one of pity, as Bhavabhūti himself admits (cf. *URC* 3.47). This is supported by the fact that Rāma believes that he is sentencing her to death when he banishes her to the forest (cf. *URC* 1.45). Yet at the end of the play they are reunited, leaving some confusion as to the true circumstances surrounding the dominant *rasa* in the work.

study with Vālmīki, who is himself busy instructing Rāma and Sītā's children, Lava and Kuśa, as well as composing the *Rāmāyaṇa*. Unable to study with Vālmīki, she asks Vāsantī where Agastya's hermitage is, hoping to study with him instead. Vāsantī directs her through Pañcavaṭī to the Godāvarī riverbank, which stirs in her the painful memory of Sītā's absence from Ayodhyā. Ātreyī then tells Vāsantī about Sītā's fate and her banishment's aftermath in Ayodhyā. Then, after mentioning that Rāma has undertaken the Horse Sacrifice, Ātreyī tells Vāsantī about the unfortunate death of a young Brahmin boy.

> **Ātreyī**: In the midst of all of this, a Brahmin threw down his dead son at the gate and beat his chest screaming, "Sacrilege!" Then, as the compassionate Rāmabhadra was reflecting on his faults, thinking, "Untimely death does not happen among the people without misconduct on the part of the king," a disembodied voice suddenly proclaimed:
>
> > There is a Vṛṣala [Śūdra] named Śambūka practicing austerities on Earth. You are to cut off his head. Kill him and revive the Brahmin. (*URC* 2.8)
>
> As soon as he heard this, the Lord of the World, his sword drawn in hand, mounted the Puṣpaka vehicle and began to roam in all directions—cardinal and ordinal—in search of the Śūdra ascetic.
> **Vāsantī**: The smoke-inhaling Śūdra named Śambūka is practicing austerities right here in Janasthāna. So now perhaps Rāmabhadra will again grace this forest.

Rāma makes his way to Janasthāna to carry out the punishment. In Bhavabhūti's understanding of the event, however, our attention is directed away from the death and revival of the Brahmin boy (who is given little mention in the play) and onto Rāma's inner conflict and his susceptibility to sympathy as he comes face to face with the man he is supposed to execute. After the prelude to Act II ends, Rāma comes upon Śambūka right at the outset of Act II proper and the *karuṇa-rasa* reignites as Rāma hesitates to carry out the punishment.

> *Rāma enters upon the Puṣpaka chariot with his sword raised with compassion.*
>
> **Rāma**: O right hand, for the life of the deceased young twice-born, cast down the sword upon the Śūdra sage. You are a limb of Rāma. How can you have pity, you who were capable of exiling Sītā while she suffered from a difficult pregnancy? (*URC* 2.10)
> (Somehow driving the sword) A deed worthy of Rāma is done. Now let the son of the Brahmin live!

We see in this passage that in addition to the compassion on display for the audience via the curious stage direction of Rāma having his sword "raised with compassion" (*sadayodyatakhaḍgaḥ*), Rāma's pity toward Śambūka is also suggested through this plea to his hand to carry out Śambūka's execution, a task he is evidently not capable of carrying out himself. He reminds his hand of its lack of pity (*karuṇā*) based on its cavalier ability to point Sītā into exile. Rāma's blame for his hand allows him to remain at some distance from the troubling work of killing Śambūka and forces his feelings of guilt to resonate with the larger narrative frame centered on Sītā's banishment.

Bhavabhūti uses the play's predominant *karuṇa-rasa* in this passage to demonstrate that Rāma resists the inevitable execution of Śambūka for fear that it would simply add to his already dejected state rooted in his tragic separation from Sītā. The above passage trains us, as the audience, to view Śambūka's execution and Sītā's exile in the same piteous light with Rāma making an explicit connection by associating the two incidents with the cruelty of his own hand. Even Bhavabhūti's utilization of indirect language works to suggest that Rāma wishes to remove himself from carrying out this difficult act. This creates an emotional dynamic between Rāma and Śambūka that is outrightly sympathetic. Such sympathy is absent from earlier tellings of the episode. Even in the *RaV*, Kālidāsa only hints at a feeling of sympathy with the brief attention he gives to Śambūka's afterlife. All these factors in Bhavabhūti's portrayal of Rāma point us to viewing him as a conflicted character—one bound by his *dharma* but reluctant to follow through with the actions necessary to adhere to that *dharma*.

## Śambūka Speaks … in Sanskrit

Despite all the poetic, narrative, and linguistic devices Bhavabhūti employs to change the context of Śambūka's death and Rāma's involvement in it, he still made the choice to engage with the controversial episode and make it a part of his own narrative universe. However, as was the case for Kālidāsa in his *RaV*, Bhavabhūti does not accept the unequivocal denial of Śambūka's divine ambitions and he dismisses the idea that the gods would celebrate upon knowing that the Śūdra failed in his ascetic efforts. Instead, he finds opportunity in the aftermath of Śambūka's death to create an atmosphere of amicable and beneficial interaction between Rāma and the once-condemned Śūdra.

Right after Rāma's sword lands the fatal blow on Śambūka, he is immediately transformed into a divine person (*divyapuruṣa*) and he speaks his first words of the play—and he does so in Sanskrit, which may come as a surprise. Given his status as a Śūdra, we can assume that he would have otherwise been speaking Prakrit as per convention in Sanskrit drama, and something true of other socially subservient characters in the *URC* (e.g., one of Rāma's spies, Durmukha, in Act I and all non-divine female characters including Sītā). While that may have been true of Śambūka in life, we never get to hear him speak when he is alive. We only hear Śambūka speak after his death and reembodiment as a *divyapuruṣa*, whereupon he speaks in a language reserved for only the most venerable of characters. Bhavabhūti's choice to portray Śambūka as a Sanskrit-speaking *divyapuruṣa* demonstrates to his audience in an indirect way that death at Rāma's hand can elevate anyone, even a criminal Śūdra, to a position of great respect. Additionally, in having Śambūka's role effectively begin after his death, Bhavabhūti opens up the narrative for considerable innovation to Śambūka's character and he uses the space he has created to foster a dialogue of devotion and respect.

**Divine man**: (Entering) Victory be to the Lord!

> As you grant safety even from Yama and bear the rod [of justice], the boy is brought to life, as is my good fortune. Śambūka is here, bowing his head at your feet. Those things which arise from contact with the good, even one's losses, carry one through (*URC* 2.11).

**Rāma**: Both are dear to me. May you experience the result of your intense *tapas*.

> Where there is joy and delight, where there is meritorious attainment, may those brilliant worlds of Vairāja indeed be yours eternally (*URC* 2.12).

**Śambūka**: This greatness comes from your grace. What is there in *tapas*? Actually, there may be great benefit through *tapas*.

> You, the Lord of Beings who yields protection, are sought out on Earth. Yet you have traveled hundreds of leagues and arrived here, seeking me out, a mere Vṛṣala [Śūdra]; this is the grace of these austerities. If it were any other way, would you have come from Ayodhyā back to the Daṇḍaka Forest? (*URC* 2.13)

Such an interaction drastically reformulates Śambūka's death as we have known it from the *VR* and even the *RaV*, where Śambūka is silenced in death. Yet, Bhavabhūti takes Śambūka's character even further by portraying him as Rāma's guide through the Daṇḍaka wilderness and has Śambūka console Rāma as he painfully relives the memories of his time spent with Sītā in Janasthāna. After Śambūka recites v. 2.13, Rāma continues:

**Rāma**: Wait, this is Daṇḍaka? (Looking all around) Can it be?

> Now I see it. I recognize these spots in Daṇḍaka, dotted with fords, hermitages, mountains, rivers, caverns, and forests. Some of these spots have a charming darkness, others are made harsh with terrible labyrinths. Each region is resounding with the murmur of waterfalls in every corner (*URC* 2.14).

**Śambūka**: This is indeed Daṇḍaka. My lord had previously dwelt right here …

> … for fourteen years. And here Dūṣaṇa, Khara, and Trimūrdhan—a trio of Rākṣasas who had committed vile deeds—were killed in battle (*URC* 2.15).

Because of that, people of the countryside like me can roam about in this wonderful land of Janasthāna free of fear.

**Rāma**: So not only is this Daṇḍaka, but Janasthāna even?
**Śambūka**: That's right. These deep forests in the innermost parts of Janasthāna—with mountain caverns crowded with packs of cruel, frantic beasts that make the hairs of all creatures stand on end—sit in the southern direction. Indeed …

> The borderlands have a silent calm in some places and the sounds of violent beasts in others; fires blaze with the deep and frightening hiss of snakes willfully sleeping. Small thirsty lizards drink the gush of sweat from large serpents in the crevices where the shimmer of water is scarce (*URC* 2.16).

**Rāma**:

> I see Janasthāna—once the abode of Khara—and now I'm experiencing incidents of old as if they're happening right in front of me (*URC* 2.17).

(Looking all around) Vaidehī was, in all respects, Rāma's beloved. All these forests … What could be more terrifying? (Tearfully)

> [She said,] "I will live with you in these honey-fragrant forests." And she even enjoyed it here—such was the love [for me].
> Doing nothing whatsoever replaces sorrow with gladness; to love and be loved is quite treasure indeed (*URC* 2.18–19).

**Śambūka**: Enough with these troubling thoughts. May the great one now look all around at the deep, calm central forests, filled with the soft colors on the throats of impassioned peacocks and adorned with dense clusters of young trees creating a thick, dark shade, where packs of animals of all kinds stay undisturbed.

> Here, the rivers flow; their cool, clear waters made fragrant by the blooming of canes and creepers which are crowded with passionate birds and their strong currents bubbling from contact with the thickets of rose-apple trees darkened from being full of fruit (*URC* 2.20).

And also

> Here, the roars of bear cubs living in caves resound, amplified with echoes. The smell of the *śallakī* trees' juicy bunches intensifies—cooling, pungent, and sharp having been split open and scattered about by elephants (*URC* 2.21).

**Rāma**: (Still and tearfully) My friend, may your paths be favorable. Set off on the way of the gods and enter into the worlds of virtue.
**Śambūka**: I will enter the eternal abode as soon as I pay homage to Agastya, the Brahmin sage of old.

*He exits.*

After Śambūka leaves, Rāma describes his surroundings as he reminisces about his time in Pañcavaṭī and the tragedies that have unfolded since he has left there. As he laments about the rumors that forced him to cast Sītā out into the forests, Śambūka returns with a message from Agastya.

**Śambūka**: (Entering) Victory! Victory be to the Lord! My Lord, the honorable Agastya has heard that you are near and is overjoyed. He says to you, "The dear Lopāmudrā waits happily as she expects your vehicle to descend, as do all the sages. So do come and honor us. Then, after heading back to your home in the swift Puṣpaka, you will be ready for the Horse Sacrifice."
**Rāma**: As the noble one commands.
**Śambūka**: Then may the Lord turn the Puṣpaka this way.
**Rāma**: (Turning the Puṣpaka) Noble Pañcavaṭī, please excuse for a moment this transgression of Rāma, which is due to respect for his gurus.
**Śambūka**: Look, my Lord, look.

> This is the mountain Krauñcāvata, having flocks of crows muted by the tumult of the [wind in the] clusters of hollowed bamboo

> along with the hooting parliaments of owls and the buzzing forest huts. There, aggravated by the coos of the trembling peacocks, the snakes rise up into the branches of the old sandal trees (*URC* 2.29).

What's more

> Here are the southern mountains, with the waters of the Godāvarī roaring indistinctly in its caverns, and whose summits are darkened by clouds resting on the peaks. And here are the auspicious confluences of rivers, with deep water, intense with the loud sound of violently moving waves colliding with each other (*URC* 2.30).

*They both exit.*

The dialogues shared between Rāma and Śambūka in these passages—taking place in pure Sanskrit—are filled with compassion, beautiful imagery, and mutual respect. Even after death at Rāma's hand, Śambūka showers him with devotion and feels grateful for the opportunity to have had contact with him. What's more, seeing Rāma flounder as he returns to Janasthāna—flooded by memories of happier days—prompts Śambūka to feel the same pity for Rāma that we have been trained to feel for the tormented hero. Śambūka consoles Rāma, guides him through the forests, and conveys Agastya's messages thus pushing forward the play's narrative with Śambūka playing a central role in sustaining that momentum. Bhavabhūti has entirely reframed the terms of the deadly interaction and its aftermath and, through Śambūka's expanded role in this incident, we get the most elaborate insight into his state of mind that we have seen thus far in Indian literary history. Beyond that, however, we get a purpose for telling Śambūka's story; he is a major connecting figure who stabilizes Rāma and ensures that the drama stays on track to reunite Rāma with his lost love. His role in that capacity deserves a closer look.

## Śambūka's Death, It's All a Part of the Plan

The *URC* provides its audience access to Rāma's inner conflict as he inflicts his punishment on Śambūka and Bhavabhūti expands on that by giving Śambūka a significant platform to express his humble gratitude and devotion toward Rāma. These are remarkable developments to the Śambūka story, but Bhavabhūti embeds Śambūka deeply into the narrative, thus giving him an unprecedented level of importance as a *Rāmāyaṇa* character.

A Sanskrit drama cannot end in tragedy. The audience knows from the outset that Rāma and Sītā will be reunited by the end of the play. We have seen that Bhavabhūti, as a poet, ensures that each piece of the *URC* contributes to the resonant *karuṇa-rasa*. But the play's connective tissue extends beyond this. As a playwright, Bhavabhūti dedicates considerable effort to ensuring that each moment in the play connects to another—there should be no dead-end plot points.[13] This means that Bhavabhūti could not be satisfied with Śambūka's death being an isolated and inconsequential event in the broader scheme of the narrative. In order to suit the demands of the *URC*'s plot trajectory, Śambūka has to be a contributor to the eventual reunion of Rāma and Sītā.

In the prelude to Act III, we learn that a network of personified rivers (Tamasā, Muralā, Gaṅgā, Sarayū, and Godāvarī) are all involved in orchestrating a one-sided contact between Rāma and Sītā. The arranged meeting between the two separated lovers is meant to have an invisible Sītā console Rāma as he relives the memories of times spent in Janasthāna, thus rekindling her affection toward her husband. Muralā has been sent by Lopāmudrā, Agastya's wife, to deliver a message to Godāvarī urging her to watch over Rāma, who, upon entering Pañcavaṭī, is sure to be troubled by the memories of times spent there with Sītā. Tamasā tells Muralā that Sītā has retreated to the netherworlds, where she is watched over by Pṛthvī and the Gaṅgā (Bhāgīrathī). Tamasā continues,

> **Tamasā**: And now, after hearing from the Sarayū about Rāma's likely arrival in Janasthāna because of the Śambūka incident, and after suspecting the very same thing that Lopāmudrā had suspected, the Blessed Bhāgīrathī has come together with Sītā to look upon the Godāvarī as if with some customary hospitality.
> **Muralā**: That is well-considered on the part of the Blessed Bhāgīrathī. When he is in the capital, Rāmabhadra's mind is distracted and fixed on the various matters benefiting the people. It is a great misfortune that he has again entered Pañcavaṭī without distraction and only grief as his companion. How, then, might Rāmabhadra be comforted by Sītā Devī now?

We then learn that Gaṅgā had the same concerns as Lopāmudrā and has ordered the Tamasā to accompany Sītā to the Godāvarī under the pretense

13 For more on plot development of the *URC*, see Kane (1983).

of collecting flowers on the riverbank in celebration of her sons' twelfth birthday. In actuality, Gaṅgā intends that Sītā console Rāma as an invisible presence when he is overcome with memories of better days with the hope that Sītā will forgive her husband for his cruelty against her. Importantly, Gaṅgā hears from Sarayū (on whose banks Rāma's kingdom of Ayodhyā sits) that Rāma is to come to Pañcavaṭī because of Śambūka. Gaṅgā thus capitalizes on Rāma's rare visit to the wilderness of his realm and the entire plan executed by the rivers revolves around the event of Rāma's entrance into Pañcavaṭī to kill Śambūka.

When the plan is finally underway in Act III, Sītā hears Rāma's voice offstage and becomes unsettled. Tamasā, who has been sent to watch over Sītā, helps confirm her suspicions by mentioning that he is rumored to be in the area.

> **Tamasā**: I have heard that an Ikṣvāku king has come to Janasthāna to carry out a punishment on a Śūdra who has been practicing *tapas*.
> **Sītā**: How wonderful, the king has not failed in a king's *dharma*.

Sītā continually consoles Rāma throughout Act III as he falls faint time and time again with memories of times passed, united with his beloved. He suspects that Sītā is near him, but doubts his intuitions as an impossibility. Bhavabhūti exploits the one-sided interaction by often and explicitly drawing attention to the pity (*karuṇa*) of the circumstances. As Rāma struggles with the uncertainty of Sītā's presence, she becomes increasingly more affectionate toward her husband. Consider, for example, this dialogue between Sītā and Tamasā:

> **Sītā**: O noble Tamasā, I do not know why my heart reacts like it does when I see him like this, even though he abandoned me without reason.
> **Tamasā**: I know, child, I know.
>
> > Your heart is indifferent because of hopelessness, spoiled under the weight of his transgression, as if paralyzed by this sudden union in the midst of a long separation; yet it is as if in this moment your heart gushes with affection, gracious because of your kindness, filled with pity for your husband's woes (*URC* 3.13).

The pervasive *karuṇa* of the third Act reignites Sītā's feelings of reconciliation toward Rāma, setting up the anticipation for the final reunion at the end of the play and sustaining the dominant *karuṇa-rasa.*[14] At the end of Act III, Rāma takes his leave from Vāsantī to continue preparations for the Horse Sacrifice. He and Sītā are separated once again, bringing back the helplessness and *karuṇa*—especially since Rāma was never fully aware that he was being cared for by Sītā.

The rest of the play follows Rāma's post-execution exploits as he meets his son Lava (not knowing then that it is his son) and approaches Vālmīki's hermitage where the *Rāmāyaṇa* play is being performed, ultimately leading to his final reunion with Sītā. Though his death is long since over by this point, Śambūka remains a presence in the play despite his character having left the dramatic action. We see even as late as the prelude to Act VI during Rāma's encounter with Lava and Candraketu that characters outside the main action of the play are aware of and making references to events related to Śambūka (cf. *URC* 7.7).

## Śambūka's New Importance

The importance of Śambūka lies in his being used as a point of convergence for various characters in the kingdom of Ayodhyā to carry out their respective intentions regarding Rāma. Śambūka is the reason Rāma was in the region, a fact that facilitates Rāma's encounter with Sītā. Bhavabhūti uses the Śambūka episode not only as a catalyst toward the play's resolved ending, but also a means to sustain the drama's dominant *rasa* of pity. This invented importance for Śambūka serves to provide some purpose to Śambūka's death that goes beyond the revival of the Brahmin boy, making it possible for the audience to be more sympathetic to Rāma's position. We now have a character around whom the other characters can design a reunion of Rāma and Sītā. This is all motivated and sustained by the consistent feelings of pity the characters have for one another. As such, Bhavabhūti masterfully uses the structures of narrative and *rasa* to reconcile Rāma's banishment of Sītā and alleviate much of the harshness surrounding Śambūka's death.

---

14 There are numerous examples in this scene between Rāma and Sītā that evince pity. For example, Sītā at the opening of Act III is described as entering with pity and anxiety (*sakaruṇautukyam*). Later in Act III, she hesitates to approach Rāma and pulls away with panic and pity (*sasādhvasakaruṇam*). Rāma, for his part, becomes increasingly piteous as he is perplexed by Sītā's phantom presence; cf. Vāsantī's entrance in Act III when Rāma speaks with pity and anxiety (*sakaruṇautsukyam*). In his artistry, Bhavabhūti is sure to play with the muddled distinction between the two *rasas* of *karuṇa* and *vipralambha-śṛṅgāra* in this scene. Rāma is still experiencing *karuṇa* because he believes Sītā is dead while Sītā is experiencing *vipralambha-śṛṅgāra* because her affection is unrequited due to Rāma being unaware of her presence.

Bhavabhūti set an innovative and expansive precedent for taking a deep look into the Śambūka story. Even in an episode as controversial as this one, both Rāma and Śambūka seem to escape the audience's criticism through the poet's masterful manipulation of *rasa* and the resulting impact it has on the circumstances of Śambūka's death. The apologetics of Bhavabhūti's rendering of the Śambūka episode exonerate Rāma in his actions against Śambūka. He puts forward an image of a conflicted Rāma, a Rāma uncertain in his actions. Already guilt-ridden for casting out Sītā, Rāma can barely find it in himself to kill Śambūka. Additionally, Bhavabhūti creates space in his narrative to detail how exactly Śambūka's divinity came to be and what he chooses to do in his divine form. Śambūka speaks openly and respectfully, fosters an affectionate relationship with Rāma, guides him through the forest, and even consoles him. His death at Rāma's hand meant instant divinization and, in a great show of affection toward his Lord, Śambūka uses his divine voice to praise Rāma, who subsequently gives Śambūka his blessings to make his way to a higher realm. In death, Śambūka even comes to the realization that the only reason his *tapas* bore any fruit was because it garnered Rāma's attention. And perhaps most importantly, Śambūka is the first step toward reuniting Rāma and Sītā, which is the anticipated resolution of the drama. With Śambūka woven deeply into the plot of the *URC*, functioning as a crucial agent toward the inevitable reunion between Rāma and Sītā, Bhavabhūti managed to transform the image of the once-maligned Śūdra from a challenging episode of the *Rāmāyaṇa* epic into a figure of positive consequence.

However, even with this level of innovation and sympathy toward Śambūka, the *URC* still represents essentially Brahminical inclinations. Śambūka is still a criminal who has transgressed *varṇa* boundaries; Rāma is still obligated to uphold the social structures of Ayodhyā and kill the Śūdra. Curiously enough, Sītā even makes the Brahminism of the incident explicit in her comment cited above in which she is pleased to know that, having killed Śambūka, Rāma has not defaulted in his *dharma* as king. Many of these themes would continue into *Rāmāyaṇa* works from the ensuing centuries. However, many after Bhavabhūti fell short of displaying this level of energy for crafting the details of Śambūka's death. *Rāmāyaṇa* poets nevertheless had to grapple with how—and even *if*—they should include Śambūka in their work. The next chapter accounts for some of these *Rāmāyaṇas* and their various strategies for dealing with the problem of Śambūka. Many followed in the footsteps of Vālmīki, Vimalasūri, or—similar to Bhavabhūti—Kālidāsa while others treaded their own path, often by removing the story altogether. Whatever the case may be, there is a veritable explosion of *Rāmāyaṇa* creation in medieval India and, with that, the Śambūka tradition also continues to expand during this period.

# Chapter 5

# THE ACCIDENT OR THE EXECUTION

Kālidāsa and Vimalasūri mark some of the earliest and most consequential landmarks in the expansion of the *Rāmāyaṇa* tradition. I might argue that these two poets were the first to widen the boundaries of *Rāmāyaṇa* tradition as we know it today—boundaries that encompass an extensive amount of variability and adaptability as the epic enters new contexts. Through their poems, each demonstrated techniques on how to receive a narrative, push the limits of its messaging, and introduce a new take on an old story. Their respective presentations of the Śambūka episode are prime examples of such poetic dynamism. These two pioneering poets helped imbue the Rāma narrative with a flexibility by which others could cater the *Rāmāyaṇa* to their own audiences.

In the centuries leading up to and immediately following the turn of the first millennium CE, poets wrote several new *Rāmāyaṇas*. The current chapter focuses on this late classical and early medieval period of development in the *Rāmāyaṇa* tradition. With the various ways of handling the Śambūka episode acting as our gauge, it becomes clear that the *Rāmāyaṇa* tradition has many vectors of influence that are deeply intertwined with prevailing socioreligious trends, geography, and language. The pathways of that influence, however, are not always what one might expect. A dogmatic adherence to a specific way of telling the *Rāmāyaṇa* based on religious affiliation, for instance, does not seem to reflect the reality of how the *Rāmāyaṇa* traveled across India. By way of example, narratives originating in the Jain tradition went on to find their place in the Hindu tradition and it becomes increasingly clear that we should take geographic proximity and the influence of literary communities therein just as seriously as poets' potential desire to stick close to a narrative produced in their own religious community.

Here, I will chart a course through the various modes of telling the Śambūka story moving into medieval India. Some older modes of presenting the episode have survived deep into this period, though almost always with some sort of modification to better reflect the sentiments of the intended audience. There are also some new ways of dealing with the issue of Śambūka that originate in this period. Whatever the case may be, the various ways Śambūka does or does not appear in the *Rāmāyaṇas* of this period reflect a choice poets had when composing their poems on the life of Rāma. The increasingly expansive episodic pool *Rāmāyaṇa* poets had to work with ensures that the variability in the *Rāmāyaṇa* tradition reached unparalleled breadth in the second millennium of the Common Era. Two major factors contributed to the boom in *Rāmāyaṇa* production during the period under investigation here: the appearance of *Rāmāyaṇas* written in vernacular languages and the prominence of new devotional paradigms rooted in *bhakti*. I will address the vernacularization of the Rāma story periodically throughout this chapter, but I turn now to a discussion of *bhakti* and its development around India in the medieval period.

## Placing *Bhakti*

In an article discussing contributions of the Jain tradition to the depth of *bhakti*'s diversity, John Cort urges us to understand that "[b]hakti is not one single thing. It is many things, and a significant part of the study of the history of Indian religion and theology is the study of the strident disagreements over what bhakti is and how it is to be practiced. Such an understanding of bhakti helps make more sense not only of Jain bhakti but also of Buddhist bhakti-like practices and later forms such as *nirguṇ* bhakti of the Sants and Sikhs as well as forms of Vaiṣṇava, Śaiva, and Śākta bhakti that more closely approximate to the definition of bhakti as ontological participation" (2002, p. 62). *Bhakti* can refer to many practices and thought processes that run the gamut from an intellectual devotion guarded by the religious elite to a range of practices meant to advance one toward experiencing an unmediated connection to the divine. *Bhakti*, then, is a category that in and of itself is too general to have any concrete meaning—it tells us little about the specifics of worship or belief; rather, it is a paradigm that helps us describe a range of worship practices and philosophical insights for conceiving of the divine.

Earlier scholarship on *bhakti* tended to favor a South Indian origin for its development, which ultimately migrated north and circumscribed the subcontinent.[1]

Recent scholarship on *bhakti*, however, suggests that there were developments in both North and South India that materialized independently and began to spread throughout the subcontinent creating a flowering of devotional sentiments with multiple points of origin.

---

1 For a thoughtful explanation of such scholarship, see Hawley (2015, pp. 13ff., esp. 19–25).

While *bhakti* did ultimately find its way into the northern religious ethos, the process was long and drawn out, with many contributing factors. At the core of *bhakti*'s difficult absorption in the region is the fact that a tradition of imperially sponsored temple practices in the North dedicated to Rāma had been maturing as early as ca. fifth century (before *bhakti* entered the scene around the turn of the second millennium) and the catalyst for and nature of *bhakti*'s appearance is wholly different from the situation in the South. I want to spend some time delineating the development of Vaiṣṇava *bhakti* in these different regions of India, especially as it relates to the worship of Rāma.

In the South we see from early on a more directly experiential system of Vaiṣṇava devotion taking shape with the Āḻvār poets active from the sixth to ninth centuries. Their songs in praise of Viṣṇu are replete with expressions of a close personal relationship to him. A key part of engaging with Viṣṇu in this way meant blurring the line between Viṣṇu and Rāma and identifying the latter with the former. Being able to imagine Rāma and Viṣṇu simultaneously was a major theological innovation of the Āḻvārs that appears to have extended to temple worship.[2] Armed with Āḻvār understandings of the Viṣṇu–Rāma relationship, devotees could now approach temples with a Viṣṇu image and see Rāma, a double-vision which represents an early manifestation of Rāma-focused Vaiṣṇavism.

Hans Bakker has looked closely at the genesis of worship practices dedicated to Rāma in North India as evidenced by a dramatic rise in temples dedicated to him and the concurrent appearance of ritual processes articulated in prescriptive Rāma literature. Bakker argues that, while we can see evidence of Rāma worship as early as the Gupta period, a definite system of worship practices appears in the eleventh century, which was marked by a dramatic increase in temples to Rāma and a body of literature that detailed how to properly worship him. The motivations for such a shift, Bakker suggests, are part of a general shift in Vaiṣṇavism of the period that showed a greater affinity for "a more personal (humanized) conception of god that had a greater emotional appeal" (1986, p. 67). Expositions on the various expressions of religious devition—for example, recitations, hymns of praise, meditations, landmarks of worship—necessary to structure a full-fledged "Rāmaite cult" first appear in early medieval texts with a Vedānta perspective, such as the *Rāmapūrvatāpanīya Upaniṣad*, the *Rāmarakṣāstotra*, and the *Agastyasaṃhitā*.

2 It appears that the early Tamil Vaiṣṇava and Śaiva poets—Āḻvārs and Nāyanārs, respectively—composed their poetry with specific temples in mind. As such, the *bhakti* of these poets was, from an early stage, closely associated with worship practices grounded in the temple. See Veluthat (1979). For a parallel example in the Śaiva context, see Peterson (2014).

Connecting the literary and archeological records, Bakker further notes that these texts were "composed from the 11th-12th centuries, the period from which our first archaeological evidence from this new development [of a Rāmaite cult] dated" (ibid., p. 67).

We should bear in mind that the scope of Bakker's study is limited to an essentially North Indian setting with its gravity centered around major Rāma worship centers such as Ayodhyā and Vārāṇasī. The literature and worship traditions emanating from that area only spread so far and cannot account for all Rāma worship practices in India. With that in mind, we can take note of another assertion by Bakker: that Islam's entrance into the subcontinent played a significant role in shaping the developmental history of Rāma worship in the North. More particularly, the early phases of Muslim control (i.e., the eleventh–twelfth centuries) had a rather obstructive impact in terms of institutional worship (1987, pp. 22ff.).

The effects of Islam on Rāma worship (and especially the role of the *Rāmāyaṇa* therein) have also been explored by Sheldon Pollock, who has argued that the *Rāmāyaṇa*, with its demonizing of Rāvaṇa and his Rākṣasa forces, provided a convenient schematic for "othering" India's Muslim invaders and provided a mytho-historical precedent for Hindu kings now being identified as Rāma himself.[3]

Pollock's ideas have not gone unchallenged. Ajay Rao, for example, argues that the hermeneutic approach of the ŚrīVaiṣṇava commentaries on the *VR* is entirely in line with a Śrīvaiṣṇava devotionalism informed by a Maṇipravāḷa paradigm of interpretation (Rao, 2013).[4] Maṇipravāḷa in the Śrīvaiṣṇava context involved a combination of the Sanskrit and Tamil traditions whereby Śrīvaiṣṇava scholars could interpret Sanskrit culture in Tamil terms. When the Śrīvaiṣṇavas created their Sanskrit-language commentaries on the *VR*, they applied a Maṇipravāḷa gloss of the text, which amounted to a translation of the Sanskrit epic in terms of vernacular devotional sentiments. Rao contends that it is this same transposed devotionalism that characterized

3 Pollock (1993) asserts that the near-synchronous events of eleventh-century Islamic invasions into India and the solidification of a cult devoted to Rāma starting especially in the twelfth century are not coincidental but are instead linked in a causal relationship—the former being the cause of the latter. Despite centuries of literary engagements with the Rāma story since its first written expression in the *VR*, the ubiquitous identification of Indian kings with Rāma took hold only with the coming of the second millennium.

4 Maṇipravāḷa is a sociolinguistic phenomenon whereby two languages—typically Sanskrit and a vernacular—are mixed in literature, oftentimes in an effort on the part of authors writing in the vernacular to participate in an established linguistic culture including its canonical literature, genres, poetics, and grammar.

the spirit of the Śrīvaiṣṇava temple practices that operated in Vijayanagara, where Rāma's imperial image is on full display in the Rāmacandra temple at the center of their capital city (2013, pp. 96ff.).[5] On this basis, Rao's contention is that the Śrīvaiṣṇavas' motivations for engaging with the *VR* operated independently of a contentious stance against Muslims.

It is worth pointing out that the influence of Rāma in Ayodhyā, Ramtek, and Vijayanagara—the three sites Pollock explores in his article—flows primarily from the North in the case of the first two and from the South in the case of the third. This distinction is important because the northerly historical context informing the situations at Ayodhyā and Ramtek is decidedly different from the southerly context flowing into Vijayanagara. It is on this basis of regionally distinct histories and uses of Rāma imagery that Rao challenges Pollock's argument of a consistently pan-Indic motivation for the *Rāmāyaṇa*'s influence in the political sphere.[6]

Whereas these arguments are debating the relative contention surrounding Islam's initial entrance into India, several scholars have attempted to show that Islam ultimately had a constructive contribution to the character of *bhakti* in the North. John Stratton Hawley (2015) provides a detailed account of this phenomenon. He argues that the story of *bhakti*'s transit from South to North—while not entirely untrue—is incomplete and fails to account for Islamic contributions. Among other examples, Hawley describes the development of Brindavan—a quintessential locale for Kṛṣṇa-*bhakti*—under officials associated with Akbar and the city's exemplary status as a site of Hindu–Muslim collaboration (ibid., p. 75). These collaborations produced not only massive architectural testimonials of devotion toward Hindu gods, but also a performative environment that wedded literary and musical genres of

5 For a description of how Rāma fit into the royal ethos of Vijayanagara, see Dallapiccola et al. (1992).

6 Speaking more generally on the issue of a widespread antagonistic view of Islam in the second millennium, B. D. Chattopadhyaya (1998) has challenged the scholarly habit of describing Indian history as a series of diametrically opposed forces and periodizations based on the invasion of an "other." In so doing, he has attempted to demonstrate how the use of certain types of "othering" vocabulary throughout Sanskrit literature often depicts a generalized enemy, not always a specifically Islamic one. In particular, Chattopadhyaya takes issue with (1) the tendency for scholars to succumb to a tunnel vision with regard to negative portrayals of Muslims and, in the case of Pollock and Bakker in particular, (2) to overstate the importance of a few inscriptional or textual references to Rāma as signifying an adoption of the *Rāmāyaṇa* as a tool for widespread public "othering" of Muslims when there are a wealth of epigraphic sources from kings in contact with advancing Muslim forces that make no mention of Rāma.

Hindu and Islamic traditions—especially Sufism—to create what Hawley sees as "complexly connective tissues of literary religiosity that pertained within north India itself" (ibid., p. 91). Hans Bakker has also noted the eventual Islamic contribution to *bhakti*—again, especially the Sufi contribution to the de-ritualized forms of Rāma worship by the Nāths and the Cult of the Name (1987, p. 27ff.).

Ultimately, northern and southern currents of dedication to Rāma carved out very distinctive pathways. *Bhakti* has been a part of South Indian Rāma worship from some time. It appears, in fact, to have been the vehicle for bringing Rāma worship *into* the temple by creating a way of visualizing Viṣṇu as Rāma himself. The situation in the North is quite different. Starting in the first couple of centuries of the second millennium, Rāma worship had grown considerably in the North based on Brahminical control over ritual practices housed in temples donated to them and detailed in texts commissioned by them. This is perhaps part of an early reaction to Islam's initial entrance into India but as the centuries of Muslim rule went on, Islam's effect on Rāma worship charted a different course. The *bhakti* of the Sants and *sampradāys*—inspired, in part, by sustained interactions with Sufi saints—brought Rāma worship *out* of the temple, or at least out of a system of monopolizing Brahminical control.

Conceiving of *bhakti* generally as a conglomerate of numerous traditions with distinct regional, historical, and religious characteristics helps us visualize the reality of the diverse ideological foundations out of which the *Rāmāyaṇa* tradition's medieval expressions arose. Participants in the tradition from each period and each corner of India had specific ways of approaching Rāma and his story and linking the epic to their sacred and political space. The prolific *Rāmāyaṇa* poets of India during these centuries make up a patchwork placed over the contoured expanse of Rāma worship during this period, uniting these practices under a shared sense of narrative continuity while still conforming to the unique topography of each devotional universe. This understanding of Rāma's changing role in pan-Indic worship practices then sets us up to encounter the many *Rāmāyaṇas* of the late-first and early- to mid-second millennium and to contextualize the different ways in which Śambūka shows up—or fails to show up—in various texts.

## The Vernacular *Rāmāyaṇas* of Kampaṉ and Tulsīdās

The two most consequential texts that typify the effects of vernacularization and *bhakti* on the *Rāmāyaṇa* tradition would likely be Kampaṉ's Tamil-language *Irāmāvatāram* (*The Incarnation of Rāma*) and Tulsīdās' *Rāmcaritmānas* (*The Lake of the Deeds of Rāma*, henceforth *RCM*) written in Awadhi. Kampaṉ's text is the earliest known vernacular *Rāmāyaṇa* while Tulsīdās' text—written late in the premodern period—is arguably the most well known (at least in in Hindi-speaking areas of North and Central India). Each of these poets crafted their Rāma texts to reflect the philosophical and religious sentiments informing their respective cultural settings.

Kampaṉ faced a mammoth task in creating a text that properly placed his audience in a familiar devotional relationship with Rāma. The entire epic, written somewhere between the ninth and twelfth centuries, needed a new sheen of contemporary Tamil *bhakti*.[7] David Shulman (1991) very effectively demonstrates how Kampaṉ reimagines Sītā's trial-by-fire (*agniparīkṣā*), one of the most challenging moments in the Rāma story, to emphasize the overall text's constant and necessary oscillation between separation and reunion—keystones of how *bhakti* envisions association with the divine—in distinctly Tamil terms. The whole epic is pervaded with intense moments of separation and reunion between Rāma and Sītā. The cruelty of Sītā's trial is just another necessary low point marking a rejection and illustrating the flux one experiences in a relationship with the divine. The way Kampaṉ constructs his poem ensures that the audience of devotees *feels* Rāma's presence as a god and experiences it in the most personal of terms complete with the elation and frustration that may characterize any intimate relationship.

The *bhakti* of Tulsīdās' *RCM* is somewhat different. This text largely falls in line with Advaita philosophy whereby Rāma is identified as *brahman*, the singular Absolute. This *brahman* can be conceived of in two ways—the abstracted *nirguṇa* (without attributes) form and the embodied *saguṇa* (with attributes) form. These ideas are, in some sense, not altogether foreign to the *Irāmāvatāram*. However, while Kampaṉ's text operates in the Tamil *bhakti* ethos described above, the *RCM* has its own, oftentimes paradoxical way of negotiating how the divine and mundane worlds collide. A highlighting of both the *nirguṇa* and *saguṇa brahman* can be found in Tulsīdās' text, mirroring the multitude of cultural forces informing its ideas. Meditations on Rāma's name and references to his transcendent formlessness—the *nirguṇa* Rāma—recall the poetry of the *sants* of western and northern India during this period, for example, the poet Kabīr (Lutgendorf, 2016, p. xxi; McGregor, 2003, pp. 932–933, 938). However, the *RCM* is, after all, about Rāma, the prince and eventual king of Ayodhyā. This is God incarnate, a perceivable *saguṇa* deity who forms the basis of a narrative rooted in our world and interacts with all types of life within it. The *RCM* tells us a story of this *saguṇa* Rāma, but simultaneously

7 Several scholars lean toward the later date for the *Irāmāvatāram*. See Brockington (1984, p. 269), Blackburn (1996, p. 27), and Shulman (1991, p. 90).

offers explanations of how to access his formless divinity. Rāma's desperate search for Sītā throughout the epic also parallels the Persian epic form *masnavī* wherein "a lover's quest for an inaccessible beloved is likened to the Sufi path to mystical union with Allah" (Lutgendorf, 2016, p. x). Even the *RCM*'s prevailing stanza structure, a series of *caupāīs* punctuated by one or more verses in *dohā* meter, draws on, among other things, earlier Sufi romances (*prem-kahānīs*)—that are themselves influenced by the *masnavī*—thus signifying considerable Sufi influence over the text's construction (ibid., p. x).

The linguistic and philosophical traditions informing Kampaṉ's and Tulsīdās' texts are therefore quite different. Those influencing traditions, different though they may have been, inspired poets to update the Rāma story to best suit the context in which they were writing. The result was, in broad strokes, very similar. Rāma's identification with *brahman* in this medieval period placed considerable stress on earlier narratives wherein some of Rāma's actions might be considered unbecoming of a wholly divinized figure. In both texts, an update to the story meant revisiting or, in some cases, expelling these episodes altogether. Prominent examples of such contentious episodes include Rāma's killing of Vālin, Sītā's trial-by-fire, Rāma's banishment of Sītā upon returning to Ayodhyā, and, of course, the Śambūka episode.

Though Tulsīdās and Kampaṉ both left Śambūka out of their *Rāmāyaṇas*, there is a fundamental difference in how they actually deleted the episode from their tellings. Kampaṉ avoided the *Uttarakāṇḍa* altogether. This wholesale rejection of the last portion of the book circumvents Sītā's final banishment, arguably the epic's most heartbreaking moment and the one most difficult to justify. Shulman observes that the challenge to Sītā's chastity in the *agniparīksā* represents "the only … moment of overt hostility on the part of Rāma toward Sītā, for the Tamil work concludes with Rāma's happy return to Ayodhya" (1991, p. 90). This is, in some sense, a logical way to end the epic as it brings the story back full circle. Sītā is rescued from the grips of Rāvaṇa and Rāma reclaims his unjustly lost throne. With no *Uttarakāṇḍa*, there is no need to address either Sītā's banishment or Śambūka's execution, undoubtedly the most troubling deeds of Rāma's reign in Ayodhyā.

Unlike Kampaṉ, Tulsīdās did venture into what life was like in Ayodhyā after Rāma's coronation, but he nevertheless avoids the more troubling events including Sītā's banishment and the death of Śambūka in his *Uttarakāṇḍa* (or *Uttarkāṇḍ* in Awadhi). On the whole, Tulsīdās' *Uttarkāṇḍ* is distinct in its content and tone from the more punctuated, episodic, and at times unsettling *Uttarakāṇḍa* of Vālmīki. The primary focus of the *RCM*'s last book is to provide an account of the wonderful blessedness provided in Rāma's Ayodhyā. There are also numerous reflections on Rāma's life and the meaning of devotion to him by the epic's frame narrators. This book also provides long expositions on the

Advaita philosophy that pervades the work overall. It is a fitting end to a text that exalts Rāma as *brahman*. The most unsettling moments—at least from a modern reader's perspective—are perhaps the premonitions about the Kali Yuga, an age far removed from Rāma's reign but one Tulsīdās identifies with his own age. The crow Bhuśuṇḍi, for example, tells Garuḍa about a previous Kali Yuga in an earlier cycle of eons where there is rampant transgression of caste norms and constant dereliction of established customs (cf. *RCM* 7.99ff.). This would have been an opportune moment to include a telling of the Śambūka story, especially given how much Bhuśuṇḍi's thoughts on mankind's declining dharmic morality and the Yugas resembles Nārada's similar lament in the *VR* (cf. *VR* 7.65.8–23). We are, however, left without any mention of the Śūdra or his unauthorized *tapas*.

## Bringing Vālmīki into a New Era

In cases where *Rāmāyaṇa* poets harken back to the episode as it appears in the *VR*, Rāma's execution of Śambūka is definitive and detrimental to the ascetic's divine ambitions. The gods witness the execution and heap praise onto Rāma for preventing this unauthorized *tapas* and, in so doing, restoring the life of the young Brahmin boy. Alternatively, *Rāmāyaṇa* poets could elaborate on Śambūka's afterlife to demonstrate the power and benefit of contact with Rāma, even if it is deadly. The precedent for such tellings can be found in Kālidāsa's *RaV*. Further still, there existed at this time the option to include the Śambūka story in a Rāma text following the accidental death motif found first in Vimalasūri's *PC*. The remainder of this chapter details several *Rāmāyaṇa* works that make use of these various Śambūka tropes, including some texts and even poets that do not easily adhere to these rather strict categories, but rather occupy a liminal space between them. The current section deals with the first of these options: those works that adhere, in large part, to the Śambūka story as it appears in the *VR*. However, I begin with a somewhat unusual example, one that does not constitute a new *Rāmāyaṇa* work *per se*, but a new interpretation of the *VR* itself via a commentary on the text.

### *Śivasahāya's commentary on the* **Vālmīki Rāmāyaṇa**

The major Sanskrit commentaries on Vālmīki's text were produced by commentators who, according to Robert Goldman, "took up the task of the explanation and analysis of this great work during the roughly six centuries between the first manifestations of Islamic political power and the consolidation of European colonial power in the Indian subcontinent" (2005, p. 84), all of which occurred during the second millennium. The early commentaries on the *VR* were an intellectual project meant to interpret this text in terms of contemporary religious and social ideals. The authors of these commentaries had the unique challenge of receiving a narrative inherited from a period when Rāma devotion had not yet fully matured and justifying that narrative in terms of a growing affinity for Rāma as a god. Their task in formulating their commentaries was done, as Goldman points out, "in a spirit of reverence for Rama as an *avatara* of Lord Vishnu, a God made flesh, in order to punish evildoers and bring his virtuous devotees to salvation" (2005, p. 95). In the growing devotional world of premodern India, Rāma's deliverance of salvation was made to be wide-reaching and available even to transgressive figures—including Śambūka, as one commentary makes clear.

When considering the *VR*'s Śambūka episode, it is immediately clear that the commentators are, by and large, focused heavily on the difficulties of Nārada's lament about the progression of Yugas (*VR* 7.65.8ff.). This is not surprising as the passage is confusing in both its exposition and subject matter.[8] Most commentators, though, ignore the actual moment of Śambūka's execution (*VR* 7.67.4). However, a lone commentator, Śivasahāya, in his *Rāmāyaṇaśiromaṇi* attempts to explain why—in an age familiar with Rāma's ability to deliver liberation—Śambūka was denied that liberation in the *VR*.[9] Vālmīki's original reads:

> As the Śūdra was speaking, Rāghava drew his resplendent sword from its sheath and cleanly cut off his head. (*VR* 7.67.4)

Śivasahāya's commentary on the verse is as follows:

> Rāghava drew his sword from its sheath and cut off the Śūdra's head cleanly, that is, avoiding contact with impurity. As relates to his asceticism being forbidden, the text is not saying that either a vision of the Supreme Spirit or a slaying by means of a weapon of Rāma that brings about the highest aim of mankind was prohibited because the practice of what is forbidden has results that are forbidden. It cannot say that, since there was no prohibition for him because he was relying on Truth, which brings about the highest aim of mankind. Instead, we are to understand that he simply sought to attain the Supreme Self too quickly and,

8 For a detailed account of the commentators' struggles with this passage, see Goldman and Sutherland Goldman (2017, pp. 1016ff.).

9 According to Goldman, Śivasahāya is among the later commentators of the southern recension of the *VR* (2005, p. 96, n. 1).

in so doing, undertook forbidden conduct. It is clear that this has brought him to this state of affliction.[10] It is because he did not perform obeisance, etc. to [Rāma]. If he would have offered obeisance, etc., then it is most certain that extremely gracious Rāma would not have killed him.

Śivasahāya's main concern with this verse is clarifying what the real reason was behind Śambūka's being denied his heavenly goals. Taking a hitherto unprecedented stance, he suggests that Śambūka's *tapas*—though a crime—would not have precluded him from accessing salvation following his deadly contact with Rāma because Śambūka was relying on the Truth (*satya*). Where Śambūka went wrong was in his neglect of showing Rāma his due respect. Importantly, Śivasahāya is sure to mention that death by Rāma's sword normally leads one to attain the highest aim of man. Śambūka's disrespectful oversight and Rāma's supreme authority to judge him on that basis is what ultimately blocks Śambūka's entrance into heaven. In Vālmīki's text, the gods praise Rāma for preventing Śambūka's salvation; Śivasahāya offers us a reason why without compromising Rāma's divinity. In fact, he appears to assume that nothing in what Vālmīki wrote suggests that Śambūka's status as a Śūdra would have denied him the right to share in Rāma's salvific qualities. Informed by centuries of socioreligious developments spanning the centuries between the *VR* and its medieval commentaries, Śivasahāya quite ingeniously updates the rationale behind Śambūka's failed salvation as it appears in the *VR*.

## *The* Padma Purāṇa

A perhaps surprising body of work that often deals with the deeds of Rāma but consistently omits the Śambūka story is the Purāṇas. The purāṇic corpus steadily developed from the early centuries of the Common Era well into the second millennium (Rocher, 1986, pp. 100–103). These texts became indispensable religious encyclopedias detailing divine lore and formulating an image of the gods that would help characterize *bhakti* in its various modes throughout the subcontinent, particularly in the portrayal of Viṣṇu and his *avatāras*. In his survey of purāṇic literature, Ludo Rocher notes that

10 Goldman and Sutherland Goldman translate this phrase (*etena tasyārtaprapannatvaṃ vyaktaṃ*) as "By this his [i.e., Rāma's] status as the recourse of the afflicted is made clear" (2017, p. 1033). This is a viable reading. However, I find that having this phrase refer to Rāma rather than Śambūka reads somewhat disjointedly from what I understand to be Śivasahāya's focus on Śambūka's conduct and condition in the passages both before and after this phrase.

"[a]n important element in puranic Vaiṣṇavism is *bhakti* [...] The only thing that counts in a person's life, and the sole possible way to salvation, is the total, sincere, and emotional devotion to Viṣṇu. Birth, wealth, and all other activities are irrelevant; in fact, being born in a lower caste, being poor, and abstaining from such things as performing austerities or even reciting the Veda, facilitate rather than obstruct the road toward true devotion" (1986, p. 106). Given Rāma's identity as a prominent *avatāra* of Viṣṇu, the death of Śambūka would seemingly have been a sensible moment to expound on Rāma's ability to deliver liberation to even the lowliest of subjects, and yet most of the Purānas avoid the story.

One exception to the Purāṇas' silence on Śambūka is the *Padma Purāṇa* (henceforth *PP*), which includes an elaborate Śambūka episode. The Purāṇas generally are difficult to date, with the *PP* being no exception. Many scholars have noted similarities between it and the works of Kālidāsa (e.g., *RaV*) and Bhavabhūti (e.g., *URC*), though they disagree on whether the material of the *PP* antedates these works or vice versa.[11] The Rāma story is peppered throughout the *PP*, though most of the material occurs in the *Pātālakhaṇḍa* where we find descriptions of Rāma's victory over Rāvaṇa, his return to Ayodhyā, and an especially lengthy narration of his *aśvamedha* (horse sacrifice) and its benefits.[12] If one were to take, for instance, the *VR* or the *RaV* as representing common benchmarks for the Rāma story's narrative progression, we might expect the *PP*'s Śambūka episode to have occurred in this *Pātālakhaṇḍa* prior to Rāma's *aśvamedha*. In Vālmīki's and Kālidāsa's texts, the Śambūka episode appears between Rāma's return to Ayodhyā and the start of his *aśvamedha*. Instead, the author(s) of the *PP* found it better suited as a tangent to a conversation in Chapter 37 of the *Sṛṣṭikhaṇḍa* that takes place between Pulastya and Bhīṣma wherein the former explains to the latter the merits of giving food as a gift.[13] Their discussion centers, in part, around Śveta, a king who was cursed to a life of hunger and thirst for refusing to give food to the hungry. His hunger was so severe that he ended up eating his own flesh. The Śveta story appears in the *VR* as well (7.68–69)—the sage Agastya tells it to Rāma right after he kills Śambūka.

11 For a survey of such perspectives, see Mirashi and Navelkar (1969, pp. 304–306), Mirashi (1974, pp. 264–265), Kale (1934, pp. 28–29), Chatterjee (1967, pp. 67ff. for the *URC* and 130ff. for the *RaV*), Sharma (n.d.), and Belvalkar (1915, pp. lvii–lviii).

12 For more on the locations of *Rāmāyaṇa* narrative elements in the *PP*, see Raghavan (1973, pp. 47ff.).

13 All citations of the *PP* are according to the Caukhambā Sanskrit Series edition (2007).

Several pieces of the *PP*'s Śambūka episode are taken verbatim from the *VR*.[14] Among them is Nārada's speech on man's moral decline through the ages and the gradual progression of *adharma*, which endures as vv. 37.44ff. in the *PP*'s *Sṛṣṭikhaṇḍa* (cf. *VR* 7.65.8ff.). Nārada identifies an errant Śūdra as the cause of the Brahmin boy's death and urges Rāma to avoid an afterlife in hell by putting the Śūdra to death. Once Rāma finally locates Śambūka, he approaches him in much the same way as in the *VR*, asking him to identify his *varṇa* and the intent behind his *tapas*. In the *PP*, however, Rāma has more to say on the subject of *tapas* and the right to practice it. He explains to Śambūka that:

> "*Tapas always* has truth as its essence when it comes to attaining the heavenly realm. It promotes *sattva* and *rajas* and this *tapas* has truth as its essence.
> "It is a source of benefit to the world and it is created by Viriñci. It brings about the fearsome valor of a Kṣatriya and is said to promote *rajas*.
> "And this, used for the destruction of an enemy, is said to be Āsura. Either concealing one's limbs, covering them with blood one by one …
> "… or being successful in the penance of five fires, in perfection, or even over death—this is Āsura, your state of being. Yet you do not seem to me to be a Brahmin." (*PP*, *SṛKh* 37.74–77)

Śambūka then responds:

> "Welcome to you, O Best of Kings. I see you at last, O Rāghava.
> "I am your son and you are my father, O faultless one. But it is not only like this, for the king is the father of all.
> "You are to be honored as you are, O King. We practice asceticism in your kingdom. We practice here as it was created long ago and set aside by the Self-Existent One.
> "O Rāma, we are not fortunate; you are the fortunate one, O King. It is in your kingdom that ascetics seek perfection in this way.
> "May you attain perfection through this *tapas* of mine, O Rāghava. To what you have asked me: of what birth am I and why do I practice *tapas* …

14 For example, see *PP SṛKh* 37.37ff. & *VR* 7.64.4ff.; *PP SṛKh* 37.57ff. & *VR* 7.66.1ff.; *PP SṛKh* 37.85ff. & *VR* 7.67.2ff. and the *VR* Baroda Critical Edition Appendix I, no. 11.

> "I am engaged in severe *tapas* as one born of a Śūdra womb. I seek godhood with my own body, O Rāma of firm vows.
> "I do not speak falsely, O King, out of a desire to conquer the world of the gods. Know me to be a Śūdra, O Kākutstha, Śambūka by name."
> (*PP*, *SṛKh* 37.79cd-85)

The episode then proceeds as it does in the *VR* with Rāma drawing his sword and decapitating Śambūka. The gods subsequently rejoice and inform Rāma that the Brahmin boy has been revived.

Much of the expansion in the *PP*'s take on the episode revolves around the effects of Śambūka's *tapas* as relates to the three *guṇas* (or traits—*rajas*, *tamas*, and *sattva*) inherent in all matter.[15] Rāma admires Śambūka's *tapas*, observing that his perfected ascetic action will promote the positive *guṇas* of *rajas* and *sattva*. This is a didactically valuable expansion in philosophical scope and the elaborations in the episode's exposition serve as a pretext for Rāma to comment positively on Śambūka's actions so long as caste is not at issue. However, once Rāma discovers that Śambūka is, in fact, a Śūdra, he denies him his heavenly ambitions based on a violation of *varṇadharma*, punishable by death.

Another substantial elaboration is the fact that Śambūka understands himself to be one of several devoted ascetics able to concentrate on their *tapas* under the protection of their righteous king. In this way, Śambūka demonstrates his appreciation of Rāma's rule over Ayodhyā and the protection of its citizens. In this context, he feels safe to reveal his true identity as a Śūdra given that Rāma has prompted a confession under the apparently false pretense that the truth will provide him with a state of perfection (*siddhi*), whereas a lie will cost him his life. Śambūka does, indeed, tell the truth and identifies himself as a Śūdra, which sparks the deadly punishment from Rāma taken directly from the *VR*.

Though the Purāṇas in general do much to expound on a relationship with the divine rooted in *bhakti*, the *PP* somewhat surprisingly does not utilize Śambūka's death and its aftermath to such an end. Śambūka still falls short of his aim to attain divinity and the gods still praise Rāma for the Śūdra ascetic's quick and fruitless death. There is no concern for Śambūka's afterlife. The *PP*, then, helps bring Vālmīki's Śambūka story into this new age of *Rāmāyaṇa* creation without doing much to update its sentiments.

---

15 The concept of the three *guṇas* is rooted in Sāṅkhya philosophy. *Sattva* is the quality of goodness, the highest of the three *guṇas*; *rajas* promotes activity while *tamas* resists it. All matter (*prakṛti*) contains all three of these *guṇas* in different proportions, thus accounting for the different gradations of material existence. For more on this concept, see Radhakrishnan and Moore (1957, pp. 424ff.).

## *The* Kaṇṇaśśa Rāmāyaṇa

Even as the *Rāmāyaṇa* tradition achieved an astonishing breadth and flexibility in narrative since Vālmīki penned his telling of the epic, the influence of the *VR* can be found even up to the present day (Goldman, 2019). Some texts produced within the period I am exploring here exhibit this influence to a great degree. We have already seen how the *PP* quotes extensively from Vālmīki, but it was not necessary to follow Vālmīki's sentiments by simply quoting him. The *VR*'s presentation of Śambūka's death was also retold in some regional, vernacular *Rāmāyaṇa*s as well. By way of example, one of the earlier Malayalam *Rāmāyaṇsa*s to narrate the entire Rāma story is Rāmappaṇikkar's *Kaṇṇaśśa Rāmāyaṇa* belonging to the fifteenth century.

This *Rāmāyaṇa* belongs to a relatively brief moment in Kerala's literary history wherein a family of poets, referred to as Kaṇṇaśśa or Niraṇam poets, created Sanskritized Malayalam renditions of prominent works like the *Rāmāyaṇa*, the *Mahābhārata*, and a stand-alone *Bhagavad-Gītā*.[16] These Kaṇṇaśśa texts, notes Rich Freeman, a scholar of Kerala's literary and social history, "were intended primarily for the devotional inspiration of their audiences, legitimizing the relatively greater degree of vernacularization" (2003, p. 466). Vernacularization, of course, is not just an issue of language. Bringing the Rāma story—heavily guarded, up to this point, by the relative inaccessibility of Sanskrit learning—into the languages of the masses means unprecedented engagement with the *Rāmāyaṇa* tradition within new cultural circles. Many social issues come into play when access to previously restricted material becomes widely available, not the least of which is caste. Freeman observes that "[t]he caste title of the Kaṇṇaśśan group of poets was Paṇikkar, which places them almost certainly in the Nāyar caste grade. This is significant in terms of these poets' claim to mastery of Sanskrit, since as Nāyars they would have been reckoned Shudras in the Brahmanical order" (2003, p. 467). The Śūdra-ness of the Paṇikkar poets was perhaps amplified by the fact that the Kaṇṇaśśa poetic project was running in tandem to the development of Maṇipravāḷam, which was another important moment in the Kerala socio-literary history that helped define a vernacular identity for Malayalam (ibid., pp. 448ff., 467). Maṇipravāḷam consists of a meticulously detailed unification of Sanskrit and the vernacular (*bhāṣā*) not just superficially through mixed lexicons,

16 For a concise description of the Niraṇam/Kaṇṇaśśa poets, see Freeman (2003, pp. 465ff.).

but also a melding of grammar and poetics. The alchemy of Maṇipravāḷam was overseen, for the most part, by Brahmins and Rāmappaṇikkar, as a Śūdra, would have been excluded from this heavily refined and largely Brahminical Maṇipravāḷam tradition. As expected, then, Rāmappaṇikkar's mixed-language rendering of the Sanskrit epic does not lean on the heavy eroticism (*śṛṅgāra-rasa*) typical of Maṇipravaḷam, favoring instead an independently formulated exaltation of Rāma and a rather close adherence to the Sanskrit original. Such an adherence is on display in the Śambūka episode.

The Śambūka story as narrated in the *Kaṇṇaśśa Rāmāyaṇa* (*KR*) progresses much as it does in the *VR*. Nārada delivers his speech about the gradual progression of *adharma* as the Yugas go by, making special mention that Śūdras are not to practice *tapas* in the Tretā Yuga. Indeed, he identifies a Śūdra's efforts in *tapas* during the current Tretā Yuga as being the cause of the Brahmin boy's death and tells Rāma to kill him to revive the boy. Rāma then sets out in the Puṣpaka to survey his kingdom.

> Without seeing anyone committing *adharma* in the north,
> he went to the south after wandering in the preeminent eastern direction;
> There, the Ornament of Mankind saw someone engaged in a difficult penance near a lake, continuously holding a single posture hanging upside-down.
> The Best of Men asked him, "Who are you and why are you practicing this asceticism?"
> He said "Why are you doing these strange acts? Tell me the truth of your intentions."
> "I am a Śūdra named Jambukan, Best of Men; know that I seek immortality.
> I am gracefully practicing asceticism for this today; understand that I never speak lies."
> The Śūdra said, "This is the truth for why I am doing this."
> Hearing this, the great Śrī Rāma removed his sword from its sheath;
> Understanding him to have done wrong, he severed his head and took his life;
> Indra and the others heaped praise on the great man with great satisfaction.
> "Give your blessing to have the Brahmin's boy live again and fade his sorrows; I have no other purpose—please know this, O gods," said the Best of Men.
> Then Indra said, "Because you have gained renown, Lord of Men, for killing the offender Jambukan, the twice-born boy is now alive." (*KR* 7.547–550)

The *Kaṇṇaśśa Rāmāyaṇa* is fitting for our purposes because the text, indeed the whole Kaṇṇaśśa tradition, reflects a *bhakti* inclination inherited from earlier Tamil poets. Nevertheless, this text does not seize the opportunity to imbue the Śambūka episode with the sentiments of *bhakti* by demonstrating Rāma's salvational abilities as many other *Rāmāyaṇa* poets had done by this period. Instead, this early Malayalam *Rāmāyaṇa* sticks close to the punishing outcomes of the *VR*. Rather than depicting Rāma as a gracious and benevolent bestower of Śambūka's aim of immortality, the poet chose to have Indra reiterate Śambūka's criminal status as an offender and praise Rāma as a deliverer of kingly justice. Considering Rāmappaṇikkar's caste status, his utilization of this Vālmīki-oriented telling of the story is noteworthy and perhaps even surprising.

## *Kṣemendra's* **Rāmāyaṇamañjarī**

Turning back to Sanskrit, the eleventh-century Kashmiri poet Kṣemendra presents a unique situation as relates to the Śambūka story. By looking at Kṣemendra's catalog of works, it is clear that he was not merely a poet, but a dedicated *student* of poetry and poetics. At the end of his *Bṛhatkathāmañjarī*, a concise Sanskrit telling of the Paiśācī-language *Bṛhatkathā*, he pays homage to Abhinavagupta, a prominent scholar of poetics responsible for learned commentaries on the *Nāṭyaśāstra* (entitled *Abhinavabhāratī*) and the *Dhvanyāloka* (entitled *Dhvanyālokalocana*). His recognition of a poetic theorist such as Abhinavagupta, evidently his teacher, in a non-didactic, narrative text like the *Bṛhatkathāmañjarī* is testament to his wide-ranging intellectual interests (Raghavan, n.d., pp. 118ff.). In addition to composing this abridged version of *Bṛhatkathā*, Kṣemendra also produced his own renditions of the *Mahābhārata* and *Rāmāyaṇa*—*Mahābhāratamañjarī* and *Rāmāyaṇamañjarī*, respectively—both in Sanskrit. Later in his career as a poet, he also composed a more devotional poem entitled *Daśāvatāracarita* describing the ten incarnations of Viṣṇu, which presents a notable contrast with the *Rāmāyaṇamañjarī* in its treatment of the Śambūka episode. To set up that contrast, I begin with the Śambūka episode in the *Rāmāyaṇamañjarī*.

Kṣemendra's three *mañjarī*s seem to represent some of his earlier compositions, each of them relatively lacking in their narrative or poetic innovation. In his *Rāmāyaṇamañjarī* (*RM*), for instance, he follows the *VR* quite closely, matching his predecessor in terms of tone and content. As an abridgment, much is left out or shortened, but Śambūka nevertheless finds his way into the text. Without repeating from the *VR* verbatim, Kṣemendra's telling, which spans nearly fifty verses, runs parallel to it. All the major narrative points remain, but in Kṣemendra's own words. The major development in this text comes with the lead up to Śambūka's response to Rāma's questioning. Just after Rāma asks Śambūka about his *varṇa*, Kṣemendra writes:

> So asked by Rāma, the one firm in his vow replied with his body upside down as if speaking in contradictions,
> "I have dedicated myself to *tapas* in order to go to heaven in this body.
> I am a Śūdra named Śambūka and I wish for this very much, Lord."
> (*RM* 7.1031–1032)

Kṣemendra uses the transition into Śambūka's response to offer a telling insight into Kṣemendra's perspective on a Śūdra's propriety in practicing *tapas*. In his reply to Rāma, Śambūka reveals that his *tapas* is in the service of his attempts to go to heaven. The poet introduces such a reply by offering that for a Śūdra to be saying such things, it is the equivalent of "speaking in contradictions" (*vaiparītyaṃ vadann iva*). Such an imbalance of propriety, we are then led to believe, is to be dealt with by swift and deadly action. Then, just as they do in the *VR*, the gods heap praise on Rāma for carrying out this action and restoring the life of the Brahmin boy.

## The Salvation of Śambūka

In the section that follows, I shift the discussion to texts that depict a more gracious death for Śambūka. Similar to Kālidāsa, all the texts in this section have Śambūka attain salvation due to his contact with Rāma. This trope became common in an age of flourishing Rāma-*bhakti* because it simultaneously showed the power of Rāma's grace—even toward the lowliest of transgressors—and his commitment to *dharma*. There are a wide range of texts representative of this treatment of the Śambūka episode, a few of which are covered below. I would like to open this section with another work by Kṣemendra, a unique example of a single poet who took two different approaches to the issue of Śambūka in his body of work. Kṣemendra found occasion to subject his Śambūka to both a summary execution in his *Rāmāyaṇamañjarī* discussed above and—as we are about to see—a gracious death in his *Daśāvatāracarita*.

### *Kṣemendra's* Daśāvatāracarita

As the title of his work suggests, the *Daśāvatāracarita* (*An Account of the Ten Incarnations [of Viṣṇu]*, henceforth *DAC*) deals with the Vaiṣṇava *avatāras* (Matsya, Kūrma, Varāha, Narasiṃha, Vāmana, Paraśurāma, Rāma, Kṛṣṇa, Buddha, and Kalki) and their deeds. The description of Rāma's incarnation is covered in about 300 verses, second in length only to Kṛṣṇa's.

In contrast to his *Rāmāyaṇamañjarī*, which is largely modeled on Vālmīki's mode of telling, Kṣemendra narrates the Rāma story in the *DAC* with comparatively more focus on Rāvaṇa. He starts the story in Laṅkā with a description of Rāvaṇa and the Rākṣasas and continuously directs attention toward the Rākṣasa king (Raghavan, n.d., pp. 141ff.; Bulke, 1999, p. 152).

As for the *DAC*'s Śambūka episode, it is quite brief, totaling only eight verses. Kṣemendra strips the story of many of the details that make up the pool of narrative possibilities related to this episode. As in other iterations of the story, a Brahmin father brings the corpse of his young son to Rāma—in fact, directly to his assembly. Crying out, the father launches into a diatribe against Rāma for allowing such an injustice to take place within the borders of his kingdom. As Rāma becomes consumed with the Brahmin's harsh words, Nārada appears and helps Rāma get to the cause of this tragedy. Where Vālmīki dedicates considerable space to Nārada's counsel to Rāma, Kṣemendra forgoes much of this material and, in a single verse, simply points Rāma directly to the renegade Śūdra as the direct cause of the boy's death. Revealing the Śūdra's name and location, Nārada says,

> "A Śūdra named Śambūka is practicing extreme *tapas* in the southern direction. This very lapse in *varṇāśramadharma* has caused the demise of the son of that high born man."
> He heard these words spoken by Nārada and, remembering his chariot, mounted this king of vehicles. Then, the king approached this man of the South, ignorant of the way of *dharma*, and killed him.
> When the Śūdra's neck was severed by the blade of Rāma's sword, he went forth to heaven in the vehicle. And as his son attained life right then while this was happening, the twice-born recanted his censure with praises. (*DAC*, *Rāmāvatāra* 283–285)

We never hear anything from Śambūka himself—nothing about his divine intentions or his motivations for practicing *tapas*. Rāma finds him and promptly decapitates him. That action of decapitation, however, liberates Śambūka and sends him on his way to heaven. The Brahmin, too, is pleased with the results, taking back the harsh words he said to Rāma at the assembly.

Though Kṣemendra does not dwell for long on the event of Śambūka's death in the *DAC*, he departs considerably from his earlier telling in the *Rāmāyaṇamañjarī*. As a more explicitly devotional Vaiṣṇava text, the *DAC*, and the Śambūka episode by extension, reflects a deeper commitment to presenting Rāma in a favorable light. The Brahmin is satisfied with the revival of his son and Śambūka, in the end, does achieve his aim. All of this comes to be through Rāma's enforcement of *varṇadharma* as Ayodhyā's god-king.

## *The* Adhyātma Rāmāyaṇa

The Sanskrit *Adhyātma Rāmāyaṇa* (*Esoteric Rāmāyaṇa*, henceforth *AdhR*) from around the fifteenth century is one of the most famous *Rāmāyaṇa* texts to come out of the medieval period and it is frequently cited as one of the quintessential text-based illustrations of devotion to Rāma. But that is not all. The text, notes prolific *Rāmāyaṇa* scholar V. Raghavan, is also considered to be a "philosophical version of Vālmīki, written on the background of the *Smārta Advaita* tradition synthesised with *Rāmabhakti*, bringing Śiva also into the tradition of *Rāma-bhakti*" (2009, p. 19). How closely it follows the *VR* or its label as any sort of "version" of that text is a point up for debate—there are many features of the text that make it quite distinct from the *VR*.[17] However, Raghavan's latter point about *bhakti* is quite salient and relevant for our discussion.[18]

Raghavan's observation on the symbiotic melding of Advaita and *bhakti* is based on the *AdhR*'s consistent identification of Rāma as *brahman*. Such an identification is perhaps best illustrated through Rāma's lecture to Lakṣmaṇa—known popularly as the *Rāma-gītā* (7.5.6–62)—on the subtleties of the Self (*ātman*) and an understanding of *brahman* heavily informed by an advaitic reading of the Upaniṣads.[19] By framing this Advaita perspective within the Rāma narrative (which is itself built on the frame dialogue between Śiva and Pārvatī), the *AdhR* operates at the intersection of philosophy and devotion. It gave the complexities of proper insight into the relationship between the Self and the Ultimate (i.e., an abstracted *nirguṇa brahman*) a dynamic religiosity through the familiar representation of Rāma (i.e., *brahman* in its *saguṇa* aspect). In so doing, the *AdhR* emphasizes *brahman* as a perceivable and widely acknowledged object of worship.[20]

Given the lengths the author of the *AdhR* went to in order to unite the concepts of Advaita Vedānta and Rāma-*bhakti*, we might expect that Śambūka would be portrayed as the beneficiary of Rāma's grace, thus attaining his divine ambitions.

---

17 See Brockington (1984, pp. 252–254) for a brief synopsis of the text and an account of some divergences between the *AdhR* and the *VR*.

18 Raghavan's note about Śiva being pulled into the universe of Rāma-*bhakti* is achieved by framing the entire narrative as a conversation between Śiva and Pārvatī.

19 This so-called *Rāma-gītā*—which understands the supremacy of true knowledge (*jñāna*) over action (*karma*) as a means of release from *saṃsāra*—draws (or at least claims to draw) most explicitly from the *Taittirīya* and *Bṛhadāraṇyaka Upaniṣads* (cf. 7.5.21) and attempts to put them in the service of its preference for *jñāna-yoga*. In its discourse on the syllable *oṃ* and its representation of the constituent forces that make up the Self and the Ultimate, the *Rāma-gītā* draws heavily from the *Māṇḍūkya Upaniṣad* (cf. 7.5.47ff).

20 Cf. the descriptions of *ātman* and *brahman* in Tulsīdās's *Rāmcaritmānas*, which was heavily influenced by the *AdhR* (McGregor, 2003, p. 937).

This is precisely what we get. Rāma's killing of Śambūka, or an unnamed Śūdra in this case, is passed over quickly and bundled together with some of his other divine deeds:

> He did several divine deeds across the land. Having observed a Brahmin's young son die before his time and knowing the Brahmin to be grieving, the ever-wise Rāma brought the Brahmin boy back to life by killing a Śūdra practicing *tapas* in the forest and bestowed upon the Śūdra the supreme heaven. This highest Self, best of Raghus, established millions of *śiva-liṅgas* everywhere and pleased Sītā with every divine enjoyment. (*AdhR* 7.4.24–27)

The author of the text describes Śambūka's death as a miracle, an example of Rāma's perfect rule in Ayodhyā. He strips the episode—indeed, the entire *Uttarakāṇḍa*—of any sense of misdeed on Rāma's part. The instance of Sītā's exile, for example, is nothing more than a clever ruse designed to reunite the gods with Rāma. The gods appeal to Sītā to come to heaven (*vaikuṇṭha*), whereupon Rāma, heartbroken, will be sure to follow. Rāma then plans to spread rumors of a scandal, thus exiling Sītā and creating the mirage of a rift between them. This would ultimately result in Sītā moving on to Vaikuṇṭha through a hole in the earth with Rāma not long in following her (7.4.32ff.).

The *AdhR*, then, is a prime example of a poet engaging with the most troubling aspects of the *Uttarakāṇḍa* but reorienting the subject matter in such a way that transforms blemishes on Rāma's character into opportunities to demonstrate his compassion for living beings and an ultimate control over their fate. The *AdhR* uses this portion of the text to reflect deeply on the philosophies informing devotion to Rāma and the Śambūka story fits right into that endeavor.

## ***E<u>l</u>utacchan's Malayalam* Adhyātma Rāmāyaṇam**

Exploring the Sanskrit *AdhR* also warrants a discussion of its vernacular cousin, E<u>l</u>utacchan's sixteenth-century *Adhyātma Rāmāyaṇam*. Today, the text is extremely popular in Kerala and serves as the basis of a month-long recitation called *Rāmāyaṇa-māsam* (*Rāmāyaṇa* Month) during Karkkaṭakam (July–August) and seems to serve as "the principal text for domestic devotional recitation down to the present" in Nāyar and other middle-caste homes in Kerala (Freeman, 2003, p. 480). E<u>l</u>utacchan wrote the text in Malayalam, but even a cursory glimpse at the text reveals that it is not a simple translation of the similarly titled Sanskrit text. It is, in fact, part of the *kiḷippāṭṭŭ* (lit. parrot's song) genre, which is typified by a portrayal of the text being recited by a parrot to a poet in metered couplets clearly designed for recitation (Freeman, 2003, p. 480). Some scholars have taken Eḻutacchan's adherence to the themes of the Sanskrit *AdhR* for granted, thereby reducing the Malayalam text's individual merits (Raghavan, 1988, p. 23; Smith, 1994, p. 12; Freeman, 2003, p. 480). An exception is John Brockington, who is careful to say that Eḻutacchan's *Adhyātma Rāmāyaṇam* may be based on the Sanskrit text, but that the poet "treats various incidents in a novel and more poetic manner than his original" (1984, p. 274). A close look at the Śambūka episode affirms Brockington's observation.

As noted above, the Sanskrit *AdhR*'s Śambūka reference speeds by in only a few verses and does not constitute much of an episode at all. The story as found in the *Uttararāmāyaṇam* section of Eḻutacchan's *Adhyātma Rāmāyaṇam*, on the other hand, digs much deeper into the Rāma–Śambūka interaction. The *Uttararāmāyaṇam* is less confidently attributed to Eḻutacchan than the rest of the *Adhyātma Rāmāyaṇam*, but this final book in the poem nevertheless aligns with many of Eḻutacchan's innovations—namely the Advaita Vedantic interpretation of the Rāma story, something we have seen in a few Rāma texts of this period. Additionally, Brockington notes that the *Uttararāmāyaṇam* section of this text more closely follows the *Kaṇṇaśśa Rāmāyaṇa* than the Sanskrit *AdhR* (1984, p. 274). While that may be true in a general sense, the Śambūka episode exhibits several key points of departure from the *Kaṇṇaśśa Rāmāyaṇa*, including a granting of Śambūka's heavenly ambitions, albeit in a somewhat veiled manner. Rāma's deliverance of Śambūka's salvation (*mokṣam*) via the swing of Rāma's sword, brings about Śambūka's mind's desire (*manoratham*)—that is, *mokṣam*. The moment in the text reads:

> "I am a Śūdra named Śambūka;
> This *tapas* is so that I can concentrate on *samvidrūpa*.
> "Please understand that I wish to attain salvation,
> and by God being here before me, I shall have a direct path."
> Right then, he severed his head with his sword
> and killed him, granting Śambūkan his mind's desire.
> The young god on earth [=Brahmin] came to life that moment
> as the gods were raining down flowers.
> (*Uttararāmāyaṇam*, *Mūnnām Adhyāyam* lines 949–956)

Another key deviation from the *Kaṇṇaśśa Rāmāyaṇa* is the insertion of Advaita philosophy in Eḻutacchan's Śambūka episode. This is also unlike in the Sanskrit *AdhR*, which attempts to bury the controversy of his death in a list of several miracles performed by Rāma. Here, we have Śambūka looking to concentrate on *samvidrūpa*, a state of pure consciousness promoted within some Advaita philosophical circles.[21] Finally, Eḻutacchan has the gods praise Rāma as they do in the *Kaṇṇaśśa Rāmāyaṇa*, but here they do so apparently in celebration of the Brahmin boy's revival, not the Śūdra's death.

### *The* Rāmcaritmānas' *Afterword*

Kṣemendra's *DAC*, the Sanskrit *AdhR*, and Eḻutacchan's Malayalam *Adhyātma Rāmāyaṇam* are illustrative of a body of *Rāmāyaṇa* texts that incorporate a Śambūka story that demonstrates a concern for the ascetic's life after death. The poets did not avoid the Śambūka story like Kampaṉ or Tulsīdās, nor did they adhere to the sentiments of the narrative's original exposition in the *VR* like the *PP* did. Instead, these poets embraced the challenges presented by the story and softened the harshness of Rāma's swift killing of Śambūka by framing it a way similar to Kālidāsa several centuries earlier. To these poets, Śambūka's execution was not a punishment; it was instead a fast track to the salvation he sought in the first place. Śambūka's unauthorized *tapas* drew the attention of the god Rāma. And according to these poets, contact with the divine—deadly though it may have been—meant Śambūka could instantly attain his aims in the afterlife.

While Tulsīdās does not address Śambūka in his *Rāmcaritmānas* (*RCM*), it is important to mention at this point that many editions of the text do include a version of the Śambūka story that employs the salvific tone under discussion here. As mentioned above, Tulsīdās devotes the *Uttarkāṇḍ* in his *RCM* to the intricacies of Advaita and Rāma's role therein. In so doing, he leaves little room for several details of Rāma's later life—some of them quite consequential—that audiences may have been familiar with from any number of other *Rāmāyaṇa* sources. We hear nothing, for instance, of Sītā's banishment or Śambūka's death. However, there exists a kind of afterword to the *RCM*, an interpolated ending that restores these familiar stories to the epic. This appended book is called the *Lav-Kuś-kāṇḍ*, the date and authorship of which are unclear (Stasik, 2006, p. 119). Though the *Lav-Kuś-kāṇḍ* is not a part of the original text, "the fact that many Hindus are convinced that Tulsīdās's Rām banished Sītā may testify to its popularity" (ibid., p. 119).

---

21 Advaita philosopher Vidyāraṇya deals with the term *saṃvidrūpa* extensively in his *Pañcadaśī*.

This controversial moment, left out of Tulsīdās' original, has nevertheless maintained its place in the collective understanding of devotees in Hindi-speaking areas of India. The inclusion of Sītā's banishment in the *RCM* via the *Lav-Kuś-kāṇḍ* is a likely contributing factor to such an understanding. Interestingly, however, casual Rāma devotees, for whom the *RCM* is a central text, are generally much less familiar with the story of Śambūka, which also appears in this same *Lav-Kuś-kāṇḍ*.

The Śambūka story in the *Lav-Kuś-kāṇḍ* is quite short, lasting only seven verses in various meters. In its brevity, much is left out of the episode, including Nārada's speech about the gradual intrusion of *adharma* in the world as the Yugas progress. Instead a heavenly voice informs Rāma of the transgressive *tapas* of a Śūdra, who remains unnamed. The short episode begins with Rāma presiding over his royal assembly with his brothers. A Brahmin then comes to the court, wailing and announcing the death of his son, an unprecedented occurrence in Ayodhyā. Playing the part of a human (*naralīlī kar*)—a coy reminder of Rāma's status as *brahman*—Rāma grieves at the Brahmin's sorrow. He sets out to find the Śūdra and, after several descriptions of the beauty of the areas he surveys, encounters the criminal Śūdra.

> Then, filled with rage, he released an arrow and cut off the Śūdra's head, which fell to the ground. Knowing his devotion to be pure, he gave to him a boon and went himself to a worthy place to observe a vow.
> The precious, once-deceased Brahmin boy sprang joyously to life and the Lord of Raghus, bestower of happiness who rids all devotees of fear, came to the city.
> (*Lav-Kuś-kāṇḍ sorṭhā 8, chand 2-doha* 1)

The *RCM*'s outwardly devotional ethos is rather subdued in this scene, which has otherwise been the venue for some considerable *bhakti*-aligned innovations in texts of preceding centuries, including those that have directly informed the *RCM* (e.g., the *AdhR*). This may not be too surprising given that this scene is not part of the original *RCM* and it restores an episode that Tulsīdās had omitted. Nevertheless, a few key *bhakti*-inducing details are noticeably absent. We hear no explanation as to why the Śūdra is practicing *tapas*, meaning that we hear nothing of his heavenly ambitions, which, in many other Rāma texts, provides Rāma with the opportunity to simultaneously restore *dharma* and grant the Śūdra liberation. We do, however, hear about the Śūdra's devotion to Rāma and the fact that his death results in a boon, which remains unspecified. Attaining this boon makes this Śambūka story akin to that of the *RaV*, *URC*, *DAC*, *AdhR*, and so on, but it is very limited in terms of detail.

The author of the *Lav-Kuś-kāṇḍ* fails to elaborate on what the boon entails or how Śambūka demonstrates his devotion, which are narrative attributes to which other Rāma poets devote considerable attention.[22]

## It Was an Accident!

Up to this point, we have covered versions of the Śambūka story that have circulated within Hindu-Brahminical literary circles. The *Rāmāyaṇas* discussed in this chapter so far that include the episode do so largely on the model of Vālmīki or Kālidāsa. Each adds its own contemporary specifics to the story, colored by local nuance, but the Śambūka story—if included in the work—either depicts Śambūka's death as swift and punitive (via the *VR*) or salvific and concerned, to some degree, with Śambūka's afterlife (via the *RaV*). But we have already seen the seeds of another extensive tradition of telling the Śambūka story in Vimalasūri's *PC*. This rendering of the Śambūka story lived on for centuries after the *PC*. Perhaps most intriguing is the fact that the story of Lakṣmaṇa accidentally killing Śūrpaṇakhā's son did not stay within the limits of the Jain tradition. As Jain and Hindu traditions matured side by side in India's medieval years, the epic at times flowed freely between them in an exchange of narrative detail with each tradition incorporating episodic moments into its texts that best represented how its authors knew the story of Rāma's deeds—or, in the case of Śambūka's accidental death, the story of Lakṣmaṇa's deeds. The flow of influence between communities of *Rāmāyaṇa* participants need not always have Hindu-Brahminical points of origin and non-Hindu (i.e., Jain, most often) destinations; the reverse, as we shall see, is also true.

There has been extensive work done on the implications of rendering the Rāma story into India's vernaculars, largely focusing on issues of expanded access to the epic, especially for traditionally uneducated or otherwise subjugated segments of Indian society.[23] While in no way working against these kinds of useful discussions of vernacular traditions and the social shifts that accompany them, I will be mobilizing vernacularization in the service of a different kind of argument. Perhaps moving against the prevailing current

22 For example, the *Ānanda Rāmāyaṇa* includes a long interaction between Rāma and Śambūka, wherein Śambūka pleads with Rāma to provide all fellow Śūdras with a way to attain heaven. Also, the *URC* reveals Śambūka's satisfaction at having been killed at Rāma's hand, providing him with divine fruits unattainable from his *tapas* alone. A few centuries after the composition of the *RCM*, the *Sindūragirimāhātmya* features perhaps the most elaborate interaction between Rāma and Śambūka and a fascinating display of mutual respect between the two figures (see Chapter 6).

23 Some especially pertinent works on this topic would be Lutgendorf (1991), Richman (1991a), and Richman (2001a).

of using the cosmopolitan to structure our understandings of the vernacular, I will use vernacular *Rāmāyaṇa*s to suggest what they can tell us about the *Rāmāyaṇa*s written in cosmopolitan languages like Sanskrit and the various Prakrits. After all, *Rāmāyaṇa*s in Sanskrit and Prakrit also continued to be written throughout the second millennium as vernacular *Rāmāyaṇa*s entered the literary scene. They were being produced in tandem and likely have something to say about each other. More specifically, vernacular *Rāmāyaṇa*s provide us with a solid geographic context that may be less evident in works composed in the pan-Indic languages of Sanskrit and—to a marginally less severe extent—the Prakrits. These regional-language texts can then provide a useful framework for describing narrative trends with some grounding in geography. The Śambūka narrative that employs the accidental death motif is particularly helpful for looking at how the different communities of *Rāmāyaṇa* poets did or did not interact in the medieval period because there are clear demarcations of where and in what religious communities this story has been told. The demarcations, however, are not quite what we might expect.

Tracking the accidental death motif suggests that there was considerable interaction between Hindu and Jain narrative communities, particularly in South Indian vernaculars. In North Indian vernaculars, the accidental death of Śambūka is largely limited to Jain *Rāmāyaṇa*s. Adding Sanskrit and Prakrit tellings of the Śambūka story to the conversation, it becomes clear that Jain poets writing in these languages would frequently make use of the accidental death narrative, but Hindu poets would not. The ensuing discussion attempts to sort through some of these dichotomies—vernacular-cosmopolitan, North–South, Jain–Hindu—and determine how they contribute, if at all, to a proper understanding of the *Rāmāyaṇa* tradition.

### *Nāgacandra's* Pampa Rāmāyaṇa

I begin this discussion with the Jain poet Nāgacandra, who wrote his Kannada-language *Pampa Rāmāyaṇa* (also known as the *Rāmacandracarita Purāṇa*) in the eleventh or twelfth century. This text is largely in line with the *PC* in its ideologies and expression, challenging the *VR*-esque stream of telling in much the same way as Vimalasūri did earlier (Brockington, 1984, p. 272). As part of this, we find the Śambūka episode much as we do in the *PC*. Nāgacandra inserts some of his own distinctive details, but the major plot points align with his Prakrit-language predecessor.[24] The story is as follows:

---

24 I draw my information on the *Pampa Rāmāyaṇa*'s Śambūka story from Dakṣināmūrti (1968).

During their initial days in the Daṇḍaka Forest, Rāma, Sītā, and Lakṣmaṇa settle on the banks of the Krauñcā River. Not far away is the city of Pātāla Laṅkā, ruled over by Khara, husband of Candranakhī, Rāvaṇa's sister. He and Candranakhī have two children together, Sundara and Śambūka. The latter goes to the surrounding forestland to engage in a twelve-year *tapas* with the intent of gaining the necessary ascetic power to wield the *sūryahāsa* sword. At the end of the twelve years, a *yakṣa* appears to praise Śambūka's intense *tapas* and present the *sūryahāsa* sword to him. At this moment, however, Śambūka—evidently too immersed in *tapas*—does not seem to notice. While strolling through the forests, Lakṣmaṇa comes across the sword and, fascinated with it, decides to test its sharpness on a nearby bamboo thicket. With a single slash, he cuts through the bamboo and, to his surprise, out falls the head of an ascetic. Fearing that he has committed a grave misdeed in killing the ascetic, Lakṣmaṇa becomes distressed. The *yakṣa* returns to the scene and, having observed that Lakṣmaṇa killed the powerful ascetic, prostrates before him. The ascetic, of course, was Śambūka, Candranakhī's son. She comes to the forest thinking that this would be the day that her son attains the sword. Instead of finding her son successful in his *tapas*, she finds him decapitated in a tangle of bamboo. She wails and faints at the loss of her son, but when she comes to, she sets out to find her son's killer. The trail leads to the nearby settlement of Rāma, Sītā, and Lakṣmaṇa. Catching a glimpse of Rāma, she becomes infatuated and—after assuming the form of a beautiful woman—attempts to seduce him. Her attempts fail, with even Sītā finding her doomed infatuation amusing. Candranakhī becomes jealous of Sītā and when the clouds of her desire for Rāma fade, the anger over the death of her son rolls back in. She returns to her husband and—after secretly mutilating herself—urges him to exact revenge on Rāma and his brother for violating her and murdering their child. This begins the chain of events that leads to Sītā's capture by Rāvaṇa.

The differences between this telling and the *PC* are few. The most superficial is the fact that Candraṇakhā in the *PC* becomes Candranakhī in the *Pāmpa Rāmāyaṇa*. Of slightly greater impact is the introduction of the *yakṣa* who grants the *sūryahāsa* to Śambūka upon completion of his *tapas*. This character does not appear in the *PC*. Instead, Vimalasūri describes Śambūka as entering the forest with the sword already in hand.

There are several other vernacular Jain texts that utilize the Śambūka episode in this same way (e.g., the Kannada *Torave Rāmāyaṇa* and the *Rām-Rās* in a vernacular from the Gujarat-Rajasthan region). While these have their own individual merits and introduce their own small details that warrant a close study, it is useful to take the conversation in a slightly different direction. As mentioned above, the vernacular *Rāmāyaṇas* that narrate Śambūka's accidental death are not all Jain texts, despite borrowing this episode from the *PC*, which was written by a Jain poet. While the narrative of Jain texts in Vimalasūri's lineage diverges considerably from the structure and content of Vālmīki's poem, compositions that fall outside the Jain tradition (i.e., those of a Hindu leaning) tend to resemble Vālmīki's structure in a general sense.[25] In these texts—all written in southern vernaculars—we encounter the death of Śūrpaṇakhā's son as an additional misfortune she suffers at Lakṣmaṇa's hand.

## *The* Raṅganātha Rāmāyaṇa

The earliest of the *Rāmāyaṇa* texts that fall into this category of non-Jain, vernacular Rāma stories that include the accidental death of Śūrpaṇakhā's son appears to be the Telugu-language *Raṅganātha Rāmāyaṇa* likely written during the thirteenth or fourteenth century.[26] In line with the Hindu tradition, this Rāma story unsurprisingly draws heavily from the stream of narrative that informs the compositions of poets such as Vālmīki and Kālidāsa. Rāma, for instance, is no stranger to violent acts and is responsible for the deaths of Rāvaṇa and Vālin. While much of Vālmīki's narrative structure was retained in the *Raṅganātha Rāmāyaṇa*, the author excluded the *Uttarakāṇḍa* from his text entirely, following a rather common trend among medieval *Rāmāyaṇa* poets already mentioned in the discussion of Kampaṉ and Tulsīdās. Without the *Uttarakāṇḍa*, the story ends with Rāma's coronation and Rāma's rule in Ayodhyā does not feature in the text. While the *Uttarakāṇḍa* is absent, the other six books endure. In the third of these six books, the *Araṇyakāṇḍa*, we encounter the Śambūka episode from the Jain tradition but with some key changes.

Some modifications to the episode in the *Raṅganātha Rāmāyaṇa* infuse the story with Brahminical traits. For instance, when Lakṣmaṇa accidently decapitates the ascetic, he panics thinking that he has committed Brahminicide. Terrified, Lakṣmaṇa runs to Rāma to confess what he has done. As the two brothers consider how to proceed, a group of local sages gathers there to explain who the ascetic was. One sage explains that the ascetic was none other than the demon prince Jambumālī, son of Śūrpaṇakhā and nephew of Rāvaṇa (as we will see, it is common for this character to appear with different names, though he serves the same general function in all narratives).

25 I would like to emphasize that I mean they resemble Vālmīki in terms of construction, not necessarily sentiment. These *Rāmāyaṇa* stories tend to follow a narrative arc that recalls the *VR*, but the intervening centuries and regional proclivities have ensured that much has been changed at the level of specific details.

26 For some contested opinions on date and authorship, see Nagar (2001, p. viii) and Raṅganātha (1961, *paricay* pp. 1–2).

Jambumālī was hoping to win a favor from Brahmā to exact revenge on Rāvaṇa for killing his father, Vidyujjihva—Śūrpaṇakhā's husband—who was conspiring to usurp the throne of Laṅkā. Should Jambumālī have accepted the sword and remained alive, he would have taken his revenge on Rāvaṇa and terrorized the world. Lakṣmaṇa's unintentional decapitation of the demon thus this.

There is no reference to caste in any Jain rendering of this episode, but it is central to Hindu tellings of the Śambūka story, whatever final form they take. In these tellings, the death of a Brahmin boy is symptomatic of Rāma's rule in Ayodhyā going horribly wrong and the underlying cause is a Śūdra practicing *tapas* before the Kali Yuga. The emphasis on caste disparities and the panic they elicit is heavy in these Brahminical tellings, but absent in Jain tellings. The *Raṅganātha Rāmāyaṇa*, then, adopts the Jain version of the Śambūka story but does mention Lakṣmaṇa's concern over committing a crime against a Brahmin, restoring a distinctly non-Jain social structure and making in accord with a Hindu worldview.

The *Raṅganātha Rāmāyaṇa* also restores Lakṣmaṇa's actual mutilation of Śūrpaṇakhā rather than having her mutilate herself, as happened in the *PC* and some other Jain texts in the same literary lineage. This restoration is illustrative of the ability on the part of the author of the *Raṅganātha Rāmāyaṇa*—and poets of other texts, as we will see—to draw on two narrative streams at once.

## *Eknāth's* Bhāvārtha Rāmāyaṇa

The accidental death of Śūrpaṇakhā's son also appears in the Marathi-language *Bhāvārtha Rāmāyaṇa* by the sixteenth-century poet Eknāth. He was a leader in the prominent Vārkarī *sampradāy*, a *bhakti* community in Maharashtra that flourished during the medieval period. Śambūka's death in Eknāth's work is less an accident and more of a divine scheme to prevent a demon from abusing the power of celestial weaponry. This is not unlike the *Raṅganātha Rāmāyaṇa*, but the story's specifics are a bit different.

As in the *Raṅganātha Rāmāyaṇa*, Lakṣmaṇa worries that he has committed the grave sin of killing a Brahmin ascetic. The *Bhāvārtha Rāmāyaṇa* then digs a bit deeper into the issue of caste than the *Raṅganātha Rāmāyaṇa* does. When Lakṣmaṇa confesses to Rāma what he has done, Rāma asks a single question: was the person a Śūdra, Vaiśya, Kṣatriya, or Brahmin? Without knowing, it is impossible to prescribe the appropriate atonement. Unsure, Lakṣmaṇa goes back to the body of the slain ascetic—here named Sāmba—to take a closer look. He discovers that he has killed a Rākṣasa. When he reports to Rāma, Rāma just laughs and reminds Lakṣmaṇa that killing these Rākṣasas is his highest *dharma*—something never mentioned in any Jain text.

Aside from reinstating the theme of Brahminicide as in the *Raṅganātha Rāmāyaṇa*, the *Bhāvārtha Rāmāyaṇa* also introduces the noteworthy addition of *śastra-devatās*—a deification of weaponry itself—to the episode. Rāma consoles Lakṣmaṇa by offering that, had Sāmba gotten to the sword first, he certainly would have killed Lakṣmaṇa and that the *śastra-devatās* were pleased with him and ensured his victory. The introduction of these *śastra-devatās* transforms what appears to be an accident on the surface—one that causes Lakṣmaṇa considerable anxiety—into a divine intervention orchestrated by the *śastra-devatās*. This breaks considerably from the Jain narratives, which empty the entire Rāma story of divine elements. In this sense, the addition of the *śastra-devatās* represents a re-divinization of Śambūka's (or Sāmba's, in this case) death.

Another striking feature of the *Bhāvārtha Rāmāyaṇa*'s engagement with the Śambūka narrative relates to the text's compositional structure and textual history. Eknāth fits in the growing category of writers during this period whose *Rāmāyaṇas* lack an *Uttarakāṇḍa*. In the case of Eknāth, however, it is possible that he left his work unfinished unintentionally as he seems to have left even the *Yuddhakāṇḍa* incomplete. In some cases, later contributors wrote stand-alone *Uttarakāṇḍas* (or their equivalents) to round off the *Rāmāyaṇa* works of their predecessors. As relates to the *Bhāvārtha Rāmāyaṇa*, this role was filled by as many as three authors, including Eknāth's own grandson, the poet Mukteśvar (Karandikar, 1978, p. 55). In adding this final chapter to the Marathi epic, Mukteśvar includes the Śambūka story mostly on the model of Vālmīki—here, the Śūdra's name is Jambuka.

With Mukteśvar's addition of the *Uttarakāṇḍa*, the Marathi-language *Bhāvārtha Rāmāyaṇa* becomes the only vernacular text to include both streams of the Śambūka narrative: the accidental death of Śūrpaṇakhā's son (in Eknāth's original) and Rāma's killing of a Śūdra seen as causing the death of a Brahmin child due to his *tapas* (in Mukteśvar's *Uttarakāṇḍa* addendum). I specify that the *Bhāvārtha Rāmāyaṇa* is the only *vernacular* text to include both types of the Śambūka story because there is one other important text that fits in this all-inclusive category: the Sanskrit-language *Ānanda Rāmāyaṇa*. As will become clear in the ensuing discussion, the *Ānanda Rāmāyaṇa* is a genuine storehouse of *Rāmāyaṇa* lore that, given its profuse collection of stories, is frequently the exception to whatever topic is at hand.

## *Kerala shadow puppetry:* tolpāvakūttu

Before moving on to texts written in Sanskrit and Prakrit that utilize the accidental death motif, it is worth mentioning one more vernacular take on this story that is still actively performed in Kerala. In the spring of each year, the small Māriyammaṉ temple in Koonathara, a small town outside Shoranur, Kerala, becomes the site of a multiday festival (seven, fourteen, or twenty-one days depending on sponsorship) dedicated to the goddess Māriyamman̲—known also as Bhadrakālī or Bhagavatī—who is installed there. In addition to complex Goddess worship that includes temple drums, creating images of the Goddess out of *neem* leaves, and long processions centered around possessed devotees, the festival features all-night performances of *tolpāvakūttu*, a form of shadow puppetry from Kerala dedicated to narrating the story of Rāma using leather puppets silhouetted on a screen inside a temple drama-house. According to the late K. L. Krishnankutty Pulavar, a prominent *tolpāvakūttu* puppeteer, this performative tradition is meant to depict the epic for the Goddess, who is believed to have been engaged in battle with another demon at the time Rāma was battling Rāvaṇa. She was upset having not witnessed the events herself and *tolpāvakūttu* performances are meant to reenact the story for her (Pulavar, 1987, p. v). As such the massive *Rāmāyaṇa* plays a supportive role in this annual devotional event that focuses not on Rāma himself, but on the goddess Māriyamman̲.

The Rāma text the puppeteers recite for Māriyamman̲ is Kampan̲'s *Irāmāvatāram*, though not in its entirety and with numerous episodes and details gathered from outside Kampan̲'s work (Blackburn, 1996, pp. 37–38). Puppeteers also insert long, largely improvised Malayalam commentaries in between Kampan̲'s verses meant to elucidate the densely poetic classical Tamil. Much of Kampan̲'s text changed as it made its way from Tamil Nadu to present-day Kerala. In addition to the numerous narrative changes, the spirit of Rāma-oriented devotionalism that permeates Kampan̲'s *Irāmāvatāram* is muted when it is performed in drama-houses meant to entertain the Goddess. In his detailed study of this Kerala shadow-puppetry tradition, Stuart Blackburn observes that "[c]ut off from the courts and monasteries that had supported it in the Tamil country, the *Kamparāmāyaṇam* [=*Irāmāvatāram*] underwent considerable change when it entered hinterland Palghat. This famous Rāma text is sung as ritual, but it is sung at temples where Rāma is not worshiped, a fact that would be astounding unless we remember the distinction between Rāma story and Rāma worship" (1996, p. 54). Even though the story is about Rāma, the focus remains on the goddess.

The accidental death of Śūrpaṇakhā's son is one episode that found its way into the drama-house despite being absent from Kampan̲'s original. In fact, the entirety of the *tolpāvakūttu* rendering of the Śūrpaṇakhā episode bears little resemblance to what is found in canonical editions of the *Irāmāvatāram* and instead features narrative details taken from the accidental death motif. Being that this rendering is enacted in Hindu settings, the specifics of the episode resemble those that appear in Hindu texts like the *Raṅganātha Rāmāyaṇa* and the *Bhāvārtha Rāmāyaṇa* with minor adjustments. For example, when

Lakṣmaṇa accidentally decapitates the figure in the thicket, he immediately identifies him as a demon. While he is somewhat distressed at his unintentional homicide, he ultimately dismisses it as a divine intervention, which he does not pretend to fully comprehend.

Also of note is the fact that this episode does not always appear in *tolpāvakūttu* performances of the *Rāmāyaṇa*. *Tolpāvakūttu* performances are sponsored events and their duration and content is dependent on the level of sponsorship provided for the performance. Seven-day performances, for instance, begin with the construction of the bridge to Laṅkā and leave out all preceding material, including the Śūrpaṇakhā story wherein Śambūka (or Śambukumāraṉ in the *tolpāvakūttu* rendition) dies. Fourteen-day performances, however, *begin* with the Śūrpaṇakhā episode, putting Śambūka at the center of the story's opening scene and sparking Sītā's eventual kidnapping, emphasizing the episode's importance to the overall narrative. Finally, twenty-one-day performances encompass the entire story from beginning to end.

## *Raviṣeṇa's* Padma Purāṇa

The phenomenon of vernacular compositions from non-Jain traditions using the accidental death motif appears to be limited to South India. I have been unable to locate this particular version of the Śambūka story in any text written in a northern vernacular composed by authors outside the Jain tradition.[27] Also, with the singular exception of the *Ānanda Rāmāyaṇa*, all Sanskrit or Prakrit texts that include this accidental death motif—regardless of region of composition—are explicitly Jain and they follow, in a general sense, the Rāma story as detailed in the *PC*. The ensuing discussion describes three such texts—by no means an exhaustive account—that illustrate this Vimalasūri-inspired pattern of narrative.

The poet Raviṣeṇa composed his *Padma Purāṇa* in the seventh century, modeled largely on Vimalasūri's *PC*, though he does not off any acknowledgement of the latter's influence.[28] The narrative similarity is obvious from a cursory glance at the canto colophons, which—as noted

---

27 Gregory Clines (2022) explores two *Rāmāyaṇa* works of fifteenth-century Jain poet Jinadāsa in detail: *Rām-Rās*, composed in the vernacular (*bhāṣā*), and *Padma Purāṇa*, composed in Sanskrit. Both include this accident motif. Jinadāsa thus straddles the cosmopolitan-vernacular line. I suspect there will be other Jain texts in northern vernaculars that are closely associated with canonical tellings in a manner similar to the example provided by Jinadāsa.

28 Much of my information on Raviṣeṇa's text is drawn from Kulkarni (1990, pp. 91ff.) and Clines (2022, pp. 29ff.).

by V. M. Kulkarni—align in almost every instance (1990, pp. 92–97). Raviṣeṇa composed his narration of Rāma's deeds in Sanskrit, nearly doubling the length of the *PC* by expanding several episodes and adding elaborate poetic descriptions. As in the *PC*, the *Padma Purāṇa*'s Śambūka episode occurs in the forty-third *parvan*, but—as could be expected—Raviṣeṇa's telling is longer, one hundred twenty-three verses in comparison to the *PC*'s forty-eight. Lengthy poetic descriptions of the Daṇḍaka Forest bustling with activity after the rainy season account for some of this increase in content as does the moment of Candranakhā's (cf. the *PC*'s Candraṇakhā) encounter with Rāma and Lakṣmaṇa. The description of Lakṣmaṇa's initial attraction to the *sūryahāsa* sword—drawn in especially by its wonderful fragrance—and his following the scent through the forest to find it similarly contributes to the inflation of the episode.

Simple expansion of the *PC*'s narrative, however, does not completely account for how Raviṣeṇa approaches Śambūka's death. In a notable departure from Vimalasūri, Raviṣeṇa leaves Lakṣmaṇa's role in Śambūka's death implicit by reorganizing the narrative. As is the case in the *PC*, Śambūka is in the forest practicing *tapas* to attain the famed *sūryahāsa* sword, which requires a twelve-year penance. Śambūka completes this stipulated period of *tapas* but remains in deep meditation for another four days without claiming the sword. This is when Lakṣmaṇa arrives, captivated by the sword's fragrance. But in the *Padma Purāṇa*, when Lakṣmaṇa strikes the bamboo thicket with the *sūryahāsa* sword, the gods appear and heap praise on him, yet we hear nothing of Śambūka's decapitation. It is left unclear in the text if Lakṣmaṇa is even aware that he killed anyone when he swung the sword into the bamboo. He returns to his riverside hermitage smeared with saffron paste and adorned with garlands and tells Rāma about how he came upon the sword—again, no mention of killing Śambūka. We do not find out that Śambūka has been decapitated until Candranakhā finds her son killed. This, then, is the moment in Raviṣeṇa's text where we get the first description of Śambūka's decapitated head. In the *PC*, by contrast, a similar description occurs at the moment of Śambūka's death, with Lakṣmaṇa clearly seeing it. Here are the two verses; first the verse as found in the *Padma Purāṇa* (*PadP*) followed by the verse in the *PC*:

> And then, [Candranakhā] saw his head, with its earrings looking like the sun setting behind the western mountain, and his body in the middle of some stumps. (*PadP* 43.73)
>
> And just then, [Lakṣmaṇa] saw there a fallen head, ornamented with earrings, and a body, wet with blood and mud as if the branch of a coral tree. (*PC* 43.27)

The comparison of verses clearly reflects the influence of Vimalasūri. Raviṣeṇa may have elaborated and reorganized the *PC*'s Śambūka story, but it remains the same in spirit. In contrast to some of the non-Jain vernacular texts that would appear a few centuries later, Raviṣeṇa's *Padma Purāṇa* keeps the name of Candraṇakhā's son as Śambūka and depicts Candraṇakhā as mutilating herself—but here apparently out of intense grief—before she approaches her husband, Kharadūṣaṇa, in a plea to enact revenge for the death of their son and the violation of her body and reputation. These narrative details persist in many, though not all, Jain tellings of the Śambūka story written in either Sanskrit or Prakrit.

### *Svayambhūdeva's* Paümacariu

Moving forward in time about two centuries, Svayambhūdeva explicitly acknowledges his indebtedness to Raviṣeṇa—among others, including Mahāvīra himself, but excluding Vimalasūri—in his ninth-century *Paümacariu* composed in Apabhraṃśa (cf. *Paümacariu* 1.2). Doctrinal features of the text show a greater affinity with Digambara Jainism, as is true of his stated predecessor, Raviṣeṇa (Kulkarni, 1990, p. 241; De Clercq, 2018, p. ix). Given his use of Kannada suffixes, apparently deep knowledge of southern geographic features, and references to Seuna (Yādava) country in the Deccan, Eva De Clercq believes Svayambhūdeva to have been writing somewhere in southern India (2018, pp. x–xi).

In the *Paümacariu*, unlike other Jain *Rāmāyaṇas*, we first hear about Śambūka in passing during a description of war between Rāvaṇa and Varuṇa, a Vidhyādhara king unwilling to submit to Rāvaṇa's authority. The story occurs near the end of the work's first book, the *Vidyādharakāṇḍa*. Here, Śambūka, a nephew of Rāvaṇa, is an officer in a large alliance fighting on Rāvaṇa's behalf, which includes Hanumān, son of Pavanañjaya. Once Rāvaṇa's armies are victorious and subdue Varuṇa, Śambūka departs for the forest to attain the *sūryahāsa* sword. We hear nothing more from Śambūka until Lakṣmaṇa stumbles upon his place of *tapas* as narrated in the *Ayodhyākāṇḍa*. The narrative unfolds much as it has in other texts following this stream of narration, but when Lakṣmaṇa tells Rāma that he has accidentally decapitated an innocent ascetic, Svayambhūdeva adds that Sītā—who has overheard Lakṣmaṇa's confession—chastises Lakṣmaṇa for being habitually violent and careless. He defends himself somewhat awkwardly by saying that it is his use of arms in the name of glory that gives his life purpose.

### *Hemacandra's* Triṣaṣṭiśalākāpuruṣacarita

The last text that will figure into this discussion of non-vernacular texts employing the accidental death motif is the *Triṣaṣṭiśalākāpuruṣacarita* (*TŚPC*).

Jain *Rāmāyaṇas* like the *Paümacariya*, *Paümacariu*, and *Pampa Rāmāyaṇa* understand Rāma, Lakṣmaṇa, and Rāvaṇa to be the eighth incarnation of the Baladeva–Vāsudeva–Prativāsudeva trio, who are included among Jainism's illustrious men or Śalākāpuruṣas. While the Jain *Rāmāyaṇas* limit their focus to Rāma, his brother, and his rival, there is another body of Jain texts that situate the Rāma story within the broader scope of his place among all sixty-three of these figures. The twelfth-century *TŚPC* of Hemacandra, a court poet of the Chaulukya Empire in what is now Gujarat (Dundas, 2002, pp. 133–136), is perhaps the most famous text compiling the histories of these Śalākāpuruṣas. Given the scope required to tell the stories of all sixty-three, the account of Rāma's deeds in the *TŚPC* is naturally shorter than in texts like the *PC*, which are entirely dedicated to the single narrative of Rāma's life and his interactions with the people around him. Likewise, the Śambūka story as it appears in this text is also relatively brief in relation to the Rāma-specific texts.

The Śambūka story in the *TŚPC* is positioned just before Candraṇakhā flees to Laṅkā and occurs over thirty-two verses (vv. 7.5.378–410). The narrative's trajectory stays close to the structure as laid out by Vimalasūri. The only major difference, aside from brevity, is that Candraṇakhā in the *TŚPC* remains unmutilated when she approaches Rāvaṇa to tell him of the death of her son—Rāvaṇa's own nephew—named Śambūka. Although Hemacandra did not introduce any significant narrative changes to the Śambūka story, it is notable that the *TŚPC* was composed in northern India and outside the primary region in which the accidental death motif had been circulating.

### *Who is narrating Śambūka's accidental death?*

One small part of the Jain contestation with how the *Rāmāyaṇa* story is told in Hindu circles was the assertion that Śambūka's death did not occur in the way that Vālmīki reported. It was an accident caused by Lakṣmaṇa, not an execution carried out by Rāma. This description of Śambūka's death occurred with enough frequency to spark a sort of canonization of Śambūka's death that was accepted beyond the limits of the Jain tradition. In the South, narrative elements from the Vimalasūri stream appear in Jain and non-Jain texts alike, but—as is clear from the lack of non-Jain texts in the North that make use of this story—that trend was not pan-Indic. In other words, texts that include the accidental death motif could be either Jain or non-Jain in theological orientation but all non-Jain texts using this story are of a southern origin. Another related point is that among the non-Jain communities, only vernacular poets made use of the accidental motif. Be it in the North or South, the story never caught on in Sanskrit or Prakrit outside of the Jain tradition. Our one exception to this is the *Ānanda Rāmāyaṇa*.

Given that mutual use of the accidental death motif between Jain and non-Jain Rāma poets occurs only in southern vernaculars, I contend that this particular understanding of the Śūrpaṇakhā story developed in the South as an account of the events leading to Sītā's abduction that was widely accepted by Jains and non-Jains alike. The story only took hold beyond the South within the confines of the Jain community, who reproduced the story in both cosmopolitan (e.g., Hemacandra's Sanskrit *TŚPC*) and vernacular (e.g., Jinadāsa's *Rām-Rās*) languages.

It is worth noting at this point that this telling of the story following the accidental death motif occurs in many more texts of Jain, non-Jain, and even non-Indic origin.[29] A few other prominent examples of texts making use of Śambūka's accidental death (acknowledging that he is not always named "Śambūka" or some Prakritized variation thereof) would be the *Torave Rāmāyaṇa* (Kannada), Bhadreśvara's *Kahāvalī* (Prakrit), and Sāraḷadāsa's *Mahābhārata* (Oriya). Sāraḷādāsa's stand-alone telling of the Rāma story, the *Bilaṅka Rāmāyaṇa*, deals exclusively with the entrance to Laṅkā, Rāvaṇa's defeat, and the return to Ayodhyā. The text's description of the post-exile events in Ayodhyā aligns considerably with the *Adbhuta Rāmāyaṇa* (e.g., Sīta assuming the form of Kālī and killing the thousand-headed Rāvaṇa, who had bested Rāma). Yet the *Bilaṅka Rāmāyaṇa*'s account of Rāma's rule in Ayodhyā omits the Śambūka episode.

## The Curious Case of the *Ānanda Rāmāyaṇa*

As I have shown, poets writing in medieval India followed essentially one of four ways of dealing with the Śambūka story in their own *Rāmāyaṇa* tellings. They could either remove the episode entirely, often as collateral damage in excising the entire *Uttarakāṇḍa*; they could tell the story as Vālmīki had done, by describing a deceased Brahmin boy, an errant Śūdra, Rāma's execution of that Śūdra, and the gods' praise of Rāma for doing so; they could keep the same basic narrative highlights as Vālmīki but depict Śambūka's death as a moment of salvation delivered by the god-king Rāma; and finally, they could follow in Vimalasūri's footsteps and depict Śambūka's death as an accident caused by Lakṣmaṇa just prior to Sītā's kidnapping. Nearly all *Rāmāyaṇa* texts include only a single version of the story, should they include one at all.

29 Though outside the scope of the study at hand, some *Rāmāyaṇa* texts from Southeast Asia including the Thai *Rāmakien* and the Malay *Hikāyat Serī Rāma* also make use of the accidental death motif.

For example, if the accidental death motif appears, it appears to the exclusion of the execution motif(s) and vice versa. There are two exceptions to this. The first is the *Bhāvārtha Rāmāyaṇa*, if one were to include the appended *Uttarakāṇḍa* of Mukteśvara. The core of the text includes the accidental death while the *Uttarakāṇḍa* reintroduces the execution motif. The second exception is the *Ānanda Rāmāyaṇa*, which deserves to be discussed independently.

I have alluded to the fact that the *Ānanda Rāmāyaṇa* (*Blissful Rāmāyaṇa*, henceforth *ĀR*), a text likely composed during the fifteenth century in Maharashtra (Aklujkar, 2001, pp. 83–86), has often been an exception to several points I have raised about the usage of the various iterations of Śambūka's death. When I argued that the motif of Śambūka's accidental death appears in no non-Jain *Rāmāyaṇa* written in a cosmopolitan language, I was forced to say that the *ĀR* is an exception. And just now, when I offered that all *Rāmāyaṇas* that include a Śambūka story include it in only one of two forms (the motif of the accident or the execution), the *ĀR* and the Marathi *Bhāvārtha Rāmāyaṇa*—together with its appended *Uttarakāṇḍa*—are the only texts that do, in fact, include both modes of telling the story. Not only does the *ĀR* include both renderings of this death, it also elaborates on them extensively—especially so in the case of the execution motif. The text includes devotional innovations such as the liberating efficacy of reciting Rāma's name and it frequently quotes from the Upaniṣads, leaving the spirit of the text structured around Rāma-*bhakti* and Advaita Vedānta. Additionally, the author of the *ĀR* brings together narratives from all over the *Rāmāyaṇa* tradition, prompting V. Raghavan to consider this poet as "a comparative student of the Rāma-epos and Rāmāyaṇa-versions" (1988, p. 121). It is time to dedicate some attention exclusively to this treasure trove of *Rāmāyaṇa* stories.

The first of the *ĀR*'s nine books, the *Sārakāṇḍa*, includes the scene of the accidental killing of Śūrpaṇakhā's son, here named Sāmba. The story follows much the same narrative arc as the Śambūka episode as found in many of the Jain and Jain-influenced Rāma texts. Here, Sāmba is in the forest performing *tapas*, which gets the attention of Brahmā, who gives him a divine sword (*divyakhaḍga*). Sāmba does not notice, leaving the sword out in the open for Lakṣmaṇa to stumble upon it. The moment of Sāmba's death and Lakṣmaṇa's confession to Rāma is rather abrupt.

> Picking up the sword, Lakṣmaṇa chops at the trees and creepers and kills Sāmba who was in the cluster of trees, whereupon he says to Rāghava,
> "Tell me, Best of Raghus, what is the expiation for killing a Brahmin?"
> Rāma then told him that he killed a Rākṣasa named Sāmba, not a sage. (*ĀR* 1.7.42–43)

Lakṣmaṇa is relieved, but we then hear about Sāmba's mother, Śūrpaṇakhā, who comes across the corpse of her son. She is distressed at the sight and intends to kill Rāma and Lakṣmaṇa but, after she assumes a beautiful form and approaches them, she becomes smitten. When she asks Rāma to marry her, he refuses and suggests she take Lakṣmaṇa instead. Lakṣmaṇa also rejects Śūrpaṇakhā, which angers her and she lunges toward Sītā. Rāma intervenes and tricks her into bringing an arrow to Lakṣmaṇa, which he uses to cut off her nose, ears, lips, and breasts. This then sparks the events that lead to Sītā's abduction as Rāvaṇa's revenge for mutilating his sister.

Later, in the *ĀR*'s seventh book, the *Rājyakāṇḍa*, we find a great deal of innovation to the execution motif.[30] After Rāma hears about the death of the young Brahmin from the bereaved parents, he promises the couple that he will bring their son back to life. In case he cannot, he offers that they take his son, Kuśa, instead. On top of this, Sītā—who is not only not exiled, but actively present in this scene—then offers their son, Lava, to the grieving mother should Rāma be unsuccessful in reviving the boy. When consulting with Vasiṣṭha about how to go about remedying the situation, Nārada arrives to offer his advice. The author of the *ĀR* forgoes any discussion of the Yugas or humanity's declining moral aptitude as the ages progress. Nārada does not even suggest to Rāma that a transgressive Śūdra is behind this death. Instead, he advises that Rāma survey his kingdom to find anyone engaged in unrighteous conduct (*adharmanirata*). Just as Rāma—accompanied by Sītā—sets out to find the unrighteous conduct mentioned by Nārada, a Brahmin woman approaches Rāma's court, lamenting the death of her husband. She charges Rāma, in his neglect, for being responsible for her husband's death. Rāma assures her of his assistance and orders that the woman's husband, along with the young Brahmin boy and any other bodies that may appear, be submerged in oil to preserve them while he solves the problem. And, as luck would have it, five more bodies appeared at the gates while Rāma is away from Ayodhyā whereupon Sumantra, Rāma's trusted charioteer, places them in vats of oil.

This addition of multiple deaths attributed (as we are soon to find out) to a Śūdra's transgression is already a major narrative expansion by the author of the *ĀR*, but the text goes further. These bodies were not all Brahmins. In fact, all social classes are represented in the death toll: one was a Kṣatriya, another a Vaiśya, the third was an oil-presser (*tailakāra*), another the daughter of a blacksmith (*lohakāra*), and the last—and perhaps most provocative—was a leather worker (*carmakāra*). This brings the body count to a total of seven people of varied social standing (Aklujkar, 2001, p. 95).

---

30 For an overview of the execution of Śambūka in the *ĀR*, see Aklujkar (2001, pp. 94–96).

The representation of several social classes of Ayodhyā's citizenry in this episode is taken further a bit later in the episode when Rāma actually encounters Śambūka—identified in the *ĀR* only as an unnamed Śūdra. Rāma finds this Śūdra in the Vindhyā Mountains hanging upside-down from a tree, inhaling smoke. Rāma charges him with acting like a Brahmin and violating his *dharma* and informs him of his impending demise. While *varṇa* hierarchies are clearly present in the text, the *ĀR* nevertheless demonstrates considerable concern for the Śūdras' collective ability to find their way toward the path (*gati*) of salvation. The author of this text—which operates as a compendium of devotional practices as dramatized through the Rāma story—uses the flexibility of the Śambūka story to elaborate not only on the outcome of the Rāma–Śambūka interaction, but also on how Śūdras are meant to make their way along this path.

After Rāma warns the Śūdra that he is about to die, he admits that he is nevertheless impressed with his *tapas*, which prompts the following exchange:

> "If you are satisfied with me, Rāma, destroyer of Rāvaṇa's pride, then I ask of you today that Śūdras find their path.
> "Please grant a boon whereby I too, might gain renown." Rāma was pleased upon hearing these words of the Śūdra and said,
> "May my name, Rāma, always be recited, celebrated, and constantly contemplated by the Śūdras.
> "Be devoted to me and the Path will be theirs in this way. And you will gain renown among the Śūdras through these means."
> After hearing Rāma's boon, the Śūdra said once more, "Śūdras will be ignorant in the Kali Age, Best of Raghus.
> "Their minds will be distracted by their work in agriculture and the like, Lord. How, then, will they keep their minds focused on recitations and such?
> So, upon reflection, may an appropriate boon be granted today as well." Rāma was pleased upon hearing his speech and said again,
> "Let the Śūdras always utter 'Rāma, Rāma' when greeting each other. They will find the path in this way.
> "This story about you will be famous and those born of my feet will remember you. And being killed by me today, you will go straight to Vaikuṇṭha."
> He again asked another boon of Śrī Rāma out of his own motives, "May you always dwell on this mountain together with Sītā and Lakṣmaṇa.
> "One by one, people should first receive my *darśana* and after that receive your *darśana*.

> "Doing this with devotion, they will proceed to their liberation. May you remove those mortals, Lord Rāma, who indiscriminately see you without seeking my *darśana*." Hari Rāma said, "Let it be so," and fulfilled for him this devotion.
>
> Having done so, the best of Raghus killed the overjoyed Śūdra and brought to life the seven people back in Sāketa [Ayodhyā]—the Brahmin and the rest. (*ĀR* 7.10.107–120)

This is a truly remarkable expansion of the circumstances surrounding Śambūka's death. In fact, we have here the first account of Śambūka as a spokesman for the Śūdras. He is portrayed as using his moment with Rāma to consider the betterment of his community. This symbolic use of Śambūka also occurs in the various Dalit and non-Brahmin movements of the early- and mid- twentieth century, though these movements typically depict the Rāma–Śambūka interaction as highly contentious and steeped in casteism rather than the mutual admiration depicted here. While the similarities between the *ĀR*'s Śambūka episode and the twentieth-century Dalit and other non-Brahmin social movements are rather superficial, the text does seem to be elucidating—in a much more literal fashion—the mythology connected to Ramtek Hill in modern-day Maharashtra, the site of the only temple to Śambūka (known there also by the name Dhūmreśvara, the Lord of Smoke). The Sanskrit-language *Sindūrāgirimāhātmya*, composed in the eighteenth century, is a descriptive text of Sindūragiri (also known as Rāmagiri or Tapogiri) and its sacred places. The text identifies this hill as the site of Rāma's encounter with Śambūka and includes an extensive account of the Śambūka story that details Rāma's granting of Śambūka's three requests, one of which is identical to the boon mentioned in *ĀR* 7.10.116: that Rāma dwell on the hill along with Sītā and Lakṣmaṇa. Likewise, Śambūka in the *Sindūragirimāhātmya* requests that all devotees to Rāma first visit him before proceeding up the hill to Rāma's temple lest their *darśana* with Rāma be fruitless (cf. *ĀR* 7.10.117–119). The significance of Ramtek Hill and the *Sindūragirimāhātmya* is discussed in detail in the following chapter.

## Borrowing Śambūka's Death: Narrative Exchange between Jains and Hindus

Once Kālidāsa and Vimalasūri had set new precedents for envisioning the Śambūka story in the first millennium CE, the tradition of narrating Śambūka's death took several divergent paths. What all of these have in common, however, is that they all seek to remove the tarnish the episode left on Rāma's image after Valmīki's *Uttarakāṇḍa*. In an age of Rāma-*bhakti*, however it may have been expressed or experienced in various parts and traditions of India, poets and devotees were intent on protecting Rāma's character and projecting the authority, morality, decorum, and grace that his character came to represent.

While the execution motif is contrary to Jain sentiments, Śambūka's accidental death is a story that could easily slip into Hindu or Jain tellings alike without offending either tradition. Such broad appeal contributed to its appearance in several *Rāmāyaṇas* from both the Jain and Hindu traditions. I would like to push this question a bit further and ruminate on why some vernacular poets of the Hindu tradition in the South incorporated something from the Jain tradition that is explicitly contentious toward the *VR*.

Neither the Jain nor Hindu traditions were absolutely strict in their conformity to party lines. The very fact of Jainism's inclusion of Rāma into its framework of Śalākāpuruṣas in response to Rāma's growing presence in the devotional minds of Jains and Hindus alike and the development of a reformulated Rāma story to support that inclusion is evidence of such flexibility. One of the clearest examples of Jain influence on the Hindu tradition is the Brahminical incorporation of *śramaṇa* ideals of asceticism and renunciation from the Buddhist and Jain traditions and use of that renunciant mode of life to structure the concept of *varṇāśramadharma* as crystallized in the Dharmaśāstra literature (Olivelle, 1993, pp. 58ff.). I argue that this willingness on the part of Hindus to respond to competing traditions—however clandestinely—extends to narrative exchange among *Rāmāyaṇa* poets. In other words, the development of the Rāma story between the Jains and Hindus was not a unilateral flow of influence. Poets of the Brahminical tradition were just as liable to incorporate compelling and well-known episodic elements of Rāma's deeds from the Jain tradition as Jains were in incorporating elements from the Hindu tradition. The story of Śambūka's accidental death was indeed compelling from the Hindu perspective. The Hindu poets of the South were confronted with the same issues of Rāma's portrayal as anyone else; they needed a strategy to address Rāma's swift and definitive killing of Śambūka. Their Jain neighbors had found a solution by relocating the story and placing the responsibility with Rāma's brother. There are additional examples of such borrowing on the part of Hindu *Rāmāyaṇa* poets of narrative elements from Jain tellings of the Rāma story. For instance, the motif of Sītā being the daughter of Rāvaṇa, which first appears in Jain poet Saṅghadāsa's fifth-century *Vasudevahiṇḍī* (Singaravelu, 1982, p. 235–236), is reasonably common in Hindu renderings of the *Ramayaṇa* including the *Adbhuta Rāmāyaṇa* (Brockington, 1984, p. 255).[31]

31 For an overview of different renderings of the Rāma story, including the various motifs of Sītā's birth, see Brockington (1984, pp. 226ff.).

It is admittedly somewhat uncertain that the Hindu poets were fully aware that this accidental death of Śūrpaṇakhā's son was a replacement for Vālmīki's rendering of the Śambūka story. I say this especially because they periodically change the victim's name (e.g., Jambumālī in the Raṅganātha *Rāmāyaṇa* and Sāmba in the *Bhāvārtha Rāmāyaṇa*). Nevertheless, other circumstances seem to point to a conscious awareness that one is a stand-in for the other, such as some prominent thematic similarities between both versions (most pertinent of which are asceticism and decapitation) and the fact that when this accidental death is utilized, the execution episode is almost always absent. Also, the Jain poets—from whom the Hindu poets appear to be borrowing—seem to consistently follow Vimalasūrī in his identification of the decapitated ascetic as Śambūka. It is only when the story enters a Hindu context that the name begins to change. This is perhaps a way of erasing any potential negativity surrounding a character named Śambūka and, by extension, any connection between him and Rāma.

I would like to raise one more point regarding the accidental death of Śambūka. Aside from a few relatively superficial changes—some of which I have detailed in the discussion above—this *Paümacariya*-influenced mode of telling the Śambūka story has remained remarkably consistent throughout its history. Rāvaṇa's nephew, however he may be named, attempts to attain a divine sword that falls into Lakṣmaṇa's hands. Enamored with its beauty, Lakṣmaṇa swings it about, accidentally decapitating the ascetic. Rāvaṇa's sister (also variously named) then stumbles upon her dead son, which sparks in her a desire for revenge against the perpetrators. This ultimately manifests in Rāvaṇa's abduction of Sītā. All these elements persist from version to version, from century to century. Their consistency, I contend, comes from the story's avoidance of controversy or of matters subject to social and legal debate. There is no significant mention of *varṇa*, nor is there any depiction of Rāma's involvement in violence. Relating to the latter, avoiding any controversial instances of violence assists in building up Rāma's perceived benevolence in an age of burgeoning devotion to him. As for the former, caste and *varṇa* became a social battleground, especially by the nineteenth century. Since the accidental motif largely circumvents issues of caste, it has no means of contributing in a meaningful way to the concerns of equality and representation for the lower castes—pivotal points of contention in caste revolutions of the nineteenth century and beyond. The story could easily resist change because it did not participate in these major social and religious movements.

For the reasons just highlighted, I will largely leave this account of Śambūka's accidental death in favor of those that elaborate on his calculated execution. This version of the ascetic's end follows several different paths, the most elaborate of which culminates in his role as a martyr in the non-Brahmin cause. This subject will be taken up in later chapters. However, before moving into this moment of Śambūka's history, I would like to first visit Ramtek, Maharashtra, the supposed site of Śambūka's death by Rāma's hand and a place that exemplifies the layered development of his legend over nearly two thousand years.

# Chapter 6

# ŚAMBŪKA LIVES ON RAMTEK HILL

Each year, many residents of the small town of Ramtek, Maharashtra gather at a modest temple (Figures 6.1 and 6.2) about halfway up the large, steep hill at the center of town to celebrate Maha Shivaratri—"The Great Night of Śiva." For this annual festival of devotion to Śiva, the image inside this temple—a *śiva-liṅga* known by the name Dhūmreśvara (Figure 6.3)—becomes the focus of attention despite there being several other similar images scattered about town. Śambūka and Dhūmreśvara are, in fact, one and the same. Though worshipped by a different name, Śambūka's identity as Dhūmreśvara is on full display on signs and posters and in pamphlets and inscriptions, leaving visitors to the temple fully aware that when they approach the *śiva-liṅga*, they are approaching Śambūka. I will outline in this chapter how Śambūka came to be known by this name and how, of all places, Ramtek Hill came to house the world's only temple to Śambūka. To do so, I focus on four historical periods of development in the area: the Vākāṭaka period, the Yādava period, the Marāṭhā period, and, finally, Ramtek today. Literature and structures from these periods provide us with an amalgamation of historical layers on

**Figure 6.1** The Dhūmreśvara temple viewed from the East.

**Figure 6.2** Ramtek Hill viewed from the South.

**Figure 6.3** The Dhūmreśvara *liṅga*.

Ramtek Hill spanning over one thousand years. In following this pathway through the area's history, we see how the early literary and material foundations associated with the town's central hill primed the area to welcome Śambūka as a permanent fixture of local Hindu religious life.

## Ramtek and the Vākāṭakas

Kālidāsa has already proven himself crucial to our unfolding narrative about the evolution of the Śambūka story through his innovations to the episode as it appears in his *Raghuvaṃśa* (*RaV*). Chapter 3 outlined a changing and increasingly institutionalized Vaiṣṇavism emerging in the Gupta Empire and Kālidāsa's contribution to this. In his *RaV*, Kālidāsa reimagined Śambūka's path after death through a paradigm of redemption, a striking departure from Śambūka's fate in the *VR*. We also saw that his *MD* participated in the consolidation of the Vaiṣṇava attitudes of the Guptas by framing the poem temporally around the *varṣāmāsavrata* festival and geographically around the extreme limits of the Guptas' imperial influence. This section continues this line of thinking by showing how the ingenuity of the dowager queen Prabhāvatīguptā brought a Gupta-influenced Vaiṣṇavism to Ramtek and how, in combination with the literary innovations of Kālidāsa, the stage was set for Śambūka to find his eternal home on the town's prominent hillside.

The imposing height of the hill at the center of Ramtek town—about fifty kilometers to the northeast of Nagpur—would have made it a particularly useful outpost for observing the surrounding plains of the oft-contested Deccan region. At least as early as the period of Vākāṭaka rule starting in the third century CE, the hill served as "an outstanding strategic base controlling the highway that connected, and still connects, the central and eastern part of the basin of the Ganges with the northern Deccan" (Bakker, 1989a, p. 467). As a gateway between regions, it had considerable political appeal, which was perhaps one feature that attracted the Vākāṭaka's greatest contemporary empire: the Guptas.

The Guptas had had a strained relationship with the Vākāṭakas since ca. 330 CE, when Samudragupta defeated Vākāṭaka king Rudrasena I and drove him south to what would become their new capital at Nandivardhana (Bakker, 1997, pp. 9ff.; Bakker, 2002, p. 1).[1] When the territory of the Guptas to the north of the Vindhyas and that of the Vākāṭakas to the south stabilized, the Guptas found it expedient to have a reliable alliance at the southern reaches of their territory (Bakker, 1997, p. 15). The result was the late-fourth-century marriage between the Vākāṭaka king Rudrasena II and Prabhāvatīguptā, the grandchildren of the once-contentious rulers Rudrasena I and Samudragupta respectively. This marriage brought a Gupta presence to the Vākāṭaka capital, and Prabhāvatīguptā—ever proud of her Gupta heritage—would prove herself to be a powerful force in the cultural and political course of the Vākāṭakas after her husband's short reign and death.

Prabhāvatīguptā held a long regency of nearly twenty years while her son, Pravarasena II, matured.[2] During this period, she exerted considerable

1 V.V. Mirashi postulates that the Guptas' relationship with the Vākāṭakas was friendly overall. He does concur, however, that Samudragupta's imperial ambitions shrunk Rudrasena I's holdings to the north and confined their territories, though Rudrasena I never accepted a position of suzerainty (1963, pp. xxi–xxii).

2 It appears that after Prabhāvatīguptā's regency, Pravarasena II's brother, Dāmodarasena, had a short reign of little consequence (Bakker, 1997, pp. 22–23).

influence over the religious leanings of the Vākāṭakas. The Vākāṭakas tended to favor Śaivism over Vaiṣṇavism, except during the period of Prabhāvatīguptā's regency and for perhaps a generation or two after her (Bakker, 1986, p. 62). Despite this interlude's relative brevity, her promotion of Vaiṣṇavism nevertheless left lasting effects on the Rāmagiri landscape. The initial moments and monuments of Vaiṣṇava development at Rāmagiri happened in a concentrated burst of devotion and productivity fueled by Prabhāvatīguptā's personal ambition.

Following the work of Michael Willis, we saw in Chapter 3 the importance of the *varṣāmāsavrata* festival in the Gupta Vaiṣṇava religious world, particularly at the site of Udaygiri in Madhya Pradesh near the modern city of Vidisha. That embodiment of Vaiṣṇava devotion that was emphasized at Udaygiri—an innovation of Chandragupta II—was subsequently transferred to the Vākāṭakas with Prabhāvatīguptā's entrance into their capital. For example, it would have been common to give religious gifts after the culmination of the *varsāmāsavrata*, which ends on the eleventh day of the bright fortnight of the month of Kārttika. Indeed, we find an abundant inscriptional record of gifts given on the following day. Most relevant for our purposes are the so-called "Ṛiddhapur plates," issued by Prabhāvatīguptā "from the feet of the Lord of Rāmagiri," (*rāmagirisvāminaḥ pādamūlāt*) that is, from Ramtek. This charter mentions a gift of a plot of land with a house and four huts given to Brahmins (Mirashi, 1963, pp. 33ff.). In it, she speaks as a Viṣṇu devotee who "meditates at the feet of Bhagavat" (*bhagavatpādānuddhyātā*). It is noteworthy that even though these Ṛiddhapur plates were issued from Vākāṭaka territory, they open with a genealogy of the Guptas instead of the Vākāṭakas, illustrating Prabhāvatīguptā's commitment to maintaining a connection to her ancestral home (ibid., pp. 33–34).

One of the most influential innovations to come out of Udayagiri, however, was the amalgamation of elements needed to solidify a state-sanctioned, temple-based mode of devotional worship. Willis identifies these elements as Brahmins learned in image worship (i.e., religious professionals), the rituals and texts used by these professionals, a deity to whom one directs these rituals, land given to conduct these religious practices, and a ruling class to endorse these landed ritual spaces (2009, pp. 113ff.). He argues that none of these are an innovation of the Guptas. Rather, it is their combination that first appears at Udayagiri and hence, Udayagiri becomes a space where "the rising power of theism was harmonised with ancient systems of ritual and knowledge, a place where the gods were established and made ready to dominate the religious landscape of later India" (ibid., p. 166). This new public form of temple-based, professionalized, and state-sponsored Vaiṣṇava worship is precisely what Prabhāvatīguptā took with her to the Vākāṭaka capital, and led to the formation of the Vākāṭaka holy hill of Rāmagiri, evidently inspired by Udayagiri to create her own "holy mountain" that showcased her devotion to Viṣṇu (Bakker, 2002, pp. 2–3).

Among the most important Vākāṭaka structures on Ramtek Hill are a now-ruined temple to Trivikrama (i.e., Vāmana), a shrine to Varāha, a Bhogarāma temple, and two temples dedicated to Narasiṃha: the Kevala Narasiṃha temple and the Rudra Narasiṃha temple. Given the special attention to Narasiṃha, this man-lion *avatāra* appears to have been the main Vaiṣṇava deity on the hill during the Vākāṭaka period and is likely the "*svāmin*" of the *rāmagirisvāmin* Prabhāvatīguptā mentions in her Ṛiddhapur plates (Bakker, 1990, pp. 67–69).[3] Hans Bakker places the Trivikrama temple towards the end of the fifth century, the Varāha shrine in the first half of the fifth century, the Bhogarāma temple in the end of the fifth or beginning of the sixth century, and assigns the construction of the Rudra Narasiṃha temple to Prabhāvatīguptā herself in the first quarter of the fifth century CE (Bakker, 1989b).[4] The Vaiṣṇava monuments on Ramtek Hill that survive today thus all date to Prabhāvatīguptā's lifetime or within a generation thereafter.

The Gupta presence in the Vākāṭaka court extends beyond Prabhāvatīguptā's regency and the parallels between Rāmagiri and Udayagiri. Kālidāsa was also part of the Gupta cultural legacy imprinted on the Vākāṭakas. He was no stranger to the Vākāṭaka capital, even using the region's holy site as the abode

3 The prominence of Narasiṃha does not appear to be random. There have been accounts of this rather *raudra* (terrifying) man-lion form of Viṣṇu being revered in Śaiva contexts, which would have made Narasiṃha a particularly expedient image when attempting to promote Vaiṣṇavism within a predominantly Śaiva kingdom (cf. the traditional name of one of the two Narasiṃha temples at Ramtek: Rudra-Narasiṃha); see Bakker (1992a, p. 9). Additionally, Vaishali Welankar notes considerable similarities between the pre-Vākāṭaka folk fertility goddess Lajjāgauri's frequent depiction with a lion and iconography of the Ramtek Kevala Narasiṃha. Prabhāvatīguptā appears to have capitalized on the proselytizing potential of the Guptas' purāṇic images of Narasiṃha as an *avatāra* of Viṣṇu in a region that already had lion imagery in their folk traditions (2009, pp. 113–120).

4 Bakker originally felt that the Kevala Narasiṃha Temple was constructed by Prabhāvatīguptā's daughter, Atibhāvatī in the first half of the fifth century in honor of her mother. He bases a part of his theory for dating the temple to this period on an inscription currently found in the Kevala Narasiṃha Temple (1989b, pp. 81ff.). He later conjectures, however, that the inscriptional evidence used to make the claim that Prabhāvatīguptā's daughter dedicated a temple to her mother was originally located in Ramtek's Trivikrama temple. He suggests that the inscription was then moved by the Bhonsles during restoration of the Kevala Narasiṃha Temple in the eighteenth century, with stones taken from the ruined Trivikrama Temple. He does not address any changes this may imply while dating the Kevala Narasiṃha Temple (Bakker, 2010, pp. 241–247; Bakker, 2013, pp. 169–176).

of the banished Yakṣa and the starting point for the cloud-messenger's journey in his famous *MD*. Kālidāsa understands Rāmagiri to have been blessed by the presence of Rāma and Sītā during their time together in exile, as is clear from the *MD*'s opening verse:

> There was a Yakṣa who was negligent in his duties. His greatness was brought to an end through the burden of a curse from his *guru* whereby he was to remain separated from his wife for a year. He took up residence in the *āśramas* of Rāmagiri, where the waters were purified from Janaka's daughter having bathed there and the trees provided ample shade. (*MD*, *Pūrvamegha* 1)

The question of whether Kālidāsa's Rāmagiri is, in fact, Ramtek Hill—that is, the same Rāmagiri of Prabhāvatīguptā's Ṛiddhapur charter—has been explored at length by V.V. Mirashi (e.g., 1959, pp. 26ff.; 1963 p. 35) and seems to be a likely identification. Prabhāvatīguptā's role in the Gupta-Vākāṭaka alliance and Kālidāsa's relationship to the Vākāṭakas via this alliance form the basis of Mirashi's argument. In addition to the reference to Rāmagiri in verse 1, Mirashi also draws attention to another moment in the *MD* that reflects Gupta influence at Rāmagiri. The Yakṣa in the poem enlists the help of a monsoon cloud forming around the top of the mountain to carry a message to his beloved. This mountain is "imprinted with…the footprints of the Lord of the Raghus," recalling—at least in its affinity for divine Vaiṣṇava footprints—Prabhāvatīguptā's issuance of her charter "from the feet of the lord of Rāmagiri" (Mirashi, 1959, p. 32; Mirashi, 1963, p. 35; Bakker, 1997, 64; Bakker, 1991, pp. 28ff.). The Yakṣa speaks to the cloud:

> Embrace and take leave of your dear friend, this mountain with its slopes imprinted with the praises of men and the footprints of the Lord of the Raghus. Season after season, your affection manifests as you unite with it, releasing warm tears born of a long separation. (*MD*, *Pūrvamegha* 12)

The connection between Kālidāsa and Rāmagiri as identified by Prabhāvatīguptā becomes even clearer when one considers, as Willis notes, that the entire *MD* is framed around the *varṣāmāsavrata* festival (2009, p. 32). The importance of this festival was already mentioned in Chapter 3 in the context of Candragupta II's elaborate use of Udayagiri to mark the onset of Viṣṇu's sleep and Prabhāvatīguptā's Ṛiddhapur charter, which was issued the day after this festival ended—an occasion on which to give gifts. Using the duration of *varṣāmāsavrata* as the temporal setting for the *MD* brings the work into the devotional world of the Guptas and—by way of Prabhāvatīguptā's influence—that of the Vākāṭakas. And by using Rāmagiri as the southern limit for the geographic setting of the work and the site of the Yakṣa's banishment, Kālidāsa is connecting Rāmagiri to the Himalayas by way of the prominent Gupta sites of Nīcarigiri (i.e., Udayagiri) and Ujjain, two of the cloud messenger's stops on the way to the Yakṣa's beloved. Indeed, I do not think it would be too much of a stretch to consider that Kālidāsa was poetically representing the reach of the Gupta territories, starting with Rāmagiri at the southern edge of their influence via their relationship with the Vākāṭakas.

I have discussed Kālidāsa and Rāmagiri under the Vākāṭakas—especially Prabhāvatīguptā—to give a "pre-history" of the specific narration of the Śambūka story at the site of Ramtek. Both Kālidāsa's literature and the Vaiṣṇava devotional context at Rāmagiri were major forces in the development in the Śambūka story. The institutional Vaiṣṇavism that developed under the Guptas had many consequences in the sphere of their influence. The sentiments and innovations behind Candragupta II's innovations at Udayagiri were transposed to Rāmagiri through his daughter, Prabhāvatīguptā. Though the bulk of the structural development on Rāmagiri happened within only a century or two of Prabhāvatīguptā's regency, her sponsorship of the Vākāṭaka holy sites on the hill had a lasting effect on how the hill would be received and used by future occupants of the site. Her influence was palpable even in her own time, attracting the great poet Kālidāsa to highlight the hill in one of his best-known works, the *MD*. More directly related to Śambūka, and as we saw in Chapter 3, Kālidāsa, in his *RaV*, framed the Śambūka story in a redemptive light that was more consonant with emerging conceptions of Viṣṇu and his *avatāra* in Rāma, a just and fair god-king. The punishment due to Śambūka was administered, but his contact with Rāma resulted in an access to the divine otherwise unattainable to a Śūdra rebelling against the proscriptions of his *varṇa*. This section has demonstrated that this same religious paradigm informed the composition of the *MD*, which utilizes the *varṣāmāsavrata* festival as its temporal scope and Rāmagiri as its starting point. His literary representation of Rāmagiri in the *MD* contributed to the Vaiṣṇava aura that dominated the hill through Prabhāvatīguptā's design. The religious spirit of the hill cultivated by Prabhāvatīguptā and the influence of Kālidāsa, the Guptas' greatest poet, converged in later centuries to identify Ramtek as not only the site of Śambūka's death, but also the place of his divinization and permanent residence.

## Ramtek and the Yādavas

From the *MD* and the *RaV*, it is clear that Kālidāsa knew Rāmagiri to have been blessed by Rāma and Sītā's presence and he knew Rāma to have shown a concern for Śambūka's position after death. The only trouble is that he seems to have known these two things separately. It cannot be said with any confidence that Kālidāsa knew Rāmagiri to be the site of Śambūka's death. Eventually, however, Kālidāsa's attention to Śambūka's afterlife did catch hold on Ramtek Hill. If Kālidāsa himself did not know Ramtek to be the place of Śambūka's death, the Śūdra ascetic's connection there was certainly an ingrained local belief by the Yādava period—a period that also witnessed the Yādavas' patronage of a full-fledged system of Rāma worship. If Vaiṣṇavism at Ramtek was the product of Vākāṭaka and Gupta intervention, the Yādavas refined that Vaiṣṇavism to have a particular Rāma-oriented expression, and this is when Śambūka took up firm residence at Ramtek.

The territories of the Nandivardhana branch of the Vākāṭakas were likely annexed by the Vatsagulma Vākāṭakas towards the end of the fifth century, which took the focus off Rāmagiri as a devotional center in the empire. Even Vatsagulma control of the territory was short-lived, as the Deccan became a patchwork of evolving alliances and power grabs especially among the Vākāṭakas, Nalas, Viṣṇukuṇḍins, Rāṣṭrakūṭas, Kalachuris and others (Mirashi, 1963, pp. xxxii-xxxiii; Bakker, 1997, pp. 169–171). The riptides of shifting power and relocating centers of rule resulted in a lull in development on Rāmagiri. It was not until the Yādavas took control of the hill in the twelfth century that developmental activity resumed in the area.

From the end of the twelfth century to the beginning of the fourteenth, the Yādavas ruled over what is roughly today's Maharashtra. This period witnessed several colliding social phenomena typified by the integration of devotional movements into the religious life of the region and the assertion of Brahminical ideals of social order. The former process was buttressed by an emerging vernacular tradition in Marathi,[5] while the latter reaffirmed long-standing institutions from the Sanskrit corpus, though not without its challenges from the nascent Marathi literature.[6] Yādava rule was characterized by attempts to negotiate these competing streams of devotionalism and Brahminism.

Yādava rulers favored an established social order rooted in Brahminical institutions that could maintain consistent control of the socio-religious structures within their kingdom. This aspiration would be the benchmark that would define what could be integrated into Yādava society and what had to be expelled. To this end, the Yādavas actively supported a sustained

5 Jñāneśvar, for instance, composed a Marathi commentary on the *Bhagavad-Gītā* known as the *Jñāneśvarī*, through which he quite consciously made accessible the teachings of the *Gītā* to women and Śūdras (Sontheimer, 2004, p. 306).

6 For more on the rise of vernacular Marathi, especially in terms of challenges to Brahminical orthodoxy as represented in the *Dharmaśāstras*, see Novetzke (2018).

engagement with Dharmaśāstra, epitomized in the work of Hemādri, who held high office during the rule of at least two Yādava rulers, Mahādeva and Rāmacandra. The most famous of Hemādri's works is his *Caturvargacintāmaṇi*, which is a digest (*nibandha*) of Dharmaśāstra literature meant to solidify the status of *varṇāśramadharma* in the Yādava realm.

Despite the increased emphasis on promoting a strict Brahminism rooted in *varṇāśramadharma*, the Yādavas nevertheless had to acknowledge the religious plurality inside their kingdom lest the legitimacy of their rule splinter on a cultural front. So long as these religious traditions could be integrated into their overarching conceptions of religiosity invigorated by an affirmation of the principles of Dharmaśāstra, Yādava rulers adopted a strategy of consolidating their influence and authority by patronizing regional cult centers (Bakker, 1987, p. 17). Supporting these religious centers—Ramtek and Pandharpur being two of the most prominent—required absorbing the momentum of an increasingly popular *bhakti* paradigm.[7] Bakker observes that "Ramtek, along with Pandharpur, illustrates the policy of the Yādava kings, who aligned themselves with the major religious movement of their day, the growing Vaiṣṇava *bhakti* in its modern form of devotion oriented towards either Kṛṣṇa-Gopāla or Rāmacandra" (1990, p. 74). Pandharpur became a primary center of devotion to the former via the construction of a temple to Viṭṭhal in Pandharpur by the first Yādava king, Bhillama, at the end of the twelfth century. The presence of this temple provided institutional legitimacy and support that contributed to the solidification of the Vārkarī movement (Bakker, 1990, pp. 63–64). The Vārkarī tradition is an early example of the Vaiṣṇavization of a local deity—in this case, identifying Viṭṭhal as Kṛṣṇa owing largely to the pastoral associations shared between the two (Dhere, 2011, pp. 28ff.).[8]

The situation in Ramtek is somewhat different. As should be clear from my reliance on his work thus far, Hans Bakker has examined the case of Ramtek in detail through numerous publications, so I will only make a few summarizing remarks here. Geographically, this hill sits as the most prominent geographic feature overlooking a major route connecting the Ganges basin and the northern Deccan, and thus on a highway along which armies, saints, and intellectuals

7 Bakker (1990) has compared the two sites of Pandharpur and Ramtek with each other temporally between the Yādava and Marāṭhā periods.

8 Worship of Viṭṭhal was and continues to be centered around biannual pilgrimages to his temple in Pandharpur, which draws in devotees from all over Maharashtra. The pilgrimage in its current form may be more recent, from perhaps the seventeenth century with Tukārām, though it is certainly built on some antecedent (Hawley, 2015, p. 84).

alike could travel. As we have already seen, Ramtek's connections have—since at least the Gupta period—extended far beyond the Maharashtra region. These kinds of connections brought Ramtek in line with a more pan-Indic fascination with Rāma that is quite distinct from the regional expressions of Kṛṣṇa-*bhakti* in other parts of Maharashtra. As Bakker observes, "[t]he evolution of Ramtek or Rāmagiri from a local holy place into a sacred centre of supra-regional importance has to do with the development of a form of Vaiṣṇavism in which the Rāma *avatāra* takes the central position" (1990, p. 66). This Rāma-oriented Vaiṣṇavism—complete with *mantras* (verses), *stotras* (hymns of praise), *dhyānas* (meditations), *tīrthas* (a sacred landmark), etc.—was expressed in texts like the *Rāmapūrvatāpanīya Upaniṣad*, the *Rāmarakṣāstotra*, and the *Agastyasaṃhitā*, which were composed in northern Rāma sites such as Ayodhyā. This body of literature aimed to establish Rāma worship as a clearly defined, orthodox dedication to the hero of the *Rāmāyaṇa* (Bakker, 1986, p. 67).

The devotionalism of the two sites of Pandharpur and Ramtek represented two different types of religious inheritance. Pandharpur is rooted in the folkways of Maharashtra, while Ramtek has a more sprawling history that spreads further north, connected to the remnants of the Gupta Empire and major centers of Rāma devotion. While both Pandharpur and Ramtek were actively supported and developed by the Yādavas, they existed with two distinct histories and patterns of worship. By patronizing the religious life of Ramtek, the Yādava administration was calling on a tradition of Rāma worship that superseded the Maharashtrian regional limits within which the worship of Kṛṣṇa as Viṭṭhal developed.

The supra-regional conception of Rāma devotion was nevertheless localized in Ramtek by drawing attention to the specific features and mytho-history of the hill and its inhabitants. This is best illustrated in the Yādava period by an inscription in the Lakṣmaṇa temple that serves as both an expression of Yādava commitment to the religious practices of the site and a precursor to the local *māhātmya* tradition that reveals itself to us as fully developed later during the Marāṭhā period.

The extensive but unfortunately damaged inscription appears in a temple to Lakṣmaṇa, one of two prominent Rāmaite temples on the hill crest still standing today—the other housing images of Rāma and Sītā. The orientation of Rāmaite influence at Ramtek appears to be coming mostly from the north based not only on the site's historical connections with the Gupta Empire, but also because the geographic references in this inscription tend to favor northern areas (e.g., v. 83).[9] Whatever the directionality of devotional influence,

9 For a full translation of the extant portions of the inscription, see Bakker (1989a).

it is indisputably clear that Rāma reigns supreme at this site, identified explicitly as "Rāma's hill,"[10] a place "which surpasses all other (mountains) because of its being touched by the lotus-feet of the illustrious Rāma" (v. 83).[11] Most pertinent to my purposes here, Rāma's greatness makes its way into the first clearly articulated expression of Śambūka's presence on—and enduring association with—the hill. The passage below occurs amid descriptions of several Śaivaite sites on the hill, implying that Rāma's killing of Śambūka resulted in the latter's divinization as a form of Śiva, something that would be made even more explicit in the coming centuries.

> Here the śūdra saint Śambuka [*sic*] has reached the abode of Murāri (i.e., Kṛṣṇa/Viṣṇu) after having been killed by the sword Candrahāsā that was wielded by Rāmacandra; and on this eminent mountain he became well known as Dhūmrākṣa. (86)[12]

By the time this inscription appeared in the twelfth century, only Kālidāsa and Bhavabhūti had depicted Rāma as delivering salvation to Śambūka—none of the texts covered in the previous chapter that make use of this trope had been composed yet. All other texts composed in the interim between the *VR* and the appearance of this inscription either follow Vimalasūri (e.g., Svayambhūdeva's *Paümacariu*), Vālmīki (e.g., the *Padma Purāṇa*), or excise the episode (e.g., the *Irāmāvatāram*). What we have, then, is an understanding of the Śambūka episode that aligns with the iteration promoted by Kālidāsa.

I cannot say for certain whether the Śambūka tradition at Ramtek is informed directly by Kālidāsa's *RaV*, although I find it to be a reasonable source of inspiration given the site's history in connection with the master poet of the Gupta-Vākāṭaka alliance. There is a slight discrepancy in terminology, however. In Kālidāsa's work, Śambūka attains the course of virtuous men (*lebhe…satāṃ gatim*), while here he arrives at the abode of Murāri (*prāpya padaṃ murāreḥ*)—Murāri being ambiguously situated as an epithet referring to either Kṛṣṇa or Viṣṇu. Kālidāsa's choice of words points to a more generalized conception of salvation, one not tied to Viṣṇu in particular, which could reflect the relative infancy of institutionalized Vaiṣṇavism taking shape under the Guptas. The reference in the inscription certainly reflects a more mature

10 *rāmasya girau*, v. 85. All verse numberings associated with this inscription are in accordance with Bakker (1989a).

11 Bakker's translation (1989a, p. 493); for additional expressions of Rāma's supremacy at the site, see also vv. 39–40 and 103–105.

12 Bakker's translation (1989a, p. 493); n.b. Śambūka in this inscription is written with a short *u* vowel.

Vaiṣṇava tone, which one might expect given the historical developments between the Vākāṭakas and the Yādavas, especially in Maharashtra where the Kṛṣṇa worship of the Vārkarī movement had only recently taken shape.[13] The spirit of the two Rāma–Śambūka interactions as found in Kālidāsa and in the inscription is nevertheless similar. Rāma's authority is not limited to his reign, it extends into the divine realm as well, so that Śambūka's death at Ramtek resulted not only in his own salvation but in the creation of an enduring *tirtha* or holy site occupied by Śambūka in his Śaivaite form, Dhūmrākṣa.

The Yādava period was marked by a consolidation of *vvarṇāśramadharma* on the one hand and a sponsorship of mor popular religious practices on the other. The Śambūka story provided the Yādavas with a perfect opportunity to express their support of *varṇāśramadharma* in terms of the evolving *Rāmāyaṇa* tradition and this northerly stream of Rāma worship already prevalent at the site. Rather than being modeled on the regional *bhakti* heterodoxies circulating around Maharashtra, the Rāma worship of Ramtek was structured in terms of Brahminical orthodoxy stemming from major sites associated with Rāma such as Ayodhyā that systematized Rāma worship in the post-Gupta age of Vaiṣṇavism. The reference to Śambūka in the Lakṣmaṇa temple's inscription simultaneously depicts both Rāma's authority as king to enforce the mandates of *varṇāśramadharma* and his divinely ordained grace to send Śambūka to the abode of Murāri.[14] Though I am unable to say exactly how the Śambūka story came to be so closely associated with the hill,[15] taking all the above points into consideration, the episode certainly fits the Yādava project. And ever since the Yādavas put his name in stone at the hilltop, Śambūka has taken a central role in the lived spirituality of Ramtek to the present day.

---

13 The ambiguity in the name Murāri would have been useful in the Yādava kingdom where Kṛṣṇa worship was very much in vogue, yet the site of Ramtek was calling on a Rāma-focused stream of Vaiṣṇavism.

14 This is all in addition to the less-historically-sound fact that Ramtek Hill and its surroundings resemble the description Mount Śaivala, where Śambūka is said to be practicing his *tapas* in the *VR* (7.66.12–13); see Mirashi (1959, pp. 5–6).

15 We might hope that Hemādri's *Raghuvaṃśadarpaṇa*, a commentary on the *RaV*, might help us locate the historical connection between Śambūka and Ramtek. However, Hemādri takes a more abstractly intellectual approach to the passage. As a part of that approach, he is rather preoccupied with explaining Kālidāsa's grammar in these verses. Even more than that, and being the legal scholar he is, he is mostly interested in justifying Śambūka's death. In support of his justification, He cites the *MDh* to reiterate that it is a Śūdra's duty to serve the Brahmins (*MDh* 10.123)—that is, they should not be doing *tapas*—and death by a king's punishment leads the offender to heaven (*MDh* 8.318).

## Ramtek and the Marāṭhās

The Yādavas, under Rāmacandra, accepted suzerainty under the Delhi Sultanate at the end of the thirteenth century. Rāmacandra's successor, Śaṅkaradeva, refused to accept that position and the Sultanate overthrew the Yādavas, leaving a break in development on the Ramtek Hill until the Marāṭhās took control of the site in the eighteenth century. The Marāṭhās revitalized the Hindu imperial ethos within their borders after the intervening period of Muslim rule. This manifested in a few different ways, including sponsorship for the development of monuments, literature, and scholarship that promoted an idealized Marāṭhā worldview.[16] I would like to contextualize the specifics of the Śambūka story's expansion during the Marāṭhā period at Ramtek by first commenting on the resurfacing of *varṇāśramadharma*, with particular focus on the place of Śūdras.

Śūdra exclusion—the consistently recognized exclusion of Śūdras in the idealized ritual schematic of pre-modern India detailed in Chapter 2—underwent something of a paradigm shift around the sixteenth and seventeenth centuries. The Dharmaśāstra literature prior to this period focused, for the most part, on the ritual conduct of the twice-born *varṇas*. In this body of literature, Śūdras are, through a blanket denial of a Vedic initiation (*upanayana*), excluded from the Vedic ritual universe and, by extension, Vedic education. It was never necessary to elaborate on the ritual conduct of the Śūdra because there was nothing of a Śūdra's role in Vedic ritual worth commenting on. Eventually, however, this began to change.

In Dharmaśāstra's classical period (starting around the second century CE), Śūdras received largely indirect attention, often in contexts of instruction to twice-born *varṇas* on how to conduct themselves in the presence of a Śūdra. Around one thousand years after this classical period, the *nibandha* genre of Dharmaśāstra literature emerged.[17] These *nibandha* texts are legal digests, compilations of Dharma literature organized categorically, thus synthesizing numerous texts in a manner that could be easily referred to. The rise of the *nibandha* genre coincides with a widening and increasingly competitive sectarian religious landscape in India and the expanding scope of literature dedicated to expounding on that devotionalism, especially

16 For an account of the Marāṭhā contributions to Ramtek's architectural record, see Bakker (1989b, pp. 97ff.).

17 The intervening period in this *Dharmaśāstra* literature is characterized largely by the development of a commentarial tradition on root texts to clarify points of content and grammar. For the history and motivation behind the emergence of such a tradition, see Davis and Brick (2018).

the Purāṇas. To this end, Donald R. Davis, Jr. and David Brick observe that "*Dharma*[*śāstra*] authors used the fuller range of religious life, practice, and theology in the Purāṇas and, to a lesser extent, the epics to forge a new orthodoxy for 'Vedic' Hinduism" (2018, p. 37). Hemādri's *Caturvargacintāmaṇi*, mentioned above, is one of these digests and is representative of a larger trend in central India as this literature was enthusiastically developed in the Deccan throughout the medieval period (Vajpeyi, 2010, p. 154).

Toward the end of this period, a subset of *nibandha* literature focused specifically on the conduct of Śūdras (*śūdradharma-nibandha*) appeared as a subset of the larger corpus of *nibandha* literature. Much of this literature was produced in Vārāṇasī, though a great many of its compilers are from what is now Maharashtra.[18]

A prime example of this *śūdradharma* literature, the *Śūdrācāraśiromaṇi* (*The Jewel of Śūdra Conduct*, henceforth *ŚĀŚ*), details the proper social and ritual conduct of the Śūdra community by drawing from the legal literature as well as other sources like the epics, Upaniṣads, and Purāṇas. By way of example, the prohibition of a Śūdra's access to Vedic education is reiterated in the *ŚĀŚ*, but as a *nibandha* drawing from a wide pool of literature, it complicates the picture by offering challenges to the orthodox position of flat denial. The *Bhaviṣya Purāṇa*, for instance, understands that the Śūdra, who is meant to serve the twice-born *varṇas*, will inevitably end up hearing the Vedas. As such, the Śūdra should not be prohibited from hearing the Vedas, but he must only hear them in the company of a Brahmin (Benke, 2010, pp. 119–120). The compiler goes to considerable interpretive lengths to ensure that such a message is consistent. For example, when the *Gautama Dharmasūtra* 12.4 says that molten tin or lac is to be poured into the ears of a Śūdra who listens to Vedic recitations, it means to say that it is forbidden for a Śūdra to listen to the Vedas with the *intent* of learning it. The *ŚĀŚ* itself states that "some say that merely listening to the sound of the Vedas does not constitute a fault on the listener's part" (ibid., p. 115; Benke's translation). However, surveys of the literature in search of passages relevant to Śūdras do not always reveal such lenient attitudes. For instance, a Śūdra is still expressly forbidden from learning Sanskrit or wearing the sacred thread. The idea behind this body

18 Two major *śūdradharma-nibandha* authors, Gāgābhaṭṭa and Kamalākarabhaṭṭa, come from a family that "moved to Banaras from Paithan, in Maharashtra, in the fifteenth century. Paithan used to be a center of Brahmin learning during Yādava rule, but upon the fall of the Yādava capital of Devagiri between 1295/6 and 1325 CE, its intellectuals began to migrate north to Banaras" (Vajpeyi, 2010, p. 162). The family of Kṛṣṇa Śeṣa, author of the *Śūdrācāraśiromaṇi*, hails from the same area (Benke, 2010, pp. 36ff.).

of literature, then, is not to demonstrate an improved social standing for the Śūdras. Instead, it is meant to consolidate the various legal perspectives on a Śūdra's proper way of being.

Juxtaposing these passages from across Sanskrit literature of the period, there emerges a comprehensive and at times contradictory view of Śūdra conduct. In doing this type of work, the *śūdradharma-nibandha* literature, as I see it, fulfills two roles. The first is to make Śūdra exclusion explicit in the context of the *varṇa* system. Instead of hearing about what Śūdras can and cannot do in the context of discussions on twice-born conduct, we now get specific prescriptions of Śūdra social and ritual activity. Second, this literature reflects a Brahminical assertion of legal authority after—and, in some cases during—Muslim rule in North India.[19] Vajpeyi notes that legal scholars contributing to the *śūdradharma* genre were, in a sense, hoping to "establish the trans-temporal stability and authority of the *varṇa* theory" (2011, p. 342). For instance, the rise of the Marāṭhā ruler Shivaji during a splintering Mughal rule was built on a close engagement with *varṇa* history by Gāgābhaṭṭa, one of *śūdradharma's* prominent scholars. Aside from participating in the genre of *śūdradharma-nibandha*, Gāgābhaṭṭa is perhaps most famous for his role in the legally complex coronation of Shivaji. He was tasked with establishing a Kṣatriya lineage for the soon-to-be king, born into the Bhonsle clan, considered until then to be of the Śūdra *varṇa*, thus disqualifying him from the kingship (Vajpeyi, 2010, pp. 162–164).

It is clear from the entire genre of *śūdradharma* literature in the legal context and from the coronation of Shivaji in the political context that the place of the Śūdra in society was heavily scrutinized throughout the sixteenth and seventeenth centuries in and around Maharashtra. In such a setting, and with the rise of Shivaji and the Marāṭhā Empire, the Nagpur branch of the Bhonsle family was able to take control of and develop Ramtek, which sat relatively dormant since the Yādavas began to decline under the Delhi Sultanate at the end of the thirteenth century. The most elaborate exposition of the Śambūka story to date appeared in this environment of revitalized Hindu development and rumination on the position of Śūdras.

We saw the modest beginnings of a *māhātmya* tradition at Ramtek with the Yādava-period inscription in the Lakṣmaṇa temple, but it is during the Marāṭhā period that we get a wealth of new information about Ramtek Hill and Śambūka's place there. This new narrative occurs in the *Sindūragirimāhātmya* (*The Majesty of the Vermilion Hill*, henceforth *SGM*), which presents the story of

19 Vārāṇasī, where much of this literature was being produced, saw considerable development under the Mughals. Indeed, it would be incorrect to suggest that with Muslim rule came the complete suppression of Hindu social systems. For the specific instance of how the *Śūdrācāraśiromaṇi* fits into Akbar's Vārāṇasī, see Benke (2010, pp. 41ff.).

Śambūka (identified only as a Śūdra or by the descriptive name *dhūmrapa*, "smoke-inhaler") in three extensive chapters.[20] The first chapter of the *SGM* to deal with Śambūka is Chapter 12, which begins by describing the untimely death of the Brahmin boy. After hearing the boy's father and mother lament the loss of their son, Rāma, wondering where he went wrong, seeks the counsel of the sage Nārada. At this point, Nārada gives an explanation similar in content and tone to what we find in *VR*, though vastly abbreviated and with one noteworthy addition. After identifying the ascetic Śūdra as the cause of Ayodhyā's troubles, he addresses a Śūdra's being denied access to the Vedas (*SGM* 12.19). This is the earliest instance that I have come across mentioning the sin of reciting the Vedas in the context of the Śambūka story.[21] All earlier texts know Śambūka's crime to be practicing *tapas* alone. Even the *SGM* stops short of explicitly saying that the Śūdra in question—the one responsible for the death of the Brahmin boy—is himself reciting the Vedas, though this seems implied. Instead, the poet connects this Śūdra's illegitimate *tapas* to a more generalized Dharmaśāstric discussion of a king's duty to protect the institution of *varṇadharma*, which happens to include denying Śūdras access to Vedic learning. As for why this appears in the *SGM*'s account of the Śambūka story, it may have been expedient in the mind of the poet to reiterate the long-standing denial of a Śūdra's initiation into Vedic study in this age of heightened awareness of *śūdradharma*.[22]

---

20 The extant *SGM* is sixteen chapters, but there once existed a forty-two-chapter version, now lost. V.V. Mirashi and L.R. Kulkarni appear to have been acquainted with this longer version and refer to it (1939–1949, p. 11). The shorter text is believed to have been authored by Bābū Mairāl. He spent time in service to the Gaikwads in Baroda before returning to Ramtek at the end of his life (late-eighteenth century) to compose several texts, of which only the shorter *SGM* survives. The variations in surviving manuscripts of the text (along with the existence of a long and short version) leads Bakker to believe that Mairāl did not create the *māhātmya* himself but rather built on an existing tradition. He suggests that "there may have existed a local *māhātmya* tradition in Ramtek which produced a new up-to-date recension in sixteen *adhyāyas* when the place was flourishing once again in the Marāṭhā period" (1990, p. 76).

21 More recent authors, especially Dalit and other non-Brahmin authors of the twentieth and twenty-first centuries, frequently depict Śambūka's perceived crimes as being both his practicing *tapas* as a Śūdra and—perhaps more importantly—his subversion of *varṇadharma* by learning the Vedas as a Śūdra. See Chapters 7 and 8.

22 The passage in the *SGM* also specifies that misfortune would befall the king should a Śūdra *recite* (*paṭet*) the Vedas. The nascent *śūdradharma* literature still expressly forbids the Śūdras from reciting and, by extension, learning the Vedas. But the *SGM* says nothing about whether he hears the Vedas, which had been taken up for debate in the *śūdradharma* literature of the period.

Chapter 13 involves the search for and location of Śambūka on the Sindūra hill, where he is practicing his *tapas* by suspending himself upside-down engulfed in smoke. Since the *SGM* is part of the *māhātmya* genre, accounts of the hill are replete with elaborate descriptions of the area's beauty and appeal that continue for about twenty verses (13.26–47). Included in this are lofty descriptions of various ascetics and the toil they put themselves through on this Hill of Austerities (*tapaṃgiri*).

The execution takes place in Chapter 14, though with a unique build-up. Rāma charges the offending ascetic with violating his *varṇa*, and orders him to stop his *tapas*. When the Śūdra hears Rāma's order, he attempts to save himself by grabbing an iron rod and rushing toward Rāma. Hanumān, who is also present, attempts to intervene but the Śūdra strikes him, prompting Rāma to tell the Śūdra to ready himself (14.6–8). The Śūdra then dashes towards Rāma brandishing the iron rod, whereupon Rāma cuts his head from his body. Once killed, the Śūdra proclaims Rāma's name and issues a lengthy apology asking for Rāma's forgiveness (14.10–35). The apology consists of recounting Rāma's many exploits in life and the Śūdra's repeated request that Rāma forgive him. Afterwards, Rāma then offers to restore Śambūka's life without the need for *tapas*, an offer which he ultimately refuses, saying that being seen by Rāma in his final moments is the highest reward—a reward even *yogins* have difficulty obtaining (14.38–40). Rāma, seemingly moved by Śambūka's sentiments, insists that because of his persistence in penance, he should request a boon (14.40–45). Śambūka obliges and, in fact, asks for three boons.

The content of these boons bears some resemblance to the requests granted to the Śūdra in the *Ānanda Rāmāyaṇa* (*ĀR*). By way of reminder, he asks in the *ĀR* that he gain renown among the Śūdras. Rāma grants this by saying that he will be remembered for establishing a way for Śūdras to gain access to salvation through devotion to Rāma. As a second boon, Rāma specifies this path to salvation by declaring that this path could be found simply by repeating the name "Rāma, Rāma" as a greeting, something Śūdras would be able to do even as they are distracted with worldly matters in the Kali Yuga. The third boon is where the *ĀR* and *SGM* more explicitly align. The Śūdra asks that Rāma dwell with Sītā and Lakṣmaṇa on the mountain where this exchange is taking place, adding that devotees should first see him prior to visiting Rāma. The *SGM*, as we will now see, splits this last boon of the *ĀR* into two. The first request in the *SGM* is that Rāma remain on the hill forever:

> The Śūdra said:
> "May the Sindūra mountain never be abandoned by you, Lord.
> "May you go nowhere other than this mountain, O one of firm vow, even at the end of the world. May you not leave this mountain and go on account of the gods.

> "May you not leave here and go far away now that the Kali Age has set in. Ailments related to the gods, other beings, or oneself increase in the Kali Age here upon us. Therefore, do stay here. None of these things exist where you are yourself present.
> "You have been praised respectfully by Brahmins and their attendants for *mokṣa*, O Lord. Give to me this first boon for which I have asked." (*SGM* 14.45cd-49)

Here, in the *SGM*, the Kali Yuga appears to already have arrived. All the renderings of the Śambūka episode covered thus far (excluding those in the narrative lineage of Vimalasūri) have assumed the Yuga contemporary to this incident to be the Tretā. Even the *ĀR*, which specifies that the greeting of "Rāma, Rāma" is to be utilized by Sūdras in the Kali Yuga, understands this recommendation as preemptive. The Kali Age has not yet arrived; Śambūka is just thinking ahead. However, confused the timeline may be at this point in the text, Rāma agrees to dwell on the mountain provided that he can see to the Brahmin boy's resurrection before he returns to the hill permanently.

The Śūdra (identified as the smoke inhaler, *dhūmrapa*) then requests a second boon—which does not appear in the *ĀR*—whereby he be transformed into a *liṅga*. Rāma instantly grants this request:

> Dhūmrapa said:
> "By your grace and the touch of your hand, O Lord of the World, let this body of mine become a *liṅga* fit for worship."
> On the words of the Śūdra, Rāma touched the auspicious Dhūmrapa and, by this mere touch, his body then became a girdle and his head was born as a great *liṅga* that was famous in the three worlds. (*SGM* 14.52cd-54)

This Dhūmrapa, in his *liṅga* form, is ostensibly the same "well-known Dhūmrākṣa" mentioned in the Lakṣmaṇa temple inscription. In the inscription, Dhūmrākṣa is not identified as a *liṅga* specifically, though he is mentioned in the context of several other Śaivaite monuments. What seems more certain, however, is that this *liṅga* (at the very least conceptually, if not materially) is the same *liṅga* present on the hill and known today as Dhūmreśvara (Mirashi & Kulkarni, 1939–1949, p. 11).[23]

23 Cousens mistakenly identifies him as Dharmeśvara, which is another divine figure on the hill mentioned in v. 85 of the Yādava inscription just prior to the Śambūka reference (1971, p. 7).

The last boon that the Śūdra requests in the *SGM* rounds out the second part of the Śūdra's last boon in the *ĀR*. He asks here that when pilgrims come to see Rāma on the hill, they receive no merit unless they see Śambūka first.

> Dhūmrapa said:
> "When you remain here unwavering, O Lord of the World, people will make pilgrimages here day after day.
> "Those gods, men, and seers alike who will come and approach you first without initially seeing me, let their travels bear no fruit by [your] order. Grant me this third boon, O handsome Lord." (*SGM* 14.58–60).

Rāma grants all these boons, whereupon the Śūdra enters Vaikuṇṭha; Rāma then goes to Ayodhyā to witness the Brahmin boy's resurrection (14.61–62).

These boons form the basis of how Śambūka is now incorporated into the active religious life of Ramtek, and appear to be linked to the boons found in the *ĀR*. The similarities between the *ĀR* and *SGM* in their narrations of Rāma's killing of Śambūka are indeed striking and seem to suggest that the latter was borrowing from the former. This apparent intertextuality deserves a closer look.

It is relatively rare in the *Rāmāyaṇa* tradition that the Śūdra go unnamed throughout the Śambūka episode. Aside from the *ĀR* and the *SGM*, the Sanskrit *Adhyātma Rāmāyaṇa* and the *Rāmcaritmānas* in its appended *Lav-Kuś-kāṇḍ* are the only other texts that I have encountered that narrate the story without naming the condemned Śūdra. Most telling, however, is the commonality in the Śūdra's requests to Rāma at the moment of death—most notably, the request that Rāma ought to dwell on the mountain with Sītā and Lakṣmaṇa and the request that devotees first visit him before proceeding to see Rāma. Prior to the *SGM*, the *ĀR* is the only other text to delineate such requests.[24] The *SGM*'s borrowing from the *ĀR* is not complete, however, and seems selective on the part of its author. Although the author of the *SGM* was certainly not blindly following the *ĀR*, there is room to ask if the *ĀR* was available to him and whether he would have been inclined to call on its narrative.

Most scholars tend to date the *ĀR* to the fifteenth century (Bulke, 1999, p. 134; Yardi, 1994, p. 157; Aklujkar, 1995, p. 107), though V. Raghavan places it quite late (late-seventeenth to early-eighteenth century) during the period when the Marāṭhās had established contacts with Tanjore (1988, pp. 120–121).

24 Even after the *SGM*, literature associated with Ramtek Hill is the only context in which this particular way of telling the story appears.

Regardless of date, however, there does seem to be enough evidence (e.g., geographic references and use of certain titles) that the text was composed by a poet from Maharashtra (Raghavan, 1988, pp. 120–121; Aklujkar, 2001, p. 86). The *ĀR* also seems to have had a specific purpose—to demonstrate not only the greatness of Rāma, but the greatness of Rāma relative to Kṛṣṇa, Viṣṇu's subsequent incarnation in the Dvāpara Age.

As discussed above, Vārkarī poets, under the support of the Yādavas, drew heavily on local *māhātmya* traditions in order to "Vaiṣṇavize" local deities—Viṭṭhal being the most prominent. During this process of Vaiṣṇavization, it was most common to identify these folk gods with Kṛṣṇa, owing largely to the pastoral associations he shared with the local deities. Perhaps the most salient feature of the Vārkarī community is the tradition of massive biannual pilgrimages to Viṭṭhal's temple in Pandharpur, which continue to draw in devotees from all over Maharashtra. Cakradhar, founder of the Mahānubhāv sect and a contemporary rival to the Vārkarīs, preached against attachments to any particular holy place, person, or deity, believing that a life of asceticism and itinerancy fostered a closer connection with God. On the surface, this seems to contrast significantly with the geographical sacrality promoted within the Vārkarī tradition. Cakradhar's ideal of detachment was somewhat qualified, however, since he advised those intent on such a lifestyle to remain in Maharashtra, a place he considered to be conducive to the concentration necessary for establishing this connection with the divine.

Despite their ideological differences, then, both the Vārkarīs and Mahānubhāvs demarcate Maharashtra as a sacred space that is always in motion.[25] In the case of the former, this is done through pilgrimage and in the case of the latter, this is done through Cakradhar's travels and his vocal preference for Maharashtra as a land suitable for the asceticism his devotional movement required. Thus each sect contributed significantly to a regional consciousness in the Deccan within which people—along with their ideas, philosophies, and literature—could easily circulate. It is also important to note that, although ideologically distanced from the Vārkarī brand of devotionalism, Cakradhar did accept Kṛṣṇa as one of the five incarnations of the Supreme Parameśvara. Within the limits of this dynamic and mobile Maharashtrian religious space, Kṛṣṇa was dominant.

The *ĀR* circulated within this world, though in something of an antagonistic way. While Kṛṣṇa had captured much of Maharashtra's religious imagination, the *ĀR* promoted Rāma, Kṛṣṇa's rival *avatāra* when it comes to

---

25 For a detailed look at Maharashtra as a dynamic religious space, see Feldhaus (1986, 2006).

seeking the hearts of devotees. And it seems clear that the *ĀR* was consciously challenging the dominance of Kṛṣṇa. It did so by describing the stories of these two Vaiṣṇava *avatāras* in terms of one another, juxtaposing them and presenting arguments for their relative merit. Vidyut Aklujkar (1995) has argued that, through a process of elaborate narrative recycling, the *ĀR* is an attempt at foreshadowing, with many of the characters of the Rāma story setting up a foundation for their counterparts in the story of Viṣṇu's subsequent incarnation as Kṛṣṇa.[26] Following Aklujkar's work, I would like to draw particular attention to a fascinating debate in the *ĀR* between a Rāma devotee and a Kṛṣṇa devotee (*Rājyakāṇḍa sarga* 3) that demonstrates the *ĀR*'s favoring of the Rāma *avatāra.* In this extensive debate spanning over one hundred verses, each side argues in favor of their respective *avatāras*, both touting their own preferred *avatāra* and chastising the other. The Kṛṣṇa devotee even refers in passing to Rāma's killing of an unnamed Śūdra (*Rājyakāṇḍa* 3.60). Unfortunately for us, the Rāma devotee does not offer a direct rebuttal to this point. Instead, he simply continues by reminding his opponent that Kṛṣṇa's entire lineage was doomed from a curse, presumably that of Gāndhārī at the end of the Kurukṣetra war. Suddenly, at the end of the debate (3.107ff.), after hearing a divine voice declare that it is not possible to praise anyone more than Rāma, the Kṛṣṇa devotee submits to the Rāma devotee as human and divine spectators shower flowers down on the victor. In an apparent gesture of goodwill, the Rāma devotee confesses that he sees Kṛṣṇa and Rāma as the same. He merely prefers Rāma. It would appear then, as Aklujkar notes, that "even after admitting that both [Rāma and Kṛṣṇa] are essentially the same, the scale is tilted on the side of Rāma" (1995, p. 114).[27] So what does this have to do with Śambūka and Ramtek?

---

26 Aklujkar states that, to her knowledge, "nowhere else is the mapping of these two *avatāra*-s so elaborate and deliberate, although some earlier texts cite one or two instances of the exact correspondence between the two *avatāra*-s" (1995, p. 109). While this may be true of the Hindu-Brahminical tradition, there is a similar instance of correspondence between Rāma and Kṛṣṇa in the Jain tradition, though the situations are not exactly parallel. In the *ĀR*, the exploits of Rāma and those around him influence—and change—how the corresponding characters in the Kṛṣṇa story interact. In the Jain example, Rāma and Kṛṣṇa are both figures within the Baladeva-Vāsudeva-Prativāsudeva triumvirate. Rāma is the eighth incarnation of Baladeva while Kṛṣṇa is the ninth Vāsudeva. The exploits of these Śalākāpuruṣas repeat from incarnation to incarnation, not influencing one another but actually recreating the same set of relational circumstances.

27 Aklujkar attributes the tilting in scales largely to the relative virtue of Rāma's monogamy over Kṛṣṇa's polygamy. I do not find this to be the most salient feature of the debate. Rather, the divine intervention, the submission of the Kṛṣṇa devotee, and the consolation on the part of the Rāma devotee seem to set up a stronger power dynamic between the two interlocutors.

The author of the *SGM* seems to have had motive and opportunity to use the *ĀR* in conceiving of his rendering of the Śambūka story. As a text produced in and reflecting the social world of fifteenth-century Maharashtra, the *ĀR* provided a precedent for the *SGM*'s exaltation of Rāma and the expansion of the Śambūka story. In a region smitten by devotion to Kṛṣṇa, the *ĀR* also provided a language of debate in support of the Vaiṣṇava *avatāra* Rāma, a figure who was enshrined on Ramtek Hill. Moreover, the *ĀR*, more than any other *Rāmāyaṇa* text, provided a paradigm for Rāma worship, which could easily and most completely be integrated into the active temple life in Ramtek. This would have certainly been appealing to the author of the *SGM* when expanding on the brief reference to Śambūka inside the Lakṣmaṇa temple.

In creating a *māhātmya*, the author of the *SGM* had to address the numerous *tīrthas* inscribed on the wall of the Lakṣmaṇa temple, including Śambūka's presence there. It seems probable to me that the *SGM* expanded this brief mention of Śambūka by using Rāma's granting of boons in *ĀR* as a model for that expansion. The *SGM* does not follow the *ĀR* precisely, however. The *SGM* had to fit the story to an existing material culture, most notably Śambūka's transformation into the Śaivaite figure of Dhūmrākṣa as found in the Lakṣmaṇa temple. Hence, instead of achieving fame for establishing a path for Śūdras to attain salvation (as in the *ĀR*), he asks that he be transformed into a *liṅga* for all worshippers to visit. The author of the *SGM* thus localizes selected elements of the *ĀR*'s rendering of the story and does so in terms of Śambūka's role on the hill as etched in stone in the Lakṣmaṇa temple. By the time the *SGM* was written, Śambūka had been known on the hill for roughly five hundred years and the *ĀR*, with some careful modification, provided a way of articulating how he got there.

## Ramtek Today

The temple complex at the crest of Ramtek's prominent hill is, without question, the center of activity in town and consciously promotes devotional and historical tourism alike. An eighteenth-century fortification encloses structures dating as far back as the Vākāṭaka period, providing visitors with a survey of the hill's imperial occupants layered one on top of the other. It is important to keep in mind, however, that the range of structures and images on Ramtek Hill are not viewed with museum-like passivity. The temples are active, even those extending back to the Vākāṭaka period. The images inside them are, for the most part, still available for worship. In many cases, the original images of older temples have been replaced with more recent ones, but both Narasiṃha temples just outside the fortification still have their original Vākāṭaka-period *mūrtis*.

The Yādava-period Rāma temple at the very edge of the steep slope on the hill's far western edge is the largest draw for visitors. Rāma is, after all, the namesake for the town, whose name means "Rāma's promise."[28] Several local worshippers attest that the promise refers to Rāma's assurance to sage Agastya when he first arrived in Daṇḍaka that he would rid the area of Rākṣasas. Most would not hesitate to agree, however, that the promise simultaneously refers to Rāma's granting of a boon to Śambūka whereby Rāma promises to dwell on the hill in a mutually reverential relationship with Śambūka in his form as a *śiva-liṅga*. These two promises represent Rāma's two visits to the hill, the two moments that define Ramtek's most significant religious history. Indeed, for most of Ramtek's residents, both the perceivable history and the devotional spirit of the Ramtek region are deeply intertwined and not mutually exclusive—it is possible to explain one in terms of the other. In his Dhūmreśvara manifestation, Śambūka is very much a part of this thriving devotional atmosphere and has a large role in the mytho-history of the region. Several contributors utilize the space on and around Ramtek Hill and a variety of modes of expression to both explain Śambūka's presence on the hill and sustain an awareness of his role in the hill's devotional atmosphere.

The earliest extant mention of Śambūka in a permanent and publicly visible way is the Yādava-period inscription in the inner sanctum of the Lakṣmaṇa temple. Being marked off with plexiglass in the inner sanctum of the temple, the inscription plays a double role as a historical monument and a religious text inside a sacred space. It is hard to miss as a feature of the temple's interior. Nevertheless, it does not call much attention to Śambūka or his presence on the hill. The inscription is visibly obscured by damage and the glare reflecting off the scratched plexiglass meant to prevent further decay and damage. Aside from this, Śambūka's name is mentioned only once and it is itself buried in elaborate descriptions of the hill's other *tīrthas* and virtues, all written in Sanskrit. For present-day visitors, this early proclamation of Śambūka's association with the hill is easily passed over.

A more accentuated reminder of Śambūka's presence at Ramtek comes with a small metal sign just outside the entrance to the large Kālidāsa memorial on the hill. A noteworthy feature about this sign is the fact that it was placed there by the Śrī Dhumreśvar Mahāśivarātrī Yātrā Mahotsav Samitī, the same group responsible for organizing the Maha Shivaratri festivities in Ramtek wherein Śambūka figures prominently as the town's main object of worship for the day. From its position outside the memorial to Kālidāsa near the midpoint of the ascent up the hill, the hand-painted sign points visitors

28 The word *ṭek* is taken in this case to mean "promise." The other possibility would be that it is derived from the Hindi/Marathi word *tekaṛī*, meaning hillock.

towards the Dhūmreśvara temple and explains why they should go there. It identifies the Dhūmreśvara temple as housing a *śiva-liṅga* established by Rāma himself and that one should visit before going to see Rāma, an instruction having its origins in Śambūka's boons from the *SGM.* Just below this, a red arrow filled in with the phrase roughly translated as "this way to Dhūmreśvara's temple" points readers towards Dhūmreśvara's small, white-washed shrine just beyond the Kevala Narasiṃha Temple and a cluster of trees. Between this explicit directionality and the statement urging devotees to visit Dhūmreśvara before seeing Rāma, this sign clarifies the proper way of moving through the hill's religious environment in a way that no other public expression of Śambūka's place at Ramtek does. This sign never actually mentions the name Śambūka. He is instead only referred to as Dhūmreśvara. However, numerous other sources from around the site make Śambūka's identification with Dhūmreśvara abundantly clear.

Among these additional sources of Śambūka lore is a large green sign outside the main entrance to the temple complex, prominently visible in the midst of the bustling hilltop fort that functions simultaneously as a religious institution and tourist attraction. Maharashtra Tourism Development Corporation Ltd., a government body, placed this large, English-language signboard here to explain several structures in the area. Though the bold heading at the top of the sign reads "Ram Temple," the very first structure mentioned on the sign is the "Dhomreshwar Mahadeo temple." The text of the sign is in two paragraphs. The entire first paragraph is dedicated to the Dhūmreśvara temple while the second paragraph briefly describes some of the fortification's featured structures. The initial portion of the sign reads as follows:

> The Dhomreshwar Mahadeo temple marks Lord Ram's promise to a Shudra named Shambuka who lived in Ramtek in primeval times. The Shudra had prayed that Lord Rama abide at Ramtek forever, and that he, the Shudra, might also be worshipped there. It is believed that Lord Ram took up abode on the hill, and the Shudra turned into a *linga* over which the temple of Dhomreshwar Mahadeo was built.

The sign then goes on to describe the other structures inside the fortification, but none (even the Rāma temple itself, despite the "Ram Temple" heading on the sign) get as much attention as the Dhūmreśvara temple, which Maharashtra Tourism goes to great lengths to contextualize in largely religious terms. The rest of the signboard maintains a largely historical or otherwise mundane tone. Setting the description of the Dhūmreśvara temple off from the other structures of the site visually by giving it its own paragraph at the top of the sign and conceptually by describing it in a religious paradigm not used for other structures demonstrates Maharashtra Tourism's participation in the ongoing project of aligning Śambūka's story with the literary tradition circulating in the area and affirming the site's identification as the location of Śambūka's death. The space that the signboard dedicates to Śambūka's story agrees with the mythology of the hill, which acknowledges that Rāma promised to live there, transform Śambūka into the *liṅga* now known as Dhūmreśvara, and proclaim that Śambūka be worshipped in his own right. A noteworthy omission from the sign's account of the Śambūka story, however, is the detail that Rāma killed Śambūka. The sign instead promotes the story that Śambūka was merely praying to Rāma.

A final example of Śambūka visibility on Ramtek is a 2002 Hindi inscription etched into the wall inside the walled-off complex housing the Rāma-Sītā temple along with temples and shrines dedicated to Lakṣmaṇa and several other deities, most of whom are associated with the *Rāmāyaṇa*. The inscription describes much of Ramtek's mythology, including a description of "the glorious best of sages, Dhūmreśvara." In elaborating on the existence of Dhūmreśvara, who is openly identified as Śambūka, the inscription details the same three boons described elsewhere on the hill and in the *SGM*, but it leaves out the fact that Śambūka was a Śūdra. This is not uncommon, as several local descriptions of Śambūka's place on Ramtek Hill also avoid identifying him as a Śūdra, as will be clear from the ensuing discussion of Ramtek's locally produced temple literature. Somewhat more glaring, however, is the complete omission of any mention of Śambūka's death. The Rāma–Śambūka interaction is entirely predicated on Śambūka's impressive austerities, which lead Rāma to grant him the boons. Violation of *varṇa*, punishment, and death have nothing to do with why these two figures come together in the inscription's account of their meeting.

Both the Dhūmreśvara sign and the Maharashtra Tourism signboard advertise the Dhūmreśvara shrine explicitly—the former by directing visitors to it, the latter by contextualizing it in relation to the site's other features. The Dhūmreśvara sign is small and a bit out of the way, but the Maharashtra Tourism signboard is prominently placed in a high-traffic area, making its message more prominent. Similarly visible is the inscription inside the Rāma temple complex. This inscription takes up five marble slabs each with dimensions of about two feet by three feet. The description of Śambūka is only a small part of this, but the inscription as a whole is a visibly striking feature near the Rāma-Sītā temple, Ramtek's biggest attraction.

Visitors to Ramtek can also get information on Śambūka and his connection to the area through literature produced in Ramtek and sold in and around the temple complex. This literature is, to an extent, publicly visible—and certainly publicly available—but it differs from the signage and inscriptions just covered in that it requires people to purposefully acquire it.

Another difference between these two types of information on Śambūka is the amount of space available to present their accounts of his relationship to the area. All the publicly displayed references to Śambūka are restricted in terms of space, which, in turn, limits how detailed they can be in terms of his life and purpose on the hill. The literature describing the hill, on the other hand, has the luxury of space to ruminate on the details of Śambūka's story. Much of the information on Śambūka found in this literature is within descriptive accounts of various attractions and landmarks in Ramtek and surrounding areas. Some of these places—for example, Pench National Park and a large reservoir often used for swimming and water sports—are entirely secular in nature. Many sites of religious interest, however, are contextualized in terms of the mytho-history of the *Rāmāyaṇa*, especially Agastya's residence on the hill and Rāma's visits there. Always included among these accounts of Rāma's visit to Ramtek is the Śambūka story.

How the Śambūka story is contextualized and what details are provided in the booklets available for purchase around the hilltop varies considerably.[29] Some mention him by merely reproducing content available elsewhere in Ramtek. One booklet, for example, simply reproduces the 2002 inscription just discussed. Other booklets expand considerably on the Śambūka narrative, anchoring it firmly within the specific *Rāmāyaṇa*-based mytho-history of Ramtek. For example, at least two booklets make special mention of Hanumān's participation in the Śambūka's killing, which is also expressed in the town's sacred geography. To this day, a unique image of Hanumān wielding a bow appears at the foot of Ramtek Hill, marking the spot from where Hanumān is believed by some to have intervened in Rāma's killing of the ascetic (Figure 6.4). One booklet, *Tapobhūmī Rāmṭek Mahātmya* (*The Legend of Ramtek, Land of Asceticism*), offers the following account of Hanumān's role in the incident:

> Rām ji's servant Hanumān had the idea that the death of an ascetic by Rām's hands would be a blemish on his good name as an honorable person. That being the case, he also stealthily made his way there. The Lord gave his bow to Hanumān ji and took out his sword before heading to kill Śambūk.[30] Just before he could do it, Hanumān ji took Rām's bow in his hands, perfectly nocked an arrow, and released it towards Śambūk, striking him before Rām could swing his sword. But because of the strength of his *tapasyā*, he did not lose his life. (2014, p. 66)

---

29 My observations are based on three booklets obtained during various trips to Ramtek in 2017. They are *Maharṣi Agastya evaṃ Mahādevī Lopāmudra: Tapobhūmī Rāmṭek Mahātmya* (2014), *Tapogiri Rāmṭek Mahimā* (n.d.), and *Rāmṭek Darśan* (n.d.).

30 Śambūka's name appears as Śambhūk in this text. Because the original language is Hindi, lacking final *a* vowels, I have substituted Śambūk to maintain consistency with Hindi passages in the rest of this study.

**Figure 6.4** Hanumān *mūrti* wielding a bow at Rām Talāī.

The booklet then goes on to describe the *murti* of Hanumān connected to this incident as well as where it can be found in Ramtek.

> The place where Hanumān ji held Lord Rām's bow was a small tank. Hanumān ji took the bow and arrow, faced East, and shot the arrow towards Śambūk. Hence, an image of Hanumān was made there wherein he is holding a bow and facing east. This tank is known as a *tapobhūmī* [ascetics' area] or a *dhārmik maidān* [religious ground] and the tank is called Rām Talāī. (2014, pp. 66–67)

A similar account appears in *Tapogiri Rāmṭek Mahimā* (*The Greatness of Ramtek, Hill of Austerities*). Here, however, Hanumān merely holds the bow for Rāma.

> From a distance of three hundred meters (approximately) from Śambūk's place of *tapas*, Śrī Rām saw that he was hanging upside-down, inhaling

> smoke and absorbed in reciting Rām's name. Lord Rām said to Hanumān, "keep my bow with you, I will wake him from his meditation just by releasing an arrow." The spot where Śrī Rām and Hanumān were is known as "Rām Talāī." There is no image of Hanumān in India where he is holding a bow in his hand. Only in Ramtek is there such an image holding a bow, which Śrī Rām had given to him at the time of bestowing salvation upon Śambūk. (n.d., pp. 21–22)

Rāma, in this account, does not kill Śambūka. Rāma's intent is to disrupt Śambūka's *tapas*, not to kill him. In fact, Rāma admires Śambūka's ascetic prowess but is forced to end it because of the damage it has done to his kingdom. *Tapogiri Rāmṭek Mahimā* describes the moment of their interaction as follows:

> Lord Rām approached Śambūk and said, "Śambūk, you've undertaken severe *tapas* against the rules of the kingdom, the result of which is terrible. This is why I have released a harmless arrow to break your *tapasyā*. As the arrow struck, you were proclaiming the name Rām in a piteous voice. Just then I abandoned the form of King Rām and came to you in the form of God." (n.d., p. 22)

Aside from avoiding the issue of Śambūka's death, there is a similar avoidance in both this booklet and in *Tapobhūmī Rāmṭek Mahātmya* of the *varṇa* dimension of the story. Neither booklet mentions Śambūka's *varṇa* and *Tapogiri Rāmṭek Mahimā* goes so far as to avoid revealing the *varṇa* of the deceased boy. The author instead recounts that a citizen (*nāgarik*) brought the body of his son to Rāma (n.d., p. 21). Such redaction of the caste details of the characters involved is somewhat typical of the way the Śambūka narrative is presented around Ramtek, but the avoidance of the subject is inconsistent. Some accounts circumvent the issue, others embrace it. What remains consistent, however, is that Śambūka is the recipient of Rāma's grace, no matter the caste dynamics or degree of injury inflicted on his worldly body.

In light of all the above references to the Śambūka story, the episode of his death is well integrated into the sacred space around Ramtek Hill, and visitors have numerous opportunities to become acquainted with the reasons for Śambūka's presence in the area. Beyond the literary manifestations of the story in small booklets sold in and around the hilltop temple complex, descriptions of Śambūka are very publicly displayed in several spaces. He is even actively incorporated into the Maha Shivaratri festival each year. The story is fully embraced on the hill and the details of its contribution to the dynamism of the hill's religious atmosphere is nearly impossible to miss. But the accessibility of and openness to the Śambūka story around the hill are not to be mistaken for conditions of complete consistency in the narrative's expression, even when limiting the scope of source materials to those produced within the small town of Ramtek. Residents and visitors may have a demonstrable awareness of Śambūka's death and its circumstances, but the details of the story's narration vary from place to place, work to work, and person to person—and at times, the details vary considerably.

However fully his story is explained in a given context depends on the explanation's intent, source, timing and, in many instances, who you are as an inquirer, observer, or participant at any given moment. The precise details of Śambūka's death at Ramtek are rarely agreed upon at all times and by all tellers. Despite this fluidity, however, an important commonality endures: Śambūka is always the beneficiary of Rāma's benevolence by way of a series of boons. These boons explain Rāma's presence on the hill, Śambūka's transformation into a *liṅga*, and the benefits of visiting Śambūka on the way to seeing Rāma. His divinization into this *liṅga* form, now known by the name Dhūmreśvara, is representative of Rāma's grace, Śambūka's humble devotion to the god-king, and the immortalizing benefits of submission to him. Visitors to Ramtek Hill are encouraged to act out this submission as well by first seeking out Śambūka in his form as Dhūmreśvara, an example of submission to the worldly and divine authority of Rāma. Only then does a vision of Rāma bear the sweetest of fruits.

## Śambūka's Layered History on Ramtek Hill

As the location of the world's only temple to Śambūka, Ramtek has embraced and dramatized his story as no other place has. Through Rāma's grace, Śambūka has become an integral part of the dynamism of the hill and the daily religious experiences of residents and visitors alike. Aside from having a specialized and central role in the town's Maha Shivaratri festivities each year, he also figures into the worship protocol each day as the key to bringing about the efficacy of a visit to Rāma's temple. Even more fundamentally, Śambūka is the very reason Rāma has even taken up residence on the hilltop in the first place. With their relationship being highlighted in this way, Śambūka's death does not typically dominate accounts of his interaction with Rāma. Instead, his salvation receives the focus.

It is uniquely possible to peel back the layers of history on Ramtek to see how this once-condemned criminal came to be celebrated on the hill as an example of Rāma's benevolence. The prevailing explanation in recent years as to how and why Śambūka exists on Ramtek in the form that he does clearly derives from the *SGM*, a narrative account of Ramtek's holy places from the Marāṭhā period. This text itself localizes a telling of the Śambūka story that resembles what is found in the *ĀR* of a few centuries earlier. That incredibly rich *Rāmāyaṇa* text was most certainly known in Maharashtra, providing the author of the *SGM* with the vocabulary necessary to challenge the dominance of Kr̥ṣṇa devotion in vogue in the region since the Yādava period. Ramtek, after all, has long since reflected a Rāma-focused expression of Vaiṣṇavism stemming from the supra-regional Rāma devotion of the post-Gupta age.

Ramtek is a case study in how social trends and political ambitions intersect to animate a living tradition—a tradition that breathes, changes, and represents the socio-political concerns of the day. The site gives us enough to connect the observable and lived *Rāmāyaṇa* tradition today to the historical record left behind over the centuries. Indeed, being able to follow the *Rāmāyaṇa* tradition as it moves from antiquity to the present day is the spirit of this study as a whole. It is in this spirit that I now follow Śambūka as he takes on a new role in modernity. Up to this point in the episode's development, Śambūka has largely been a conduit for demonstrating Rāma's aptitude in simultaneously upholding *dharma* and providing all his devotees with a path towards liberation. Unsurprisingly, Śambūka is always subordinated to the primacy of Rāma, playing a supporting role as Rāma worship and devotion took shape during the first two millennia of the *Rāmāyaṇa's* life. With the nineteenth century, however, we see a drastic shift in the social undercurrents propelling Śambūka's path through the *Rāmāyaṇa* tradition. Less than one hundred years after the *SGM* was written in Maharashtra, for example, Jotirao Phule emerged in this very same region as an anti-caste activist who changed the course of identity politics surrounding what it means to be a Śūdra. His activism as well as that of many others, including Dr. B.R. Ambedkar some four or five decades later, served as a driving force that energized the non-Brahmin and other anti-caste movements of the past two centuries, and continues to mobilize caste and *varṇa* issues lurking beneath the Śambūka story today.

# Chapter 7

# THE ANTI-CASTE REVOLUTIONARY

Adjustments to the Śambūka episode covered up to this point have largely been part of a calculated reframing of this controversial moment in the *Uttarakāṇḍa* in order to protect Rāma's image. The intent had not been to empathize with Śambūka, but rather to elevate Rāma and update the circumstances of their interaction to match prevailing religious sentiments regarding Rāma and his divinity. Throughout the twentieth century, however, we see a new battleground for the details surrounding Śambūka's death. In this new context, Śambūka is the central figure, not Rāma; the protagonist, not the antagonist. One reason for the shift in focus is the fact that new contributors to the Śambūka tradition came from the same social position as Śambūka himself, and their primary purpose in calling on his narrative was to present powerful challenges to the caste system. It is necessary to keep in mind, however, that the perspectives on Śambūka—or even on how to approach the problem of caste—within these groups have never been monolithic. Anti-caste ideation has had many different expressions throughout history and figures in the twentieth century representing numerous activist groups sought to reframe the details of the Śambūka story to promulgate their specific anti-caste messaging. In formulating such messaging, some made references to a generalized, skeletal Śambūka narrative in hopes of evoking the tragedy of his death to expose long-standing casteism in Indian society. Others created entirely new works on Śambūka, digging deep into the narrative and adjusting its nuances to suit the exact type of message they were promulgating. While the precise message varied, the narrative framework within which these authors were working was often the same: Śambūka was a charismatic leader and teacher of the oppressed classes of India and he died a martyr.

In this chapter, I detail the sociopolitical background that allowed for activists to mobilize the Śambūka narrative against the caste system and I provide several examples of how such mobilization manifested. The anti-caste activism covered here operated largely in the realm of literature, which featured new ruminations on the Śambūka story coming from India's socially oppressed communities. However, given that this body of literature advocated for the abolition of caste and typically—though not always—depicted Rāma in an unfavorable light, it often encountered robust challenges from more dominant segments of India's religious and political society. Those challenges produced a lively debate over the details of the Śambūka story and thrust this debate into the public eye. Throughout the twentieth century, Śambūka appeared in dramas, impassioned speeches, and censorship battles in court, a sampling of which are covered below. First, however, understanding Śambūka's position as a figurehead of anti-caste mobilization requires an overview of the social and political setting of early twentieth-century India.

## The Politics of Caste

There is much to be said for the heterogeneity of social assertion movements spearheaded by the lower castes all around India, especially in the first few decades of the twentieth century. In setting up the specific set of circumstances in Andhra, Uma Ramaswamy places the region's anti-caste movements in the context of sweeping social changes happening throughout India by noting that "[i]n the 1920s and 1930s there was not just one social movement aimed at the uplift of the disprivileged in peninsular India, but several. To classify all of these under a blanket term stands in the way of understanding the cleavages which always existed between them" (1978, p. 291). These cleavages were extensive and even finding a blanket term is a troubling task. "Non-Brahmin" is perhaps a close approximation of the scope of these movements, but it falls short as an appropriate appellation due in large part to the contentious relationship between lower-caste Hindus and Dalits or so-called Untouchables. The former, generally speaking, fall within the *varṇa* system but are relegated to a position of social subjugation. The *varṇa* system stipulates the latter as being so ritually impure as to exclude them from that system altogether. The Dalits and lower-caste Hindus found themselves in frequent conflict as they articulated the nature of their respective struggles against caste hegemony. The two groups' movements, though sharing a decidedly non-Brahmin thrust, came to fruition under different circumstances and for different purposes. For example, non-Brahmin caste Hindus, especially in South India, sought proportional political representation in a governmental system dominated by the upper castes, while Dalit movements more frequently focused on social uplift outside the political arena (at least initially). When the two streams of "non-Brahmins" converged, it was often to the disappointment of the Dalit community, which frequently felt the two groups' shared representation as non-Brahmins was dominated by the higher non-Brahmin castes. A prominent example of the unrealized potential of these two groups' political unification was the disconnect between the Justice Party and the Adi Dravida movement.

In 1907, Iyothee Thass, "a Buddhist by conviction and a Paraiah by birth" (Geetha & Rajadurai, 1998, p. 42), started the Tamil weekly *Oru Paisa Tamizhan*. In their sweeping account of non-Brahmin movements in Tamil Nadu, V. Geetha and S.V. Rajadurai note that the journal fast became a venue to consider a number of issues pertinent to the socially marginalized "Pariah" community of the Madras Presidency, including concerns about casteism within the nationalist movement as well as the declaration of a particular Dravidian identity by recalling "the glories of a forgotten past when Tamils had lived far and wide in the subcontinent and achieved a level of culture unmatched by anything that succeeded this golden age" (1998, pp. 46–47). According to Thass, the Tamils of this period were Buddhists, the Adi Dravidas, the "original Dravidian culture."[1] For him, the decline of Buddhism and the installation of the concepts of caste and untouchability were the direct result of an Aryan invasion (ibid., pp. 91ff.). This conceptualization of origins of caste in Indian history was shared among several anti-caste movements from different parts of the subcontinent during the early twentieth century.

The anti-Brahminical sentiments of the Adi Dravidas made their movement a probable partner with the non-Brahmin movement taking shape at the time in the Madras Presidency. The non-Brahmin movement aimed at political representation through the founding of the Justice Party in 1916. This nascent political party claimed to represent the interests of all non-Brahmins within the Madras Presidency including the Dalits, who had up to this point been focused primarily on acquiring social concessions in education and public service rather than political representation (Geetha & Rajadurai, 1998, p. 175). Influential Adi Dravida leaders like M.C. Rajah thus welcomed this path towards political representation offered by the Justice Party, which won a major electoral victory for the Madras Legislative Council in 1920 thanks, in part, to a Congress boycott of the elections (Ram, 1974, p. 219; Basu, 2011, p. 18). However, regardless of this electoral success and despite their common ground as non-Brahmins, the relationship between the non-Brahmin caste Hindus and the various Dalit groups within the Justice Party was always tense due to the social stigmas associated with the two groups' interaction.

Related to this, representation of Dalits within the Justice Party was always an issue of significant contention largely because, as Mohan Ram offers in his account of E.V. Ramasami's involvement in Tamil Nadu social movements, the Party "drew its leadership from the elite of the various contiguous linguistic regions…

1 Iyothee Thass is also responsible for the push for Dalits to register as casteless Dravidians in the 1891 census, the same year he founded the Dravida Mahajana Sabha (Teltumbde, 2017, p. 57).

that comprised the sprawling [Madras] Presidency" (1974, p. 219) and the voice of the Dalits within the party was frequently stifled due to underrepresentation. These tensions ignited into caste-based violence during the Buckingham and Carnatic Mills Strike in 1921, when the lower-caste Hindus attacked the Adi Dravidas who willingly returned to work first (Geetha & Rajadurai, 1998, pp. 181ff.; Patankar & Omvedt, 1979, p. 420). The trust between the two groups was irreparably damaged, leading to M.C. Rajah and several other Adi Dravidas leaving the party and pursuing their own political ambitions represented by groups like the Adi Dravida Mahajana Sabha (The Great People's Assembly of the Original Dravidians).

North Indian Dalit communities experienced similar disillusionment with Hindu reform movements like the Arya Samaj. Within the Samaj, caste Hindus worked towards establishing equal access to Hinduism's tenets regardless of caste—an outwardly noble cause. However, such inclusion involved attempts to bring Dalits into the Hindu fold through purification committees called "Shuddhi Sabhas" aimed at preventing their conversion into other religions. A prominent example of Dalit disillusionment with the Arya Samaj is well exemplified with the formation of the Adi Hindu movement, founded by Swami Achhutanand in 1920s-United Provinces. In a near parallel experience to the Madras Presidency's Adi movements' relationship to the Justice Party, the Adi Hindu movement was formed out of frustration with the failures of the Arya Samaj's method of reform. In the North and South alike, the inability to fully abandon caste hierarchies accounts for the miscalculations in the Arya Samaj's and Justice Party's efforts to represent—either politically or religiously—the interests of the Dalit communities they had hoped to embrace. Another key parallel is the Adi Hindu movement's claim to the glories of a prosperous pre-Aryan civilization to aid in identity formation among their Dalit constituents. As was the case with the Adi Dravidas in the South, the Adi Hindu movement in the North established an identity for its followers as descendants of India's original inhabitants in order to circumvent the group's unwanted ties to the Hindu religion.

Ultimately, both the non-Brahmin movements in the South and the Hindu reform movements in the North failed to maintain the Dalits' enthusiasm because of vested interests among the more socially dominant communities within those movements. However, despite their disagreements on an ideological front, the two groups—the Dalits and other non-Brahmins—found the Śambūka story to have considerable propagandizing potential. The episode helped these movements' leaders articulate the scope of systemic subjugation by the upper *varṇas* by placing Śambūka in a position of authority among India's oppressed and transforming him into a martyr. The historical paradigm around which such an image of Śambūka developed was the Aryan invasion theory.

In the 1840s and 1850s, Orientalist philologists undertook extensive explorations into the alleged "Aryan race," which, as Joan Leopold notes in her account of such explorations, "maintained that the speakers of Indo-European languages in India, Persia, and Europe were of the same culture and race, descendants of one primitive tribe of proto-Indo-European speakers which had lived north of the Hindu Kush and dispersed after 2000 BC to the south and west to conquer and colonize. This people had called itself 'arya' or noble in the Rigveda and Avesta" (1970, p. 271). Friedrich Max Müller, one of these scholars, "used the theory to praise the literature and philosophy of ancient India, to emphasize 'the common descent and... legitimate relationship between Hindu, Greek, and Teuton' and the blood tie between the Englishman and Bengali, and to reveal the providential nature of British rule in India" (ibid., p. 272).[2] Indian intellectuals and reformers employed the terms "Arya" and "Aryan" to define what was best about Hindu tradition. By extension, however, this excluded the Śūdras—those not from twice-born *varṇas*—from representing Aryan values. Rosalind O'Hanlon observes that such a conception of Hinduism's value system was quickly challenged by the lower castes, most notably by Jotirao Phule, who "turned this interpretation of the Aryan past upside-down" (1985, p. 149). For Phule, O'Hanlon notes, "[t]he 'golden age' of India had been the pre-Aryan realm of *Kshatriyas*, under the benign rule of King Bali. The most important values of this society were those of the warrior and the peaceful landholder and cultivator" (ibid., p. 149) represented by the Śūdras and the Atiśūdras, the latter of which includes groups from what are now termed India's Dalit and tribal populations.

Phule's reconfiguration of the past of India's oppressed classes invigorated low-caste identity formation in numerous regions of India as the country moved towards Independence. In the face of increasing nationalist discourse, the lower castes feared that an independent India would bring nothing more than upper-caste dominance in all areas of social and political life, simply replacing colonial oppressors with Brahminical ones (Murthy, 2016, p. 241; Basu, 2011, p. 12; Jaffrelot, 2005, p. 202). Widespread non-Brahmin and Dalit movements at the turn of the twentieth century used the theory of an Aryan invasion as a means of fostering self-respect and political mobilization that led to nearly as many iterations of this pre-Aryan past as there were movements staking a claim to it.

The Aryan invasion theory as a means of challenging upper-caste overrepresentation in an increasingly self-governing India found its earliest expression in the Madras Presidency. In his study of the Ad Dharm movement

---

2 Leopold quotes from Friedrich Max Müller (1854, p. 129) and (1861, pp. 214–215).

in Punjab, Mark Juergensmeyer briefly touches on some Dalit assertion movements' common claims about pre-Aryan civilization in India by noting that "[t]he Adi Dravida movement [of the Madras Presidency] seems to have been the first to formulate the concept that the Scheduled Castes were the original inhabitants of India, and from there, apparently, the idea spread north and lent its name to the Ad Dharm movement in the Punjab and the Adi Hindu movement in what is now Uttar Pradesh" (1982, p. 24). These circumstances of the Scheduled Castes' claim to aboriginal status within India noted by Juergensmeyer are built upon an account of early Indian history rooted in Orientalist scholarship from the nineteenth century.[3] Such theorizing ultimately became an extremely important factor in low-caste identity formation throughout India, and accounts of the Śambūka episode likewise came to incorporate the thematics of the Aryan invasion.

In the pages that follow, I cover the contributions of six anti-caste activists who incorporated the Śambūka story into their work in one form or another. First is the Andhra playwright Tripuraneni Ramaswami Chaudari, who composed a drama centered around a drastically transformed Śambūka narrative that he framed with contemporary theorizing about an Aryan invasion that took place millennia ago. This new scaffolding for the Śambūka episode was subsequently utilized by several other dramatists of subsequent years from various regions of the subcontinent. Two such dramatists were Swami Achhutanand and Santram B.A., whose plays are also covered in the coming pages. Both maintain the same overall spirit of the Śambūka narrative utilized by Ramaswami Chaudari, but adjust it to better suit the nuances of their own anti-caste movements. Santram, for his part, borrows this narrative frame while simultaneously abandoning the Aryan invasion theme, setting it far apart from works that utilize this new historical paradigm for imagining Śambūka's history. Santram also had an indirect role in the creation of one of India's most consequential anti-caste texts, *Annihilation of Caste*, written by Dr. B.R. Ambedkar, the fourth anti-caste activist covered below. It was Santram's group, the Jat-Pat Todak Mandal (Society for the Demolition of Caste), that invited Ambedkar to speak at their annual convention on the subject of caste and subsequently disinvited him when the two parties could not agree on the precise content of Ambedkar's speech,

3 The term Scheduled Caste (or SC) is a governmental term used to classify a particular segment of India's socially disadvantaged population. Though not always the case, SCs are often Dalit groups. Other governmental terms for the various disadvangated communities in India include the Other Backward Classes (OBCs, often non-Brahmin groups, including Śūdras, though there are numerous execptions) and Scheduled Tribes (STs), India's tribal populations.

which the latter then published as a book. Finally, I cover the connections between anti-caste leaders Periyar E.V. Ramasami and Periyar Lalai Singh—the former from Tamil Nadu, the latter from Uttar Pradesh—and a series of censorship attempts and court battles in Uttar Pradesh surrounding the literary activities of Lalai Singh that had connections to both E.V. Ramasami and B.R. Ambedkar.

Accounts of Śambūka's life and death underwent a tectonic shift in the twentieth century as the control over his narrative fell into the hands of India's anti-caste activists. All the instances of anti-caste assertion covered in this chapter—instances that represent a much grander scope of anti-caste activity in India happening at the time—demonstrate the ever-widening scope of the Śambūka tradition as his story became a means of expressing Dalit and non-Brahmin social and political discontent.

## Tripuraneni Ramaswami Chaudari's *Śambuka Vadha*

As a prominent non-Brahmin leader from Andhra, Tripuraneni Ramaswami Chaudari (1887–1943) promoted the non-Brahmin movement in coastal districts of the Madras Presidency and used Hinduism's own texts—which he saw as the root cause of Brahmin supremacy—to destabilize what Uma Ramaswamy describes as the "deifying attitude of the common man towards the Brahmin" (1978, p. 293).[4] Ramaswami Chaudari made the *Rāmāyaṇa* work for him in this way when he wrote *Śambūk Vadha* (*Killing Śambūka*) in 1920. Following the strong currents of the Aryan invasion theory circulating in Dalit and non-Brahmin communities, Ramaswami Chaudari structured his vision of the Śambūka episode around the struggle between antagonistic Aryans and victimized Dravidians. In his application of the Aryan invasion, however, he parts from Iyothee Thass' formulation of the original Dravidians being specifically Buddhist. Velcheru Narayana Rao points out that, according to Ramaswami Chaudari's Dravidian anthropology, there was an extant hierarchy among South Indian (i.e., Dravidian) castes prior to an Aryan invasion wherein the landed castes in Andhra like the Kammas, the Reddis, and the Velamas (all analogous to the Aryan Kṣatriyas) were at the top and the priestly castes like Golla, Palli, and Kummaris (all analogous to the Aryan Brahmins) were subordinate to them. When the Aryans invaded, they placed their own priests in the dominant position and relegated the formerly royal warrior castes like the Kammas and Reddis to the Śūdra *varṇa* in the foreign Aryan social hierarchy known as the *cāturvarṇya* (Narayana Rao, 2001, p. 176).

4 See also Narayana Rao (2001, p. 173ff.).

In Ramaswami Chaudari's broader conception of the *Rāmāyaṇa*, the Aryans under the leadership of Rāma are the enemies of the Dravidians, who had Rāvaṇa as their king.[5]

*Śambuka Vadha* depicts Śambūka as a Dravidian, a race of aboriginal Indians vanquished by the Aryans. Śambūka acquires identification as a Śūdra only in this Aryan-dominated context. By practicing his austerities as a Dravidian, Śambūka is threatening the authority of the Aryans and Rāma's Brahmin ministers concoct a conspiracy to have him killed. These details already separate Ramaswami Chaudari's framing of the Śambūka story from any account already covered in this study, but some of his most influential innovations come with the specific character traits of Śambūka himself and Rāma's role in his death.

For Ramaswami Chaudari, Śambūka was a revolutionary who dedicated his efforts toward organizing the Dravidians under a unified goal of asserting their equal access to Vedic systems of asceticism. In *Śambūka Vadha*, Vasiṣṭha, a royal sage in the court of Ayodhyā, informs Rāma that Śambūka is soon to establish a hermitage near Ayodhyā that would provide a space for non-Brahmins to preach against the Smṛtis and insist that the Śūdras are equal to the Aryans. Śambūka's followers are then to take his message from town to town. Rāma hesitates to deliver any sort of punishment to Śambūka without proof of his guilt. He even engages in a scholarly debate with Śambūka structured around the Vedas on Śambūka's request. Rāma is impressed with Śambūka's depth of knowledge and the two part on good terms with Rāma even granting Śambūka permission to continue with his austerities. He also defers to Śambūka's knowledge of the Vedas on matters of a Śūdra's right to practice penance and gives Śambūka his word that he will not kill him. When Rāma returns to Ayodhyā, Vasiṣṭha prods Rāma into beheading the Śūdra ascetic by convincing him that his leniency towards Śambūka would weaken the Brahmin-Kṣatriya governance over the Dravidians, leading, in turn, to the demise of the Brahmins and Kṣatriyas alike. As king, Rāma reluctantly agrees to carry out the sentence and kills Śambūka, who attains heaven in a flash of light.[6]

5 Tripuraneni Ramaswamy had more than one work on the *Rāmāyaṇa*. In 1924, he wrote *Sūta Purāṇamu*, a major work that outlines a clear and antagonistic Aryan-Dravidian divide between the two major sides of the *Rāmāyaṇa* (Narayana Rao, 2001, pp. 173–177).

6 For more on the plot and circumstances of *Śambuka Vadha*'s composition, see Narayana Rao (2001, pp. 159–162) and Ranganayakamma (2004).

Throughout *Śambuka Vadha*, Ramaswami Chaudari attempts to demonstrate that the culpability for Śambūka's death rests with the Brahmins, not with Rāma.[7] He finds space in the story to provide audiences with an account of happenings behind the scenes of the more orthodox tellings of the *Rāmāyaṇa*. In addition to venerating Śambūka, he uses that space to criminalize the Brahmins, highlight their obsession with maintaining the *cāturvarṇya*, and create a Brahminical conspiracy that uses the military mechanisms of the state to crush Śambūka's revolution. Rāma's hesitation in killing Śambūka is an important factor in demonizing the Brahmins, as it shows their blatant antagonism as puppeteers manipulating Rāma, who is otherwise compassionate and reasonable. Rāma's struggle is well-illustrated in the following statement: "O my right hand! To you—who sent a fully pregnant royal woman to [the] forests mercilessly...—will it be difficult to take a life of a man even though he is a great sage? Will you be sympathetic?" (Ranganayakamma, 2004, p. 743), a clear reprise of Rāma's conflicted state of mind as depicted in Bhavabhūti's *Uttararāmacarita* (see Chapter 4).

Ramaswami Chaudari's revisionist drama is a clear example of his strategy to use Brahminical texts (the *Rāmāyaṇa* in this case) to criticize Brahmins. His own experiences as a non-Brahmin provided him with some resonant insights into the *varṇa*-based overtones present in the story, but those insights require some qualification.[8] Ramaswami Chaudari's own conception of pre-Aryan South Indian society had its own system of rank wherein his caste, the Kammas, was in a dominant position. He accepted the pre-Aryan pseudo-*varṇa* ranking and identified the Kammas as being part of what would now be considered the Kṣatriya *varṇa* (Ramaswamy, 1978, p. 295). The paradox of a non-Brahmin leader appropriating the *varṇa* system as a means of promoting social progress while simultaneously resisting the caste system was symptomatic of the larger trends of the higher-caste non-Brahmins embracing their status to lay claim to much of the non-Brahmin movement's leadership, as I noted earlier with respect to the Justice Party. Noting the specific case of Andhra, Uma Ramaswamy affirms that "[t]he [non-Brahmin] movement was from the beginning dominated by the upper non-Brahmins: Kammas, Reddis, and Velamas" (1978, p. 296).

---

7 Ranganayakamma draws consistent attention to this point and criticizes Ramaswamy Chaudari for trying to mold Rāma into a virtuous character who sympathizes with Śambūka. She finds him to be hypocritical in trying to develop this character of Rāma while simultaneously depicting him as murdering Śambūka on the order of Brahmins (2004, pp. 738ff.).

8 For some examples of Tripuraneni Ramaswamy Chaudari's experiences as a non-Brahmin, see Ramaswamy (1978, p. 292) and Rao (1988, pp. 23–24).

I consider Ramaswami Chaudari's perceptions of himself and the make-up of the non-Brahmin movement to be important when considering the motivations behind creating a work like *Śambuka Vadha*. A prominent Kamma leader within the non-Brahmin movement writing a drama like *Śambuka Vadha* seems to reflect non-Brahmin leaders' ambitions of attracting the lower castes into their movement by establishing a common Dravidian origin for themselves and the Dalit communities that was distinct from the overbearing Aryan castes. There is a clear push in the drama towards emphasizing equality among castes by attempting to reveal a double standard: that austerities and learning are pious actions when undertaken by Brahmins but sinful actions when pursued by Śūdras. Śambūka's revolutionary portrayal as a Dravidian leader also provides the broadest scope for non-Brahmins with a protagonist who is emblematic of their ideals.

The propagandizing potential of *Śambuka Vadha* is further strengthened by Ramaswami Chaudari's resistance to turning Rāma—a widely venerated figure—into a villain and his emphasis on the Dravidians' status as cultivators of a flourishing pre-Aryan civilization, a theme that had been circulating in the Madras Presidency among the Adi Dravidas since at least the early twentieth century. *Śambuka Vadha*'s ability to speak to the lower-caste non-Brahmins without alienating those who were still drawn to Rāma's divinity imbued Ramaswami Chaudari's work with the ability to reach a broad audience in an effort to attract them to the Non-Brahmin movement. Whether any of this potential was actually realized is another matter. The non-Brahmin-Dalit coalitions in the Madras Presidency were consistently impeded by caste prejudices and opportunistic alliances that best suited the aims of their respective movements.[9]

Whatever the case may be regarding *Śambuka Vadha*'s efficacy in non-Brahmin politics of the Madras Presidency, the themes present in the drama do appear in anti-caste movements of the North, where Śambūka continued to be framed as an advocate for pre-Aryan prosperity, especially in the United Provinces (later Uttar Pradesh). Authors engaging with the Śambūka episode as a means of anti-caste protest seem transpose the most expedient details from drama to drama to allow the Śambūka story to fit the exact ideological specifications of

9 The range of non-Brahmin and Dalit movements in the Madras Presidency were characterized by shifting allegiances depending on what was most beneficial to their specific goals. This is especially so in the case of the Adi Dravida and Adi Andhra movements, which would align with Hindu reform movements or nationalist movements so long as they could lend their influence in service of the ambitions of the Adi communities. For the case in Tamil Nadu, see Basu (2011); for the case in Andhra, see Murthy (2016).

their movement. These changes in details adhere to a consistent schematic of the story wherein Śambūka is the main protagonist and vocal representative of anti-caste ideology. It is noteworthy that this schematic is identifiable despite variance in region, language, or even religion. Śambūka's transferability in such circumstances is well-represented in two examples from North Indian anti-caste and Hindu reform movements: the Adi Hindu movement and the Jat-Pat Todak Mandal.

## *Comparing Śambūka's Crimes: Swami Achhutanand's* **Rām-Rājya-Nyāy** *and Santram B.A.'s* **Niraparādh kī Hatyā**

The narrative frame implemented by Tripuraneni Ramaswami Chaudari was reproduced in texts from many different areas of India and served as a vehicle for numerous distinct philosophies within anti-caste movements. Even when the authors' philosophies differed rather significantly, the nuances of this iteration of the Śambūka story were malleable enough that they could suit the needs of whatever position was being put forth. I will explore here two dramatic portrayals of the story that closely resemble each other and the narrative put forward by Ramaswami Chaudari. The two dramas I will cover here—Swami Achhutanand's *Rām-Rājya-Nyāy* (*Justice During the Reign of Rām*) and Santram B.A.'s *Niraparādh kī Hatyā* (*The Killing of an Innocent*)—are nearly identical in their narrative progression, vocabulary, and general thematic material. Their differences lie in their philosophical orientations. Achhutanand founded Adi Hinduism, a Dalit assertion movement based in the United Provinces (today's Uttar Pradesh), while Santram B.A.'s anti-caste ideals are marked by the influence of the Arya Samaj, a group within which Achhutanand was also highly active before breaking free and starting his own movement. Their texts reflect the philosophies of their respective movements and a close look at them side-by-side reveals how Śambūka's death was used to illustrate different expressions of anti-casteism. A glimpse into their authors' lives as activists contextualizes their respective portrayals of Śambūka and the anti-caste messaging he is meant to embody.

Santram B.A. (1887–1988) belonged to the Kumhar caste of potters, a class of Śūdras (Gupta, 2017, p. 21).[10] His experiences in the lower ranks of Hinduism's caste hierarchy fueled his attraction to the caste-inclusive policies

10 Juergensmeyer refers to him generally as belonging to a Scheduled Caste (SC), which could be true as the Kumhars are classed as either an Other Backwards Class (OBC) or SC depending on region (1982, p. 38). Gupta never specifies his official status as either an OBC or SC, instead relying on the *varṇa* category of "Śūdra."

of the Arya Samaj, a reform movement within Hinduism founded in 1875 by Dayanand Saraswati and an organization in which he was active for several years. Santram saw the Samaj's limitations, particularly when it came to caste, but he wanted to see Hindu reform policies succeed and strengthen the religion's image among the lower castes. Santram sought the full eradication of the caste system and he encouraged the Samaj to follow suit, which was the impetus for him to found the Jat-Pat Todak Mandal (Society for the Demolition of Caste, henceforth JPTM) in 1922 as an organization within the Samaj. In her account of Santram's life and work, Charu Gupta notes that JPTM's "first priorities were to break the birth-based caste system and to promote intercaste marriages" (2017, p. 26) in an effort to dilute the system's social efficacy. The Arya Samaj may have been inclusive of all castes, but—to the frustration of many of the group's lower-caste members—it still maintained caste as a feature of its reformist Hinduism. Santram's commitment to eradicating caste was thus met with considerable resistance from the group (ibid., p. 28). The tensions between the Samaj and his own JPTM reached a breaking point in 1924, ultimately leading Santram to dissociate from the Samaj (Juergensmeyer, 1982, pp. 38–39), though he still continued to draw inspiration from the organization, using its language selectively to suit his purposes (Gupta, 2017, pp. 29–30, 39). He still believed in reforming Hinduism and would continue to do so as a Hindu, but a Hindu outside the Arya Samaj. Indeed, Gupta suggests that "Santram could never bring himself to move away from a Hindu paradigm and often enacted a language of caste respectability with ambiguous implications" (2017, p. 29). This ambiguity continued to affect the JPTM after it separated from the Arya Samaj, as will become clear with respect to the JPTM's role in Ambedkar's famous *Annihilation of Caste* and Santram's own *Niraparādh kī Hatyā*, both discussed in detail below.

Swami Achhutanand "Harihar" (1879–1933) was an anti-caste activist and literary figure working in the United Provinces (U.P.) during the early years of the twentieth century. He was educated in the military's cantonment school in Devali, U.P. on account of his father's employment there. Later, he began associating with mendicant saints who stressed an adherence to *bhakti*, which would later become a major component of his Adi Hindu philosophy.[11] His experiences with the Arya Samaj, though rife with contention, also proved invaluable to the trajectory of his activism and the formation of his religious and social ideals.

A primary focus for the Arya Samaj was to revitalize Hinduism on a platform of reform and inclusiveness encouraging equal access to Vedic and other Aryan

11 For details of Achhutanand's early life and education, see Hunt (2017, pp. 34–35) and Narayan & Mishra (2004, pp. 17–18).

literatures among all castes (Hunt, 2017, p. 37; Van der Veer, 1994, pp. 65–66). Unlike many other reformist groups, the Arya Samaj encouraged the lower castes and Dalits to participate within its functions and the mission statement of caste equality within the Arya Samaj was promising. In addition to providing a network of schools spanning the primary, secondary, and college levels, the aims of the organization promoted an unprecedented access to Hindu institutions by translating the Vedas into vernacular languages and de-ritualizing Hindu ceremonies (Juergensmeyer, 1982, p. 38). What became clear, however, was that despite the emphasis on equality of caste, caste was still maintained as a palpable and active structure within the Samaj's expression of Hinduism. The imprint of caste is typified especially by the Arya Samaj's Shuddhi Sabhas (Purification Committees), which were campaigns meant to purify people from any number of "impure" or non-Hindu communities—including Dalits, Muslims, and others—in order to bring them into the Hindu fold; Achhutanand was himself involved in these campaigns from 1905 to 1912 (Teltumbde, 2017, p. 59; Hunt, 2017, pp. 37, 75 n. 19). His participation ultimately led to his parting ways with the Samaj, feeling that the organization was nothing more than the upper castes' disingenuous use of the lower-caste population to save Brahminism by preventing conversions to Christianity or Islam (Jigyasu, 2004, pp. 105ff.).

Achhutanand's disillusionment led him to champion his Adi Hindu movement, which gained significant traction by the 1920s thanks to his tireless efforts to promote it through his own publications and journals (Narayan & Mishra, 2004, pp. 17–19).[12] Also key to Adi Hinduism's initial success was his presentation of seventeen demands to the Prince of Wales in 1922 in front of over ten thousand Dalits (Teltumbde, 2017, p. 60).[13] This strategy of appealing to the British government is another noteworthy commonality shared between the northern and southern Non-Brahmin assertion movements.[14]

12 Though the 1920s saw Adi Hinduism's first real momentum, Achhutanand's efforts in formulating his Adi Hindu movement extend back to 1917 when he started expressing the movement's philosophies through poetry (Jaffrelot, 2005, pp. 201ff.).

13 Gandhi had boycotted this visit by the Prince of Wales as part of his non-cooperation movement. Achhutanand's presentation to the Prince, then, stood to counter Gandhi's nationalist efforts as a representative of Congress, whom Achhutanand saw as a twice-born interest group as foreign to India as the British. Indeed, "[Achhutanand] argued that the Untouchables should not oppose the British; on the contrary, the colonial era was an opportune time for demanding their basic rights" (Jaffrelot, 2005, p. 202).

14 A near parallel to the Prince of Wales' visit to India can be found in the 1917 visit to Madras by Viceroy Lord Chelmsford and Secretary of State Edwin Montagu. Non-Brahmin communities raised their concerns, especially as they related to political representation, which helped formulate the Montagu-Chelmsford Reforms (Basu, 2011, pp. 13ff.).

Sarah Beth Hunt observes in her meticulous account of Hindi Dalit literature that the Adi Hindu movement adopted the Aryan invasion theory to suggest that "the so-called 'untouchables' had once ruled over a thriving civilisation; however, this 'golden age' in Indian history came to an end when invading Aryans overpowered the peace-loving Adi Hindus and oppressed them by imposing Brahmanical Hinduism and, with it, the hierarchical system of caste" (2017, p. 32). Adi Hinduism's tenets this way share considerable commonality with the views of Phule. Hunt also clarifies that these explorations into a pre-Aryan past are not the only manifestation of Phule's impact on Achhutanand. She explains that "Achhutanand seems to have been influenced not only by [the Aryan invasion theory] but also by Phule's use of drama as a means of spreading his message" (2017, p. 33). I would like to add to this by suggesting that he was also heavily influenced by Jotirao and Savitribai Phule's educational campaigns with the Satyashodhak Samaj (Society of Truth-Seekers), which Jotirao founded in 1873. Commenting on this particular aspect of the Phules' activism, Gail Omvedt offers that "[t]he effects of the Satyashodhak 'awakening'...were to generate a wide range of educational and economic mobilization among the non-Brahman communities throughout Maharashtra" (2011, p. 179), though its influence was certainly not limited to this central Indian state. All of these characteristics—assertion of a pre-Aryan golden age in India, use of drama as a vehicle for propagating ideas, and emphasis on educating the lower castes—form the basis of Swami Achhutanand's Hindi drama *Rām-Rājya-Nyāy (Nāṭak): Śambūk-Muni-Balidān (Justice During the Reign of Rām (A Drama): The Sacrifice of Sage Śambūk*, henceforth *Rām-Rājya-Nyāy*), originally written in 1931.[15] I have discussed this play and its influence on Śambūka narratives in and around U.P. elsewhere (Sherraden, 2021), but a few details are worth reiterating here to set up the comparison with Santram B.A.'s *Niraparādh kī Hatyā*.

*Rām-Rājya-Nyāy* functions as a conduit for expounding the principles of Adi Hinduism through the easily understood and dynamic medium of drama. Its characters represent differing perspectives and levels of understanding on various subjects including caste, authority, and religion. The Aryan invasion theory provides the framework for the way the *Rāmāyaṇa* story is presented, thus placing Śambūka—representing India's aboriginal population—in the role of the protagonist and Rāma—representing the Aryans—in an antagonistic role. Śambūka is an enlightened leader and teacher among the aboriginal communities oppressed under Aryan rule and Rāma has been dispatched by the Brahmins to silence him, lest there be an uprising against their social and

15 I take this dating of *Rām-Rājya-Nyāy* from Swaroop Chandra Bauddh's introduction to the Samyak Prakashan edition of the play (2006, p. 27). Hunt estimates its composition as occurring somewhere between the late 1920s and early 1930s (2017, p. 97).

political authority. The play is rather short, consisting of a single act of five scenes plus a prologue. However, even in this short span, it contains a great deal of information about Adi Hinduism. Its structure, though, is not unique. A later play composed by Santram B.A. entitled *Niraparādh kī Hatyā* (*The Killing of an Innocent*) unfolds almost identically as *Rām-Rājya-Nyāy*.

Santram's *Niraparādh kī Hatyā* appears as the seventh chapter of his 1949 book, *Hamārā Samāj* (*Our Society*). The book is a critical look at Hinduism, authority, and the origins of caste, with particular focus on the position of Śūdras. In fact, the chapter immediately preceding *Niraparādh kī Hatyā* is called *Varṇ-Vyavasthā meṃ Śūdroṃ kī Sthiti* (*The Position of Śūdras within the Varṇa System*). In it, Santram takes a critical look at several citations from the *MDh*, various *Dharmasūtra*s and other Smṛti texts, and the *Śatapatha Brāhmaṇa* that are especially detrimental to the social well-being of Śūdras. He ends the discussion with a look at the *Rāmāyaṇa*. After giving an account of the Śambūka episode as it appears in the *VR* (though taking some introspective and creative liberties), Santram concludes the chapter by saying,

> I do not know whether Śambūk's killing is an historical event or mere fiction. If Rām really did kill the Śūdrarāj Śambūk because he was worshipping God as a Śūdra, then it is difficult to imagine a greater injustice and atrocity than this. Shri Dwijendralal Ray and Shri Jogesh Chandra Chowdhury of Bengal have each described this incident in a very heartfelt way in their plays entitled *Sītā*. (1949, p. 57)

The reasoning behind the reference to the two Bengali plays becomes clear when one notices that at the end of Chapter Seven (i.e., *Niraparādh kī Hatyā*), Santram acknowledges the material comprising the chapter to be from Radha Mohan Kavyatirth's Hindi translation of Jogesh Chandra Chaudhuri's *Sītā*, originally written in Bengali in 1924.[16] Sushil Kumar Mukherjee notes the volatility of the question of untouchability at the time of the play's composition and states that "[i]n *Seeta* this problem was highlighted through the Sambuka episode" (1982, p. 441). For the purposes of this book, I will be concerned only with the play as it appears in *Hamārā Samāj* and will use the title *Niraparādh kī Hatyā* whenever referring to the material found in Chapter Seven of Santram's book.[17]

16 The play was premiered on August 6, 1924 at the Natyyamandir under the direction of Sisir Kumar Bhaduri. He had Jogesh Chandra Chaudhuri write the play "since he could not get D.L. Roy's [i.e., Dwijendralal Ray, see above] *Seeta*, the copyright of which Art Theatre had already acquired" (Mukherjee, 1982, p. 187; see also p. 650).

17 This chapter was isolated and released as a separate work with the title *Niraparādh kī Hatyā* in 2016 by the New Delhi publishing house Samyak Prakashan.

The plot structure of *Niraparādh kī Hatyā* progresses precisely as it does in *Rām-Rājya-Nyāy*,[18] though it is shorter than Achhutanand's play (three scenes instead of five). The former also does not include a prologue or any songs as does the latter. Other than that, the plays are so strikingly similar, it is more productive to describe how they depart from each other than catalog their similarities. The two plays even share entire dialogues with only trivial changes to language.

In its brevity, *Niraparādh kī Hatyā* loses a few dimensions of plot development emphasized in *Rām-Rājya-Nyāy*. Two of these are particularly noteworthy. First, Rāma does not exhibit a paranoia over the welfare of the Brahmins in *Niraparādh kī Hatyā* as he does in *Rām-Rājya-Nyāy*. Second, Rāma does not defend Śambūka when Vasiṣṭha explains his culpability in the Brahmin boy's death. Hence, Rāma is much more complicit within the *cāturvarṇya* system and the flow of influence from Brahmin to Kṣatriya is never questioned in *Niraparādh kī Hatyā*. The most telling differences between the two works, however, come with the delineation of their respective philosophies. Where Achhutanand focused on the Adi Hindu philosophies he championed in *Rām-Rājya-Nyāy*, *Niraparādh kī Hatyā* is centered around the right to Vedic ritual and sacrifice, demonstrating Santram's somewhat more sustained, albeit contentious, relationship with the Arya Samaj and his commitment to inclusive policies within Hinduism.

Everything in *Niraparādh kī Hatyā* has a parallel in *Rām-Rājya-Nyāy* though the reverse is not the case. *Niraparādh kī Hatyā* does not depict Rāma with a constant concern for the welfare of the Brahmins, thereby removing hierarchical pressures of the *varṇa* system from its plot. Here I will focus on Rāma's lament regarding the difficulties of ruling in the opening scene of each play (not counting *Rām-Rājya-Nyāy*'s prologue). Note in the case of *Niraparādh kī Hatyā* that he expresses no specific concern about the condition of Brahmins where he does in *Rām-Rājya-Nyāy*. Each passage is quoted in full.

---

18 Achhutanand was himself familiar with both Hindi and Bengali, and even mentions in the prologue to *Rām-Rājya-Nyāy* that the play is a recounting of the Śambūka story as told by Vālmīki, Bhavabhūti and "the Bengali and Dravidian *Rāmāyaṇas*" (1995, p. 6). It is possible that Achhutanand, like Santram, knew Jogesh Chandra Chaudhuri's *Sītā* in either its original Bengali or the Hindi translation, perhaps accounting for the remarkable similarities between *Rām-Rājya-Nyāy* and *Niraparādh kī Hatyā*. Considering this and *Rām-Rājya-Nyāy* and *Śambuka Vadha*'s similar characterizations of Śambūka as a revolutionary leader promoting a pre-Aryan identity for himself and his followers, it is conceivable that Achhutanand could be thinking of Tripuraneni Ramaswamy Chaudari's *Śambuka Vadha* and Jogesh Chandra Chaudhuri's *Sītā* when he mentions the "Dravidian and Bengali *Rāmāyaṇas*."

***Niraparādh kī Hatyā***

**Rām:** This kingdom, managing the course of the kingdom's rule is no laughing matter. I don't know why people always look to the royal throne with greedy eyes. They don't consider that it is covered in thorns, not flowers. I destroyed everything I had by taking on this kingdom. I sent my beloved Jānakī into exile in order to please my subjects. But alas, my subjects are still not happy. Famine has struck everywhere. People are lamenting. What do I do now? (Santram, 2016, pp. 14–15)

***Rām-Rājya Nyāy***

**Rām**: The kingdom! Looking after its subjects! Ah! This is no laughing matter. Who knows why people always look to the royal throne with greed-filled eyes. They don't consider that it's covered in thorns, not flowers. Ah! I destroyed everything I had taking on this kingdom and its governance. Following the orders of the Brahmins, I sent my beloved Jānakī into exile just to keep my subjects happy and I struck lightning into my own life. But alas! Even with all that, the harsh Creator feels no compassion. He is committed to the destruction of my subjects. People all over the kingdom are lamenting wildly because of this drought. The Brahmins aren't getting the ghee, milk, or grains they need for their sacrifices. The cows aren't getting any grass. My life has become insufferable from the difficulties of the cows and Brahmins. A king is bound for hell if the Brahmins of his kingdom are seeing difficult times. What do I do now? I must have some immense funds that I can give away to my subjects and spare them of their troubles and satisfy the twice-born. (Achhutanand, 1995, pp. 8–9)

A conversation between Śambūka and his wife, Tuṅgabhadrā, that appears in both *Rām-Rājya-Nyāy* and *Niraparādh kī Hatyā* serves as a venue to clearly lay out the ideologies informing each play. Śambūka is the spokesman for those ideologies and Tuṅgabhadrā plays the role of the relatively uninformed interlocutor.

***Niraparādh kī Hatyā***

**Tuṅgabhadrā**: Āryaputra![19]
**Śambūk** My dear, I am no Āryaputra, I am a vile Anāryaputra. Do you not know? My father stayed in a Brahmin's house and herded his cattle. He stayed there for twelve years but still he did not have permission to touch the water pot.

19 The term Āryaputra is an honorific title in Aryan culture literally meaning "son of an Aryan."

**Tuṅgabhadrā**: What is this you're saying? Does a water pot become impure from touch too?
**Śambūk**: That's what the people who created the Śāstras say. Yes, there is some flexibility to this because of some basic differences. The water in the pot becomes impure to the touch, but not that of the pond.
**Tuṅgabhadrā**: I see, so what then? You've studied so much, done so many sacrifices, and yet you still cannot become an Aryan?
**Śambūk**: No, the Brahmins could never accept such a thing. Still, I can say what I want to whom I want on the basis of my own will.
**Tuṅgabhadrā**: So be it. The Brahmins can call you an Aryan or a non-Aryan, but I will call you Āryaputra. I can never accept that my husband is at all a lesser person than some Brahmin, Kṣatriya, or Vaiśya. (Santram, 2016, pp. 19–20)

### *Rām-Rājya-Nyāy*

**Tuṅgabhadrā**: Āryaputra! [...]
**Śambūk**: My dear, I am no Āryaputra, I am an Original Inhabitant of India. Do you not know? It was the twice-born who looted my father and drove him into poverty. And taking everything away from him, they stuck him with the job of herding the cows in a Brahmin's house. He kept carrying on as a slave for twelve years. And that Brahmin would degrade him horribly; he wouldn't even let him touch the dishes.
**Tuṅgabhadrā**: What is this you're saying, lord? Do dishes become impure from somebody's touch, too?
**Śambūk**: My dear, those are the rules in the *dharma* of the Aryan twice-born. Now, there is some hierarchy based on a distinction in the type of vessel. For instance, water from an earthen pot becomes impure from touch, but water from a lake does not.
**Tuṅgabhadrā**: But now you are a most wise ascetic sage. You have hundreds of thousands of followers. People come from miles away to take advantage of your profound knowledge and hear your lessons. There is nobody in this Daṇḍaka Forest who can compare to you in yoga or *tapas*—I hear this every day. Do these twice-borns still think you are an Untouchable, a servant, and a slave even now?
**Śambūk**: Yes, my dear, these Brahmins can never consider me to be an Aryan twice-born or equal to them. I can get as far ahead as I want through my ascetic strength and my accomplishments. But remember, I don't want to become an Aryan twice-born and erase my Adi Lineage or my Adi Dharma.

**Tuṅgabhadrā**: May it be so. The Brahmins can call you an Aryan if they wanted, or a non-Aryan. But I could never accept that my husband is in any way lesser than some Aryan twice-born.
**Śambūk**: What is this lesser or greater, my dear? The truth is that people belonging to the Adi Lineage are themselves the religious gurus to the twice-borns. They have created their Vedānta after learning our knowledge of understanding the *ātman* and now they have started to propagate it as Brahmā-vidyā. Yet they still don't understand its secret. Only the virtuous Original Inhabitants understand it. These people are very ungrateful. They learned this knowledge from us and have the nerve to write about us in their texts as being Śūdras, low, slaves, servants, and mixed-caste; and they disgrace and torment our people everywhere. (Achhutanand, 1995, pp. 17–18)

The passage in *Niraparādh kī Hatyā* outlines a concern of inclusion of the lower castes into the Hindu fold, something Santram advocated given his efforts towards welcoming all castes into Hinduism and his frustrations with the Adi Hindu movement and similar groups (e.g., Ad Dharm in Punjab) attracting the lower castes away from Hinduism. In *Niraparādh kī Hatyā*, Śambūka has put in the time and the work, dedicating himself to study and sacrifice, a fact that should present anyone with an opportunity to succeed based on their personal merits. Still, the Brahmins are not ready to accept a Śūdra into their religious mode of life. Achhutanand's passage, on the other hand, is not concerned with this inclusion. In fact, Śambūka explicitly denounces any desire to take part in Aryan culture at the expense of his own, depicting the more radical view of figures like Achhutanand, who aimed at solidifying an independent Adi identity within India's oppressed communities.

Another key moment in both plays comes just after Śambūka finds out about Rāma coming to deliver punishment. In each case, Śambūka refers to a sacrifice (*yajña*) that he will conduct. Both plays even make use of Vedic terminology relating to sacrifice. The circumstances of the sacrifice and the way of framing it, however, are vastly different. In *Niraparādh kī Hatyā*, the sacrifice is a Vedic sacrifice in a literal way. The catch is that Śūdras will perform all the roles involved in such a sacrifice, thus subverting Brahminical supremacy over ritual action. Śambūka's vision of this sacrifice in *Rām-Rājya-Nyāy*, however, centers around self-sacrifice and the legacy of what Śambūka understands to be his impending martyrdom. Achhutanand makes use of Vedic terminology as a criticism of Vedic sacrifice in order to portray Śambūka himself as the sacrificial offering. Even the stage directions following Śambūka's pronouncement of his sacrifice are telling in each play.

### *Niraparādh kī Hatyā*

> **Śambūk**: Today, there will be a sacrifice unique in all the world wherein not a single Brahmin will be involved. A Śūdra will be the ritual overseer [*purohit*], a Śūdra will be the reciter [*hotṛ*], and a Śūdra will be the priest [*ṛtvij*]. Be it in the ages of a near or distant past, nobody must have ever conducted such a sacrifice.
> [Then several men and women who had been summoned enter and start working on the altar. The Śūdra reciters [*hotṛ*s] sit around the altar. There is Vedic chanting. As the Śūdra sage Śambūk starts offering the oblations to the sacrificial fire as he recites Vedic mantras, Rām and Lakṣmaṇ enter]. (Santram, 2016, pp. 21–22)

### *Rām-Rājya-Nyāy*

> **Śambūk**: (To himself) Today, a new kind of sacrifice, ancient though it may be, will be completed wherein not a single twice-born will take part. Only people of the Original Lineage will be its chanter [*udgātṛ*] and its priest [*ṛtvij*]. Certainly nobody has ever done such a sacrifice across the entire country—from the Himalayas to Kanyakumari.
> Ghee, milk, grains, and medicines are wasted in Brahmins' sacrifices and meek cattle are killed and offered during the fire rite. But I will be offering myself as an oblation in this sacrifice of mine. There will be songs of service to one's caste, the priests will be bent on serving their caste, and there will be a complete offering of my ephemeral worldly life.
> [Just then, Sage Śambūk's followers come to the penance grove along with a crowd of Original Inhabitant men and women and they greet the great sage Śambūk before sitting down facing him. The great sage asks learned questions and his followers play the *iktārā*, tambourine, and *kartāl* as everyone gets together to sing a bhajan of Original Lineage knowledge on the essence of experiencing *ātman*.] (Achhutanand, 1995, pp. 20–21)

Comparing *Rām-Rājya-Nyāy* and *Niraparādh kī Hatyā* in their entirety is a useful exercise for witnessing the flexibility of the Śambūka story and its suitability as a vehicle for a range of ideologies. Though the two have the same narrative arc, they foster vastly different messages by changing the circumstances leading to Śambūka's death. Achhutanand used the Śambūka story to bolster his promotion of Adi Hinduism, itself an anti-caste movement centered around the claim that India's most subjugated populations are, in fact, the subcontinent's original inhabitants. Śambūka's revolution in *Rām-Rājya-Nyāy* is an attempt to reclaim their land, culture, and religion from the invading Aryans.

Śambūka's revolution in Santram's *Niraparādh kī Hatyā*, however, seeks to subvert the caste system and incorporate Śūdras and other disenfranchised communities into the religious structures of Hinduism. Thus, these two dramas, though nearly identical in structure, present notably different understandings of Śambūka's life and anti-caste messaging.

## Dr. B.R. Ambedkar on Śambūka

Santram B.A.'s Jat-Pat Todak Mandal (JPTM) was the group responsible for inviting and eventually disinviting Dr. B.R. Ambedkar to speak at their annual conference in Lahore in 1936. As mentioned above, the JPTM had formed as a staunchly anti-caste faction within the Arya Samaj but broke away from the Samaj in the 1920s when the JPTM's views on caste bred strife with their parent organization. Aggressively anti-caste though it may have been, the JPTM continued to fall within the Arya Samaj's sphere of influence, even after the two groups separated. As an illustration of such commitment to the Samaj's underlying philosophies on religion, the JPTM claimed that they rejected Ambedkar's speech because he would not redact his criticisms of the Veda and he said this would be his last speech as a Hindu, thus working against the goals of JPTM, which sought to reform Hinduism, not abandon it.[20] Ambedkar printed the speech anyway, publishing it under the title *Annihilation of Caste*, which has arguably become the most well-known piece of anti-caste writing in India's history. In it, we find a brief mention of Śambūka.

Starting with Chapter Fifteen of his undelivered speech, Ambedkar discusses the *cāturvarṇya* as an ideal of the Arya Samaj. Up to this point, he had been speaking about a more variegated sense of caste based on birth, occupation, and parentage known as *jāti*.[21] One must keep in mind that Ambedkar meant to deliver this speech to the JPTM, which, S. Anand reminds us in his annotated edition of *Annihilation of Caste*, "was originally affiliated to the Arya Samaj and continued to have several important Arya Samaj leaders of the Punjab leading it" (2014, p. 263 n. 82). Even though the speech was to be delivered to the JPTM, the influence of the Arya Samaj would have been palpable in their overarching religious philosophies. To that point, Ambedkar uses his discussion of *cāturvarṇya* to question the Arya Samaj's intentions behind reforming Hinduism while maintaining *cāturvarṇya* by simply redefining it. Ambedkar

20 Claiming this was his "last speech as a Hindu" is actually a misreading of Ambedkar's speech. He said that the speech "would probably be my last address to a Hindu audience, on a subject vitally concerning the Hindus" (2014a, p. 311), not that this would be his last speech as a Hindu. See also Anand (2014, p. 330 n. 12).

21 For more on the concept of *jāti*, see Chapter 1, note 7.

charges that such a redefinition would consist of (1) doing away with concepts of caste and maintaining only the four *varṇa* categories; (2) making classification into one of the *varṇa*s as being based on worth, not birth; and (3) being able to uphold a system of *cāturvarṇya* through some kind of penal system. He criticizes all these points as being impossible to maintain and it is this last point on a system of penalization that leads Ambedkar to discuss Śambūka.

Ambedkar insists that the *cāturvarṇya*—a system that, in his view, constantly faces the problem of transgression—can only be upheld through enforcement. In Ambedkar's own words, this social structure "cannot subsist by its own inherent goodness" (2014a, p. 268). If, for example, the Arya Samaj would like to institute *cāturvarṇya*, they would have to commit to enforcing it through penalty. To illustrate his point, he cites Rāma's execution of Śambūka as a symptom of the system and its need for violent enforcement.

> Some people seem to blame Rama because he wantonly and without reason killed Shambuka. But to blame Rama for killing Shambuka is to misunderstand the whole situation. Ram Raj was a raj based on chaturvarnya. As a king, Rama was bound to maintain chaturvarnya. It was his duty therefore to kill Shambuka, the Shudra who had transgressed his class and wanted to be a Brahmin. This is the reason why Rama killed Shambuka. But this also shows that penal sanction is necessary for the maintenance of chaturvarnya. Not only penal sanction is necessary, but the penalty of death is necessary. [...] The supporters of chaturvarnya must give an assurance that they could successfully classify men, and that they could induce modern society in the twentieth century to re-forge the penal sanctions of the *Manusmriti*. (2014a, pp. 268–270)

Ambedkar's point about Śambūka's death being the result of the *varṇa* system rather than Rāma himself is an important one and it is taken up by many authors, including Ramaswamy Chaudari and Achhutanand. We have already seen in *Śambuka Vadha* that the Brahmins exploited a king's obligations to the system of *cāturvarṇya* to manipulate Rāma into killing Śambūka and we have seen in *Rām-Rājya-Nyāy* that Rāma was a figure constantly aware of the plight of the Brahmins (and hence, the system as a whole) who even defended Śambūka's actions upon first hearing of his supposed crimes. We often find Rāma as the subject of Brahminical pressure to maintain a *status quo* based on the *cāturvarṇya*. He does so through the same recourse to punishment as identified by Ambedkar in the above passage. In reality, Rāma's obligation to uphold *varṇadharma* and punish Śambūka harkens back to the same idealization of *rājadharma* discussed in Chapter 2.

Ambedkar takes up the subject of Śambūka in other works as well, including *Riddles in Hinduism*, which was published posthumously by the Government of Maharashtra via the series "Dr. Babasaheb Ambedkar: Writings and Speeches" (BAWS) in 1987, just over three decades after Ambedkar died in 1956 (Anand, 2016, p. 14). The book was formed out of a file of loose papers that sat neglected after Ambedkar's death and changed hands many times before reaching the Government of Maharashtra, with whom they sat for many years before they were finally published.[22] It is a deep critique of Hinduism and, in particular, of the hold Ambedkar believed the Brahmins maintain over the religion. He presents his critique in the form of twenty-four riddles divided into three categories: religious (fifteen riddles), social (five riddles), and political (four riddles). Included in the BAWS publication of *Riddles in Hinduism* as an appendix was a chapter entitled "The Riddle of Rama and Krishna," though the chapter's exact relationship to the base text is unclear given that there is no mention of it in a listing of the book's intended contents (Anand, 2016, p. 7). The chapter's inclusion in *Riddles in Hinduism* led to rioting by the Shiv Sena, which, in turn, led to the Government of Maharashtra excising the chapter from the publication. Dalits all around Maharashtra engaged in a counter-protest, the result of which was to have "The Riddle of Rama and Krishna" included yet again in *Riddles in Hinduism*, though the Government of Maharashtra absolved themselves of responsibility by stating that it did not share the views expressed in the chapter (Anand, 2016, p. 14). The Navayana Publishing Pvt Ltd edition—which itself is an abridgment of the BAWS edition, selecting ten of the original twenty-four riddles—includes this material as an appendix entitled "The Riddle of Rama and Krishna" and it is here that Ambedkar again mentions Śambūka.

In "The Riddle of Rama and Krishna," Ambedkar systematically deconstructs Rāma's image to demonstrate that he is not a figure worth emulating; he subjects Kṛṣṇa to similar scrutiny. He attacks Rāma's parentage, the legitimacy of his marriage to Sītā, and his conduct as an individual and king. To illustrate Rāma's improper behavior as an individual, Ambedkar cites the death of Vālin and his treatment of Sītā in the aftermath of her rescue—that is, her trial-by-fire and subsequent exile upon returning to Ayodhyā—as examples. Ambedkar charges Rāma with being negligent in his kingly duties and giving in to the trappings of the throne: luxurious comforts, lavish meals, liquor, etc. Rāma, Ambedkar argues, was almost wholly neglectful of his responsibility to the public. The only example of Rāma hearing from

22 For more on the circumstances of *Riddles in Hinduism*'s publication, see Anand (2016).

his subjects is none other than the father of the deceased Brahmin boy, and at this point Ambedkar presents his views on Rāma's execution of Śambūka.

In providing his summary of the Śambūka episode, Ambedkar largely sticks to the basic outline we find in the *VR*. His tone and descriptive choices reveal his sympathy for Śambūka and critical view of the reasoning for his death. For instance, Ambedkar refers to Rāma's killing of Śambūka as a "murder" (2016, p. 230) and describes the moment of Śambūka's decapitation by saying "and with no more ado than to enquire of him and inform himself that he was a Shudra by the name Sambuka, who was practicing *tapasya* with a view to going to heaven in his own earthly person and without so much as a warning, expostulation or the like addressed to him, cut off his head. And lo and behold! That very moment the dead Brahman boy in distant Ayodhya began to breathe again" (ibid., p. 231). Unfortunately, however, Ambedkar offers little actual analysis of the episode and appears to be satisfied in letting the story speak for itself. Immediately after recounting the story, he simply states "Such is Rama"—meant to encapsulate his entire litany of criticisms, not just his killing of Śambūka—before moving on to Kṛṣṇa. *Annihilation of Caste* is a much richer source for his deeper thoughts on what Śambūka represents for Indian society.

## Two Periyars Censure the *Rāmāyaṇa*

The Government of Uttar Pradesh exerted considerable effort during the late-1960s and early-1970s attempting to halt two literary projects created under the supervision of the non-Brahmin activist Lalai Singh Yadav. Singh, who dropped his Yadav surname in 1967 after he converted to Buddhism because it identified him as an OBC,[23] oversaw the production and distribution of a compilation of Dr. B.R. Ambedkar's speeches and the Hindi translation of E.V. Ramasami's *The Ramayana (A True Reading)*. The bans were ultimately unsuccessful and the processes by which they were overturned involved using the *VR* itself as legally viable justification for the critical viewpoints expressed in these works. E.V. Ramasami's blessings for the Hindi translation of his seminal book brought him into a working relationship with Lalai Singh. These two figures and their efforts in literary activism—both separate from and in concert with one another—had a profound effect on anti-caste movements representing large swaths of India.

Periyar E.V. Ramasami (1879–1973) was a well-known anti-caste activist from Tamil Nadu. In addition to his involvement with institutionalized political

23 This in not unlike E.V. Ramasami, who himself renounced his caste name Naicker.

organizations like the Justice Party, E.V. Ramasami launched a continuous stream of vitriolic attacks on the *Rāmāyaṇa* throughout his life, which gave him a particular infamy even amid the cacophony of other Dalit and non-Brahmin voices exclaiming their resentment of Brahminical oppression. Recognizing that E.V. Ramasami's voice carried a special kind of weight, Paula Richman cautions us: "Although one might be tempted to dismiss E.V. Ramasami as an isolated eccentric, this would be unwise, for his exegesis of the *Rāmāyaṇa* was pivotal" (1991c, p. 194). Ramasami saw the *Rāmāyaṇa* as the quintessential representation of North Indian (i.e., Aryan) subjugation of South India and used his criticisms of the epic as propaganda for his views. For him, the entire *Rāmāyaṇa* is a story of Aryan conquest of a prosperous Dravidian society ruled over by the virtuous Dravidian king Rāvaṇa. This perception of the Rāma story in combination with what Ramasami considered a series of North Indian aggressions (e.g., the attempt by the Congress ministry to make Hindi compulsory in schools) formed the basis of his demand for a separate Dravidian nation. Richman has made the observation that, "[i]n much the same way that other South Asians sought…the creation of a separate Islamic state (Pakistan), E.V.R. desired a separate Tamil state and identity for South Indians, linking the articulation of that identity with a critique of the *Rāmāyaṇa*" (1991c, p. 179). The epic, then, became Ramasami's ready-made allegory for his ideas on the Aryans' incessant subjugation of India's indigenous population.

Ramasami's sustained campaign of attacks on Rāma and his epic—starting as early as the 1920s—made him an object of reverence for some and disdain for many others. This campaign manifested in many ways, including his infamous campaign in 1956 to burn images of Rāma at the Madras marina (Richman, 1991c, pp. 175ff.). Also included in Ramasami's steady series of criticisms is the publication of his Tamil-language booklet *Irāmāyaṇappātiraṅkaḷ* (*The Characters of the Rāmāyaṇa*) in 1930. The pamphlet is a biting manifestation of his critical stance on the epic and its supposed heroes. In it, notes Richman, "E.V.R. vehemently attacks the respect with which Tamilians have traditionally viewed the *Rāmāyaṇa*, arguing that the story is both an account of and a continuing vehicle for northern cultural domination. Reversing the conventional understandings of villain and hero, he also calls upon readers to abandon their 'superstitious' beliefs and embrace a desacralized view of the world" (1991c, p. 181). His booklet thus became a sort of manifesto detailing his views on Dravidian history, the state of the Dravidian community today, and the effect of Aryan culture, all of which he filtered through the lens of the *Rāmāyaṇa*.

As the leader of South India's arguably most prominent non-Brahmin movement, Ramasami in *Irāmāyaṇappātiraṅkaḷ*, "reserves his greatest outrage…for Rāma's treatment of Śūdras" (Richman, 1991c, p. 185), who made up a significant portion of South India's population and were his primary audience. Among his criticisms of Rāma, Ramasami is sure to include the execution of Śambūka as illustrative of Rāma's true sentiments toward them.

> Looking at his hand Rama said the Sanskrit slogan—"O Right hand, you kill this Asche[24] Sudra unhesitatingly as killing this Sudra is the only way to get back the life of the deceased Brahmin boy. Are you not one of the limbs of Rama?" (Valmiki Ramayanam)[25]
> Note: This Rama who mercilessly took away the life of Sambuka for no other fault than that he was making penance is held to be the Avatar (Incarnation) of Vishnu! If there were kings like Rama now! Alas! What would be the plight of those who are called "Sudras" (1972, p. 22)?

India's patchwork of vernaculars significantly limited *Irāmāyaṇappātiraṅkaḷ*'s reach on a pan-Indic scale. In 1959, only a few years after Ramasami's 1956 campaign to burn images of Rāma, the English translation of *Irāmāyaṇappātiraṅkaḷ* appeared under the title *The Ramayana (A True Reading)* (henceforth *True Reading*). Though this title is not an exact translation of the Tamil, Richman observes that it is "in some ways more illuminating, for it indicates E.V.R.'s goal of revealing to the reader the 'correct' interpretation of the *Rāmāyaṇa*" (1991c, p. 180). The English-language *True Reading* gave Ramasami's views of the *Rāmāyaṇa* a much broader reach. It was this version of the text that moved beyond the borders of Tamil Nadu and the stability with which the *Rāmāyaṇa* is imbedded in the cultural fabric of all parts of India ensured that Ramasami's ideas would solicit reactions—both positive and negative—even far away from home. His engagement with the *Rāmāyaṇa* paired with the wide range of his other political and social exploits made Ramasami increasingly well-known across India as a non-Brahmin leader. Indeed, his promotion of a pre-Aryan golden age of Dravidian culture would have resonated deeply with similar anti-Aryan theorizing happening in various regions of North and South India alike. His framing of the Aryan invasion

24 The term "Asche" is unclear and could perhaps be a typographical error. There are many such errors in the text due to the translation's hasty completion in one week (Ramasami, 1972, p. vii). The Hindi version of *True Reading* includes the word *nirdoṣ* (innocent) to describe the Śūdra, apparently in place of this word "Asche," which survives in English editions.

25 Ramasami attributes this verse to the *VR*. However, this bears more resemblance to Rāma's line at the opening of Act II in Bhavabhūti's *URC* as Rāma prepares to decapitate Śambūka. Cf. Tripuraneni Ramaswami Chaudari's use of a similar line in his own *Śambuka Vadha*, written in 1920 around the same time that Ramasami was starting his pointed attacks on the *Rāmāyaṇa*.

in terms of the *Rāmāyaṇa* would have made this resonance even more potent. This gave Ramasami the opportunity to travel across India.

Kanwal Bharti, a prominent Dalit writer and literary critic from Uttar Pradesh, notes how Ramasami's visit to Lucknow sometime around 1967 for a convention on minorities brought him into contact with Lalai Singh, who had already made a significant name for himself as one of two major writer-activists revered within the "Bahujan" community (Bharti, 2016).[26] Bharti considers the other to be Chandrika Prasad Jigyasu. Singh admired Ramasami a great deal and the two formed an amicable relationship, as is evidenced by Singh's invitation to speak on the occasion of Ramasami's death in 1973. It is said that Ramasami's followers were moved by Singh's impassioned eulogy and dubbed him the next Periyar, leading to Singh adopting the Tamil honorific "Periyar" before his own name and forever solidifying their mutual respect and the connection between anti-Brahminical movements of the North and South (Aditya, 2011, p. 52).

Lalai Singh (1911–1993) was born in Jhinjhak, Kanpur District, Uttar Pradesh. His father, a proud Arya Samaji, inculcated in Singh a strong sense of anti-casteism and support not only for his fellow OBCs, but for Dalits as well.[27] Singh subsequently found his own voice in activism during his government service. In 1933, for example, while an officer with the Gwalior Armed Police, he organized an agitation against the abysmal living conditions of his company. These activities got him dismissed from service, though this dismissal would later be overturned on appeal (Bharti, 2016; Vāgh, 2016, p. 87). Singh retired from government service in 1950, whereupon he shifted his focus to literary activism, which became his most significant contribution to the push for eliminating caste.

Singh was a key player among anti-Brahminical activist-publishers in U.P. through his press, Ashok Pustakalaya (now run as the Periyar Lalai Singh Charitable Trust), in Kanpur District. Like many other non-Brahmin publishing houses in U.P., which combined to form a tight network of

26 Bharti's use of the word "Bahujan" implies a unified community of Dalits, OBCs, and, to some extent, India's tribal population. The term (literally meaning majority) was popularized by Phule in the nineteenth century through his conceptualization of a *bahujan samāj*—that is, the unification of all Śūdras with the Atiśūdras (Dalits, tribals, and all women), who, if combined, would form a consolidated majority in opposition to the twice-borns. See Jaffrelot (2005, p. 155) and Hunt (2017, p. 39). I use quotations around the term because its applicability as an identifying term has been subject to debate, especially in relation to the concept of a Bahujan literature (Kostka & Ranjan, 2016).

27 Singh's various biographers highlight several accounts of his father's involvement in anti-caste and anti-untouchability issues along with his experiences in the Arya Samaj (Aditya, 2011, pp. 19ff.; Bauddh, 2009 pp. 10–13; Vāgh, 2016, pp. 86–87).

like-minded literary activists, Ashok Pustakalaya focused on the dissemination of affordable and readable works relating to prominent anti-caste activists and their lives, opposition to caste discrimination, and reinterpretation of conventional histories of India and accounts of Hinduism. Singh himself had a propensity for using dramatic portrayals of epic themes as a vehicle for spreading his messages, and even wrote one on the subject of Śambūka entitled *Śambūk Vadh* (*The Killing of Śambūka*), coauthored with Ram Avtar Pal in 1962.[28] This play shows considerable influence of Achhutanand's *Rām-Rājya-Nyāy*, which was written in the same region a few decades earlier. The weight of Achhutanand's influence on *Śambūk Vadh* is obvious in the latter's use of several aspects of the Adi Hindu worldview as well as certain characters and plot points that are either imports from or developments on *Rām-Rājya-Nyāy*.[29]

Singh's anti-caste literary activism led to numerous contentious interactions with the U.P. Government, which even involved two attempts to ban projects conducted under his supervision. One attempt was related to a Hindi translation of E.V. Ramasami's *True Reading* and the other was in connection with a compilation of Ambedkar's speeches.

During Singh's first encounter with E.V. Ramasami in Lucknow, the two discussed *True Reading* and Singh expressed interest in publishing a Hindi translation of it. Ramasami initially told Singh not to go forward with publication because Chandrika Prasad Jigyasu, who ran the publishing house Bahujan Kalyan Prakashan out of Lucknow, was already assigned to the task.[30]

---

28 His other dramas include *Aṅgulimāl*, *Vīr Sant Māyā Balidān*, *Nāg Yajña*, and *Eklavya*. *Eklavya* and *Śambūk Vadh* in particular illustrate a continuance of the early twentieth-century trend of calling on the epics to challenge the caste system. As a Niṣāda and Śūdra respectively, Ekalavya and Śambūka are both within the broadly conceived non-Brahmin community of the modern day (consisting of Dalits, Adivasis, and Other Backward Classes/OBCs) and were easily portrayed as martyrs and exemplars of a history of systemic subjugation of India's socially oppressed communities enacted by the higher castes.

29 I have explored the connections between *Śambūk Vadh* and *Rām-Rājya-Nyāy* elsewhere (Sherraden, 2021).

30 Chandrika Prasad Jigyasu was also a close follower of Achhutanand and ensured that Achhutanand's ideas carried on through his own publishing house, Bahujan Kalyan Prakashan, by publishing his own works attempting to historicize the theories of the Adi Hindu movement as well as posthumous editions of Achhutanand's work. He is also associated with Periyar Lalai Singh and Ram Avtar Pal's *Śambūk Vadh* via an introductory note that expounds on the perceived association of the *Rāmāyaṇa* and an Aryan invasion prevalent among several non-Brahmin publisher-activists at the time. In so doing, Jigyasu "connects *Śambūk-Vadh* to the wider network of Dalit and non-Brahmin publishing houses in Uttar Pradesh and places it in the literary lineage of Achhutanand's *Rām-Rājya-Nyāy*" (Sherraden, 2021, p. 72).

Jigyasu, however, could not follow through and the project was passed on to Singh (Bharti, 2016; Aditya 2011, p. 50).

The original *Irāmāyaṇappātirankaḷ* was clearly meant for a Tamil audience. Aside from the fact that it was written in Tamil, Ramasami states on numerous occasions that the victims of Aryan violence and deception are specifically Dravidians. This presents an interesting problem in translation, which was solved by redefining, in a sense, what Dravidian means. Each time the word Dravidian appears in *True Reading,* the Hindi translation adds a parenthetical elaboration: "(Śūdras and Mahā-Śūdras)," that is, Śūdras and Dalits, Tribals, etc. (cf. Phule's Śūdras-Atiśūdra).[31] This universalizes Ramasami's intent behind his use of the term "Dravidian" in a way that would be more applicable to a Hindi-speaking audience. In other words, this translation strategy forces Ramasami's conception of the Dravidians to fall in line with a more generally applicable idea that the Dalits and non-Brahmins are the victims of an Aryan invasion and they all share a common heritage, be they from the North or the South. While the specifics of this universalization of the term "Dravidian" could have been up for debate, Ramasami's own idea of what would comprise a separate Dravidian state suggests that he may have embraced such a pan-regional openness. Along these lines, Geetha and Rajadurai suggest that, more than an identity based on geography, the Dravidian-ness that defined Ramasami's conceptual state "signified an openness, an acceptance within its fold of all those who consented to the destruction of caste and who wished to found a rational egalitarian order" (1998, p. 327). After a meeting with Ambedkar in 1944, wherein Ambedkar posited that the idea of an anti-Brahmanical Dravidian nation with such a mission statement was applicable India-wide, Ramasami himself began promoting his Dravidianism as broadly inclusive rather than regionally limited (ibid., p. 327).

*True Reading* was translated into Hindi by Ram Adhar and published in 1968 under the title *Saccī Rāmāyaṇ* (*The True Rāmāyaṇa*) by Ashok Pustakalaya in Kanpur under the directorship of Lalai Singh. The U.P. Government promptly placed a ban on both the English and Hindi editions of Ramasami's work, effective December 8, 1969. The announcement of the ban first appears publicly in the U.P. Government Gazette released on December 20, 1969 claiming that passages in these books "are deliberately and maliciously intended to outrage the religious feelings of a class of citizens of India, namely, the Hindus by insulting their religion and religious

31 Even when E.V. Ramasami uses the phrase, "our men," the Hindi translation elaborates by saying "our men, the Dravidians (Śūdras and Mahā-Śūdras)." See, for example, Ramasami (1972, pp. 2–3) and its parallel passage in Adhar (2011, pp. 14–15).

beliefs" (1969, p. 5154). The publication was therefore punishable under section 295-A of the Indian Penal Code (IPC), 1860 (Act no. 45 of 1860), which prescribes a punishment of up to three years' imprisonment, a fine, or both for anyone who offends the religious sentiments of any Indian citizen through speech, writing, signs, or visual representations.[32] The Gazette then lists the locations of thirty-six passages in both *Saccī Rāmāyaṇ* and *True Reading* that they consider to be objectionable on these grounds. The government then confiscated copies of the books citing section 99-A of the Code of Criminal Procedure, 1898 as granting such authority. Singh appealed the forfeiture with the Allahabad High Court, which ruled in favor of Singh on January 19, 1971.[33] The U.P. Government decided to challenge the ruling before the Supreme Court of India, which upheld the Allahabad High Court's ruling on September 16, 1976.[34]

While these battles over *True Reading* and *Saccī Rāmāyaṇ* were still ongoing, the Government of U.P. placed a ban on another book: *Sammān ke liye Dharm Parivartan Kareṃ* (*You Must Change Your Religion to Find Respect*, henceforth *Sammān*), a collection of Dr. Ambedkar's speeches edited and translated into Hindi and published while Lalai Singh was president of the Dr. Bhim Rao Ambedkar Literature Committee (Kumar, 2009, pp. 51–53). The ban appeared in the U.P. Government Gazette on September 12, 1970, though the government instituted the ban earlier, on August 25.[35] As was the case with *True Reading* and *Saccī Rāmāyaṇ*, the U.P. Government cited section 295-A of the IPC 1860, but, in order to strengthen their case against the publishers, they additionally invoked section 153-A, which includes a potential punishment of three years imprisonment, a fine, or both for causing disharmony between communities. Pulling almost verbatim from IPC 153-A, the exact charge in the Gazette states that material found throughout the book "promotes or attempts to promote on grounds of religion, caste or community disharmony or feelings of enmity, hatred or ill-will between different religions, castes or communities and insults

32 At this point in history, IPC 295-A would have included modifications as of 1961 (Act no. 41 of 1961).

33 Lalai Singh Yadav v. State of Uttar Pradesh, 1971 Cri LJ 1519 All. (January 19, 1971)

34 State of Uttar Pradesh v. Lalai Singh Yadav, 1977 AIR 202, 1977 SCR (1) 616 (September 16, 1976).

35 Because appeals must be made within two months of the initial announcement, this long delay between the U.P. Government's ban and its publicly available appearance in the massive tome of the Gazette caused a hiccup in Lalai Singh's appeal. After Singh's counsel provided sufficient reason as to why he had missed the appeal deadline, Singh's case was ultimately accepted. See Lalai Singh Yadav v. State of Uttar Pradesh 1971 Cri LJ 1773.

or attempts to insult the religion or religions [*sic*] beliefs of a class" (1970, p. 4450). As such, the Government's claim was similar to the case against *Saccī Rāmāyaṇ*, but it added the new angle of inciting enmity between communities in addition to promulgating religious insults. Again, Lalai Singh appealed to the Allahabad High Court to overturn the ban and, again, he was successful as per a High Court ruling on May 14, 1971.[36] The U.P. Government did not further appeal this ruling.

In their attempted ban of *Sammān*, The U.P. Gazette includes a list of twenty-four objectionable passages from the text. One of these passages appears to have come from Dr. Ambedkar's speech for the second session of the All India Scheduled Castes Federation in Kanpur on January 30, 1944.[37] In its totality, the speech was a scathing critique of Hinduism and its promotion of untouchability. The following passage addresses the issue of Śambūka specifically and the apparent contradiction between being a Śūdra and worshipping Rāma:

> Śambūk was an untouchable. That is why Rām killed him. Untouchables and Śūdras worship as a god that killer Rām, whose very duty as a god is to kill learned Śūdras—how can they worship him? (2014b, p. 32)

While referring to this passage along with two others, which were all deemed objectionable by the U.P. Government due to their criticism of Hindu gods, Allahabad High Court Justice William Broome, who presided over the case with Y. Nandan and S. Malik, writes the following in his judgment overturning the ban:[38]

> The author [i.e., Ambedkar] states that Hindus think it right to despise others on account of the arrogance based on caste, and hope to attain salvation thereby; and the gods and goddesses of Hinduism are modelled on these same repulsive ideals. He then gives the story of Shambuk, a Sudra who dared to become an ascetic and was killed by

36 Lalai Singh Yadav v. State of Uttar Pradesh 1971 Cri LJ 1773 (May 14, 1971).

37 The original edition of *Sammān* to which the U.P. Gazette refers is not easy to locate and later editions of the text released by different publishers do not coincide with the text referred to in the Gazette, which only lists the passages by their location in the original edition. The edition to which I had access was published by Samyak Prakashan in 2014.

38 The three passages are identified in the U.P. Gazette respectively as p. 37 lines 4–7, p. 37 lines 23–29, and p. 38 lines 1–6 of *Sammān* as published by R.N. Shastri, New Delhi (no date given).

> Ram on that account; and he asks how anyone can worship a god like Ram, who considered it his duty to commit the murder of a sage in this fashion. … The original text of the Valmiki Ramayan [*sic*] has been shown to us and we find that it describes…the killing of Shambuk by Ram. … That being the case, it is difficult to see how the repetition of these stories can be said to be an insult to the Hindu religion or to promote disharmony and hatred. In the eyes of orthodox Hindus the Valmiki Ramayana has the status of a holy book or scripture; and nothing that is mentioned therein can possibly be taken offence to or construed as an insult to Hinduism, however much it may be at variance with modern ideas of morality and ethics. (Yadav v. State of U.P., 1971, p. 1776).

Lalai Singh's legal victories in these cases provided the perspectives promoted by Ashok Pustakalaya and other non-Brahmin publishing houses with a legally recognized legitimacy. News of these successes spread quickly in Dalit and OBC circles, creating a heroic aura for the future "Periyar of the North," Lalai Singh. In contrast to the rather mild scholarly attention these cases have received, accounts of Singh's legal battles appear in nearly every one of Singh's biographies or other accounts of his life that I have read.[39] Recalling the first time he met Lalai Singh, Kanwal Bharti notes,

> On 11 March 1973, Dalai Lama gave "diksha" in Buddhism to around 20,000 Dalits at a function in Ramlila Maidan, Delhi. I was one of them. That is where I saw Periyar Lalai Singh for the first time.[40] A slight man wearing a sky-blue kurta-pyjama was selling books, hawking them in his sharp voice. He was Periyar Lalai Singh. Having won the *Sachchi Ramayan* lawsuit, he had already become a hero of the Dalits and OBCs. … Many people had surrounded him, which was natural. (Bharti, 2016)

## A Battle over the Details: Śambūka in the Twentieth Century

The twentieth century was a transformative period in the history of the Śambūka episode. For the first time in the story's history, we get perspectives

39 Kumar (2009) covers the *Saccī Rāmāyaṇ* case and the *Sammān* case respectively on pp. 47–49 and pp. 51–53. For some biographers' accounts of these cases see Aditya (2011, pp. 51–52), Bauddh (2009, pp. 30–31), and Vāgh (2016, pp. 88–89).

40 Though deeply influenced by Ambedkar's life and work, Singh did not officially convert to Buddhism until 1967, over ten years after Ambedkar converted at Deekshabhoomi in Nagpur in 1956.

on the story that originate from the same social community as Śambūka himself. That paradigm shift led to a broadening of the message the story could deliver. The name Śambūka began appearing in contexts far beyond mainstream narrations or enactments of the *Rāmāyaṇa* such as those that were considered in earlier chapters. In addition to literary, dramatic, and poetic contexts within which Śambūka had been appearing for centuries, he was now a focal point in new genres of expression such as speeches and legal battles as a symbol of anti-caste mobilization. In becoming such a symbol, the narrative of his death had to change dramatically.

One of the most palpable innovations of this period came with framing the Śambūka story in terms of concurrent theorizing about an Aryan assault on India's indigenous population. In presenting the *Rāmāyaṇa* in terms of an Aryan invasion, twentieth-century anti-caste activists reversed the typical organization of antagonist-protagonist and, in so doing, presented fierce critiques of what the *Rāmāyaṇa* supposedly represents. Critical engagements with the Śambūka episode often meant putting Rāma's character at issue. Taking aim at Rāma on behalf of Śambūka typically meant situating him firmly under the thumb of Brahmin overseers as we saw in the case of Swami Achhutanand's *Rām-Rājya-Nyāy* or more directly challenging his ethics or the ethics of the social system he is meant to represent as we saw in the case of Ambedkar's *Riddles in Hinduism* and *Annihilation of Caste*. Criticisms of Rāma became the flashpoint for riots and lawsuits. Rāma's supporters in Maharashtra lashed out when the government there circulated Ambedkar's "The Riddle of Rama and Krishna." And, as we have seen, the government of Uttar Pradesh unsuccessfully attempted to quash the publication of E.V. Ramasami's piercing attack on the *Rāmāyaṇa* and its Hindi translation overseen by Lalai Singh. The U.P. Government also attempted to stop publication of a collection of Ambedkar's speeches wherein, among other things, he questions how Śūdras can be devoted to Rāma despite his execution of Śambūka. Those unabashed reproaches of Rāma do not represent all challenges to the Śambūka episode, however. Both Tripuraneni Ramaswami Chaudhari and Santram B.A. managed to empathize with Śambūka while simultaneously working to preserve Rāma's image. Rather than attack the man, they attacked the system to which he was beholden. Ramaswami Chaudari, despite his measured portrayal of Rāma, advocated for a restoration of a pre-Aryan society, which Śambūka's character was meant to represent. Santram B.A. carefully avoided such a backdrop for his Śambūka narration. His allegiances remained with the Hindu reformist platform wherein the deepest critiques were reserved for the strict prescriptions and proscriptions of the *varṇa* system, but not necessarily for the religious milieu within which *varṇa* was conceptualized.

In this case, Śambūka's rebellion was not against Ayodhyā as the symbol of an invasive foreign force, but rather against the social system that Ayodhyā promoted.

These diverse interventions show that twentieth-century developments in the Śambūka tradition could harness the societal dissonance depicted in the episode to serve many purposes. The episode could be effectively molded to promote several solutions to the problem of caste.

# Chapter 8

# ŚAMBŪKA IN THE TWENTY-FIRST CENTURY

One of the most polarizing moments in India's recent history came with the central government's attempts to implement the recommendations of the Backward Classes Commission, also known as the Mandal Commission. The Commission was set up in 1979 headed by B.P. Mandal and, a year later, it issued its recommendation that just under 50% of available seats in educational institutions and government jobs be allocated to India's OBC, SC, and ST populations—Articles 15(4) and 16(4) of the Constitution prevent the totality of reserved spots from exceeding 50%. Acknowledging that the recommendations will cause some pain to those who fall outside the reservation schematic proposed by the Commission, the report's authors question whether it is appropriate that "the mere fact of this heart burning be allowed to operate as a moral veto against social reform" (1980, V.1, p. 58). Speaking in the context of OBC reservations, the Mandal Commission attempts to argue that a top-heavy practice of reservation that favors the higher castes has always been in practice in India. In the process, the Commission even refers to Ekalavya and Śambūka, two oft-cited examples of caste-based violence in situations where one wishes to illustrate the injustices of the caste system. The document reads:

> In fact the Hindu society has always operated a very rigorous scheme of reservation, which was internalised through caste system [*sic*]. Eklivya [*sic*] lost his thumb and Shambhuk [*sic*] his neck for their breach of rules of reservation. The present furore against reservations for OBCs is not aimed at the principle itself, but against the new class of beneficiaries, as they are now clamouring for a share of the opportunities which were all along monopolised by the higher castes. (*Report of the Backward Classes Commission*, 1980, Part 1, p. 58)

The Mandal Commission's recommendations remained dormant for nearly a decade before Prime Minister V.P. Singh attempted to implement them in 1989. The shift from a purely merit-based (and upper-caste dominated) system of admissions to this legally ordained positive discrimination ignited a controversy that engulfed India's urban centers, Delhi in particular. In addition to widespread riots, the Mandal Commission protests were famously characterized by multiple cases of self-immolation. Those most visibly opposed to the recommendations were students, typically of higher castes, who felt that the admissions process and their own eventual job prospects were being encroached upon by supposedly undeserving students from underprivileged backgrounds. On the other side of this struggle, access to education has been of great concern to anti-caste movements starting as early as the mid-eighteenth century and the Mandal Commission protests in the 1990s demonstrated that the concern has remained justified.

We saw in the previous chapter how the Śambūka episode was reformulated to encompass the concern over education through various endeavors in anti-caste literature and activism. Author-activists thrust Śambūka into a leadership role wherein he was a teacher of the downtrodden. Education quickly became central to the story's messaging. This image of Śambūka holds true in the twenty-first century as well. The reality of societal volatility and casteism in contemporary India—and Śambūka's role in expressing it—provides the backdrop for this chapter. Here, I explore how, built on the foundation of the anti-caste movements of the previous century, Śambūka remains a symbol of Dalit and non-Brahmin struggles for equal access to education. At the same time, he also remains an anchor to India's mythological past that anti-caste activists mobilize while they draw societal parallels between ancient times and the present and seek to demonstrate that the casteist violence of old persists today. Those parallels were drawn yet again and in different contexts in the wake of Rohith Vemula's suicide in January 2016. His death bound together these two concerns—the right to education and casteist violence—and evocations of Śambūka provided an expedient vocabulary for illustrating the connections between them. I will detail three instances in which anti-caste activists and artists have invoked Śambūka to help articulate the tragedy and injustice of Rohith Vemula's death. The first is a speech given by Darshan "Ratna" Raavan, leader of the Aadi Dharm Samaaj on the occasion of Mahāmuni Śambūk Balidān Divas (The Martyrdom Day of the Great Sage Śambūka); the second is a street play put together by the Delhi-based street theater group, Jana Natya Manch; and the third is a poem by the Kerala-based poet Chandramohan S. These three examples demonstrate the wide applicability of the Śambūka story to different genres of artistic and activist activity and they all share the common theme of using the timeless and widely known *Rāmāyaṇa* epic to frame a problematic current event. Before proceeding to these, it is necessary to first describe the circumstances of Vemula's passing and its aftermath.

Rohith Vemula was a member of the University of Hyderabad's chapter of the Ambedkar Students' Association (ASA), which placed him at the center of the antagonism between that activist organization and the Akhil Bharatiya Vidyarthi Parishad (ABVP), a student affiliate of the Hindu nationalist Rashtriya Swayamsevak Sangh (RSS) and the right-wing Bharatiya Janata Party (BJP). The events leading to Vemula's suicide revolve around his suspension and eviction from the university hostel following a conflict between several ASA members, including Vemula, and the president of the university's chapter of the ABVP, Susheel Kumar. The ASA students were accused of assaulting Kumar in response to his online provocation condemning two contentious stances of the ASA. The first was the ASA's protest against the death penalty imposed on Yakub Menon, who in 2007 was convicted of criminal conspiracy for his role in the 1993 Bombay bombings. The second was the ASA's support of a controversial screening on the Delhi University campus of the documentary *Muzaffarnagar Baaqi Hai*, which covers the 2013 communal riots in Muzaffarnagar, Uttar Pradesh. The day after the alleged assault, Kumar was admitted to the hospital for appendicitis, though rumors circulated that his hospitalization was the result of the ASA confrontation. BJP MP Bandaru Dattatreya wrote a letter to the Minister of Human Resource Development, Smriti Irani, in support of Kumar and accusing the University of Hyderabad as being a "den of casteist, extremist and anti-national politics,"[1] and listing the ASA's protest against Yakub Menon's execution as an example of such politics. When the letter was forwarded to the university vice-chancellor, P. Appa Rao, Vemula and four others were suspended and evicted from university housing. After a series of challenges, the suspension was upheld on January 3, 2016. Two weeks later, on January 17, Vemula was found dead.

The aftermath of his death was defined, in large part, by an outpouring of anger at the systemic casteism that drove him to suicide on the one hand and character assassination on the other. Much of the negativity targeting Vemula after his death involved attempts to undermine his Dalit identity in an attempt to expose fraudulent acquisition of caste-based scholarships and university admission. The media frenzy surrounding Vemula's death—whether positive or negative—brought this particular tragedy into the spotlight, where it received the attention of numerous artists and activists, especially those working on behalf or in support of the Dalit community. Rohith Vemula quickly became a household name and any mention of him in 2016 and beyond

1 Bandaru Dattatraya, Letter to Smriti Zubin Irani dated August 17, 2015.

easily colored any conversation, speech, article, poem, etc. with impassioned thoughts on systemic casteism and its deadly consequences. One such mention was provided by Darshan "Ratna" Raavan, leader of the Adi Dharm Samaaj, on October 30, 2016, a day known as Mahāmuni Śambūk Balidān Divas.

## The Aadi Dharm Samaaj and The Martyrdom Day of the Great Sage Śambūka

In their own words, "AADI DHARM SAMAAJ 'AADHAS' is not an organisation rather it is a Social, Cultural, Spiritual and Educational Movement of oppressed among Aboriginals (Dalits as they are called today), who were the Original inhabitants and once the Rulers of Bharat/India before the advent of Aryans" (AADHAS, 2022). Led by the charismatic Darshan "Ratna" Raavan for the past twenty-five years or so, the group consists primarily of members of the Valmiki community of Dalits.[2] To this day, Raavan and a core group of AADHAS members travel extensively conducting seminars and other events, organizing door-to-door campaigns, and meeting with individual families in many North Indian cities and villages in order to spread their messages and connect to the wider community of Dalits. Their main goal is to convince families of the value of education, even in the face of widespread discrimination that makes it hard to convince children to keeping going to school. Part of this fight for education involves changing the habits of parents, so AADHAS also frequently addresses issues of widespread substance abuse, culturally fed superstitions, and illiteracy, all of which have a negative effect on their children's support network and hinder their educational aspirations.

The group also focuses much of its energy on community building and inculcating a sense of self-pride among its membership. In a way not dissimilar to other Dalit and non-Brahmin movements around India, AADHAS has developed an entirely new system of symbols, rituals (including marriages), calendars, etc. that promote a distinctive "Aadi Culture" so that the Valmiki community can move away "from faded identity to [the] Acceptance of Dignified Dalit Identity based on the teachings of Srishtikarta Valmeki Dayavaan and Dr. Bheem Rao Ambedkar ji" (AADHAS, 2022).[3] For AADHAS, the most crucial aspect of this shift from a faded identity to one of dignity is awareness and education. And the struggle for education is epitomized

2 For more on the Valmikis (also called the Balmikis), see Prashad (2000, pp. 65–111) and Leslie (2003, esp. pp. 25–76).

3 The English phrase "Acceptance of Dignified Dalit Identity" here is a slightly jumbled translation of part of the Hindi slogan *dalit astitva kī sammānajanak svīkṛti hetu* (for the dignified acceptance of Dalit identity), which appears on nearly all AADHAS posters, books, and so on.

in the punishment and death of Śambūka, to whom Raavan drew a parallel with Rohith Vemula on Mahāmuni Śambūk Balidān Divas, a day Raavan uses year after year to articulate for his audience the connections between a Brahminically doctored *Rāmāyaṇa* and long-standing Dalit subjugation.

When AADHAS held Mahāmuni Śambūk Balidān Divas on October 30, 2016, it had been about nine and a half months since Vemula's passing. His death and the events leading to it had long since been scrutinized in the media and debates about who was responsible had been raging for months. The reality of Vemula's death was still very much alive in October—so much so that Raavan made it a point to mention him and other victims of institutionalized casteism during his seminar on the life and death of Śambūka.

> Whenever Dalit children are discriminated against in schools and colleges—and Rohith Vemula was driven to suicide; and after that, a girl was brutally murdered in Rajasthan; and this also happened in Madras—a question comes to my mind. People say, "Take to the streets, let's fight." But then I remember Great Sage Śambūk. I think, "No." What happened is terrible, but now is not the time to go all out and fight in the streets. I usually give this as an example: a lot of bricks have to be broken in order to build a building. Many of them fall and break, many are broken in order to fit them in. But will the building ever be made if we take all of the bricks and go fight with them? No, it will never be made. Those children that are studying now, those bricks that have to be fit into the building—that have to make the building magnificent—let them do their work. If a brick cracks in half, the person who bought the brick will be upset when it breaks. But the other side of this is that a building is being made. So Great Sage Śambūk said that we need to think of raising up this building. We need to raise up a system… an entire system. (Raavan, 2016a)

Raavan's thoughts on Vemula are challenging. He wants to resist the inflamed sentiments of those who were angered by Vemula's death to the point of direct action and instead urges his audience to keep the bigger picture in mind. For Raavan, Vemula was an unfortunate casualty of the same societal overhaul that he believes Śambūka was trying to enact in his own time. Śambūka's educational revolution is slow and painful, but it is noble and the battle is still being fought today. So long as Dalit students face discrimination in their schools and their communities, the message of Śambūka remains relevant. It is easy to consider Vemula and Śambūka to be victims of systematic oppression, but the more hopeful understanding of their sacrifice is that they are both martyred heroes of the revolution meant to drive out that oppression. Raavan seems to acknowledge an underlying truth in both ways of seeing these figures, but the latter always gets the last word as it is most mobilizing for the Dalit community at large. If one characterizes Śambūka or Vemula as mere victims, then casteism emerges unchallenged and their deaths lack any greater meaning. If they are remembered as heroes, however, then Śambūka's message of revolution remains animated in the present day and there is some impetus to continue chipping away at the obstacles of caste.

The day on which Raavan said these words about Vemula is deserving of some attention as well. Mahāmuni Śambūk Balidān Divas is an annual commemoration of Śambūka's death and martyrdom and an occasion on which Raavan is able to reiterate the importance of Dalit education. In 2016, the occasion was marked on October 30, a day most of India celebrated as Diwali. That Mahāmuni Śambūk Balidān Divas happens close to Diwali (and on Diwali itself when I attended in 2016) is no coincidence. According to AADHAS, Śambūka has an intimate connection to this festival of lights. A book published by the group poses a question: "Is Diwali related to the killing of Śambūka?" The response begins by comparing a guru to a lamp that casts light on ignorance and Śambūka—along with his wife, Tuṅgabhadrā—were two such gurus working on behalf of the downtrodden. They were both killed to keep those whom they were trying to educate in the dark. The book continues:

> The killing of Great Sage Śambūk and Mother Tuṅgabhadrā was seen as being connected to the education (lamp) of the Dravidians and Nagavanshis.
> When news of Great Sage Śambūk's death arrived in Ayodhyā four days later, the Aryans, overjoyed, lit lamps in celebration and said, **"Look, you Dravidians and Nagavanshis are in the dark and we (Aryans) are in the light, even on a night [as dark as] Amāvas."** This is the meaning of Diwali. There are many such Hindu festivals that are connected to the slaughter of our ancestors. (Raavan, 2014, pp. 72–73)[4]

With Diwali and Śambūka's death being so closely related according to AADHAS, Raavan insists that AADHAS always hold Mahāmuni Śambūk Balidān Divas on the Sunday closest to Diwali (Raavan, 2016b). In fact, AADHAS always holds their seminars on Sundays as it allows for families to come regularly and does not interfere with work or—most importantly for AADHAS—school (ibid.).

Mahāmuni Śambūk Balidān Divas is, on the whole, much like many of AADHAS' events. It is primarily a seminar delivered by Raavan that focuses

4 The emphasis and parenthetical remarks are original to the text.

on promoting education among its membership, especially young girls, which is AADHAS' most palpable concern. You get a sense of education's importance at this and other events through posters that often line the walls, poles, doors, and windows in and around the venues hosting AADHAS. The posters feature images of Darshan Raavan himself, Ambedkar, Nelson Mandela, Martin Luther King, Jr., Vālmīki, Raidās, and Ekalavya, among others. They either have empowering quotes spoken by or attributed to these figures or statements on the importance of reservations and persistence in getting oneself and one's children educated. During the 2016 event, AADHAS also placed a large poster as a backdrop to the stage that featured a graphic depiction of Śambūka's decapitation on one side and images of Ambedkar and Darshan Raavan on the other.

After Raavan took his seat on the stage, AADHAS members came up to pay their respects to him accompanied by *bhajans* and other songs describing Dalit identity, education, and the supremacy of Rāvaṇa. When Raavan began speaking, he used the occasion to clarify and correct numerous misconceptions and misrepresentations about Śambūka's life in a way that resembles many of the themes associated with his story that have been developing over the last century. As an orator, however, he elaborated on these themes considerably. He described a beautiful *āśrama* run by Śambūka and a Brahminical conspiracy against Śambūka meant to shut down his push for educating Dalits. In describing the aftermath of the Brahmin boy's death and the frantic search for a cause, Raavan explained to his audience that "it is *adharma* when a Śūdra—an Untouchable (*achūt*)—would get himself educated. And then to go settle [in the mountains looking] to establish an *āśrama*. This is *adharma*, right? This is written in our Śāstras" (Raavan, 2016a). The beauty and order of Śambūka's *āśrama*, Raavan was sure to point out, captivated and impressed Rāma. The *āśrama* was a place of learning—a place that Śambūka created to follow his own pursuit of knowledge and to help others do the same. However, this quest for knowledge brought with it a gradual disavowal of the Brahminical social order culminating in intellectual challenges to that order. Because of that, it had to be destroyed.

As for why Śambūka wanted to build his *āśrama* and start his revolution, Raavan recited the following verse:

> He crafted the birds' beak like a tool;
> Śambūk [says], do praise such a noble man.[5]

5 The appearance of Śambūka (Hindi, *śambūk*) here, I believe, is not part of the grammar of the verse. Rather, I believe that this verse is attributed to Śambūka and has inserted his name into the verse as a signature. This verse is part of a series known as the Vālmīki

In explaining its meaning, Raavan said:

> There are many kinds of birds that peel tree trunks, that dig at trees. When they dig inside these trees, they take out [the insects], the bugs and eat them. But first they actually have to dig into the tree. And how do they do this? They don't have a saw, they don't have an axe. They don't have anything except for their beak. So Great Sage Śambūk is saying that God gave them a beak that they can use to take insects out from inside the tree trunk. If we were made to be slaves, if we were born to sweep, if were born to clean up trash […] then we wouldn't need these [kinds of] hands. Instead, your hand would be a broom's [brush], and just as your nails keep growing, its bristles would keep growing. […] You would have a long pole here [on your arm], really long. […] But it's not [like that]. He gave you the same hands that a Brahmin has. […] Great Sage Śambūk thought about this at that time. He said "If God made us equal, then who is spreading these divisions? Who is teaching us about this?" He said, "No, I am not going to believe this, I am not going to accept this anymore. I cannot believe this." And Great Sage Śambūk built his *āśrama*. (Raavan, 2016a)

For Raavan, Śambūka's intellectual endeavors and challenges to the social order of his day are the reason for the Brahmins' conspiracy against him—and the conspiracy runs deep, even into the reception of the *Rāmāyaṇa* text itself. Raavan believes that the *Rāmāyaṇa* as we know it today is nothing more than a Brahminical redaction. Vālmīki's words have been manipulated and misrepresented through Brahmins' additions and, just as important, deletions. The *Rāmāyaṇa*, according to Raavan, is massively reduced in content by thousands of verses (Raavan, 2017b). The excision of this material has transformed Vālmīki from an impartial witness to the story's events into a Brahminical sympathizer; it has transformed Śambūka from a revolutionary educator and charismatic orator into a passive ascetic and voiceless victim.

By way of example, we find in the *VR* we know today that Śambūka is hanging upside-down and practicing *tapas* in hopes of attaining divinity with his body (cf. 7.67.2). What we do not know, according to Raavan, is that this is all

---

Akṣar-mālā, which appears in the *Ādi Nityanem*, an AADHAS scriptural text. This Vālmīki Akṣar-mālā is structured around the Devanāgarī alphabet praising figures like Īśvara, Vālmīki, Rāvaṇa and outlining the AADHAS community's aims in life.

fabricated. Śambūka was not simply hanging upside-down practicing *tapas*. Rāma hung Śambūka upside-down from a tree and proceeded to slowly draw his sword across his neck to get him to confess to his crimes (Raavan, 2016b). Raavan considers Rāma's ability to judge Śambūka's crimes to be further misrepresentations. He discredits Rāma's capacity in this regard on both authoritative and personal grounds. To the former point, Rāma is a worldly king and his domain is his kingdom on earth. He has no place in determining whether someone is worthy of heaven. That authority lies with God (*parameśvara*) alone, a point that Raavan reiterated during his speech. As to the latter, Raavan charges Rāma with mistreating his wife, thus disqualifying him from exhibiting sufficient moral fortitude to be able to judge another person (2014, pp. 71–72).

Just before Raavan took the stage for another AADHAS event commemorating Ambedkar Jayanti in 2017, I asked him to elaborate on the issue of Śambūka's *tapas* and what about this story is misrepresented in the *Rāmāyaṇa* as we have it today. I asked whether the story about Śambūka's *tapas* was just a lie that was added to the *Rāmāyaṇa*. If so, how and why was it added, and by whom? He responded:

> it was *changed* by Brahmins—not added—changed. Consider this: If someone is hanging upside-down doing *tapasyā*, praying upside-down, then who are you or I to object? If he is doing it in his house—even if he's doing it upside-down—then we should have no objection to it. But I might object if I feel that there is some threat to my authority. And there was a threat to Brahminical authority because he [Śambūk] was educating children. And Brahmins are feeling quite threatened even today. This same thing is happening today. Today he says that when Dalits—the SCs—learn, if an OBC were to learn, then it will be a threat to a Brahmin's authority. The CM of U.P. [Yogi Adityanath] has just done this very thing. As soon as he became CM he put an end to reservations for SCs in private institutions. [...] So Śambūk was not hanging upside-down doing *tapasyā*. His *tapasyā* wasn't even *tapasyā*. *Tapasyā* here means that he was educating children—he established an institute. After that those children were massacred. There is a river in the South, the Tungabhadra. The story goes that it was formed from the blood of those children. (Raavan, 2017b)

Raavan's response here gets to the heart of the Brahminical conspiracy that he believes is muted in the *Rāmāyaṇa* with which most people are familiar.

The issue is not a Śūdra practicing asceticism—this is a coverup by Brahmin redactors.[6] The real problem is the threat of education, a subject that never appears in this doctored *VR*. Though Raavan emphasizes it as being mischaracterized as *tapas* more pointedly than others, the argument that education is at the center of the Brahminical conspiracy against Śambūka is nothing new. Several Dalit and non-Brahmin movements of the twentieth century contributed to such an understanding of the Śambūka story, a history about which Raavan is certainly aware. That history, however, comes with some contention. Being the leader of a social community and religious movement that reveres Vālmīki, Raavan is at odds with some Dalit and non-Brahmin leaders for overstepping their criticisms of the *Rāmāyaṇa* and Vālmīki's role in its creation.[7] In explaining that Vālmīki is to be praised, not scorned, for telling the story, Raavan notes that "if the Gracious Vālmīki, ocean of compassion, had not revealed this instance of [Śambūk's] killing, then several Dalit writers, along with Periyar Ramasami, would never have made the mistake of saying such [degrading] things [about Vālmīki] as they try to elevate themselves by chastising Rāma for murdering Great Sage Śambūk and Mother Tuṅgabhadrā" (2014, p. 107).[8] What he is suggesting here is that Vālmīki exposed the situation that Dalit and non-Brahmin activists are now using to criticize their oppressors. Without such an account, they would have lost their ammunition against Brahminical supremacy. Hence, their criticism of Vālmīki is unfounded and misplaced. Vālmīki is an ally, not an enemy.

One notices throughout Raavan's descriptions of Śambūka's death, especially when he speaks to a live audience, that he constantly brings the circumstances of Śambūka's death in line with relevant current events or experiences. Sometimes the parallels are very clear and out in the open, as was the case with his connecting Śambūka's death with Rohith Vemula's and his finding commonality between Yogi Adityanath rolling back reservations

6 In fact, Darshan Raavan explained to me on multiple occasions that Śambūka would never have practiced *tapas* in the first place. In the AADHAS philosophical understanding, *tapas* is not a path towards salvation. Knowledge (*jñāna*) is the only way to get there. Śambūka, Raavan notes, would have realized the inefficacy of *tapas* in reaching his goal (Raavan, 2016b, 2017b).

7 The devotion towards Vālmīki is prevalent at many AADHAS functions. For example, regardless of the specific purpose of any particular AADHAS event, Darshan Raavan often concludes them by leading his congregation in a series of prayers and prostrations toward an image of Vālmīki.

8 Raavan is similarly critical of E.V. Ramasami's *The Ramayana (A True Reading)* and its Hindi translation (2014, pp. 101–102).

upon being elected CM of Uttar Pradesh and the Brahminical conspiracy against Śambūka's educational endeavors. Sometimes, though, the parallels are more subtle: his explanation, for example, of Śambūka's verse about the practicality of a bird's beak by guiding his audience in imagining their hands and arms taking the shape of brooms and discrediting the validity of the casteist designation of occupations such as scavenging and sweeping.

## Śambūka in *The Last Letter*

The second example of a connection drawn between Śambūka and Rohith Vemula comes with the short street play entitled *The Last Letter*, created and performed by Jana Natya Manch, Janam for short. Safdar Hashmi founded the group, an unapologetically left-wing drama troupe dedicated to bringing plays to the people, in 1973. Most often, Janam conducts short, impromptu performances riddled with satire and political commentary in outdoor, public locations. Members of the group may stop at a crowded section of a market or a busy intersection of narrow pedestrian-filled gullies where they call attention to themselves with drumming and boisterous slogans meant to rouse people's interest and announce the performance. With many of their performances unfolding in unaccommodating areas like this following snap decisions, the bulk of their repertoire consists of flexible and easily staged street plays, of which *The Last Letter* is one example.

The group is still active today—some fifty years after its founding—though they have spent the last few decades without their founder. Janam was attacked on January 1, 1989 during a performance of the play *Halla Bol!* in support of the Communist Party of India (Marxist) candidate in an upcoming election. The attackers were supporters of a rival candidate whose procession passed by the performance space in an industrial area to the northeast of Delhi. Safdar was beaten unconscious in the chaos and died a day later. Janam returned to the space on January 3 to finish their performance of *Halla Bol!*.

With its leftist values, Janam holds progressive views on the eradication of social stratification of any kind, especially when rooted in caste. Safdar, though, did not live to see his organization take an official stance on caste. The catalyzing event that pushed Janam towards taking such a stance would come just months after his untimely death: the Mandal Commission riots discussed at the outset of this chapter.

While India was dealing with the Commission and its backlash in the early 1990s, Marathi Playwright G.P. Deshpande was developing a proscenium play entitled *Satyaśodhak* (*Seekers of the Truth*) based on the life of Jotirao Phule. Among the major themes addressed in *Satyaśodhak*—and particularly relevant to the aftermath of the Mandal Commission recommendations—are the right to education and an assertion of a prideful history and culture. Arjun Ghosh writes in his close look at Janam that, "based on available resources and on Phule's own writings, Deshpande weaves a plot in which Jyotirao Phule becomes a pioneering voice in the battle against the caste system, charting the strategy of countering the brahmanical hegemony through the spread of knowledge and a sovereign culture" (2012, p. 172).

As Deshpande wrote the play, it was simultaneously being translated into Hindi by Chandrakant Patil and rehearsed by members of Janam. With its sympathetic stance on Phule's activism and anti-caste sentiments, the play marked Janam's first official foray into the realm of caste politics nearly twenty years after its founding. Not only had Janam been silent on caste issues, the entire political Left, for which it was an active voice, "had often been criticized for not having taken a clear position on the question of caste-based exploitation" (Ghosh, 2012, p. 171). *Satyaśodhak* served as Janam's—and the CPI(M)'s, to some extent—stance against casteist oppression.[9]

Janam, it is worth noting, also created an entire proscenium play focused on caste issues while utilizing the Śambūka story as a conduit for its messaging. The play, written in 2004 by playwright and Janam member Brijesh, is entitled *Śambūk Vadh* (*Killing Śambūka*). It features several narratives from Sanskrit literature that are woven together with the Śambūka story to create a complex narrative and cast of characters that represent a wide range of views on caste. The play's director, Sudhanva Deshpande, has written about the play and the process of its creation at length elsewhere (Deshpande, 2021), but a few aspects of its creation are noteworthy in the present context. In producing a play centered on Śambūka, the urban middle-class status and the leftist, caste- and creed-blind position of Janam and its membership bring the issues underlying the story into an entirely different creative schematic than other depictions we have explored so far in the modern period. Unlike Śambūka's depiction in the plays of figures like Achhutanand or Lalai Singh, who each show him as a valorous hero, martyr, and spokesman for a glorious and prosperous Adivasi past, Janam's take on the Śambūka story places him as a representative of just one kind of Dalit liberation—one based on a measured dismantling of the Brahminical *varṇa* project through education, understanding, and, to some extent, faith that the State has the lower castes' best interest in mind. Śambūka's stance in the play is controversial not just for those characters who subscribe to the Brahminical worldview, but also for Śambūka's peers who find his methods ineffective or misguided. Brijesh's depiction of

9 For more on *Satyaśodhak*, its development, and its implications for Janam's politics, see Ghosh (2012, pp. 170–173).

such divisions even among Dalits is an analytical take on the larger issues of caste in modern India that comes from his and the Janam organization's particular social, political, and economic positioning within Indian society.

Today, Janam's stance on caste is unambiguous, especially after the creation of two large-scale productions focused on the issue (i.e., *Satyaśodhak* and *Śambūk Vadh*). For them, its institutions and oppressions should not exist; it is dehumanizing not just for the oppressed, but for the oppressor as well. It reduces all people to a plot point on a gradation of purity and inherent worth and the system indoctrinates the higher castes into buying in to their superiority. One should not think that the upper castes are oppressive, but the system itself is oppressive and must be eradicated.[10] For Janam, caste has created an artificial divide between communities that is justified on grounds of purity and supremacy and maintained through acts of violence. The view that caste is an all-encompassing agent of dehumanization permeates Janam's production of *The Last Letter*.

Janam created *The Last Letter* about one month after Vemula's suicide in early 2016 to address his death and its circumstances. The play, about fifteen minutes in length, consists of a series of quotations from Vemula's own suicide note interspersed with excerpted exchanges between government officials, university administrators, and Vemula himself regarding his university suspension. As is the case with many of Janam's street plays, *The Last Letter*'s staging is extremely minimal and suggestive, allowing for the script to communicate the play's meanings and intentions. Not only is the staging limited to make room for the sentiments of the play, Janam purposefully muted its own intervention in the script. None of its members wrote a single word of the script; the original sources are meant to speak for themselves. Providing such agency to the sources is not merely an artistic choice, but a social and political one as well. Janam does not represent the Dalit community. While their left-leaning political views often put them in a position of sympathy with Dalit issues, most of the group's members are not Dalits. Janam speaks in support of Dalits, not for them.

By not adding any material of their own creation attempting to contextualize the words present in the play, Janam puts Vemula's own voice at center stage. His voice is then placed in opposition to antagonizing authority figures and barbed with powerful works of Dalit poetry that echo the sentiments expressed by Vemula in his note. One such work is author and

10 While such a stance is evident throughout their work, such a clear articulation as presented here is based on my conversation in December 2016 with Sudhanva Deshpande.

poet Omprakash Valmiki's *Śambūk kā Kaṭā Sir* (*Śambūka's Severed Head*),[11] which appears in *The Last Letter* immediately after an actor reads the opening of Vemula's suicide note. The poem positions Śambūka's death as a symbol of an insurmountable obstruction hindering India's oppressed communities in their social progress, the consequences of which are tragedies like Vemula's suicide. Śambūka is a constant reminder that society's complacency has, for centuries, ensured that India's oppressed populations have remained suppressed in their ambitions. Below is an excerpt.

Whenever I wanted
to sit in the shade of a lush tree
horrible screams began to echo
in my ears
as if there were countless corpses
hanging from every branch
and Shambuk's severed head lay on the ground,
I want to get up and run
Shambuk's head blocks my path
It cries out—
I have been hanging from this tree for ages
Ram has killed me time and time again
My words flutter like a bird
with severed wings—(Valmiki, 2021, p. 63)[12]

Through his poem, Valmiki depicts a frustration and persistent self-doubt among India's Dalits that has started to fester into a consequential revolution. The poem concludes with:

Shambuk, your blood has seeped
into the ground and any day now
it will erupt
in a volcanic explosion! (ibid., p. 64)

11 In addition to being a poet, Omprakash Valmiki was a major contributor to Dalit literature as an author. His most widely known work is *Jūṭhan* (Delhi: Radhakrishna Prakashan, 1997), a path-breaking autobiography about his experiences growing up as a Dalit.

12 For a complete translation into English, see Valmiki (2021). For the Hindi original, see Valmiki (2012).

Janam's pairing of Valmiki's poem on Śambūka with Vemula's words results in a mutual amplification of their respective messages, resulting in a harmony that elevates both expressions of abhorrence against casteist oppression. Calling on the weight of Śambūka's death in this situation glosses the entire context with the familiar *Rāmāyaṇa* frame while turning the mainstream conceptions of the epic upside down. *The Last Letter* in this way challenges complacency with respect to how Indian society understands the *Rāmāyaṇa* in a wholesale fashion and how it views caste. The play implores audience members to refuse to accept the *Rāmāyaṇa* as an unassailable monolith and, perhaps most importantly, Rohith Vemula's death as an unavoidable circumstance of contemporary caste politics.

## Śambūka, Rohith Vemula, and the Lynching of African Americans in the United States

A final example of Rohith Vemula's portrayal as a modern parallel to Śambūka comes in the form of a poem written by Chandramohan S., a Dalit poet from Kerala who writes exclusively in English. As we already saw in the case of Omprakash Valmiki's *Śambūk kā Katā Sir*, poetry provides an especially vibrant and flexible vocabulary whereby one can make veiled allusions to the shared set of circumstances that surround these two figures. Chandramohan S. takes this parallel further and seeks to connect not only Vemula and Śambūka to each other, but also connect the common circumstances of their deaths to similarly oppressed communities from elsewhere the world; in this case, to Black victims of lynching in the United States. Frustrated by the circumstances of Vemula's death, Chandramohan S. wrote *Killing Shambuka* to address the incident. I cite the short poem in its entirety:

**Killing Shambuka**
Jim Crow segregated hostel rooms,
Ceiling fans bear a strange fruit,
Blood on books and blood on papers,
A black body swinging in mute silence,
Strange fruit hanging from tridents.[13]

It is worthwhile to place *Killing Shambuka* in the context of Chandramohan's work as a whole. Much of his subject matter relates to caste, but that does not constitute the full extent of his work. He devotes considerable anger and vulnerability to addressing and empowering victims of patriarchy, globalization,

13 This poem appears on p. 4 in Chandramohan S.'s *Letters to Namdeo Dhasal: Poems by Chandramohan S* (Vadodara: Desirepaths Publishers, 2016).

sexism, objectification, greed, violence, exploitation, homophobia, and casteism. The aggressive bluntness of Chandramohan's poetry is often punctuated by a pointed brevity and numerous references to the legal injunctions, mythology, and history of his surroundings that have converged into a long-building momentum of oppression aimed at the communities he features in his work. In addition to invoking the casteism underlying Śambūka's death, Chandramohan also addresses the misuse of the Unlawful Activities (Prevention) Act,[14] the whiplash of High Court and Supreme Court rulings associated with Sec. 377 of the IPC,[15] and the revolutionary actions of prominent figures in Kerala like Ayyankali and Nangeli.[16]

As for *Killing Shambuka* itself, the poem traverses a massive amount of geographic, temporal, and mytho-historical space with just five lines and a title. The most explicit paradigm of comparison is between Rohith Vemula's twenty-first-century suicide and early twentieth-century lynchings of Black Americans. Such a comparison is accomplished by modeling the entire poem on *Strange Fruit*, a fact that Chandramohan acknowledges at the bottom of the page where the poem appears in his volume, *Letters to Namdeo Dhasal* (2016). He writes: "This poem draws its inspiration from the poem 'Strange Fruit' (1937) by Abel Meeropol and is on the suicides of Dalit-bahujan students in institutions of higher education in India. Rohith Vemula is the most recent victim" (2016, p. 4).

Meeropol's *Strange Fruit* was popularized in 1939 as a song performed and recorded by Billie Holiday. However, prior to its life as a song, it was first published as a poem in 1937 under the title *Bitter Fruit* in a monthly union publication, *The New York Teacher*. The opening stanza reads:

> Southern trees bear a strange fruit,
> (Blood on the leaves and blood at the root,)
> Black body swinging in the southern breeze,
> Strange fruit hanging from the poplar trees. (Meeropol, 1937)

---

14 The Unlawful Activities (Prevention) Act of 1967 or UAPA was intended to provide a means of preventing terrorism, but it is frequently misused to circumvent freedom of speech protections and quash revolutionary activity in areas of social justice.

15 Indian Penal Code sec. 377 is the section of the IPC that serves as the basis for deeming homosexuality a criminal offense in India.

16 Ayyankali was a social reformer from Kerala who advocated for the social and educational advancement of the untouchable castes, especially the Pulayars, a group to which he himself belonged. See Francois Houtart and Genevieve Lemercinier (1978, pp. 22–25). Nangeli was an Ezhava woman believed to have lived in the nineteenth century who cut off her breasts in protest of the breast tax (*mulakkaram*) imposed by the Kingdom of Travencore on low-caste women as soon as they reached adolescence. Whether or not Nangeli existed historically is a matter of debate, but her legend is increasingly evident in Kerala today.

The origin of *Bitter Fruit* (or *Strange Fruit*) provides yet another basis of comparison—an especially visual one—between lynching cases in the United States and Dalit-Bahujan deaths in India. In 1971, Meeropol wrote a letter to Linda Kuehl, who had intended to write a biography of Billie Holiday, describing how he came to write the poem. In it, he writes:

> Way back in the early Thirties, I saw a photograph of a lynching published in a magazine devoted to the exposure and elimination of racial injustice. It was a shocking photograph and haunted me for days. As a result, I wrote "Strange Fruit." (Kovaleff Baker, 2002, p. 45)[17]

Kovaleff Baker notes that the photograph mentioned in the letter is not among Meeropol's papers housed in a special collection at Boston University and it could have been any one of many photos that drove him to compose his poem (2002, p. 45). Acknowledging this uncertainty, the literature at large and the Internet are, nevertheless, peppered with several unsubstantiated claims that the photograph is that of Thomas Shipp and Abram Smith taken by Lawrence Beitler after they were lynched and gawked at by a crowd of white onlookers in 1930. This popular assumption of Meeropol's inspiration seems to have informed the graphic design choices of the cover of Chandramohan's *Letters to Namdeo Dhasal*, the volume of poetry in which *Killing Shambuka* appears. On this cover, several lifeless men suspended in the air recall this infamous photo. Above each of these lynching victims hovers a ceiling fan draped in a blue flag, an image of the Ambedkar Students' Association banner that Rohith Vemula used to hang himself from the hostel ceiling fan at the University of Hyderabad. Both the poem's content and the cover art combine to draw deep connections between histories of oppression shared by Indian Dalits and African Americans. The comparison is given an extra dimension of atemporal mytho-history through the poem's title, *Killing Shambuka*. This image extends into the cover art as well. Beneath the hanging victims, a blue-skinned, multi-armed figure frantically and violently decapitates a condemned man kneeling before him with a cartoonish flood of blood spilling out across the cover. And so, with *Killing Shambuka*'s few lines, we see two simultaneous images superimposed: the Black victims of Jim Crow-era lynchings in the United States and the Dalit-Bahujan victims of recent suicides in India, all packaged in an aura of epic mythology by way of its concise title.

---

17 Kovaleff Baker cites the letter as follows: Lewis Allen, letter to Miss [Linda] Kuehl, July 28, 1971, in the Meeropol Collection.

## Controlling the Narrative: Śambūka's Slaughter

This chapter and the previous one have outlined an enormous change in control over the details of the Śambūka story when anti-caste activists take charge of the narrative's nuance. That control extends not only to how the story is told, but also to how it is talked about. We have seen throughout this chapter how Śambūka can be framed in terms of recent events such as the death of Rohith Vemula. Darshan Raavan, Janam, and Chandramohan S. each identify the circumstances surrounding Vemula's suicide as abetted by caste discrimination, which exists as an institutionalized and continually lived obstacle for countless Dalit, OBC, and Adivasi students. They borrow the vocabulary of the Śambūka story to help elucidate this reality and make their message more powerful. In each iteration of the Śambūka story highlighted in this chapter, the Śūdra's death operates as an allegory for instances of silencing the oppressed, quashing revolution, and perpetuating instances of caste-based violence that are still happening today. The activists from this chapter have identified a commonality between Śambūka's death and contemporary Dalit and non-Brahmin experiences. In this way, and in the hands of these activists, the Śambūka story has moved away from being a purely didactic narrative meant to demonstrate the greatness of Rāma or the personal benefits of his salvific qualities to a cathartic narrative meant to speak to the experiences of those who share in Śambūka's pain. In contexts such as those highlighted over the last two chapters, the Śambūka story is meant to teach its audience about the importance of education, the necessity of sacrifice and challenges to the social *status quo*, and the power of connecting histories and common experiences.

There is yet another, slightly more subtle way in which the discourse around Śambūka has changed in recent years. When those representing Śambūka's same social position analyzed and reflected on the consequences of the narrative, the vocabulary used to describe how Rāma and Śambūka interacted began to evolve. Before attending Mahāmuni Śambūk Balidān Divas in 2016, I sat down to discuss Śambūka with AADHAS chief Raavan, seeking his insights on some of the material I had been collecting. I had brought with me several plays and other literature including Achhutanand's *Rām-Rājya-Nyāy*, Santram B.A.'s *Niraparādh kī Hatyā*, Periyar Lalai Singh and Ram Avtar Pal's *Śambūk Vadh*, and Brijesh's *Śambūk Vadh* written for Janam. I also had with me a collection of songs entitled *Rām Rājya banām Śambūk Vadh* (*The Reign of Rāma versus the Killing of Śambūka*) by Buddha Sangh "Premi" and a narrative poem entitled *Śambūk kā Balidān* (*Śambūka's Sacrifice*) by R.V. Suman. When I showed these to Raavan, he made a telling observation almost immediately. Without opening any of the pamphlets, he singled out the works of Singh and Pal, Janam, and Buddha Sangh "Premi" as having misleading titles.

Each of these titles characterize Śambūka's killing by using the Hindi term *vadh*. For Raavan, this word suggests that Rāma was enacting a punishment to match an equally severe crime. But in his understanding of the story, Śambūka had committed no crime and, as such, *vadh*, which to Raavan implies more of an execution, is a wholly inappropriate term to use when describing the circumstances of his death. In place of words like *vadh*, Raavan generally refers to Śambūka's killing as *qatl*, an Arabic word that might be better translated as "slaughter." After explaining to me his preferred vocabulary for discussing how Śambūkda died, Raavan then pointed to R.V. Suman's work, *Śambūk kā Balidān* as a work that captured the appropriate sentiments that surround Śambūka's death. The term *balidān* conveys the sacrifice that Śambūka gave in his push for the education and uplift of his followers (Raavan, 2016b).

About a month after meeting with Darshan Raavan, I discussed the production of Janam's *Śambūk Vadh* with its director, Sudhanva Deshpande. I showed him the same set of materials that I showed Raavan. The first thing he mentioned after looking through them was that some Dalit friends of his immediately questioned Janam's use of the term *vadh* in the title of their own production. Though the play had already been completed by the time he received this feedback, Deshpande mentioned that they would have rather seen his death referred to as "*hatyā*," a term best rendered as "murder" (Deshpande, 2016). Deshpande and I, as non-Dalits, had never considered this aspect of classifying the Rāma-Śambūka interaction. But for Darshan Raavan and some of Deshpande's Dalit friends, the idea of referring to his death as a *vadh* was entirely untenable and elicited some criticism.

The power of those from the same social group as Śambūka to stake a claim over how to define his death at the level of preferred word choice is a hallmark of the shift in momentum surrounding the tradition's evolution in the twenty-first century. That control over vocabulary and how the episode is *discussed* is extrapolated to control over the narrative itself and how it is *portrayed*. Developments to the Śambūka episode during the twentieth and twenty-first centuries—a sampling of which I have covered in the last two chapters—carried out by anti-caste activists from a similar social community as Śambūka have entirely redirected the story's messaging to be more sympathetic to and resonant with the Dalit and non-Brahmin experience. The most pressing concerns from within these communities—education, violence, muted histories, persistent subjugation, revolution, sacrifice—have shown up time and time again as central themes in recent iterations of the Śambūka narrative. By introducing expedient social issues of current times into the Śambūka story, activists have been able to seamlessly apply its messaging to current events like Rohith Vemula's death and use the episode as an illustration of the longstanding and ongoing prevalence of casteism.

# Chapter 9

# CONCLUSION: ŚAMBŪKA AND THE *RĀMĀYAṆA* TRADITION

The continued expansion of the *Rāmāyaṇa* tradition for the past two millennia and the flexibility of its expression hinges on the fact that the *Rāmāyaṇa*—as A. K. Ramanujan reminds us—is "always already" (1991, p. 46). The trouble is not in locating its stories. The trouble comes with trying to negotiate all the different ways the stories coexist—all the ways in which they have "already" existed and will continue to "already" exist. Throughout the course of this study, I have tried to connect some of these stories to each other and to the contexts of their creation to demonstrate just how complex the inner workings of the *Rāmāyaṇa* tradition really are. We must not take for granted the stories we receive; they have been through a long history of change and it is in the social propulsions behind such change that we locate literature's deeper meanings and its effects on the people who create it, read it, pass it on, and bring it into new avenues of expression.

Since the beginning of the *Rāmāyaṇa* tradition, whenever that may have been, people have evoked the *Rāmāyaṇa* and the many morals, controversies, truths, and fabrications buried within its stories to bolster any number of social, religious, and political viewpoints. The focus here has been one story that has splintered into numerous modes of narration depending on the needs and intentions of its tellers. As Śambūka's death toll climbs, his narrative tradition gets broader, more complex, and more all-encompassing. Each new iteration carries with it a new message and a fresh perspective on the meaning behind his life and death. Śambūka has died over and over again in a near endless stream of stories, poems, paintings, speeches, dramas, dances, movies, and more. With his story uniquely situated at the intersection of artistic innovation, caste politics, religion, and violence, each expression of his death is poised to comment on a range of social issues and even on the nature of the *Rāmāyaṇa* itself.

The purpose underlying Śambūka's death has been evolving since the first time his story was penned in the *Vālmīki Rāmāyaṇa*. By showing some concern for Śambūka's afterlife, Kālidāsa used the story to demonstrate Rāma's graciousness and authority in alignment with the Gupta Empire's religious innovations and political ambitions. Vimalasūri employed the story in his simultaneous projects of correcting what he believed to be Vālmīki's Brahminical lies and maintaining Rāma's position as an illustrious figure who embodies the nonviolent ideals of the Jain tradition. In the centuries that followed these initial responses to this troubling episode, the seemingly unassuming character of Śambūka helped express numerous ideologies in the works of many medieval authors as Rāma-*bhakti* flourished as a conduit for social, religious, and intellectual expression. Śambūka's death even helped Bhavabhūti sustain a sentiment of pity in his *Uttararāmacarita*, illustrate Rāma's conflicted state of mind, and ignite an emotional reunion of Rāma and Sītā. But the impact of Śambūka's story did not always come exclusively through its expression in literature. For centuries, Śambūka has contributed substantially to the lived religious experience of Ramtek, Maharashtra. His story has been used there as an exemplary demonstration of Rāma's grace and the unwavering redemption one receives from devotion to him—and that devotion is reenacted daily as visitors stop by Śambūka's modest temple on their way up the hill to see Rāma. He has even become a central figure in the realm of social justice with numerous Dalit and non-Brahmin activists and authors in the twentieth and twenty-first centuries calling on the Śambūka story to help consolidate a common identity, establish a prideful history, and generate a momentum toward social revolution among India's most oppressed communities. And before all of these highlights to Śambūka's narrative career, his story was there to help a hungry jackal in the *Mahābhārata* convince a grieving family to hold on to the hope that their son might spring back to life.

The Śambūka story has exhibited an extraordinary versatility throughout its two-thousand-year history. For each new way the story has been told, a new purpose has been fulfilled and as the story stands at the ready to accommodate new needs in an ever-evolving social landscape, I have no doubt that people will always be able to find new relevance buried in the tale. I find the Śambūka episode's adaptability in this regard to be especially well illustrated in the painting that serves as the cover for this book. Created by artist Murali T. in August 2012, it is entitled *Śambūkamokṣam* (*The Salvation of Śambūka*) in Malayalam or *Shambuka Moksham—May 2012*, Murali's chosen English title (henceforth, *Shambuka Moksham*). The color palette is distinctly Murali: bold blue, purple, and red supplemented with metallic silver. The painting features two blindfolded figures towering over a man draped in a red cloth. Each of these towering men wields weapons. The first holds a machete in his right hand and an axe in the other; the second holds a bow in his left hand and a machete in his right. The man beneath them has his eyes closed and his hand raised in the *abhaya* gesture, a gesture of reassurance. Near him is a wheel.

In the background are two monkeys, also blindfolded, standing near a car. Both are holding clubs in their right hands. The monkey on the left also holds a machete while the monkey on the right carries a flag for the Communist Party of India (Marxist), or CPI(M). The choice of weaponry in the painting is intimately tied with Hindu imagery of mythic heroes and anti-heroes. The clubs resemble the *gadā* which is traditionally associated with Hanumān. The axe identifies the man on the left as Paraśurāma ("Rāma with an axe") while the bow marks the man on the right as Rāma, hero of the *Rāmāyaṇa*.[1] The title of the painting leads us to understand the man foregrounded at the bottom of the canvas to be Śambūka, unarmed and fallen victim to the violence of the painting's other subjects. At the same time that we see Śambūka in the man at the bottom, the wheel (*cakra*) near the man's head, his topknot, his closed eyes, and his hand making the *abhaya* gesture all suggest the Buddha.

If one considers only the foregrounded scene, it is easy to see this painting as not only a depiction of Rāma's actions against Śambūka, but also Brahminism's violent dominance over Buddhism, which is a recurring theme in much of Murali's work.[2] Leaving it at this, however, does not account for the imagery that pulls us into the modern era: the car and the CPI(M) flag. To understand those features of *Shambuka Moksham*, we need to take a closer look at the man at the bottom of the painting. The face of the man draped in the red cloth is not taken from Murali's own imagination of how Śambūka—or even the Buddha—might have looked. That face belongs to T. P. Chandrasekharan, a political leader in Kerala who was murdered in 2012.

T. P. Chandrasekharan, ex-CPI(M) party member and founder of the rival Revolutionary Marxist Party (RMP), was found hacked to death on May 4, 2012. He was run off the road by a car as he rode his motorcycle near Onchiyam, Kerala. While he was on the ground, a group of men armed with machetes surrounded and killed him. A total of twelve people were found guilty of killing Chandrasekharan, including some prominent members of

1 Paraśurāma, also an *avatāra* of Viṣṇu, is believed to have been sent to earth to rid the world of an arrogant ruling class of Kṣatriyas. He does so violently by killing all male Kṣatriyas and reestablishing Brahminical order.

2 According to Murali, Kerala society starting in the third century is characterized by the intellectual atheism of Buddhism and Jainism—the "*śravaṇa*" culture. For Murali, even Kerala's Namboothiri Brahmins are converted scholars who were once included in the Buddhist intellectual tradition. Once Brahminical culture spread into Kerala by the eighth century, Murali contends that these scholars were forced to convert, lest they be killed. Several of Murali's paintings depict massacres of Buddhist monks and scholars (Murali, 2017).

the CPI(M). The motivation was found to be political. Chandrasekharan's RMP was encroaching on CPI(M) influence, which led the CPI(M) to hatch a plot to murder him.[3]

Though the specific case of T. P. Chandrasekharan's murder inspired Murali to create *Shambuka Moksham*, he did so aiming to depict a larger culture of violence both in northern Kerala and in India at large. His explanation of *Shambuka Moksham* in his book *Amaṇa* clarifies his thoughts on Kerala's potential for nonviolence, even in the face of political hypocrisy, and the messages contained in his painting. He writes that

> [s]o far as society is concerned, the position [of the CPI(M)] is actually something of a cultural shift and a hopeful development. A catalyzing event has awakened us to the possibility of a democratic revolution in society and, because of that, a cultural platform has arisen in our society. I have created the painting Shambuka Moksham under such circumstances as a reminder that the main causes of violence are not resolved by criminal investigation and punishment of yet another political murder. I have given a warning through the creation of this painting that it is not enough to simply believe that society can be made free of violence through politics, authority, and judiciaries; it will be possible to eliminate this issue forever only through the reformulation of culture. (2019, pp. 97–98)

Chandrasekharan may have been the victim of violence, but Murali understood his death to be a catalyst for a genuine push toward a true spirit of nonviolence. For Murali, this reformulation of culture means, at least in part, understanding the place of Hindu mythology in society's taste for violence.[4] As it relates to *Shambuka Moksham* specifically, Murali describes the Śambūka incident and

3 For more on the political tensions in Kerala around the time of T. P. Chandrasekharan's death, see Chaturvedi (2012).

4 In addition to violence, much of Murali's work attempts to expose an obsession in Indian society with casteism, slavery, complacency, superstition, and oppression. The BBC, for example, highlighted a series of Murali's paintings on Nangeli; see the BBC (2016), see also Chapter 8, note 17 in this study. He also has a work depicting Ekalavya (*Ekalavyan̲ṯĕ Tyāgam*, *Ekalavya's Sacrifice*), about which Murali writes: "Ekalavya shows how it is that, as champions of the *Manusmṛti* [=*MDh*], the Brahmins' ideas of *varṇa* and *jāti* put an end to learning and educational endeavors and replaced them with a system of racial exploitation; he shows us how it is that these people concocted a martial discipline using of the bows and arrows of India's tribal population—they Sanskritized it by calling it *dhanurvidyā* [archery], pilfered it, and claimed their own educational monopoly over it" (2019, p. 119).

frames it as a representation of Brahminical oppression and an example of pervasive violence underlying Hindu culture.

> The situation that caused the premature death of a Brahmin boy during the reign of Śrī Rāma—said to be the result of a corruption of the king's righteousness—was resolved through the killing of Śambūka as found in the *Uttararāmāyaṇam.* Śambūka was accused of the horrendous crime of practicing *tapas*, thus defying social law that such knowledge is prohibited to Śūdras. The divine sage Nārada Muni came down from heaven to address the accusation of the Brahmin, who was wailing out of grief for his son. We must recognize that the foundational knowledge of Hindu/caste culture is vile when it gives a divine ordinance for agreeing to the summary execution of Śambūka, sifting through the entire country in the Puṣpaka Vimāna, seeking out the Śūdra, and the horribly disgusting act of decapitating him for engaging in *tapas*, which all [supposedly] attest to the fact that the death of the Brahmin boy happened because of a decline in righteousness brought about by a Śūdra practicing *tapas*. The violence of the ideal man, Śrī Rāma—acting as an obedient servant and custodian of Brahminical caste politics—is following us even into the present day. Even now, caste-Hindu culture is persisting, brutalizing our minds by giving justification for the repetitions of all types of violence—political or otherwise. (2019, p. 99)

Understanding Murali's thoughts on violence in India, especially as exacerbated by the murder of Chandrasekharan, sheds new light on the imagery found in his painting. The two figures in the back are monkeys in Rāma's army ready to do the bidding of their leader and quash Śambūka's revolution. They are also CPI(M) goons, exiting their vehicle as they move in on Chandrasekharan. They represent the complacency and mob mentality that fuels pervasive outbursts of violence. The wheel at the bottom is not just the Buddha's *cakra*, it is also a motorcycle wheel—a very mechanical symbol of the attack on Chandrasekharan. The wheel is a timeless symbol of the Buddhist tradition and a connection to the specific and fleeting moment of Chandrasekharan's death. The man at the bottom is obscured by a red cloth with only his head and right hand visible. This is certainly symbolic of Śambūka's bloody decapitation, but it also suggests the Buddha's robe and T. P. Chandrasekharan's red burial shroud. The painting tells us many stories simultaneously: Rāma's killing of Śambūka, Hindu subjugation of Buddhism, the CPI(M)'s elimination of T. P. Chandrasekharan, and the result of complacency in the face of the violence plaguing India.

Murali's *Shambuka Moksham* perfectly captures the spirit of the Śambūka tradition. The painting shows how the story—just like the *Rāmāyaṇa*—transcends any single time period, religious tradition, or set of political circumstances. Even though the image borrows the cultural weight of the *Rāmāyaṇa* to make its point—criticizing the epic in the process—the focus is on Śambūka. This troubled synchronicity between Śambūka and the *Rāmāyaṇa* is where I find Murali's painting to be a fitting allegory for the overall tradition. Though the Śambūka episode began its narrative history intimately connected to the *Rāmāyaṇa*, it has grown to support a tradition all its own. Its connections to the *Rāmāyaṇa* will always imbue it with an ability to comment on the mythology of South Asia, but it no longer needs to be a part of any particular *Rāmāyaṇa*. The Śambūka tradition is therefore paradoxically part of and independent of the *Rāmāyaṇa* tradition, making it a useful tool for measuring the sweeping impact of the *Rāmāyaṇa* and its capacity to be everywhere, "always already." By being situated squarely within this paradox of participation within and rebellion against the *Rāmāyaṇa* tradition, Murali's *Shambuka Moksham* serves as an appropriate conclusion for this book, which has explored how the Śambūka episode evolved alongside a cascade of social, political, and religious developments in South Asia over the course of nearly two thousand years. Murali's painting lays out visually the layered history of the Śambūka tradition and its wide applicability to innumerable issues. *Shambuka Moksham*'s meaning gets its cultural force from the understood connections—however hostile or adulatory they may be—that Śambūka has to the *Rāmāyaṇa* and the *Rāmāyaṇa* has to South Asian society at large.

I can confidently say that the increasing willingness to engage with the Śambūka story rather than ignore it or wish its controversies away will undoubtedly continue to produce new works and new thoughts on old works. I have tried to show the breadth of Śambūka's reach, but I have regrettably had to leave some things out of this particular path through the historical development of the Śambūka tradition. Acknowledging that the work is not done—and never will be—my intention has been to provide a solid understanding of why the Śambūka story is such an important piece of the *Rāmāyaṇa* tradition and how it came to possess a tradition all its own. As new ways of addressing the complicated history of the story continue to appear, my hope is that I have given readers the context necessary to place these new narratives within the continually morphing framework of *Rāmāyaṇa* and Śambūka stories.

# BIBLIOGRAPHY

## Primary Sources

### *English*


Ambedkar, B.R., 2014a. Annihilation of Caste: The Annotated Critical Edition. New Delhi: Navayana.

———, 2016. Riddles in Hinduism: An Exposition to Englighten the Masses. Delhi: Navayana.

Chandramohan S., 2014. Warscape Verses. Delhi: Authorspress.

———, 2016. Letters to Namdeo Dhasal: Poems by Chandramohan S. Vadodara: Desirepaths Publications.

Deshpande, S, 2016. Interview with Sudhanva Deshpande on December 14, 2016 in New Delhi.

Meeropol, A., 1937. "Bitter Fruit." *The New York Teacher*, 1(12), p. 17.

Murali, T. (Ṭi. Muraḷi), 2017. Interview with T. Murali on May 26, 2017 in Kannur, Kerala.

Ramasami, Periyar E.V., 1972. The Ramayana (A True Reading). Trihcy: Periyar Self-Resepect Propaganda Institution Publications.

———, 2001. The Ramayana (A True Reading). New Delhi: Samyak Prakashan.

Valmiki, O. (Omprakāś Vālmīki), 2021. Shambuk's Severed Head, trans. A. Sherraden. In: P. Richman & R. Bharucha, eds. *Performing the Ramayana Tradition: Enactments, Interpretations, and Arguments*. New York: Oxford University Press, pp. 63–64.


### *Hindi*


Achhutanand, Swami (Śrī 108 Svāmī 'Harihar' Achūtānand), 1995. *Rām-Rājya-Nyāy (Nāṭak): Śambūk-Muni-Balidān*. Lucknow: Bahujan Kalyan Prakashan.

———, 2006. *Rām-Rājya-Nyāy (Nāṭak): Śambūk-Muni-Balidān*. New Delhi: Samyak Prakashan.

Adhar, Ram (Rām Adhar), trans., 2011. *Saccī Rāmāyaṇ*. Nāgpur: Nyāyālay Kṣetra.

———, n.d. *Saccī Rāmāyaṇ*; bound with Lalaī Siṃh Yādav. *Rāmāyaṇ kī Cābhī*. New Delhi: Mangaldeep Prakashan.

*Ādi Nityanem*, n.d. [New Delhi]: Aadhas Sanvaad Publication.

Ambedkar, B.R., 2014b. *Sammān ke liye Dharm Parivartan Kareṃ*. New Delhi: Samyak Prakashan.

Brijesh (Bṛjeś), 2006. *Śambūkvadh*. New Delhi: Jana Natya Manch.

Deshpande, G.P. (Govind Puruṣottam Deśpāṇḍe), 2011. *Satyaśodhak*, trans. Candrakānt Pāṭil (Chandrakant Patil). New Delhi: Jana Natya Manch.

Pal, Ram Avtar & Lalai Singh Yadav (Rām Avtār Pāl & Lalaī Siṃh Yādav), 1990. *Eklavya (Nāṭak)*. Kanpur: Ashok Pustakalaya (Periyar Lalai Singh Charitable Trust).
———, 2009. *Eklavya (Nāṭak)*. New Delhi: Samyak Prakashan.
Raavan, Darshan "Ratna" (Darśan "Ratna" Rāvaṇ), 2014. *Ādikavi Vālmīki ke Kuśī-Lav Kyoṃ Hue Rakṣas se Bhaṅgī (Savāl-Javāb)*. Naī Dillī: Ādhas Saṃvād.
———, 2016a. Speech delivered during Mahāmuni Śambūk Balidān Divas on October 30, 2016 in Shahabad, Haryana.
———, 2016b. Interview with Darshan "Ratna" Raavan on October 30, 2016 in Shahabad, Haryana.
———, 2017a. Speech delivered during Ambedkar Jayanti on April 16, 2017 in Faridabad, Haryana.
———, 2017b. Interview with Darshan "Ratna" Raavan on April 16, 2017 in Faridabad, Haryana.
Ramasami, Periyar E.V. (Periyar Ī. Vhī. Rāmāsāmī), n.d. *Saccī Rāmāyaṇ*, trans. Ram Adhar (Rām Adhar); bound with Lalai Singh Yadavn (Lalaī Siṃh Yādav). *Rāmāyaṇ kī Cābhī*. New Delhi: Mangaldeep Prakashan.
Santram, B.A. (Santrām Bī.E.), 1949. *Hamārā Samāj*. Bombay: Nalanda Prakashan.
———, 2016. *Niraparādh kī Hatyā*. Naī Dillī: Samyak Prakāśan.
Singh, Periyar Lalai (Periyar Lalaī Siṃh), n.d. *Rāmāyaṇ kī Cābhī*; bound with Periyar E.V. Ramasami (Periyar Ī. Vhī. Rāmāsāmī). *Saccī Rāmāyaṇ*, translated by Ram Adhar (Rām Adhar). New Delhi: Mangaldeep Prakashan.
Singh, Periyar Lalai & Ram Avtar Pal (Pairiyar Lalaī Siṃh & Rām Avtār Pāl), 1985. *Śambūk Vadh (Nāṭak)*. Kanpur: Ashok Pustakalaya (Periyar Lalai Singh Charitable Trust).
———, 2013. *Śambūk Vadh (Nāṭak)*. New Delhi: Samyak Prakashan.
Tulsīdās, 1990. *Śrīrāmcaritmānas*, ed. and trans. R.C. Prasad. Delhi: Motilal Banarsidass.
———, 1966. *Gosvāmī Tulsīdāsjī Kṛt Rāmāyaṇ*. Bambaī: Śikṣā Granthāgār.
———, 2016. *The Epic of Ram*, trans. P. Lutgendorf. Cambridge: Harvard University Press, Murty Classical Library of India.
Valmiki, Omprakash (Omprakāś Vālmīki), 1997. *Jūṭhan*. Delhi: Radhakrishna Prakashan, 1997.
———, 2012. Śambūk kā Kaṭā Sir. In: *Pratinidhi Kavitāeṁ: Omprakāś Vālmīki*, ed. Rāmcandra. Delhi: Shilpayan Publishers and Distributers, 2012.

## *Malayalam*

Eḻuttacchan, 1977. *Adhyātmarāmāyaṇam*, ed. Pi. Karuṇākaran Nāyar. Tṛśśūr: Keraḷa Sāhitya Akkādami.
———, 2001. *Adhyātmarāmāyaṇam Kiḷippāṭṭŭ*, ed. Em. Es. Candraśekhara Vāriyar. Kottayam: DC Books, 2001.
Murali, T. (Ṭi. Muraḷi), 2019. *Amaṇa: Caritrattilillātta Citraṅṅaḷ*. 2nd ed. Kannur: Amana Books.
Rāmappaṇikkar̲, Niraṇattu, 2013. *Kaṇṇaśśarāmāyaṇam*, studied and interpreted by Putuśśeri Rāmacandran̲. Thiruvananthapuram: The State Institute of Languages, Kerala.

## *Sanskrit & Prakrit (and Translations)*

*Adhyātma Rāmāyaṇ: Hindī-Anuvādasahita*, n.d., trans. Munilāl. Gorakhpur: Gita Press.
*Adhyātma Rāmāyaṇa*, 1913, trans. Rai Bahadur Lala Baij Nath. Alahabad: Sudhīndra Nātha Vasu.
*Adhyātmarāmāyaṇam: Text with Introduction & English Translation*, 1999, trans. K.P.A. Menon. 2 vols. Delhi: Nag Publishers.

*Ānanda Rāmāyaṇa Attributed to the Great Sage Vālmīki (Sanskrit Text with English Translation)*, 2006. 2 volumes, trans. S. Nagar. Delhi: Parimal Publications.

Bhavabhūti, 1915. *Rama's Later History of Uttara-rama-charita: An Ancient Hindu Drama by Bhavabhūti*, trans. S.K. Belvalkar. Cambridge: Harvard University Press.

———, 1934. *The Uttararāmacarita of Bhavabhūti*, trans. M.R. Kale. Delhi: Motilal Banarsidass.

———, 2007. *Rāma's Last Act by Bhavabhūti*, trans. Sheldon Pollock. New York: New York University Press and the JJC Foundation.

Hemacandra, 1990–2012. *Triṣaṣṭiśalākāpuruṣacaritamahākāvyam.* 5 vols. Amadāvāda: Kalikālasarvajña Śrīhemacandrācārya Navama Janmaśatābdī Smṛti Śikṣaṇa Saṃskāranidhi.

Jinasena, 1965. *Ādipurāṇa [=Mahāpurāṇa], Second Part with Hindi Translation, Appendices, etc.*, ed. Pannālāl Jain. Varanasi: Bharatiya Jnanapitha.

Kālidāsa, 1979. *Meghadūtam*, ed. Saṃsāracandra. Dillī: Motilāl Banārsīdās.

———, 1987. *Raghuvaṃśa-Mahākāvya (Sampūrṇa)*. Dillī: Motilāl Banārsīdās.

Kṣemendra, 1985. *Rāmāyaṇa-Mañjarī*, ed. Pt. Bhavadatta Shastri. Delhi: Chaukhamba Sanskrit Pratishthan.

———, 1989. *Daśāvatāracaritam*, ed. K.D. Giri. Varanasi: Chaukhambha Sanskrit Sansthan.

*Padmapurāṇam Part III: Sṛṣṭikhaṇḍa*, 1894. Poona: Ānandāśrama Press.

*Padma Purāṇam Part I Containing Sṛṣṭi Khaṇḍam*, 2007. Varanasi: Chowkhamba Sanskrit Series Office.

Raviṣeṇācārya (Raviṣeṇa), 1977. *Padmapurāṇam (Padmacaritam)*. 2 vols. Vārāṇasī: Bhāratīya Jñānapīṭha Prakāśana.

———, 2008. *Jain Rāma Kathā or Padma Purāṇa (Padmacarita) Volume 1–2: Composed in Sanskrit by Raviṣeṇācārya*, trans. S. Nagar. Delhi: Eastern Book Linkers.

*Śindūragirimāhātmya*, 1989, ed. Sa. Mo. Ayācit. Nāgpur: Amogh Prakāśan.

*Śivamahāpurāṇam* 1981, ed. N.S. Singh. Delhi: Nag Publishers.

*Śrīmad-Bhāgavata-Mahāpurāṇam (Mūla-Mātram)*, 1999. Gorakhpur: Gita Press.

Svayambhūdeva, 1989. *Paümacariu.* 2 vols., ed. Ec. Sī. Bhāyāṇī. Nayī Dillī: Bhāratīya Jñānapīṭha.

———, 2002. *Jain Rāmāyaṇa—Paumacaryu: Rendering into English from Apabhraṁśa*, trans. S. Nagar. Delhi: B.R. Publishing Corporation.

——— 2018. *The Life of Padma Volume 1*, ed. and trans. E. De Clercq. Cambridge: Murty Classical Library of India and Harvard University Press.

*Taittirīya-Saṃhitā*, 1957. Pāraḍī: Svādhyāya Maṇḍala.

Vālmīki, 1960–1975. *The Vālmīki Rāmāyaṇa: Critical Edition.* 7 vols., ed. G.H. Bhatt and U.P. Shah. Baroda: Oriental Institute.

———, 1983. *Rāmāyaṇa of Vālmīki with the Commentaries Tilaka of Rāma, Rāmāyaṇaśiromaṇi of Śivasahāya and Bhūṣaṇa of Govindarāja Vol. VII: Uttarakāṇḍa*, ed. Shastri Shrinivasa Katti Mudholakara. Delhi: Parimal Publications.

———, 1984–2017. *The Rāmāyaṇa of Vālmīki: An Epic of Ancient India.* 7 vols., ed. R.P. Goldman, trans. R.P. Goldman, et al. Princeton: Princeton University Press.

Vidyāraṇya Svāmin, 1949. *Pañcadaśī* with the commentary of Rāmakṛṣṇa. Mumbai: Nirnayasagar Press.

Vimalasūri, 2005. *Paümacariyaṃ.* 2 vols., ed. H. Jacobi, trans. S.M. Vora. 2nd ed., revised by Muni Shri Punyavijayaji. Ahmedabad: Prakrit Text Society.

## *Primary Sources in Other Languages (and Translations)*

Eknāth, 1962. *Bhāvārth Rāmāyaṇ (Saṅkṣep) arthāt Nāthāṃcā Rām.* Auraṅgābād: Śrī Baḷvant Girirāv Ghāṭe. [Marathi]

Mukteśvar, 1963. *Bhāvārth Rāmāyaṇ: Uttarkāṇḍ*, ed. Vasant Sa. Jośī. Puṇeṃ: Vhīnas Prakāśan. [Marathi]

Raṅganātha, 1961. *Raṅganāth Rāmāyaṇ: Rājā Gonbuddh-racit Mūl Telugu se Anūdit*, 1961, trans. E.Sī. Kāmākṣi Rāv. Paṭnā: Hār-Rāṣṭrabhāṣā-Pariṣad. [Telugu; translated into Hindi]

Raṅganātha, 2001. *Śrī Raṅganātha Rāmāyaṇa: Rendering into English from Telugu*, 2001, trans. S. Nagar. Delhi: B.R. Publishing. [Telugu; translated into English]


## *Court Rulings, Government Gazette Notifications, Policy, etc.*


Criminal Appeal No. 11/2011 (Arising out of Special Leave Petition (Crl) No. 10367 of 2010).

Lalai Singh Yadav v. State of Uttar Pradesh, 1971 Cri LJ 1519 All. (January 19, 1971).

Lalai Singh Yadav v. State of Uttar Pradesh, 1971 Cri LJ 1773 (May 14, 1971).

Law Commission of India. *Indian Penal Code 1860* (Act no. 45 of 1860).

———. Code of Criminal Procedure 1898 (Act no. 5 of 1898).

*Report of the Backward Classes Commission, Parts 1 & 2* [=Mandal Commission Report]. Government of India, 1980.

State of Uttar Pradesh v. Lalai Singh Yadav, 1977 AIR 202, 1977 SCR (1) 616 (September 16, 1976).

U.P. Government Gazette Dec. 20 1969, 5154. Notification no. 9722-R/VIII-B-II-1346-68 (December 8, 1969).

U.P. Government Gazette Sep. 12, 1970, 4450. Notification no. 4431-R/VIII-B/II-1163–70 (August 25, 1970).


## Secondary Sources


AADHAS, 2022. *About Us*. [Online] Available at: http://www.aadhasbharat.com/about-us.php [Accessed 28 January 2019].

Aditya, J. E., 2011. *Mahāprāṇ Karmvīr Pairiyar Lalāī Siṃh kā Jīvan Saṅghaṛṣ*. Kanpur: Periyar Lalai Singh Charitable Trust.

Aklujkar, V., 1995. Rāmāvatāra Recycled. *Annals of the Bhandarkar Oriental Research Institute*, 76(1), pp. 107–118.

———, 2001. Crying Dogs and Laughing Trees in Rāma's Kingdom: Self-Reflexivity in *Ānanda Rāmāyaṇa*. In: P. Richman, ed. *Questioning Ramayanas: A South Asian Tradition*. Berkeley: University of California Press, pp. 83–103.

Anand, S., 2014. *Annihilation of Caste: The Annotated Critical Edition*. New Delhi: Navayana.

———, 2016. Preface. In: S. Anand & S. Iyer, eds. *Riddles in Hinduism: An Exposition to Enlighten the Masses*. New Delhi: Navayana, pp. 7–16.

Bakker, H., 1986. *Ayodhya*. Groningen: Egbert Forsten.

———, 1987. Reflections on the Evolution of Rāma Devotion in the Light of Textual and Archeological Evidence. *WZKS*, 31, pp. 9–42.

———, 1989a. The Ramtek Inscriptions. *Bulletin of the School of Oriental and African Studies, University of London*, 52(1), pp. 467–496.

———, 1989b. The Antiquities of Ramtek Hill, Maharashtra. *South Asian Studies*, 5, pp. 79–102.

———, 1990. Ramtek: An Ancient Centre of Viṣṇu Devotion in Maharashtra. In: H. Bakker, ed. *The History of Sacred Places in India as Reflected in Traditional Literature*. Leiden: E.J. Brill, pp. 62–85.

———, 1991. The Footprints of the Lord. In: D. L. E. Mallison & F. Mallison, eds. *Devotion Divine: Bhakti Traditions from the Regions of India: Studies in Honour of Charlotte Vaudeville*. Groningen: Egbert Forsten, pp. 19–37.

———, 1992a. Memorials, Temples, Gods, and Kings: An Attempt to Unravel the Symbolic Texture of Vākāṭaka Kingship. In: A. van den Hoek, D. Kolff & M. Oort, eds. *Ritual, State and History in South Asia*. Leiden: Brill, pp. 9–16.

———, 1992b. The Manbaus' Seat on Ramtek Hill. In: R. McGregor, ed. *Devotional Literature in South Asia: Current Research, 1985–88*. Cambridge: Cambridge University Press, pp. 11–25.

———, 1997. *The Vākāṭaka: An Essay in Hindu Iconology*. Groningen: Egbert Forsten.

———, 2002. Religion and Politics in the Eastern Vākāṭaka Kingdom. *South Asian Studies*, 18(1), pp. 1–24.

———, 2008. *Mansar: The Discovery of Pravaresvara Temple and Residence of the Vākāṭaka King Pravarasena II*. Groningen: University of Groningen.

———, 2010. Trivikrama: Word and Statue: A New Interpretation of Rāmagiri Evidence. *Acta Orientalia Academiae Scientiarum Hungaricae*, 63(3), pp. 241–247.

———, 2013. The Trivikrama Temple: A New Interpretation of Rāmagiri Evidence (3). *South Asian Studies*, 29(2), pp. 169–176.

Basu, R. S., 2011. The Making of Adi Dravida Politics in Early Twentieth Century Tamil Nadu. *Social Scientist*, 39(7/8), pp. 9–41.

Bauddh, K. N. B., 2009. *Uttar Bhārat kā Periyār: Dalit aur Picharoṃ kā Masīhā Lalaī Siṃh Yādav*. New Delhi: Samyak Prakashan.

Bauddh, S. C., 2006. Introduction to *Rām-Rājya-Nyāy (Nāṭak): Śambūk-Muni Balidān*. New Delhi: Samyak Prakashan.

Belvalkar, S., 1915. *Rama's Later History of Uttara-rama-charita: An Ancient Hindu Drama by Bhavabhūti*. Cambridge: Harvard University Press.

Benke, T., 2010. *The Śūdrācāraśiromaṇi of Kṛṣṇa Śeṣa: A Sixteenth-Century Manual of Dharma for Śūdras*. Philadelphia: University of Pennsylvania.

Bharti, K., 2016. *Lalai Singh Yadav: Fiery Hero of Rebel Consciousness*. [Online] Available at: https://www.forwardpress.in/2016/09/lalai-singh-yadav-fiery-hero-of-rebel-consciousness/ [Accessed 26 February 2017].

Bhatt, G. & Shah, U., eds., 1960–1975. *The Vālmīki Rāmāyaṇa: Critical Edition*. Baroda: Oriental Institute.

Blackburn, S., 1996. *Inside the Drama House: Rama Stories and Shadow Puppets in South India*. Berkeley: University of California Press.

Bose, M., ed., 2004. *The Rāmāyaṇa Revisited*. Oxford: Oxford University Press.

Brockington, J. L., 1984. *Righteous Rāma: The Evolution of an Epic*. Delhi: Oxford University Press.

———, 1998. *The Sanskrit Epics*. Leiden: Brill.

Bronkhorst, J., 2016. *How the Brahmins Won: From Alexander to the Guptas*. Leiden: Brill.

Bronner, Y., 2010. *Extreme Poetry: The South Asian Movement of Simultaneous Narration*. New York: Columbia University Press.

Bulke, Father C., 1999. *Rāmakathā: Utpatti aur Vikās*. Allahabad: Hindi Parishad Prakashan.

Chatterjee, A., 1967. *Padma-Purāṇa: A Study*. Calcutta: Sanskrit College.

Chattopadhyaya, B., 1998. *Representing the Other? Sanskrit Sources and the Muslims (Eighth to Fourteenth Century)*. New Delhi: Manohar.

Chaturvedi, R., 2012. North Kerala and Democracy's Violent Demands. *Economic and Political Weekly*, 47(42), pp. 21–24.

Clines, G. M., 2022. *Jain Rāmāyaṇa Narratives: Moral Vision and Literary Innovation*. London and New York: Routledge.

Cort, J. E., 1993. An Overview of Jain Purāṇas. In: W. Doniger, ed. *Purāṇa Perennis: Reciprocity and Transformation in Hindu and Jaina Texts*. Albany: State University of New York Press, pp. 185–206.

———, 2002. Bhakti in the Early Jain Tradition: Understanding Devotional Religion in South Asia. *History of Religions*, 42(1), pp. 59–86.

Cousens, H., 1971. *Antiquarian Remains in the Central Provinces and Berar*. Varanasi: Indological Book House.

Dakṣināmūrti, E., 1968. *Pampa-Rāmāyaṇ kī Kathā*. Maisūr: Vijaynivās.

Dallapiccola, A. L., Fritz, J. M., Michell, G. & Rajasekhara, S., 1992. *The Ramachandra Temple at Vijayanagara*. New Delhi: Manohar, American Institute of Indian Studies.

Davis, D. R., Jr. & Brick, D., 2018. Social and Literary History of Dharmaśāstra: Commentaries and Legal Digests. In: P. Olivelle & D. R. Davis, Jr., eds. *Hindu Law: A New History of Dharmaśāstra*. New Delhi: Oxford University Press, pp. 30–45.

De Clercq, E., 2018. *The Life of Padma*. Cambridge: Murthy Classical Library of India & Harvard University Press.

Deshpande, S., 2021. The Killing of Shambuk: A Retelling from a Director's Perspective. In: P. Richman & R. Bharucha, eds. *Performing the Ramayana Tradition: Enactments, Interpretations, and Arguments*. New York: Oxford University Press, pp. 83–93.

Dhere, R. C., 2011. *The Rise of a Folk God: Vitthal of Pandharpur*. Oxford: Oxford University Press.

Dumont, L., 1980. *Homo Hierarchicus*. Chicago: University of Chicago Press.

Dundas, P., 2002. *The Jains*. London: Routledge.

*Epigraphia Indica*, 1909–1910. Vol. X., ed., S. Konow and Rai Bahadur V. Venkayya. Bombay: British India Press.

Erndl, K. M., 1991. The Mutilation of Śūrpaṇakhā. In: P. Richman, ed. *Many Rāmāyaṇas: The Diversity of a Narrative Tradition in South Asia*. Berkeley: University of California Press, pp. 67–88.

Feldhaus, A., 1986. Maharashtra as a Holy Land: A Sectarian Tradition. *Bulletin of the School of Oriental and African Studies*, 49, pp. 532–548.

———, 2006. Religious Geography and the Multiplicity of Regions in Maharashtra. In: R. Vora & A. Feldhaus, eds. *Region, Culture, and Politics in India*. New Delhi: Manohar, pp. 189–209.

Fitzgerald, J. L., 2004. *The Mahābhārata: Book 11, The Book of the Women and Book 12, The Book of Peace*. Chicago: University of Chicago Press.

Fleet, J. F., 1960. *Corpus Inscriptionum Indicarum Vol. III: Inscriptions of the Early Gupta Kings and their Successors*. Varanasi: Indological Book House.

Freeman, R., 2003. Genre and Society: The Literary Culture of Premodern Kerala. In: S. Pollock, ed. *Literary Cultures in History: Reconstructions from South Asia*. Berkeley: University of California Press, pp. 437–500.

Geetha, V. & Rajadurai, S., 1998. *Towards a Non-Brahmin Millennium: From Iyothee Thass to Periyar*. Calcutta: Samya.

Gerow, E., 1971. *Indian Poetics*. The Hague: Mouton.

———, 1984. Sanskrit Dramatic Theory and Kālidāsa's Plays. In: B. Stoler Miller, ed. *Theater of Memory: The Plays of Kālidāsa*. New York: Columbia University Press, pp. 42–62.

Ghosh, A., 2012. *A History of the Jana Natya Manch*. New Delhi: Sage Publications.

Gillingham, S., 2018. *Psalms through the Centuries: A Reception History Commentary on Psalms 1–72*. Hoboken: John Wiley & Sons.

Goldman, R. P., 1984. *The Rāmāyaṇa of Vālmīki: An Epic of Ancient India, Volume I: Bālakāṇḍa*. Princeton: Princeton University Press.

———, 2001. Rāvaṇa's Kitchen: A Testimony of Desire and the Other. In: P. Richman, ed. *Questioning Ramayanas: A South Asian Tradition*. Berkeley: University of California Press, pp. 105–116.

———, 2003. The Ghost from the Anthill: Vālmīki and the Destiny of the Rāmakathā in South and South-East Asia. In: M. Bose, ed. *The Rāmāyaṇa Culture: Text, Performance and Iconography*. New Delhi: D.K. Printworld, pp. 11–35.

———, 2005. Historicising the Ramakatha: Valmiki's Ramayana and its Medieval Commentators. *India International Centre Quarterly*, 31(4), pp. 83–97.

———, 2019. Vālmīki's Children: Adulation, Imitation and Ethical Critique in Poets of the Rāmakathā. *Rivista Degli Studi Orientali*, XCII(92), pp. 93–102.

Goldman, R. P. & Sutherland Goldman, S. J., 2017. *The Rāmāyaṇa of Vālmīki: An Epic of Ancient India, Volume VII: Uttarakāṇḍa*. Princeton: Princeton University Press.

Gupta, C., 2017. Speaking Self, Writing Caste: Recovering the Life of Santram BA. *Biography*, 41(1), pp. 16–43.

Guruge, A., 1991. *The Society of the Rāmāyaṇa*. New Delhi: Abhinav Publications.

Hawley, J. S., 2015. *A Storm of Songs: India and the Idea of the Bhakti Movement*. Cambridge: Harvard University Press.

Herman, D., 2009. *Basic Elements of Narrative*. Oxford: Wiley-Blackwell.

Hiltebeitel, A., 2001. *Rethinking the Mahābhārata: A Reader's Guide to the Education of the Dharma King*. Chicago: University of Chicago Press.

———, 2010. *Dharma*. Honolulu: University of Hawai'i Press.

Houtart, F. & Lemercinier, G., 1978. Socio-Religious Movements in Kerala: A Reaction to the Capitalist Mode of Production: Part One. *Social Scientist*. 6(11), pp. 3–34.

Hunt, J. M., Smith, R. A. & Stok, F., 2017. *Classics from Papyrus to the Internet: An Introduction to Transmission and Reception*. Austin: University of Texas Press.

Hunt, S. B., 2017. *Hindi Dalit Literature and the Politics of Representation*. New Delhi: Routledge.

Ingalls, D. H., 1976. Kālidāsa and the Attitudes of the Golden Age. *Journal of the American Oriental Soceity*, 96(1), pp. 15–26.

Ivanova, G., 2018. *Unbinding the Pillow Book: The Many Lives of a Japanese Classic*. New York: Columbia University Press.

Jaffrelot, C., 2005. *India's Silent Revolution: The Rise of the Lower Castes in North India*. New York: Columbia University Press.

Jaini, P. S., 1979. *The Jaina Path of Purification*. Delhi: Motilal Banarsidass.

Jamison, S. W. & Brereton, J. P., 2014. *The Rig Veda: The Earliest Religious Poetry of India*. New York: Oxford University Press.

Jha, S., 1978. *Aspects of Brahmanical Influence on the Jaina Mythology*. Delhi: Bharat Bharati Bhandar.

Jigyasu, C. P., 2004. Shree 108 Swami Achhutanandji 'Harihar'. In: B. Narayan & A. Mishra, eds. *Multiple Marginalities: An Anthology of Identified Dalit Writings*. New Dehli: Manohar, pp. 101–129.

Joshi, J. & Sharma, A., 2005. Mansar Excavations 1998–2004: The Discovery of Pravarapur. *Puramanthana*, 3, pp. 1–26.

Juergensmeyer, M., 1982. *Religion as Social Vision: The Movement against Untouchability in 20th-Century Punjab*. Berkeley: University of California Press.

Kaelber, W. O., 1989. *Tapta-Mārga: Asceticism and Initiation in Vedic India*. Albany: State University of New York.

Kale, M., 1934. *The Uttararāmacarita of Bhavabhūti*. Reprint 2010. Delhi: Motilal Banarsidass.

Kane, M. L., 1983. *The Theory of Plot Structure in Sanskrit Drama and Its Application to the "Uttararamacarita"*. Cambridge: Harvard University.

Karandikar, M., 1978. Eknath. In: V. Raghavan, ed. *Ramayana, Mahabharata, and Bhagavata Writers*. New Delhi: Ministry of Information and Broadcasting, Government of India, pp. 51–62.

Knight, W. J., 1956. *Virgil: The Aeneid*. London: Penguin Books.

Kostka, I. & Ranjan, P., 2016. *The Case for Bahujan Literature*. Wardha: The Marginalised.

Kovaleff Baker, N., 2002. Abel Meeropol (a.k.a. Lewis Allen): Political Commentator and Social Conscience. *American Music*, 20(1), pp. 25–79.

Krishnamoorthy, K., ed., 1991–1993. *A Critical Inventory of Rāmāyaṇa Studies in the World*, Vols. 1–2. New Delhi: Sahitya Akademi.

Kulkarni, J.M., 1959. The Origin and Development of the Rāma Story in Jaina Literature. *Journal of the Oriental Institute*, 9, pp. 189–204, 284–304.

———, 1990. *The Story of Rāma in Jain Literature (As Presented by the* (Leslie, 2003) *bara and Digambara Poets in the Prakrit, Sanskrit and Apabhraṁśa Languages)*. Ahmedabad: Saraswati Pustak Bhandar.

Kumar, G., 2009. *Censorship in India*. New Delhi: Har-Anand.

Lacey, H., 2014. Nandivardhana and Nagardhan: Preliminary Analysis of the Surface Evidence from Nagardhan and Hamlapuri in the Eastern Vākāṭaka Territory near Rāmṭek, Maharashtra. *South Asian Studies*, 30(2), pp. 116–132.

Lal, H., 1908. A Visit to Ramtek. *Indian Antiquary*, Volume XXXVII, pp. 202–208.

Leonard, J., 2013. *Faithful Labourers: A Reception History of Paradise Lost, 1667–1970*, Oxford: Oxford University Press.

Leopold, J., 1970. The Aryan Theory of Race. *The Indian Economic & Social History Review*, 7(2), pp. 271–297.

Leslie, J., 2003. *Authority and Meaning in Indian Religions: Hinduism and the Case of Vālmīki*. London: Routledge.

Lieb, M., Mason, E. & Roberts, J., 2011. *The Oxford Handbook of the Reception History of the Bible*. Oxford: Oxford University Press.

Lubin, T., 2013. Aśoka's Disparagement of Domestic Ritual and Its Validation by the Brahmins. *Journal of Indian Philosophy*, 41(1), pp. 29–41.

———, 2018. The Vedic Graduate: *snātaka*. In: P. Olivelle & D. R. J. Davis, eds. *Hindu Law: A New History of Dharmaśāstra*. New Delhi: Oxford University Press, pp. 113–124.

Lutgendorf, P., 1991. *The Life of a Text: Performing the Rāmcaritmānas of Tulsidas*. Berkeley: University of California Press.

———, 1994. My Hanuman Is Bigger Than Yours. *History of Religions*, 33(3), pp. 211–245.

———, 2001. Dining out at Lake Pampa: The Shabari Episode in Multiple Ramayanas. In: P. Richman, ed. *Questioning Ramayanas: A South Asian Tradition*. Berkeley: University of California Press, pp. 119–136.

———, 2016. *The Epic of Ram*. Cambridge: Harvard University Press, Murty Classical Library of India.

Martindale, C., 1993. *Redeeming the Text: Latin Poetry and the Hermeneutics of Reception*. Cambridge: Cambridge University Press.

McClish, M., 2009. *Political Brahmanism and the State: A Compositional History of the Arthaśāstra*. Austin: University of Texas at Austin.

———, 2019. *The History of the Arthaśāstra: Sovereignty and Sacred Law in Ancient India*. Cambridge: Cambridge University Press.

McGregor, S., 2003. The Progress of Hindi, Part 1. In: S. Pollock, ed. *Literary Cultures in History: Reconstructions from South Asia*. Berkeley: University of California Press, pp. 912–957.

Mirashi, V. V., 1959. *Meghdūt meṃ Rāmgiri arthāt Rāmṭek*. Nagpur: Vidarbha Sanshodhan Mandal.

———, 1963. *Corpus Inscriptionum Indicarum Vol. V: Inscriptions of the Vākāṭakas*. Ootacamund: Archaeological Survey of India.

———, 1974. *Bhavabhūti; His Date, Life and Works*. New Delhi: Motilal Banarsidass.

Mirashi, V. V. & Kulkarni, L., 1939–1949. Ramtek Stone Inscription from the time of Ramachandra. *Epigraphia Indica*, Volume XXV, pp. 7–20.

Mirashi, V. V. & Navlekar, N. R., 1969. *Kālidāsa: Date, Life and Works*. Bombay: Popular Prakashan.

Mukherjee, S. K., 1982. *The Story of the Calcutta Theatres 1753–1980*. Calcutta: K.P. Bagchi & Company.

Müller, F. M., 1854. The Last Results of the Sanskrit Researches in Comparative Philology. In: C. Bunsen, ed. *Christianity and Mankind*. London: Longman, Brown, Green, and Longmans, pp. 128–142.

———, 1861. *Lectures on the Science of Language*. London: Longman, Green, and Roberts.

Murthy, N. C. B., 2016. Identity, Autonomy and Emancipation: The Agendas of the Adi-Andhra Movement in South India, 1917–30. *The Economic and Social History Review*, 53(2), pp. 225–248.

Nagar, S., 2001. *Śrī Raṅganātha Rāmāyaṇa: Rendering into English From Telugu*. Delhi: B.R. Publishing.

Narayan, B., 2001. Heroes, Histories and Booklets. *Economic and Political Weekly*, 36(41), pp. 3923–3934.

Narayan, B. & Mishra, A., 2004. *Multiple Marginalities: An Anthology of Identified Dalit Writings*. New Delhi: Manohar.

Narayana Rao, V., 2001. The Politics of Telugu Ramayanas: Colonialism, Print Culture, and Literary Movements. In: P. Richman, ed. *Questioning Ramayanas: A South Asian Tradition*. Berkeley: University of California Press, pp. 159–185.

Nath, V., 2001. From 'Brahmanism' to 'Hinduism': Negotiating the Myth of the Great Tradition. *Social Scientist*, 29(3/4), pp. 19–50.

Novetzke, C. L., 2018. Vernacularization. In: P. Olivelle & D. R. J. Davis, eds. *Hindu Law: A New History of Dharmaśāstra*. New Delhi: Oxford University Press, pp. 480–495.

Obeyeskere, G., 1990. *The Work of Culture: Symbolic Transformation in Psychoanalysis and Anthropology*. Chicago: University of Chicago Press.

O'Hanlon, R., 1985. *Caste, Conflict, and Ideology: Mahatma Jotirao Phule and Low Caste Protest in Nineteenth-Century Western India*. Cambridge: Cambridge University Press.

Olivelle, P., 1993. *Āśrama System: The History of Hermeneutics of a Religious Institution*. New Delhi: Munshiram Manoharlal Publishers.

———, 1999. *Dharmasūtras: The Law Codes of Āpastamba, Gautama, Baudhāyana, and Vasiṣṭha*. Oxford: Oxford University Press.

———, 2005. *Manu's Code of Law: A Critical Edition and Translation of the Mānava- Dharmaśāstra*. Oxford: Oxford University Press.

———, 2006. *Between the Empires: Society in India 300 BCE to 400 CE*. New Delhi: Oxford University Press.

———, 2017. *A Dharma Reader: Classical Indian Law*. New York: Columbia University Press.

———, 2019. *Gṛhastha, Āśrama,* and the Origin of Dharmaśāstra. In: P. Olivelle, ed. *Gṛhastha: The Householder in Ancient Indian Religious Culture.* New York: Oxford University Press, pp. 107–123.

Omvedt, G., 2011. *Cultural Revolt in a Colonial Society: The Non-Brahman Movement in Western India.* New Delhi: Manohar.

Pai, S., 2002. *Dalit Assertion and the Unfinished Democratic Revolution: The Bahujan Samaj Party in Uttar Pradesh.* New Delhi: Sage.

Parasher, Aloka, 1991. *Mlecchas in Early India: A Study in Attitudes towards Outsiders upto AD 600.* New Delhi: Munshiram Manoharlal Publishers.

Patankar, B. & Omvedt, G., 1979. The Dalit Liberation Movement in Colonial Period. *Economic and Political Weekly,* 14(7/8), pp. 409–411, 413, 415, 417, 419–421, 423–424.

Peterson, I. V., 2014. *Poems to Siva: The Hymns of the Tamil Saints.* Princeton: Princeton University Press.

Pollock, S., 1984a. *The Vālmīki Rāmāyaṇa: An Epic of Ancient India, Vol. II: Ayodhyākāṇḍa.* Princeton: Princeton University Press.

———, 1984b. *The Vālmīki Rāmāyaṇa: An Epic of Ancient India, Vol. III: Aranyakāṇḍa.* Princeton: Princeton University Press.

———, 1993. Ramayana and Political Imagination in India. *The Journal of Asian Studies,* 52(2), pp. 261–297.

———, 2006. *The Language of the Gods in the World of Men: Sanskrit, Culture, and Power in Premodern India.* Berkeley: University of California Press.

———, 2007. *Rāma's Last Act by Bhavabhūti.* New York: New York University Press and the JJC Foundation.

Prashad, V., 2000. *Untouchable Freedom: A Social History of a Dalit Community.* Oxford: Oxford University Press.

Pulavar, K. K., 1987. *Tolpava Koothu: The Traditional Shadow Puppet Play of Kerala, Vol. I Balakandam.* Koonathara: All Kerala Puppeteers Sangham.

Radhakrishnan, S. & Moore, C. A., 1957. *A Sourcebook in Indian Philosophy.* Princeton: Princeton University Press.

Raghavan, V., 1966. *The Great Integrators: The Saint-Singers of India.* New Delhi: Ministry of Information and Broadcasting.

———, 1973. *The Greater Ramayana.* Varanasi: The All-India Kashiraj Trust.

———, 1988. *Sanskrit Rāmāyaṇas other than Vālmīki's: The Adbhuta, Adhyātma, and Ānanda Rāmāyaṇas.* Chennai: Dr. V. Raghavan Centre for Performing Arts.

———, 2009. *Studies on Rāmāyaṇa.* Chennai: Dr. V. Raghavan Centre for Performing Arts.

———, n.d. *The Rāmāyaṇa in Classical Sanskrit and Prākṛt Mahākāvya Literature.* Chennai: Dr. V. Raghavan Centre for Performing Arts.

Ram, M., 1974. Ramaswami Naicker and the Dravidian Movement. *Economic and Political Weekly,* 9(6/8), pp. 217, 219, 221–224.

Ramanujan, A., 1991. Three Hundred *Rāmāyaṇas*: Five Examples and Three Thoughts on Translation. In: P. Richman, ed. *Many Rāmāyaṇas: The Diversity of a Narrative Tradition in South Asia.* Berkeley: University of California Press, pp. 22–49.

Ramaswamy, U., 1978. The Belief System of the Non-Brahmin Movement in India: The Andhra Case. *Asian Survey,* 18(3), pp. 290–300.

Ranganayakamma, M., 2004. Tripuraneni Ramaswamy Chowdary's '*Murder of Sambuka*'. In: *Ramayana: The Poisonous Tree [Stories, Essays and Foot-Notes],* trans. B. R. Bapuji et al. Hyderabad: Sweet Home Publications, pp. 738–746.

Rao, A., 2013. *Re-Figuring the Rāmāyaṇa as Theology: A History of Reception in Premodern India.* New York: Routledge.

Rao, A. S., 1988. *Tripuraneni Ramaswamy: A Herald of Philosophical Renaissance*. Hyderabad: Telugu University.

Rao, P. A., 1995. Changes in the Theme and Characters of the Ranganatha *Ramayana*. In: G. Pollet, ed. *Indian Epic Values: Rāmāyaṇa and Its Impact*. Leuven: Peeters Press & Department of Oriental Studies, pp. 59–65.

Richman, P., 1991a. *Many Rāmāyaṇas: The Diversity of a Narrative Tradition in South Asia*. Berkeley: University of California Press.

———, 1991b. Introduction: The Diversity of the *Rāmāyaṇa* Tradition. In: P. Richman, ed. *Many Rāmāyaṇas: The Diversity of a Narrative Tradition in South Asia*. Berkeley: University of California Press, pp. 3–21.

———, 1991c. E.V. Ramasami's Reading of the *Rāmāyaṇa*. In: P. Richman, ed. *Many Rāmāyaṇas: The Diversity of a Narrative Tradition in South Asia*. Berkeley: University of California Press, pp. 175–201.

———, 2001a. *Questioning Ramayanas: A South Asian Tradition*. Berkeley: University of California Press.

———, 2001b. Questioning and Multiplicity Within the Ramayana Tradition. In: P. Richman, ed. *Questioning Ramayanas: A South Asian Tradition*. Berkeley: University of California Press, pp. 1–21.

———, 2004. Why Can't a Shudra Perform Asceticism? *Śambūka* in Three Modern South Indian Plays. In: M. Bose, ed. *The Ramayana Revisited*. New York: Oxford University Press, pp. 125–148.

———, 2008. *Ramayana Stories in Modern South India: An Anthology*. Bloomington: Indiana University Press.

Rocher, L., 1986. *The Purāṇas*. Wiesbaden: Harrassowitz.

Sathaye, 2015. *Crossing the Lines of Caste: Viśvāmitra and the Construction of Brahmin Power in Hindu Mythology*. Oxford: Oxford University Press.

Sattar, A., 2016. *Uttara: The Book of Answers*. Gurgaon: Penguin Random House India.

Sharma, H., n.d. *Padmapurāṇa and Kālidāsa*. Calcutta: Calcutta Oriental Series.

Sherraden, A., 2019. *Gṛhasthas* Don't Belong in the *Rāmāyaṇa*. In: P. Olivelle, ed. *Gṛhastha: The Householder in Ancient Indian Religious Culture*. Oxford: Oxford University Press, pp. 204–221.

———, 2021. Recasting Shambuk in Three Hindi Anti-Caste Dramas. In: P. Richman & R. Bharucha, eds. *Performing the Ramayana Tradition: Enactments, Interpretations, and Arguments*. New York: Oxford University Press, pp. 65–82.

Shulman, D., 1991. Fire and Flood: The Testing of Sīta in Kampaṉ's *Irāmāvatāram*. In: P. Richman, ed. *Many Rāmāyaṇas: The Diversity of a Narrative Tradition in South Asia*. Berkeley: University of California Press, pp. 89–113.

———, 2001. Bhavabhūti on Cruelty and Compassion. In: P. Richman, ed. *Questioning Ramayanas: A South Asian Tradition*. Berkeley: University of California Press, pp. 49–82.

Singaravelu, S. 1982, Sītā's Birth and Parentage in the Rāma Story. *Asian Folklore Studies*, 41(2), pp. 235–243.

Smith, W. L., 1994. *Ramayana Traditions in Eastern India: Assam, Bengal, Orissa*. New Delhi: Munshiram Manoharlal Publishers.

Sontheimer, G.-D., 2004. God, Dharma and Society in the Yādava Kingdom of Devagirī according to the *Līḷācaritra* of Chakradhar. In: H. Brückner, A. Feldhaus & A. Malik, eds. *Günther-Dietz Sontheimer: Essays on Religion, Literature and Law*. New Delhi: Manohar, pp. 305–326.

Stasik, D., 2006. In the world of Tulsīdās's *rām-kathās*. *Rocznik Orientalistyczny*, 58(2), pp. 114–131.

Teltumbde, A., 2017. *Dalits: Past, Present and Future*. London: Routledge.

Thapar, R., 1989. The Ramayana Syndrome. *Seminar*, 353, pp. 71–75.

———, 2000. *Cultural Transaction and Early India: Tradition and Pilgrimage*. New Delhi: Oxford University Press.

The BBC, 2016. *The woman who cut off her breasts to protest a tax*. [Online] Available at: https://www.bbc.com/news/world-asia-india-36891356 [Accessed 22 January 2019].

Thiel-Horstmann, M., 1991. *Rāmāyaṇa and Rāmāyaṇas*. Wiesbaden: Otto Harrasowitz.

Thompson, D. P., 2004. *The Trojan War: Literature and Legends from the Bronze Age to the Present*. Jefferson: McFarland & Company.

Vāgh, S. M., 2016. *Picharā Varg aur Uskā Mahāpuruṣ*. Delhi: Gautam Book Centre.

Vajpeyi, A., 2010. *Śūdradharma* and legal treatments of caste. In: T. Lubin, D. R. J. Davis & J. K. Krishnan, eds. *Hinduism and Law: An Introduction*. Cambridge: Cambridge University Press, pp. 154–166.

———, 2011. The Śūdra in History: From Scripture to Segregation. In: Y. Bronner, W. Cox & L. McCrea, eds. *South Asian Texts in History: Critical Engagements with Sheldon Pollock*. Ann Arbor: Association for Asian Studies, pp. 337–358.

Van Buitenen, J.A.B., 1973. *The Mahābhārata: Book 1, The Book of the Beginning*. Chicago: The University of Chicago Press.

———, 1975. *The Mahābhārata: Book 2, The Book of the Assembly Hall and Book 3, The Book of the Forest*. Chicago: The University of Chicago Press.

Van Daalen, L., 1980. *Vālmīki's Sanskrit*. Leiden: E.J. Brill.

Van der Veer, P., 1994. *Religious Nationalism: Hindus and Muslims in India*. Berkeley: University of California Press.

Veluthat, K., 1979. The Temple-Base of the Bhakti Movement in South India. *Proceedings of the Indian History Congress*, 40, pp. 185–194.

Vijayavardhana, G., 1970. *Outlines of Sanskrit Poetics*. Varanasi: The Chowkhamba Sanskrit Series Office.

Welankar, V., 2009. The Iconography of Kevala Narasimha: A Reappraisal. *South Asian Studies*, 25(1), pp. 113–130.

Willis, M., 2009. *The Archaeology of Hindu Ritual: Temples and the Establishment of the Gods*. New York: Cambridge University Press.

Yardi, M., 1994. *The Rāmāyaṇa: Its Origin and Growth, A Statistical Study*. Poona: Bhandarkar Oriental Research Institute.

Yazdani, G., 1961. *The Early History of the Deccan, Vol. I & II*. London: Oxford University Press.

Ziolkowski, T., 2011. *Gilgamesh Among Us: Modern Encounters with the Ancient Epic*. Ithaca: Cornell University Press.

# INDEX


Aadi Dharm Samaaj (AADHAS) 202, 204–211, 218
Abhinavagupta 109
Achhutanand, Swami 172, 177–180, 182n18, 186, 188, 194n30
  and his *Rām-Rājya-Nyāy* (*See Rām-Rājya-Nyāy* of Swami Achhutanand)
  Involvement with the Arya Samaj 170, 177–179
Ad Dharm movement 172, 185
*Adbhuta Rāmāyaṇa* 128, 133
*adharma* 105, 108, 116, 130, 207
*Adhyātma Rāmāyaṇa* (Sanskrit) 9, 112–116, 112n17, 155
  *bhakti* in 112
  *Rāma-gītā* of 112n19
*Adhyātma Rāmāyaṇam* of Eḻutacchan (Malayalam) 115
Adi Andhra movement 176n9
Adi Dravida movement 168–170, 172, 176n9
Adi Hindu movement 170, 172, 177–182, 179n12, 185, 186, 194n30
*Ādipurāṇa* (*Mahāpurāṇa*) of Jinasena 67n14
Adityanath, Yogi 209, 210
Adivasis 193n26, 194n28, 212, 218
Advaita Vedānta 99, 101, 112, 114–115, 115n21, 129
*Aeneid* of Virgil 6–7
Agastya 59, 86–88, 104, 159, 162
*Agastyasaṃhitā* 95, 146
Allahabad High Court (Uttar Pradesh) 196–198
Āḻvārs 95
Ambedkar, B. R. 166, 173, 190, 194–197, 198n40, 199, 204, 207
  Ambedkar Jayanti 209
  Ambedkar Students' Association (ASA) 203, 217
  and his *Annihilation of Caste* (*See Annihilation of Caste* of B. R. Ambedkar)
  and the Jat-Pat Todak Mandal (JPTM) 172, 187
  and his *Riddles in Hinduism* (*See Riddles in Hinduism* of B. R. Ambedkar)
  on Śambūka 188–190, 197
*Ānanda Rāmāyaṇa* 117n22, 122, 124, 127–132
  *bhakti* in 129
  Comparison with *Sindūragirimāhātmya* 132, 153–158, 166
Andhra 168, 173, 175, 176n9
*Annihilation of Caste* of B. R. Ambedkar 172, 178, 187–190, 199
*Āpastamba Dharmasūtra* 32–33, 33n17, 37
*Araṇyakāṇḍa* 23, 120
Arjuna 39
*Arthaśāstra* 28, 33, 36–38, 40, 41, 42n28, 43
Arya Samaj 177–178, 182, 188, 193n27
  Dalit disillusionment with 170
  and "Shuddhi Sabhas" 170, 179
Aryan invasion theory
  Conceptions of a pre-Aryan society 170–173, 175, 176, 180, 182n18, 191, 192, 199
  Scholarly interventions into 171
  Use in anti-caste movements and literature 169, 171–172, 174n5, 181, 191, 192, 194n30, 195, 199, 204, 206
Āṣāḍha, month of 65
Ashok Pustakalaya 194, 195, 198
Aśoka 29, 30, 35

*āśrama* (hermitage) 46, 85, 125, 142
of Agastya 59, 82
of Śabarī 44–45
of Śambūka 174, 207–208
of Vālmīki 90
*āśrama* (life-mode) 41–42, 42n27, 60, 111, 133, 145, 148, 149
Atiśūdras 171, 193n26, 195
*ātman* 112n20, 185, 186
Ayodhyā 17, 19, 21, 23–25, 44n31, 49, 57, 60n1, 79, 82, 84, 89, 90, 100, 104, 128, 130–132, 155, 174, 189, 200, 206
as a center of Rāma-*bhakti* 96, 97, 146, 148
Decline of *dharma* in 3, 45, 46, 54, 116
and the destruction of the Babri Masjid 10
Rāma's rule in 24n6, 26
Śambūka's disruption of peace in 14, 43, 45, 54, 152
*Ayodhyākāṇḍa* 23
Ayyankali 216n17

Bahujan (and Dalit-Bahujan) 193n26, 216, 217
Bahujan literature 193n26
Bahujan Kalyan Prakashan 194, 194n30
*Bālakāṇḍa* 24n6, 25n8, 27, 49, 64, 66, 69
*Bhagavad-Gītā* 39, 107, 144n5
*Bhāgavata Purāṇa* 60n1
*bhakti* 94, 121, 145, 178
in the *Adhyātma Rāmāyaṇa* (*See Adhyātma Rāmāyaṇa* (Sanskrit))
in the *Ānanda Rāmāyaṇa* (*See Ānanda Rāmāyaṇa*)
Development of 94–98
in Kampaṉ's *Irāmāvatāram* (*See Irāmāvatāram* of Kampaṉ)
in the *Kaṇṇaśśa Rāmāyaṇa* (*See Kaṇṇaśśa Rāmāyaṇa*)
Kṛṣṇa-*bhakti* 97, 146, 148, 166
in the Purāṇas 103, 106
Rāma-*bhakti* 17, 58, 95–98, 110, 112n18, 132, 146, 148, 222
in Tulsīdās' *Rāmcaritmānas* (*See Rāmcaritmānas* of Tulsīdās)
Bharti, Kanwal 193, 198
Bhavabhūti 61n4, 75n1, 147, 182n18
and his *Uttararāmacarita* (*See Uttararāmacarita* of Bhavabhūti)
and Kālidāsa 76–79, 78n6
*Bhāvārtha Rāmāyaṇa* of Eknāth 121–123, 134
Mukteśvar's addendum to 122, 129
*Bhaviṣya Purāṇa* 150
Bhīṣma 4–5, 104
*Bilaṅka Rāmāyaṇa* 128
Brahmā 121, 129, 185
*brahman* 99–101, 112n20, 116
*Brahmāṇḍa Purāṇa* 41
Brahminism 16, 28, 30–31, 34, 38, 40, 42n28, 43, 45n33, 51, 53, 54, 57, 58, 61, 66–68, 67n14, 68n15–16, 69n21, 71n23, 72, 91, 98, 117, 133, 144–145, 144n6, 148, 151, 179, 207, 212, 223n1–2, 225
Brahmins 9, 28, 29, 32n15, 35, 45, 54, 68, 108, 121, 140, 148n15, 154, 173, 189
Anxiety with respect to the welfare of 24–25, 25n8, 120, 121, 182–183
Brahmin boy in the Śambūka episode 1, 3, 8, 12, 14, 21, 22, 41–43, 45–46, 54, 59, 78, 82, 90, 101, 105, 106, 108, 110, 111, 113–116, 121, 122, 128, 130, 132, 152, 154, 155, 190, 192, 207, 225
Brahminicide 46, 120–122, 129
Conspiracy to kill Śambūka 174–175, 175n7, 180, 207, 208, 210–211
Rāma questions Śambūka about being a Brahmin 21, 105
Redaction of the *Rāmāyaṇa* by 205, 210
Social supremacy of 29–33, 32n14, 37n21, 40, 43, 150, 173, 183–186, 210, 223
*Bṛhadāraṇyaka Upaniṣad* 112n19
Buddha 110, 223, 225
Buddhism 29–30, 64n11, 67, 94, 133, 169, 173, 190, 198n40, 223n2, 225

*caṇḍālas* 49–51
Candranakhā (*See* Śūrpaṇakhā (and Candraṇakhā, Candranakhā, Candranakhī))
Candraṇakhā (*See* Śūrpaṇakhā (and Candraṇakhā, Candranakhā, Candranakhī))
Candranakhī (*See* Śūrpaṇakhā (and Candraṇakhā, Candranakhā, Candranakhī))
Caste (*See also jāti*; *varṇa*) 3n7, 12–13, 19, 30, 32n14, 51, 101, 104, 106, 107, 109, 121, 132, 134, 164, 166–181, 185–188, 193–206, 194n28, 211–216, 216n17, 218–219, 221, 225
*Caturvargacintāmaṇi* of Hemādri 145, 150
Chandrasekharan, T. P. (Politician in Kerala) 223–225, 224n3
Chaudari, Tripuraneni Ramaswami 172–177, 199
  and his *Śambuka Vadha* (*See Śambuka Vadha* of Tripuraneni Ramaswami Chaudari)
Christianity 179
Communist Party of India (Marxist) or CPI(M) 212, 223–225

Dalits (*See also* Bahujan (and Dalit-Bahujan)) 19, 32n14, 132, 152n21, 168–173, 172n3, 176, 177, 179, 189, 191, 193n26, 194n28, 195, 198, 202–214, 216, 218, 219, 222
  and African-Americans 217
  Dalit literature 12–13, 18, 180, 194n30, 215
Daṇḍaka Forest 84–86, 119, 125, 159, 184
Daśaratha 63
  Kills young ascetic 42, 46–48, 52
*Dasāvatāracarita* of Kṣemendra 109–111, 115, 116
Delhi 202, 211
  Delhi University 203
Delhi Sultanate 149, 151
*dharma* 5, 29–33, 38–40, 44, 45, 60n1, 83, 110, 116, 121, 131, 166, 184
  in the *Arthaśāstra* (*See Arthaśāstra*)
  in Ayodhyā (*See* Ayodhyā)
  Complexities of 79
  in the Kali Yuga 21, 41, 72n25, 121, 153
  of kings (*See rājadharma* (the *dharma* of kings))
  of Kṣatriyas (*See* Kṣatriyas, and their *dharma* (*kṣatradharma*))
  Lapses in 26, 39, 54, 111
  in the *Mānava Dharmaśāstra* (*See Mānava Dharmaśāstra*)
  Nārada's lament on (*See* Nārada, laments the decline of *dharma*)
  of Śūdras (*See* Śūdras, and their *dharma* (*śūdradharma*))
  and *varṇa* (*See varṇadharma*)
Dharmaśāstra 26, 33–35, 37–38, 41, 47, 133, 144–145, 149, 152
  *nibandha* literature 145, 149–151
Dravidians 169, 173–174, 176, 182n18, 191, 192, 195, 206
Dvāpara Yuga 156

Ekalavya 194n28, 201, 207, 224n4

Gāgābhaṭṭa 150, 151
*Gautama Dharmasūtra* 33, 150
Guha (Niṣāda king) 44n29–31
Gujarat 119, 127
Gupta Empire 22, 27, 28, 33, 34, 38, 57, 61–66, 62n5, 78, 138–144, 146, 147, 222
  Candragupta II 62n5, 63n9, 64n11, 142, 143
  Chandragupta II 140
  Inscriptions of the 62–63
  and Kālidāsa (*See* Kālidāsa, Relationship to the Guptas)
  Kumaragupta 63n9
  Prabhāvatīguptā (*See* Vākāṭaka Empire, Prabhāvatīguptā)
  Samudragupta 62n5, 63n9, 139
  Skandagupta 62n6, 63n9
  Socio-religious developments under the 16, 57, 64–65, 95, 140–141, 147

Hanumān 9, 10, 24, 126, 223
  Involvement with the death of Śambūka 153, 162–164
Hemādri 144–145, 148n15, 150
*Hikāyat Serī Rāma* 128n29

Holiday, Billie 216–217
Horse Sacrifice (*aśvamedha*) 62, 82, 86, 90, 104

*Iliad* and *Odyssey* of Homer 6
Indian Penal Code (IPC) 196, 216
*Irāmāvatāram* of Kampaṉ 72n24, 98–101, 115, 120, 123, 147
  *bhakti* in 99, 123
*Irāmāyaṇappātiraṅkaḷ* of E. V. Ramasami 191, 192, 195
Islam 96n3, 97–98, 97n6, 101, 179, 191
  Sufism 97–98, 100

Jainism 17, 29, 66–69, 67n14, 73, 94, 126, 223n2
  Ethics of 67–69, 67n13, 68n16, 71, 80, 222
  Hindu deities in 16, 67–68, 68n15, 71, 127, 133, 157n26, 222
  Lay community within 66–67, 72
  *Rāmāyaṇa* in (*See also Padma Purāṇa* of Jinadāsa, *Padma Purāṇa* of Raviṣeṇa, *Pampa Rāmāyaṇa* of Nāgacandra, *Paümacariu* of Svayambhūdeva, *Paümacariya* of Vimalasūri, *Rām-Rās* of Jinadāsa, *Triṣaṣṭiśalākāpuruṣacarita* of Hemacandra, and *Vāsudevahiṇḍī* of Saṅghadāsa) 12, 16–18, 58, 67, 68n16, 80, 93, 117–122, 124n27, 126–129, 133–135
Jana Natya Manch (Janam) 202, 211–215, 218, 219
  *The Last Letter* of (*See The Last Letter* (street play by Janam))
  *Śambūk Vadh* of (*See Śambūk Vadh* (proscenium play performed by Janam))
Janasthāna 77, 82, 84–85, 87–89
*jāti* 3n7, 187, 224n4
*Jātiviveka* 41n25
Jat-Pat Todak Mandal (JPTM) 172, 177–178, 187
Jigyasu, Chandrika Prasad 193, 194
Justice Party 168–170, 175, 191

Kali Yuga 21, 41, 72n25, 101, 121, 131, 153–154
Kālidāsa 16, 18, 58–66, 72–73, 75, 76, 79, 91, 93, 115, 117, 120, 132, 138–139, 143–144, 147, 148n15, 159, 221
  and Bhavabhūti (*See* Bhavabhūti, and Kālidāsa)
  and his *Meghadūta* (*See Meghadūta* of Kālidāsa)
  and his *Raghuvaṃśa* (*See Raghuvaṃśa* of Kālidāsa)
  Relationship to the Guptas 16, 61–66, 141
*Kaṇṇaśśa Rāmāyaṇa* 107–109, 114–115
  *bhakti* in 109
Kausalyā 46, 47
Kerala 72n24, 107–108, 113, 122–123, 202, 215, 216n17, 223–224, 223n2, 224n3
*Kiṣkindhākāṇḍa* 23, 44n31
*krauñca* bird 26
Kr̥ṣṇa 17, 39, 67, 68n15, 110, 145–147, 156–158, 189, 190
  as Vāsudeva (*See* Jainism, Hindu deities in)
Kr̥ta Yuga 24
Kṣatriyas 29, 31, 32n15, 35, 37, 39, 44n31, 50–52, 105, 121, 130, 151, 171, 173, 175, 184, 223n1
  and their *dharma* (*kṣatradharma*) 4, 37, 39, 40
  and their relationship to Brahmins 4n8, 25n7, 31, 39, 42n28, 174, 182, 188, 223n1

Lakṣmaṇa 25n8, 44, 45, 50, 53, 60n1, 112, 125, 131, 132, 153, 155, 186
  accidentally kills Śambūka 12, 70–71, 73, 117, 119–122, 124–130, 134
  Temple in Ramtek 146, 148, 151, 154, 158, 159, 161
  as Vāsudeva (*See* Jainism, Hindu deities in)
*The Last Letter* (street play by Janam) 211, 213–215

Lava and Kuśa 26, 82, 90, 115–117, 130, 155
Lynching 215–217
of Thomas Shipp and Abram Smith (photograph by Lawrence Beitler) 217

Madras Presidency 169–171, 173, 176–177, 176n9
*Mahābhārata* 2–5, 9, 39, 41, 45n33, 77, 107, 109
*Rāmopākhyāna* of 2–3, 3n5, 5n10
Relationship to the *Rāmāyaṇa* 2
Śambūka mentioned by a jackal in 1–5, 8, 222
of Sāraḷadāsa 128
Mahāmuni Śambūk Balidān Divas (The Matrydom Day of the Great Sage Śambūka) 202, 204–209, 218
Mahānubhāvs 156
Maharashtra 18, 66, 121, 129, 132, 135, 137, 144–146, 148, 150, 151, 156–158, 160–161, 166, 180, 189, 199, 222
Mahā-Śūdras (*See also* Atiśūdras) 195n31
Māllinātha, his commentary on the *Raghuvaṃśa* 60
*Mānava Dharmaśāstra* 28, 33–41, 42n28, 43, 60, 63n10, 148n15, 181, 188, 224n4
Mandal Commission 201–202, 211–212
*Māṇḍūkya Upaniṣad* 112n19
Maṇipravāḷa 96–97, 107–108
Manu (*See Mānava Dharmasāstra*)
Marāṭhā Empire 137, 145n7, 146, 149, 151, 152n20, 155, 165
Shivaji 151
Māriyammaṉ 122–123
Maurya Empire 22n2, 27–30, 33, 38, 40, 53, 54, 57
Meeropol, Abel 216–217, 217n18
*Meghadūta* of Kālidāsa 65, 66, 139, 141–143
Mount Śaivala 148n14

Nangeli 216n17, 224n4
Nārada 111, 152, 225
instructs Rāma to kill Śambūka 21, 39–41, 43, 45, 59, 105, 108, 130
laments the decline of *dharma* 21, 41, 48, 59, 72n25, 78, 101, 102, 105, 108, 116, 130
*Nāradīya Purāṇa* 41n25
Narasiṃha 110, 141n3–4, 158, 160
Nāyanārs 95n2
*Niraparādh kī Hatyā* of Santram B. A. 177, 178, 181–187, 218
Comparison with *Rām-Rājya-Nyāy* of Swami Achhutanand 180, 182–187, 182n18
Influence of Arya Samaj philosophy in 182
Niṣādas 44, 45n33, 194n28
Non-Brahmin movement(s) 132, 135, 166, 168–177, 176n9, 179n14, 190–192, 202, 204, 210, 222
Literature of (*See also Niraparādh kī Hatyā* of Santram B. A., *Rām-Rājya-Nyāy* of Swami Achhutanand, *Śambūk kā Katā Sir* (*Śambūka's Severed Head*) of Omprakash Valmiki, *Śambūk Vadh* (drama by Periyar Lalai Singh and Ram Avtar Pal), *Śambūka Vadha* of Tripuraneni Ramaswami Chaudari, and *The Ramayana* (*A True Reading*) of E. V. Ramasami (translation of *Irāmāyaṇappātiraṅkaḷ*)) 12–13, 18, 19, 152n21, 193, 194n30, 195, 198, 218, 219

Other Backwards Classes (OBCs) 172n3, 177n10, 190, 193n26, 194n28, 198, 201, 209, 218

*Padma Purāṇa* (Hindu Purāṇic text) 104–106, 147
*Padma Purāṇa* of Jinadāsa 124n27
*Padma Purāṇa* of Raviṣeṇa (Jain Purāṇic text) 80, 124–126
*Pampa Rāmāyaṇa* of Nāgacandra 118–120, 127
Pañcavaṭī 82, 86, 88–89
Pandharpur, Maharashtra 145n7–8, 146, 156

Paraśurāma 110, 223n1
*parivrājaka* 42n26
*Paümacariu* of Svayambhūdeva 126, 127, 147
*Paümacariya* of Vimalasūri 16, 17, 58, 66, 68–72, 69n18, 71n23, 72n24, 101, 117–121, 124–127, 134
Periyar Lalai Singh Charitable Trust (*See* Ashok Pustakalaya)
Phule, Jotirao 166, 171, 180, 193n26, 195, 211–212
Phule, Savitribai 180
Purāṇas (general) 9, 26, 38, 39, 67, 103–104, 106, 150
Puruṣasukta of the *Ṛg Veda* 29
Puṣpaka Vimāna 82, 86, 108, 225

Raavan, Darshan "Ratna" (Leader of AADHAS) 202, 204–211, 218–219
*Raghuvaṃśa* of Kālidāsa 16, 58–64, 62n6, 66, 72–73, 75, 83, 84, 101, 104n11, 110, 116, 117, 139, 143, 147, 148n15
*rājadharma* (the *dharma* of kings) 37, 40, 41, 43, 45, 48, 53–55, 60, 71, 89, 91, 188
Rajah, M. C. 169, 170
Rajasthan 119, 205
Rāma
  as an *avatāra* of Viṣṇu (*See* Viṣṇu, Rāma as an *avatāra* of)
  as Baladeva (*See* Jainism, Hindu deities in)
  banishes Sītā (*See* Sītā, banishment of)
  as *brahman* 99–101, 112, 116
  Dejected state of 79–87, 89–90, 175, 222
  delivers salvation to Śambūka 12, 16, 59–61, 73, 76, 84, 91, 101, 102, 111, 113, 114, 116, 117n22, 128, 131–132, 143, 147, 153–155, 221
  and his *dharma* as king 26, 40–41, 43, 45, 48, 53–55, 57, 61, 79–80, 82, 83, 91, 111, 188, 189, 209
  enters heaven 50
  executes Śambūka 3, 11, 13, 19, 39, 41, 43, 44, 51, 52, 57, 66, 71, 76, 101, 106, 108, 128, 133, 188, 190, 192, 197, 209, 225
  Exile of 2, 9, 44, 47, 68, 76, 77
  grants boons to Śambūka 18, 116, 131–132, 153–155, 158–161, 165
  hesitates in killing Śambūka 17, 76, 82–83, 174, 175
  kills Vālin (*See* Vālin)
  as a leader of the Aryans 174, 180
  in the *Mahābhārata* (*See also Mahābhārata*, *Rāmopākhyāna* of) 1, 3, 8
  praised for killing Śambūka 48, 59, 103, 106, 110, 115, 128
  Rāma-*bhakti* (*See bhakti*, Rāma-*bhakti*)
  refrains from killing Śambūka 162–164
  Relationship with Guha (*See* Guha (Niṣāda king))
  Relationship with Śabarī (*See* Śabarī)
  as a representative of Ayodhyā's ruling class 39, 44n31, 46, 48n38
  Rule in Ayodhyā 2, 16, 23–25, 43, 45, 48, 53, 70, 78, 79, 91, 99, 100, 106, 111, 113, 120, 121, 128
  under the influence of Brahmins 174, 175n7, 180, 182–183, 188, 199
*Rāmakien* 128n29
*Rāmapūrvatāpanīya Upaniṣad* 95, 146
*Rāmarakṣāstotra* 95, 146
Ramasami, E. V. (Periyar E. V. Ramasami) 169, 173, 190–193, 195n31, 199, 210
  Criticism of the *Rāmāyaṇa* in *The Ramayana* (*A True Reading*) (*See The Ramayana* (*A True Reading*) of E. V. Ramasami (translation of *Irāmāyaṇappātiraṅkaḷ*))
  Relationship with Lalai Singh 190, 193
Rāmāyaṇa
  Anti-caste tellings of 13, 18–19, 167, 173–177, 180–187, 190–193, 195–200
  in Jainism (*See* Jainism, *Rāmāyaṇa* in)

Relationship to the *Mahābhārata* (*See Mahābhārata*, Relationship to the *Rāmāyaṇa*)
Tradition of 5–19, 25, 55, 58, 59, 66, 72, 73, 76, 80, 93–94, 98, 107, 118, 129, 148, 155, 166, 221, 225–226
TV serializations of 10n14
of Vālmīki (*See Vālmīki Rāmāyaṇa*)
*The Ramayana* (*A True Reading*) of E. V. Ramasami (translation of *Irāmāyaṇappātiraṅkaḷ*) 190, 192–196, 210n9
*Rāmāyaṇamañjarī* of Kṣemendra 109–111
*Rāmcaritmānas* of Tulsīdās 99–101, 112n20, 117n22, 120, 155
*bhakti* in 99
*Lav-Kuś-kāṇḍ* and the inclusion of Śambūka in 115–117, 155
*Rām-Rājya-Nyāy* of Swami Achhutanand 180–188, 180n15, 182n18, 194n30, 199, 218
Adi Hindu philosophy in 180–182, 184–185
Comparison with *Niraparādh kī Hatyā* of Santram B. A. (*See Niraparādh kī Hatyā* of Santram B. A.)
Connection with *Śambūk Vadh* of Periyar Lalai Singh and Ram Avtar Pal 194n29–30
Depiction of an Aryan invasion in 180–181, 186
*Rām-Rās* of Jinadāsa 119, 124n27, 128
Ramtek, Maharashtra 18, 66, 97, 132, 135, 137–166, 222
Identity with Rāmagiri in Kālidāsa's *Meghadūta* 142–143
Maha Shivaratri celebrations in 137, 159, 165
as the site of Śambūka's death 18, 144, 147, 148, 153–155, 161–165
Temple to Śambūka in 137, 160–161, 165
as a tourist site 158, 160–161
*Raṅganātha Rāmāyaṇa* 120–123, 134
*rasa*
in Bhavabhūti's *Uttararāmacarita* 76, 79–81, 90, 91
*karuṇa-rasa* (*rasa* of pity) 80, 81n12, 82–83, 88, 90n14
*śānta rasa* (*rasa* of peace) 80
*śṛṅgāra-rasa* (erotic *rasa*) 81, 90n14, 108
Theory of 75–76, 76n2, 81n11
Rāvaṇa 2, 23–26, 64, 68n16, 69, 70n22, 71, 79, 96, 100, 104, 111, 119, 120–121, 123, 126–128, 130, 131, 133, 134
as a Dravidian king 174, 191
as Prativāsudeva (*See* Jainism, Hindu deities in)
as a venerated figure 207, 208n6
Revolutionary Marxist Party (RMP) 223–224
*Ṛg Veda* 29, 171
*Riddles in Hinduism* of B. R. Ambedkar 189–190, 189n22, 199

S., Chandramohan 202, 215–218, 215n14
Śabarī 42, 44–46, 44n32, 45n33
*Saccī Rāmāyaṇ* (Hindi translation of E. V. Ramasami's *The Ramayana* (*A True Reading*)) 190, 192, 194–197, 195n31, 198n39
Śaivism 64n11, 94, 95n2, 140, 141n3, 147, 148, 154, 158
Śalākāpuruṣa 17, 68, 72, 127, 133, 157n26
Rāma, Lakṣmaṇa, and Rāvaṇa as (*See* Jainism, Hindu deities in)
*Śambūk kā Katā Sir* (*Śambūk's Severed Head*) of Omprakash Valmiki 214, 215
*Śambūk Vadh* (drama by Periyar Lalai Singh and Ram Avtar Pal) 194n28, 194n30, 218
Connection with *Rām-Rājya-Nyāy* of Swami Achhutnand (*See Rām-Rājya-Nyāy* of Swami Achhutanand, Connection with *Śambūk Vadh* of Periyar Lalai Singh and Ram Avtar Pal)
*Śambūk Vadh* (proscenium play performed by Janam) 212–213, 218, 219

Śambūka
Accidental death of (*See* Lakṣmaṇa, accidentally kills Śambūka)
Afterlife of (*See* Rāma, delivers salvation to Śambūka)
as an anti-caste revolutionary 13, 19, 167, 168, 180, 182n18, 202, 207, 208, 212, 222, 225
as a devotee of Rāma 11, 84–87, 91, 116, 131–132
as an educator 13, 19, 167, 180, 202, 206, 208
Execution of (*See* Rāma, executes Śambūka)
in dialogue with Rāma 21–22, 83–87, 105–106, 108–110, 114, 131–132, 153–155, 164
identified with Dhūmrākṣa (*See also* Śambūka, identified with Dhūmreśvara) 147, 148, 154, 158
identified with Dhūmreśvara 18, 132, 137, 147, 154, 159–161, 165
as a martyr 11, 13, 19, 135, 167, 170, 185, 194n28, 205, 212
as a spokesman for Śūdras (*See also* Śambūka, as an anti-caste revolutionary) 132
*tapas* of 3, 21–22, 40–41, 44, 45, 47, 51, 52, 59, 61, 70, 72n25, 73, 78–79, 82, 84, 89, 91, 101, 103, 105–106, 108, 110, 111, 113–116, 117n22, 119, 121, 122, 125, 126, 129, 131, 148n14, 152n21, 209–210, 210n7, 225
Tradition of 10–15, 17, 19, 61n4, 76, 91, 132, 147, 167, 173, 200, 219, 221, 225–226
*Śambūka Vadha* of Tripuraneni Ramaswami Chaudari 173–177, 182n18, 188, 192n25
Santram B. A. 172, 177–178, 181–187, 199
as founder of the Jat-Pat Todak Mandal 172, 177–178, 187
Involvement with the Arya Samaj 177–178
and his *Niraparādh kī Hatyā* (*See Niraparādh kī Hatyā* of Santram B. A.)
Relationship with B. R. Ambedkar 172, 187
Sarasvatī 59, 78n6
Scheduled Castes (SCs) 172n3, 177n10, 197
Scheduled Tribes (STs) 172n3
*Sindūragirimāhātmya* 117n22, 132, 151–158, 152n20, 152n22, 155n24, 160, 161, 165, 166
Comparison with the *Ānanda Rāmāyaṇa* (*See Ānanda Rāmāyaṇa*, Comparison with *Sindūragirimāhātmya*)
Singh, Lalai (Periyar Lalai Singh, Lalai Singh Yadav) 173, 190, 193–198, 212
as coauthor of *Śambūk Vadh* (*See Śambūk Vadh* (drama by Periyar Lalai Singh and Ram Avtar Pal))
Legal battles of 173, 194–199
Literary activism of 193–194
Relationship with E. V. Ramasami (*See* Ramasami, E. V. (Periyar E. V. Ramasami), Relationship with Lalai Singh)
Sītā 9, 10, 17, 23, 26, 44, 45, 69n18, 77, 81n12, 84, 88–90, 90n14, 100, 113, 119, 126, 128, 131, 132, 133n31, 142, 143, 146, 153, 155, 161, 189, 222
Abduction of 2, 25, 70, 71, 119, 124, 128, 130, 134
Banishment of 5n10, 17, 24, 25, 54–55, 60, 69n18, 76, 79–83, 81n12, 86, 100, 115–116, 189
Present at Śambūka's killing 130
as Rāvaṇa's daughter 133
Trial-by-fire (*agniparīkṣā*) of 99, 100
*Sītā* (drama by Jogesh Chandra Chaudhuri) 181n16, 182n18
Śiva 1, 112n18, 137, 147
Śambūka as a *śiva-liṅga* (*See* Śambūka, identified with Dhūmreśvara)
*śiva-liṅga* 18, 113, 137, 154, 158–161, 165

*Śiva Purāṇa* 60n1
Śrīvaiṣṇavas 96–97
*Śūdrācāraśiromaṇi* of Kṛṣṇa Śeṣa 41n25, 150n18, 151n19
Śūdras
and their *dharma* (*śūdradharma*) 32n14, 37, 41–42, 41n25, 106, 143, 148n15, 149–151, 150n18, 152n22, 207
Exclusion from initiation into Vedic education (*upanayana*) (*See also upanayana* (initiation into Vedic education); Vedas, Śūdras' access to) 33, 35, 149, 150, 152
Forbidden from practicing *tapas* (*See* Śambūka, *tapas* of; *tapas*, Forbidden for Śūdras)
and the greeting "Rāma, Rāma" 131, 153, 154
A path to salvation for 117n22, 131, 158
Position in the *varṇa* system 3, 12, 21, 29, 33, 36, 40, 43, 47, 52, 121, 173, 176, 185
Social position of 14, 33n17, 47, 51, 52, 83, 103, 107–108, 144n5, 151, 166, 171, 172n3, 174, 181, 185, 187, 195
speak Prakrit in Sanskrit drama 83
*Sundarakāṇḍa* 23
Supreme Court of India 10, 19, 196, 216
Śūrpaṇakhā (and Candraṇakhā, Candranakhā, Candranakhī) 70–71, 117, 119–130, 134

T., Murali 222–226
*Taittirīya Upaniṣad* 112n19
Tamil Nadu 123, 169, 173, 176n9, 190, 192
*tapas* (austerities) 21–22, 39, 41–42, 42n27, 44–48, 51, 52, 59, 70, 71, 73, 78–79, 84, 91, 104–106, 108, 111, 114, 116, 119, 125, 126, 129, 131, 152–153, 161–164, 174, 176, 184, 192, 209–210, 210n7
and *āśrama* (life-mode) 41–42
Forbidden for Śūdras 3, 21, 40–41, 42n26, 45, 47, 48, 51, 61, 82, 89, 101, 103, 108, 110, 111, 113, 115, 116, 121, 122, 148n15, 152, 153, 190, 225
Thass, Iyothee 169n1, 173
*Tolpāvakūttu* (Kerala shadow puppetry) 72n24, 122–124
*Torave Rāmāyaṇa* 119, 128
Tretā Yuga 51, 108, 154
Triśaṅku 48–53, 50n40
*Triṣaṣṭiśalākāpuruṣacarita* of Hemacandra 126–128
Trojan War 6–7
Tuṅgabhadrā, wife of Śambūka 183–185, 206, 210

United Provinces (*See* Uttar Pradesh)
Unlawful Activities (Prevention) Act (UAPA) 216, 216n15
Untouchables (*See also* Dalits) 32n14, 168, 169, 179n13, 180, 181, 184, 193n27, 197, 207, 216n17
*upanayana* (initiation into Vedic education) 33, 35, 42, 149, 152
Upaniṣads 112, 129, 150
Uttar Pradesh 62n7, 172, 173, 176–178, 180, 190, 193–199, 194n30, 203, 209, 211
*Uttarakāṇḍa* 5n10, 14, 16, 17, 22–27, 24n5, 25n9, 39, 42n28, 53–55, 57–58, 61, 64, 66, 69, 72, 75, 76, 78, 79, 113, 115, 129, 132, 167, 225
appended to an existing text 122, 129
and its fit within the *Vālmīki Rāmāyaṇa* 25–27
known to Vimalasūri 72
Late addition to the *Vālmīki Rāmāyaṇa* 14, 23–24, 41, 49, 66
Plot of 24–25
Removal of 73, 100, 120, 122, 128
*Uttararāmāyaṇam* of Eḻutacchan 114

*Uttararāmacarita* of Bhavabhūti 17, 73, 75–91, 104, 175, 192n25, 222
  Use of *rasa* in (*See rasa*, in Bhavabhūti's *Uttararāmacarita*)

Vaiṣṇavism 16–17, 57, 61, 64–66, 73, 94–97, 95n2, 104, 110, 111, 138–148, 141n3, 148n13, 156–158, 166
Vaiśyas 29, 32n15, 35, 37, 46, 47, 121, 130, 184
Vākāṭaka Empire 137–144, 139n1, 141n3, 147, 148, 158
  Prabhāvatīguptā 139–143
Vālin 38–39, 44n31, 48n38, 69, 100, 120, 189
Vālmīki 18, 69n17, 90, 91, 117, 120
  Author of the *Rāmāyaṇa* 2, 26
  and the creation of the *śloka* meter 26
  as teacher to Lava and Kuśa 82
  Veneration of 207–210, 208n6, 210n8
Valmiki, Dalit community (*See* Aadi Dharm Samaj (AADHAS))
Valmiki, Omprakash 213–215, 214n12
  and his poem, *Śambūk kā Katā Sir* (*Śambūka's Severed Head*) (*See Śambūk kā Katā Sir* (*Śambūka's Severed Head*) of Omprakash Valmiki)
*Vālmīki Rāmāyaṇa* 2n4, 3, 14, 16, 17, 21–22, 22n1, 25n7–8, 44n29, 44n32, 46n34–35, 47n36–37, 48n38, 49n39, 50n40, 57–60, 60n1, 64, 69n18, 71, 96n3, 100, 105n14, 111, 120n25, 128, 147, 192
  Challenges to 58, 66, 68–70, 68n16, 72, 73, 118, 127, 133, 181, 190, 210, 222
  used in court rulings 190, 198
  Development of 2n3, 3n5, 22–24, 23n3, 35, 38, 42n28, 43, 48, 52, 54, 66
  Deviations from 59, 60, 79, 84, 112n17, 115, 139
  as the earliest account of the Śambūka episode 4, 11, 16, 21–22, 221
  Explorations of *dharma* in 38–43
  as a model for later texts 73, 101–111, 117, 120, 122, 147, 152, 182n18
  Śambūka in 38–55, 61, 66, 71–73, 76, 79, 148n14
  Śivasahāya's commentary on 101–103, 102n9
  Śrīvaiṣṇava commentaries on 96–97
*vānaprastha* 42n26
Vārkarīs 121, 145, 148, 156
*varṇa* 3n7, 4n8, 38, 39, 47, 49–52, 59, 60, 66, 71, 76, 78, 91, 105, 110, 131, 134, 143, 151, 153, 161, 164, 166, 170, 175, 177n10, 212, 224n4
  Origins of 29
  Social system of (*cāturvarṇya*) 3, 12, 21, 29, 40, 43, 151, 168, 175, 181, 182, 187–188, 199
  Twice-born (*dvija*) *varṇa*s 33, 149, 150, 171
*varṇadharma* 27–31, 33, 35–41, 42n28, 43, 45, 47, 53, 54, 57, 106, 111, 152n21
  *varṇāśramadharma* 60, 111, 133, 145, 148–149
*varsāmāsavrata* 65, 139, 140, 142, 143
Vasiṣṭha 49, 50n40, 51, 60n1, 130, 174, 182
*Vasudevahiṇḍī* of Saṅghadāsa 133
Vedas 29, 34, 104, 174, 179, 187
  Śūdras' access to 33, 150, 152n21–22
Vedic sacrifice (*yajña*) 25n8, 29–30, 35–36, 49, 51, 52, 183–186
Vemula, Rohith 202–206, 210, 211, 213–219
Vernacular languages 94, 96n4, 99, 107, 113, 119–120, 122, 124n27, 126–128, 133, 144n6, 192
  Vernacularization 17, 94, 98, 108, 117–118, 179
Vimalasūri 16–17, 58, 66–73, 69n17, 71n23, 75, 80, 91, 93, 118–120, 126–128, 132, 147, 154, 222
  and his *Paümacariya* (*See Paümacariya* of Vimalasūri)
Vindhyā Mountains 131

Viṣṇu 57, 64–66, 103, 104, 109, 110, 140, 141n3, 147, 156, 157, 223n1
Rāma as an *avatāra* of 50, 57, 64, 67, 95, 98, 104, 110, 143
Slumber of 65, 142
Viśvāmitra 25n8, 39, 49–52, 49n39, 50n40
Viṭṭhal 145n8, 146, 156
Yādava Empire 126, 137, 143–148, 145n7, 148n13, 149, 150n18, 151, 154n23, 156, 159, 166
*Yuddhakāṇḍa* 23, 24n6, 25, 26, 122
Yudhiṣṭhira 4–5, 4n9, 5n10

www.ingramcontent.com/pod-product-compliance
Lightning Source LLC
Chambersburg PA
CBHW021138230426
43667CB00005B/174
* 9 7 8 1 8 3 9 9 9 4 9 4 4 *